MYTHS AND LEGENDS OF THE POLYNESIANS

Johannes C. Andersen

DOVER PUBLICATIONS, INC.
NEW YORK

Published in Canada by General Publishing Company, Ltd., 30 Lesmill Road, Don
Mills, Toronto, Ontario.
Published in the United Kingdom by Constable and Company, Ltd., 3 The Lanches-
ters, 162–164 Fulham Palace Road, London W6 9ER.

Bibliographical Note

This Dover edition, first published in 1995, is an unabridged republication of *Myths &
Legends of the Polynesians*, originally published by George G. Harrap & Company Ltd.,
London, in 1928. Some of the illustrations have been repositioned for this edition. The
illustrations now facing pages 54, 65, 113, 128, 129, 164, 202, 248, 260, 261, 268, 295, 310, 342,
405 and 440, originally in color, were painted by the artist Richard Wallwork.

Library of Congress Cataloging-in-Publication Data

Andersen, Johannes Carl, 1873–1962.
   Myths and legends of the Polynesians / Johannes C. Andersen — Dover ed.
     p.   cm.
   Originally published: London : George G. Harrap, 1928. With illustrations
repositioned.
   Includes index.
   ISBN 0-486-28582-0 (pbk.)
   1. Mythology, Polynesian. 2. Legends—Polynesia. 3. Folklore—Polynesia.
4. Polynesia—Religion. I. Title.
BL2620.P6A53 1995
299'.92—dc20   95-9840
                                                            CIP

Manufactured in the United States of America
Dover Publications, Inc., 31 East 2nd Street, Mineola, N.Y. 11501

PREFACE

THE Polynesians were bold navigators long before the Phœnicians ventured out of the Mediterranean; they had explored and settled the Pacific long before Columbus groped across the Atlantic. Having left one continental area, as is conjectured, they thereafter took as their heritage the islands of the Pacific, crossing and recrossing its wide waters, but avoiding settlement on its bordering continents.

They are not of the Far East, nor of the Far West. Kipling's *mot* has lost its point, and will surely be refuted—the East and West may yet meet and assimilate in the Farther East, the Farther West, in the storm-bred peace of the Pacific.

The Polynesian is regarded as the Caucasian of the nadir; it is recognized that he is the finest of the uncivilized races; and the past century has seen, as it were, a tropic dawn—the stride of a people from barbarity to enlightenment; from the past Stone Age to the present age of civilization. White men even now living have spoken with white men who were daily eye-witnesses of the barbarity and cannibal feasts of the grandfathers of Polynesians who are now honoured and esteemed as among the foremost of our legislators, the most finished of our orators, models in a culture and a language not originally their own.

Is it any wonder that a few have found it worth while to study the history, the customs, the mythology, the arts, of such a people as the Polynesians? It is said that they have no literature; they have a splendid one, but it has hitherto and through the ages been circulated only by word of mouth, retained, as all civilized literature was originally, in the memory. That has been the difficulty; even those who had the desire had not always the ability to tap the reservoir, and even with the ability had yet to win the confidence of its guardian. Odin gave an eye for a draught from the well of wisdom of Mimer; who has offered as much to the Mimer of the Polynesians?

3

MYTHS OF THE POLYNESIANS

We have for some time realized that even those who have collected some of the ancient lore have done so with only half understanding; the acquisition of the language is but the first step. It is only by living in close contact with them for many years, as Elsdon Best has done in the case of the Maori, that it is realized how different are the points of view of the two peoples, the Polynesians and ourselves. Most of us are, as most of our collectors have been, outside unsurmountable palisades. We cannot think as they think; they cannot think as we think; and the result has been much misunderstanding, much misinterpretation. Something can yet be gleaned, and a brighter day is dawning; in the Polynesians themselves there is a re-awakening of the pride of race; they themselves are beginning to place on record their histories, their legends, their songs; they themselves are striving for a renaissance of their arts; and when the Polynesian workers themselves enter the field, as they surely will, we stammering, thumb-fingered *pakeha* may stand aside and rejoice in the day-dawn.

Personally, I came so late in the day that I have been able to gather but little, but I have tried to be as a trumpet through which the musical Polynesian voice might make itself heard and attract attention to the power and personality behind the voice; and it is in this capacity that I have gathered together these gleanings of other men's harvests, so that my navigators and poets and orators, and savages, if the reader wills, may stand before him as do the Greeks of old, splendid even in the ruin of what they were.

The list at the end of the book gives the names of those to whom I am indebted for my gleanings, and there is no need to particularize, though I must acknowledge especial indebtedness to Cook, Moerenhout, Grey, Gill, Fornander, Kalakaua, and Percy Smith. I have not included Elsdon Best among these, as I wish to acknowledge his assistance more particularly, and also that of the Venerable Arch-deacon Williams, both of whom have ever been ready with their help and criticism pungent and salutary. I should

4

PREFACE

also like to acknowledge help from two towers of strength, the Bernice P. Bishop Museum of Honolulu, under the directorship of Professor Herbert E. Gregory, and the Maori Board of Ethnological Research, under the guidance of Sir Apirana T. Ngata.

J. C. A.

WELLINGTON
1928

CONTENTS

ILLUSTRATIONS

9

MYTHS OF THE POLYNESIANS

10

ILLUSTRATIONS

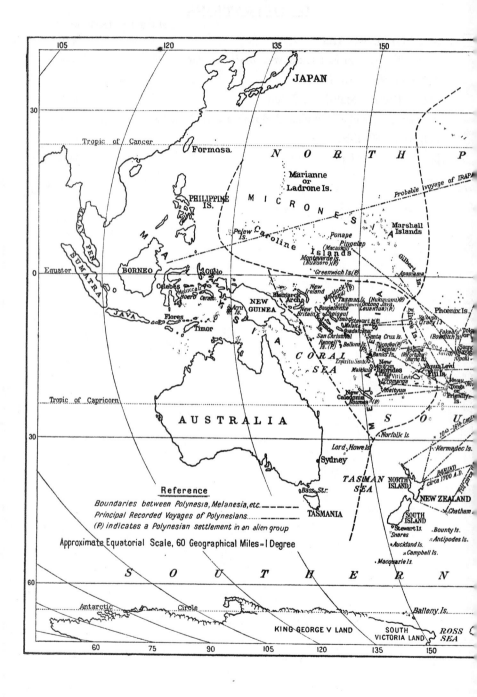

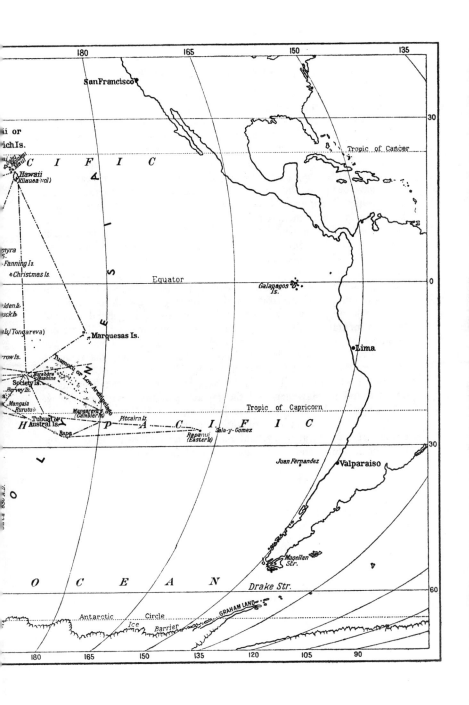

San Francisco

Tropic of Cancer

ki or
ich Is.

C I F I C

Hawaii
(Kilauea vol.)

myra
s.
Fanning Is.
Christmas Is.

Equator

Galapagos
Is.

lden Is.
uck Is.
Is.(Tongareva)

Lima

Marquesas Is.

row Is.

Tuamotu or Low Archipelago

Borabora
Tahitine
Society Is.

Hervey Is.

Mangaia
Rurutu

Tropic of Capricorn

Tubuai
Austral Is.

Mangareva Is.
(Gambier Is.)

Pitcairn Is.

Rapa

Sala-y-Gomez

Rapanui
(Easterly)

H

P — A — C — I — F — I — C

Juan Fernandez

Valparaiso

Magellan
Str.

O C E A N

Drake Str.

GRAHAM LAND

Antarctic Circle

Ice Barrier

NOTE ON PROPER NAMES

PROPER names have been spelt according to the particular dialect from which they have been collected, transliterations being made in the text in some cases for reasons of comparison when the names occur in widely separated localities. The transliterations can always be followed by reference to the table on p. 17. Hyphens have been used with reluctance, as unless the history of the name is known it is not known what actually are the components; they may be quite other than those they appear to be. They have been used, however, so that readers may not be staggered with a name like Tamanuiaraki, which, while quite simple, may not be so at first sight in this form, but is really simple enough as Tama-nui-a-raki. Moreover, as it is not necessary to give the name in full every time it appears, names have been contracted (as is the custom among Polynesians themselves), Tama-nui-a-raki appearing as Tama-nui', Tu-te-Koropanga as 'Koropanga, and so on. It is as well to remember, however, that although names have been broken with hyphens, they are not broken in sound, the voice flowing from vowel to vowel, giving each its full sound while coalescing them. The vowels have one sound in general—that of the Continental vowels—though they may be long or short. There are instances where they are not coalesced, as in Lu'ukia. Here the apostrophe represents a catch in the breath, the catch being the remnant of a dropped consonant—in this instance *k*. The Maori form of the word explains it—Rukutia. There is a remark in the text on the dropping of one *k* sound in Hawaiian and the replacing of the *t* with another *k*. The Maori alphabet contains the letters *a, e, h, i, k, m, n, o, p, r, t, u, w, ng, wh*. It is the same throughout Polynesia, allowing for the letter-changes referred to at p. 17, and remembering that *ng* in Maori and *g* in Samoan, etc., stand for the same *ng* sound, as in 'singer.'

CHAPTER I: POLYNESIA AND ITS PEOPLE

EARLY voyagers were surprised to find, scattered over the islands of the Pacific Ocean, a race that appeared homogeneous in physical characteristics, language, customs, and religion, and all observing the powerful institution of the *tapu*. They occupied a definite part of the great ocean, extending from Hawaii in the north to New Zealand in the south, a distance of 3200 miles, and from the Ellice Islands in the north-west to Easter Island in the south-east, a distance of 4000 miles—or, roughly, from 25° north latitude to 45° south, and from longitude 170° east of Greenwich to 110° west, or, say, an area of 3500 miles by 4000—that is, 14,000,000 square miles.

The area occupied has been called Polynesia, and roughly it lies east of a line drawn from New Zealand through the Friendly Islands to Samoa, thence north-east to Hawaii, all the islands mentioned being included. Within this area there are a few islands occupied by non-Polynesians, the principal groups and islands occupied by Polynesians being as follows: the Hawaiian Islands (6500 sq. m.), Samoa (1200 sq. m.), the Friendly or Tongan Islands (390 sq. m.), Rotuma (20 sq. m.), Niue (100 sq. m.), the Cook Islands, including the Hervey Islands and Rarotonga (120 sq. m.), the Austral Islands (75 sq. m.), the Society or Tahitian Islands (650 sq. m.), the Low Archipelago, or Tuamotu group (formerly Poumotu, mispronounced Paumotu) (30 sq. m.), the Marquesas (480 sq. m.). The Ellice Islands (30 sq. m.) lie 400–500 miles north-west of Samoa, and outside the western boundary of Polynesia as defined above; but with this exception, and the exception of a few scattered places in the New Hebrides, the Loyalty Islands, and the north-east and south-east coasts of New Guinea, the Polynesian is not found unmixed west of the line described.

The other great divisions according to racial characteristics are Indonesia, including the East Indian islands, Sumatra, Borneo, Java, the Philippines, Celebes, and the

Moluccas, etc.; Melanesia, including Australia, New Guinea, and the string of islands running south-east from the latter—the Bismarck Archipelago, the Solomon Islands, Banks Islands, the New Hebrides, New Caledonia, and Fiji; and Micronesia, including the small islands in the scattered groups north-east of Indonesia and Melanesia— the Mariannes, the Caroline Islands, the Marshall Islands, and the Gilbert Islands. While the Polynesians once occupied the Indonesian islands and the Micronesian, their occupation was rather that of sojourners than settlers, and they do not now live among the Indonesians and Micronesians, nor do they mix with them.

As a race the Polynesians are somewhat above middle height, 5 feet 9 inches or 5 feet 10 inches, usually well formed, with well-developed limbs and muscles. The women, however, are inclined to be short and stout, and over-developed as regards the lower limbs. In colour they vary from a light to a dusky brown, the lighter shades being found nearer the equator, the darkest being at the two extremes, Hawaii in the north and New Zealand in the south. The children when born are as fair as Europeans, but darken on exposure. In Tahiti a fair skin was esteemed, and women, and men too, would live as much in the shade as possible in order to retain the fairness. Their hair is thick and strong and black, with a slight tendency to curl or wave. The beard is scanty, and does not appear till toward middle life. The hair under the arms and on the breast was often eradicated for cleanliness' sake. In many of the islands there is, or was, a great difference between what are commonly called the upper and lower classes, the former being much superior in size and build, often showing strains of men over 6 feet in height, and of fine physical development. The lower classes were also darker in hue.

In character they showed the general gaiety of a happy disposition and good humour, with a desire to please and a willingness to be amused. They were, however, fickle in their passions and their desires. They showed great susceptibility to new impressions, and a readiness to adopt

14

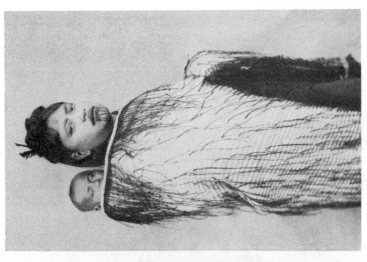

WOMAN CARRYING CHILD

(See page 14)

MAORI MAN

FIGURE OF A TATTOOED NATIVE OF THE MARQUESAS

From Captain David Porter's *Journal of a Cruise made to the Pacific Ocean in the U.S. Frigate "Essex" in 1812-13-14*

(See page 16)

new customs and modes of thinking, and their intellectual endowments were good. Their domestic affections were weak, they were fond of war, and, while not deliberately cruel, were callous to the sufferings of others. They were licentious, extremely so in some of the islands, and showed a general lack of conscientiousness. They were incapable of keeping a secret, so that in warfare each side usually knew what the other intended. It was his secretive nature that made Te Rauparaha such a remarkable Maori warrior ; no man knew his thought. They had strong religious feelings, which could not be called fear or superstition since many had no images or idols, and those who had used them as symbols only, as Christians use the Cross. It was this religious feeling that gave the system of *tapu* so firm a hold, and there is no doubt that *tapu* effectively took the place of conscience and civil law, and was more implicitly obeyed.

There were, of course, great variations of these general characteristics, due to locality and circumstance. The finest physique was found among the Marquesans ; the most estimable people were found among the Samoans ; the most poetical and gentle among the Tahitians ; the most religious and romantic among the Hawaiians ; the most intellectual, and the most formidable warriors and military strategists, among the Maori.

They were a race of navigators ; not only because of being island-dwellers, but because their ancestors were navigators ; and for this reason they have ever shown a great fondness for travel.

They were not universally cannibals : the avowed cannibals were found in New Zealand, the Hervey Islands, the Gambier Islands at the south-east extremity of the Low Archipelago, and in the Marquesas. Cannibalism was known to occur in Samoa and the Friendly, Society, and Hawaiian Islands, but was not commonly practised there, being rather regarded with aversion, if not horror. *Kava*-drinking was practised widely, but chiefly in Samoa and Tonga ; and usually it was a ceremonial custom confined to the chiefs. It was quite unknown in New Zealand.

Tattooing was practised in most of the islands, but the style differed very considerably; only touches here and there, as on the finger-joints, in Hawaii; the body was ornamented, as if to simulate clothing, in the more tropical islands; in New Zealand, where the climate caused the body to be generally covered, the face-tattoo reached its highest development, though the body was also heavily tattooed.

Cook noted the great cleanliness of the people, both in eating and in the care of the body. He noted that their sanitary arrangements were superior to those of many European cities, and that in cleanliness the Polynesian women could teach many of their European sisters. When their houses were crowded for hours during one of their many entertainments Cook noted that the only inconvenience experienced was from the excessive heat.

The sea-temperature permitted of the ceaseless sea-bathing and surf-riding in which the Hawaiians and Tahitians in particular were so enthusiastically expert; between the latitudes of 45° north and 45° south the surface-temperature is always above 50° Fahrenheit; it reaches 80° in summer between Japan and New Guinea. In that part of the Pacific south of the equator the temperature of the surface-water is apparently higher than that of the air.

The speech of the Polynesians consists of dialects of one language, with a limited alphabet, and all syllables ' open '; and at the time of their discovery there was no other single language that covered so great an area. A great many words are the same, so that Cook was able to employ a Tahitian as interpreter in all the islands from New Zealand to Hawaii. A Grimm's law operates here as in Teutonic tongues, so that it may be said with certainty what letter-changes, if any, a word will take when transplanted from Hawaiian to Samoan, or from Samoan to Maori, or from Maori to Rarotongan. There were sounds that might indifferently be represented by *l*, *r*, or *d*, and these various sounds have been stabilized according to the ear of the one who first fixed them by giving their alphabet-equivalent. In the Maori the sounds of *l* and *d* have been eliminated in favour of *r*, and words which actually may have had the sound of *d*, as Kidikidi, are now pronounced by even most Maoris, if not all, as Kirikiri. So, too, the sound that may have been the *l* sound is now *r*, but under the stress of excitement the former may slip out, as the present writer has heard, ' lecord ' being said instead of ' record ' (the noun). The Maori *r* is properly formed by a single contact of the tongue with the palate, without any ' roll '; this would approximate to *d* or *l* according as the tongue was more or less flattened, but would never actually be *d* or *l*. The Maori, realizing a difference between his and the English *r*, will often, in the endeavour to reproduce this difference, mispronounce an English *r* as *l*. There is no *g* sound in Polynesian ; but in some of the dialects, such as Samoan, *g* has been employed to represent the nasalguttural which in Maori is represented by *ng*—the sound being that of the *ng* in ' singer,' not in ' finger.' A special sign, *ŋ*, was devised for this sound, but has not been adopted. It is unfortunate that two signs, *ng* and *g*, should be used for the one sound.

The following table, showing the interchange of consonants, is quoted by Tregear from Hale, of the Wilkes Expedition.

Maori of New Zealand	Samoa	Tahiti	Hawaii	Tonga	Rarotonga	Marquesas	Mangareva	Tuamotu
h	*s* or *f*	*h*	*h*	*h*	Wanting	*h*	*h*	*h*
k	' (a break)	Wanting	Wanting	*k*	*k*	*k*	*k*	*k*
ng	*g*	Wanting	*n*	*g*	*ng*	*k*	*g*	*g*
p	*p*	*p*	*p*	*b*	*p*	*p*	*p*	*p*
r	*l*	*r*	*l*	*l*	*r*	Wanting	*r*	*r*
t	*t*	*t*	*k*	*t*	*t*	*t*	*t*	*t*
w	*v*	*v*	*w*	*v*	*v*	*v*	*v*	*v*
wh	*f*	*h* or *f*	*h*	*f*	Wanting	*f* or *h*	*h*	*f* or *h*

The remark above regarding the *g* of Samoan applies also to the *g* of Tonga, Mangareva, and Tuamotu; the sound is nasal as in Maori—*g* has the same significance as *ng*. Both *m* and *n* are pronounced by all without variation. There is an anomaly in Hawaiian : the *k* is dropped, but another *k* is substituted for the Maori *t*, so that the word *tangata* (man) becomes *kanaka*—*n* taking the place of *ng*. It would seem that the dropped *k* must have had a different sound from the *k* that takes the place of *t*, or there would be no reason for the dropping. So in Maori the *k* had two sounds—the sound of English *k* in the North Island, and a hard sound like *kh* in the South Island among the Ngati-mamoe, who also substituted this *k* for the North *ng*, making *kainga* (a village) *kaika* ; and the final *a* being breathed only, the word became *kaik* ; and a writer hearing the name Kaik Hill, and not knowing the Maori word, wrote it Caique Hill, substituting Peruvian for Maori.

In the stories following the spelling of the dialect from which the story was first collected has been retained ; thus the god Tangaroa (Maori) may appear as Tagaloa (Samoan), Kanaloa (Hawaiian), Ta'aroa (Tahitian), so that he is Protean in spelling as in other respects.

On the east the Polynesians are bordered only by the Pacific Ocean until the continent of America is reached, about 2000 miles away. On the west they are bordered by the Micronesians and Melanesians.

It is difficult to say what the original Polynesian type was—there has been so much crossing with darker and perhaps fairer races during their wanderings ; but S. Percy Smith thinks the nearest to the original Polynesian is the handsome, tall, oval-faced, high-browed, lithe, active, light brown, black-straight-haired, black- or very-dark-brown-eyed, cheerful, dignified individual so frequently met with in various parts of the Pacific. This type predominates in some branches more than in others, and perhaps Samoa contains a larger proportion than any other island ; but it is found everywhere—from Hawaii to New Zealand, from Samoa to Easter Island.

There are here and there islands among the bordering fringes of non-Polynesian islands which are altogether, or

18

in part, occupied by settlements of Polynesians, as in the neighbourhood of the Friendly Islands, where the two races, Polynesian and Melanesian, are blended, the Fijians being about half and half, as are the New Hebrideans. In some islands farther to the west both races live, the Polynesians occupying the shore-line, the Melanesians living in the interior mountain fastnesses. There are remnants of their occupation in the Caroline Islands, but the population itself, about 30,000 in number, includes black, brown, and yellow races. There are also isolated islets, as Nukuoro (Monteverde) and Greenwich Island, occupied by Polynesians in Melanesian areas.

The Polynesian population of the groups enumerated above amounted in 1922 to approximately 184,000; in 1900 it was, according to Percy Smith, about 182,000; in 1838, according to Wilkes, 375,000; at the end of the eighteenth century, according to Cook, Forster, and others, 1,290,000. Even if this last estimate were double the actual number, the decrease is a terrible one, more especially when it is remembered that it is largely due to the presence of the white man. A heavy price has been paid by the Polynesian for the blessings of civilization.

The Pacific Ocean was first seen by Europeans at the end of the fifteenth century, when Vasco da Gama, for the first time rounding the Cape of Good Hope, then the Cape of Storms, established Portuguese trading-stations in India, and in the East Indies, including the Moluccas. It was first seen from the eastern side by the Spaniard Balboa, from the Panama isthmus, in 1513. It was first sailed and named by the Portuguese navigator Magellan, sailing under the Spanish flag, in 1520. The calm weather experienced by him after discovering and sailing the strait named after him caused him to call it *Mare pacificum*. The first Englishman to follow him, Drake, in 1577, found occasion to call it *Mare furiosum*. Its behaviour, and that of its people, ranges between these extremes. In crossing it Magellan missed the Hawaiian group, and discovered first the Ladrone Islands, then the Philippines, in 1521.

19

MYTHS OF THE POLYNESIANS

The Polynesians had inhabited the islands of this great ocean, which occupies about half the water-surface of the globe, for at least 1500 years before it was sailed by a European. While the Norsemen were penetrating the Arctic seas and the North Atlantic, discovering Iceland, Greenland, and America, and sailing up the Old World rivers, harrying all Europe, the Polynesians were exploring the far wider Pacific, even venturing into the stormy Antarctic seas, as Cook ventured centuries later.

Almost every navigator has perceived the kinship of the widely scattered Polynesians; almost every navigator has speculated on the reasons for this scattering, and on the position of the land from which the race originally came. If that land still exists, it is not inhabited by Polynesians, for no Polynesians are known outside the Pacific. A comparatively highly civilized people, with characteristics such as those possessed by the Polynesians, could hardly, one would suppose, have failed to leave traces of their occupation in the land of their origin, yet hardly a trace can be found.

There are four theories as to their origin, all as different as they well could be. One theory derives the Polynesian from America, relying principally on the fact that the prevailing winds are from the east, and that as European circumnavigators have usually crossed the Pacific from the east the Polynesians with their comparatively fragile craft must have come from the east. Minor arguments are the similarity of certain customs, such as the use of the earth-oven. While, however, the prevailing trade-winds make it easier to sail from the east, navigators, whalers, and others have shown that sailing from the west is almost equally practicable, and this theory is not now held seriously.

The second theory, which finds widest acceptance, is that the Polynesians came from some part of Southern Asia. Taking the word Uru, found in old traditions of the Maori, as a place-name, and not merely as a cardinal point, 'the west,' which is its usual meaning, the part of Asia from which the most ancient traditions derive them has tentatively been identified as Ur of the Chaldees, on the

MAORI BOY AND GIRL

Photos Iles, Thames, N.Z.

(See page 20)

TE HAUHAU, A TYPICAL OLD MAORI WARRIOR
(See page 26)

river Euphrates. This Asiatic theory has been worked out most fully by Percy Smith and A. Fornander on the traditional and genealogical side, by W. Churchill on the linguistic, and by A. C. Haddon on the sociological. Briefly, it is suggested that the movement of a great body with Aryan affinities began toward India at a period between 4000 and 2000 years B.C., Indo-Aryans appearing in the Panjab in 1080 B.C. They settled in Lower Panjab in 850 B.C., and in Mid-Ganges in 800 B.C. There were great disturbances in India from 500 to 400 B.C., and Javan traditions say that in 300 B.C. 20,000 families were led by Arishtan Shar from North-west India, most of whom dispersed *en route*, probably in Malabar, Maladiva, and Malagassar (Madagascar, many of whose words show a Polynesian affinity). Ten years later there was a second invasion of Java by 20,000 families from the Kling coast. Indian Malas, or Malays, Yauvas, or Javans, Bali, and others were all over the peninsula and archipelago in 125 B.C. If the Rarotongan records are correctly interpreted, reference is made in them to the leaving of India by the Polynesians about the fourth or fifth century B.C.

There are extant traditional accounts, or log-books, as Percy Smith calls them, of three of these emigration streams. The first consisted of Samoans, Tongans, and probably the many islanders occupying the outlying islands along the coasts of the Solomon and New Hebrides groups, from Leuaniua (or Ontong Java), Futuna, Uvea, and Niue Islands to, possibly, New Zealand. The second, consisting of the so-called Tongafiti branch of the race, included Rarotongans, Tahitians, Tuamotuans (Poumotuans), Marquesans, Mangarevans, and most of the Maori of New Zealand. The third consisted of the east coast Maori of New Zealand and many, if not all, of the Hawaiians. Percy Smith quotes from these log-books in his work *Hawaiki*, and many strange movements of ancient peoples are seen dimly in the far past by means of the fitful gleams given by these long-preserved oral traditions. More will be said of these later.

The third theory maintains that the Polynesians came neither from the eastern nor from the western continent, but were scattered from some centre, now no longer existing, in the Pacific itself, from some continental area of which the many scattered groups of islands are the unsubmerged remnants. The able champion of this theory is Dr J. Macmillan Brown, though he first considered that they came from some western region by way of Siberia, Japan, and the Caroline Islands; and he urges that the Polynesians could not have been in long or close contact with the Indonesians without becoming acquainted with the art of pottery and carrying it with them into the Pacific; they could never have used rice, a grain they must have known if they had lived in India or Indonesia, or they would not have abandoned that easily carried food; they would hardly have escaped the betel-chewing habit had they lived any length of time in Malaysia before being urged farther on by the incursions of Malayans from South-east Asia; their language would show more trace of the languages of the peoples among whom or on whose coasts they sojourned than it does, the dialects into which it is divided being no more than the dialects of a continental people speaking a common language. It is possible, however, that even had they known the art of pottery the manufacture might have been abandoned on their occupying lands that supplied little suitable material, especially when the migrations were, as some of them were, composed principally of men. Moreover, Cook found a few articles of pottery on Ewa, in the Friendly Islands (spelled Eaoowe by him, formerly Middleburg), but so few that he thought they must have been brought from some other island; and on New Caledonia the natives made earthen jars, so that the Polynesians could not have been altogether ignorant of the art, and it almost appears as though they had no great desire for such articles. Pottery is also found in Fiji, New Guinea, and in two places in the New Hebrides. As will be seen later, they probably did know rice, but abandoned its use in favour of other abundant and natural foods found

MAORI CARVED WOODEN BOWLS

Photos Dominion Museum, Wellington, N.Z.

(See page 22)

in the areas to which they migrated. It need not necessarily follow that the knowledge of betel-nut-chewing meant its adoption; many civilized people, for instance, know of the existence of the tobacco-chewing habit, but do not themselves adopt it. There is no continental area now known where one language is spoken in varied dialects. On the other hand, the diffusion of a language like the English has taken place from a small centre by successive waves in various directions; so the Polynesian language appears to have spread from its Asiatic source, a small migration entering Madagascar, another entering Japan, so that the languages of those countries are a little tinged with the Polynesian of the few migrants absorbed by them.

These are ethnological considerations, and they appear to make the former existence of a continental area at least unnecessary. This question is, however, rather geological than ethnological, and geology affords us no evidence of the existence, in times at all recent, of a continental area in the Eastern Pacific. Before the exploration of the Pacific scientific theorizing required the existence of a southern continent to balance the northern land-mass of the globe; and long before Cook and other voyagers proved the non-existence of such an area the continent had been discovered as Bacon discovered his New Atlantis, had been mapped, and the various divisions marked off and named.

Geologically there is no evidence of a continental area in the Eastern Pacific. The mean depth of the ocean is about 2500 fathoms; it is more uniform in the east, where there are few islands, more diversified in the west, where the islands are numerous. The deepest sounding of the exploring ship *Challenger* was 4575 fathoms (nearly 5¼ miles), between the Caroline and Ladrone Islands; the American ship *Tuscarora* found 4655 fathoms north-east of Japan, and a British ship found 4500 fathoms east of Fiji. Recently, and by new methods of sounding, depths much greater than these have been found. The shallow areas indicating former land-surfaces lie among the groups of larger islands between Asia and Australia, and point to Australia having included New Guinea within its ancient land-area, while Asia included the East India Islands. A deep channel separates these two ancient continental areas.

The islands within Polynesia are volcanic or coralline, or both combined; the Hawaiian Islands and the Marquesas are volcanic, Hawaii possessing or being possessed by one of the largest active volcanoes in the world. Samoa and the Society Islands are also volcanic. The Friendly Islands, and the Austral Islands, are coralline; the larger Cook Islands are volcanic, the smaller ones coralline. Niue is an island of upheaved coral. If there had been a continental area which slowly submerged, allowing the building of coral reefs round its higher points, the submergence must have been so slow that, remembering the average depth of the ocean, at the time there was a continuous or brokenly continuous area of land there were no Polynesians. There have, besides, been periods of slow upheaval—a slow rising and falling as of a breathing Antæus; this would put the date of any land-area still further back. In 1849 Dana, the geologist of the United States Exploring Expedition of 1838–42, wrote: " We should beware of hastening to the conclusion that a continent once occupied the place of the ocean, or a large part of it, which is without proof. To establish the former existence of a Pacific continent is an easy matter for the fancy; but geology knows nothing of it, nor even of its probability."

The mythical Lemuria, a Pacific continent analogous to Atlantis of the Atlantic, is, by such as believe in it, supposed to have extended from Madagascar or its neighbourhood in the Indian Ocean to some part of the mid-Pacific, including the scattered islands of the East Indian Archipelago. Asia and Australia were then non-existent—at any rate, in anything like their present form; but there is little tangible, if much psychic, evidence of the existence of Lemuria, though its very name is intended to indicate its biological origin; it was supposed to have existed to account for the fact that the genera of lemurs are confined to Malaysia and Madagascar, a few only occurring in Africa.

The fourth theory, urged seriously by only one writer, Lesson, suggested that the Polynesians originated in New Zealand.

The two trade-winds blow fairly constantly, the one from the north-east, the other from the south-east, between them lying the equatorial belt of calm which is experienced all the year round north of the equator in the East Pacific, but which in the West Pacific is south of the equator during the Southern summer, being replaced by a regular southerly breeze during the Southern winter. There are also belts of calms with variable winds north and south of the trade-winds, westerly winds blowing toward America north and south of these again. It was on the trade-winds that the early circumnavigators sailed across the Pacific, leaving the continent in the north about California, in the south about Chili and Peru. Besides the trade-winds there are the monsoons, which blow with great regularity, their direction changing according to the season. They are more prevalent in the Western Pacific, their general direction being south-east, north-east, or north-west.

The various winds cause temporary currents, but these are no more than surface-currents and change with the wind. A cold surface-current constantly flows north from the Antarctic, dividing at Cape Horn, one branch entering the Atlantic, the other flowing along Chili and Peru, and thence westward. A great equatorial current flows west, divided into two by a counter-current flowing east; one branch on approaching the Asiatic coast flows north and north-east along Japan, the other southward along the east shores of Australia, sweeping up along the west coasts of New Zealand, thence curving east past Cape Maria van Diemen and merging in the Antarctic surface-current. The many islands diverting one or other of the currents cause minor branch currents.

After the voyage by Magellan in 1520–21 the Spaniards must have sailed the ocean and discovered various islands or groups of islands. Old native traditions seem to point to their having visited at least the Hawaiian Islands; but they were secretive regarding their discoveries, and their old maps are only beginning to be brought to light. Quiros was in the Low Archipelago in 1606; the first English vessel to visit the islands was one commanded by Wilson in 1797. Tasman visited the Friendly Islands in 1643; Cook, in 1773, was the first Englishman to do so. Roggewein visited Samoa in 1722, the *Pandora* in 1791. Wallis discovered the Society Islands in 1767; he was followed in 1769 by Cook, who also discovered Niue in 1774, and the Hawaiian Islands in 1778. It is supposed that the Spaniard Gaetano discovered Hawaii about 1555; but this is no more than conjecture.

Cook realized that permanent European settlement among the Polynesians would be most harmful to the islanders. He said that so far as the natives were concerned, a settlement might easily be established there, but this, he hoped, would never happen. The occasional visits of Europeans might benefit them in some respects; " but a permanent establishment amongst them," said he, " conducted as most European establishments amongst Indian nations have unfortunately been, would, I fear, give them just cause to lament that our ships had ever found them out. Indeed, it is very unlikely that any measure of this kind should ever be seriously thought of, as it can neither serve the purposes of public ambition, nor of private avarice; and, without such inducements, I may pronounce that it will never be undertaken."

He was wrong; nineteen years afterward, in 1796, the ship *Duff* sailed with the first missionaries for the South Seas. An attempt to form a station in the Friendly Islands was made without success, and those islands were abandoned for the Society Islands—the most charming region in the South Seas. Had it been possible to introduce a modified form of Christianity and the advantages of civilized arts and industries applicable to the regions, without the danger of the disadvantages following, it might have been well;

but the disadvantages did follow; and if one prophecy of Cook proved untrue, the other proved too true.

Cook also noted the complete change in a few years, as far as tools were concerned, from the Stone Age to the Iron Age. " By the time that the iron tools, of which they are now possessed, are worn out," said he, " they will almost have lost the knowledge of their own. A stone hatchet is, at present, as rare a thing amongst them as an iron one was eight years ago; and a chisel of bone, or stone, is not to be seen. Spike-nails have supplied the place of the last; and they are weak enough to fancy that they have got an inexhaustible store of them, for these were not now at all sought after."

He had trouble with his men, three of whom deserted when he lay in the Society Islands in 1777, as one had deserted in 1774. While he could by no means condone with the offence, he evidently sympathized with the offenders, writing in the latter year : " When I considered this man's situation in life, I did not think him so culpable, nor the resolution he had taken of staying here so extraordinary, as may at first appear. He was an Irishman by birth, and had sailed in the Dutch service. I picked him up at Batavia on my return from my former voyage, and he had been with me ever since. I never learnt that he had either friends or connexions to confine him to any particular part of the world : all nations were alike to him; where then could such a man be more happy than at one of these isles ? where, in one of the finest climates in the world, he could enjoy not only the necessaries, but the luxuries of life, in ease and plenty. I know not, if he might not have obtained my consent, if he had applied for it in proper time." It is to be wondered if, had these men succeeded in eluding Cook, and remained in their Paradise, their lot would have proved as happy as they expected. Pierre Loti found it a dream-garden, but dreams have an end; are even broken, sometimes, before fading.

The same attractions, contrasted, no doubt, with life on the ship under a martinet captain, caused the mutiny on the *Bounty* in 1790, when Bligh was set adrift in an open boat with eighteen men, and made a remarkable voyage of over 3500 miles through the West Pacific, overcoming difficulties and enduring dangers that seemed to make success miraculous. The *Bounty* was within sight of the Friendly Islands when the mutiny took place; and on Bligh being set adrift the mutineers returned to Tahiti, sailing finally, all but ten men, to Pitcairn Island, taking with them six Polynesian men and a dozen women. They ran the *Bounty* ashore and burned her, and their retreat was not discovered for eighteen years, and then only by chance. How rude was the awakening during the earlier of those eighteen years from the dreams that led to the mutiny! Of the ten men who remained at Tahiti four only were skilled mechanics, two of the four being carpenters; yet in eight months, with only a few tools and the raw material furnished by the island, they had built a small vessel which sailed those seas for many years, making the quickest passage of the time from China to the Hawaiian, then known as the Sandwich, Islands.

Still more recently, in 1913, the *El Dorado* (Captain Benson) was wrecked in the Eastern Pacific, and in a 20-foot boat eleven men weathered the storm, sighting Easter Island in nine days, but not making it till two days later. They had been three or four months on the island when the Captain, business urging him, patched up the boat and set sail in October for Mangareva, 1600 miles away, with a watch for compass and friction-sticks for matches. He arrived in sixteen days, rested two days, then set out for Tahiti, covering the extra 900 miles in eleven days more.

These events, the voyages by Bligh and Benson in the open boats, and the building of the vessel at Tahiti, are themselves sufficient to show that there is no improbability in the Polynesians having built vessels as seaworthy, or of their having made as long voyages. Besides being excellent navigators, the Polynesians were also true colonizers; indeed, the primal reason for their voyaging was no doubt the need for discovering fields for migration. They were not nomads by nature, but rather agriculturists, and wherever they went they carried with them the food-plants to which they had been accustomed. To New Zealand, for instance, they carried the *kumara*, or sweet potato, the *taro*, the yam, and the gourd, all of which, except perhaps the yam, were seen by the early colonists from Europe, and of which the *kumara* is still grown in large quantities. Neither the *kumara* nor the *taro* flowers normally in New Zealand; only one instance of each has been recorded in Poverty Bay. To New Zealand was also brought the *aute*, or paper mulberry, for the manufacture of cloth, and the finding when dredging the Whangarei Harbour of an old *tapa*-beater of the same four-sided pattern as used in the Pacific is a proof that the bark-cloth was manufactured for a time in New Zealand. An infinitely superior material being found in the *harakeke*, or Maori flax, however, the plants of which grew everywhere without trouble, the cultivation of the *aute* was soon abandoned, and the trees died out. A few were still to be seen when Cook visited New Zealand. It is also said that the coconut was brought, but failed to grow. A palm bearing a nut similar to the coconut was indigenous to New Zealand geological ages ago, fossil nuts about an inch and a half in length having been found during the last thirty years or so in one northern locality. One of these was sent to the writer while engaged on this book. The face of Tuna appears even on these nuts, which ripened and fell before man had appeared upon earth. They are supposed to be well over a million years old. The breadfruit may have been brought, but it could not have been grown so far south, and the only indication now existing that the ancestors of the present Maori knew the breadfruit at all is the occurrence of its name, *kuru*, in several old songs and place-names. The Maori dog, *kuri*, was introduced, also the Maori rat, *kiore*, a vegetable-feeder; but the pig and the fowl, so common elsewhere in the Pacific, apparently were never established in New Zealand until the pig was liberated by Captain Cook, and throve and multiplied exceedingly. To the present day pig-hunting is a sport both to Maori and European, the former especially finding wild pork a good addition to his larder. The dog, however, became extinct in the early days of European settlement.

The plants introduced had almost reached their southern limit; indeed, they could not be grown in the extreme south of the islands. The yam would grow only in the extreme north, extending no farther south than Tologa Bay, near East Cape, where it was seen in the time of Cook; the *taro* and gourd (also probably imported) came as far as Cook Strait, but could not be altogether relied on so far south; the *kumara* could be grown as far south as Temuka, near Timaru, but only in sheltered localities, for the frosts of those parts are too severe. To augment their supply of vegetable food the Maori added fern-root, baked and beaten to loosen the fibre, and the saccharine tap-root of the *ti* (*Cordyline*; not the common cabbage-tree), also making bread from the pulp of *hinau* berries and the pollen of *raupo*, the bulrush. The edible *ti* does not flower, and is probably exotic. The orange-coloured berries of the *karaka* (*Corynocarpus laevigata*) were also an important article of food.

While the Polynesians may have used rice at one time (for the Maori and the Cook Islanders preserve the name in the words *ari* and *vari*), they apparently left it behind on leaving the mysterious homeland, the many-positioned Hawaiki. They apparently abandoned its cultivation and use when the breadfruit was discovered in Java, and thereafter they carried the cuttings of the breadfruit-tree with them, planting it wherever it would flourish. As showing the little need for actual hard work in the luxuriant islands of the Pacific, it is said that if a man in his lifetime plant ten breadfruit-trees he has done his duty for posterity.

There are records of these waves of migration. There were periods of voyaging alternating with periods of rest, when the Hotspurs of the Pacific would cry, " Fie upon this quiet life! I want work," and would go a-voyaging; and there seem to have been no islands in the Pacific that were not visited by these intrepid navigators. They must

30

TYPES OF POLYNESIAN CANOES AND CHARTS

A. Outrigger canoe. *B.* Double canoe of Hawaii, with crab-claw sail. *C.* Double canoe of Tahiti, showing characteristic sail. *D.* Double canoe of Fiji, with lateen sail. *E.* Maori war canoe, with *ra kauta* form of sail. (There might be two or more such sails.) *F.* Stick and string charts.

have visited continental areas such as Australia, and New Guinea, and America, but for some reason that cannot be divined they formed no settlements on them; or, if they did, no trace of them has yet been found. The Hawaiian Islands were not occupied by the present Polynesians until about the seventh century; New Zealand about the fourteenth. There had, however, been migrations of other folk, probably other branches of Polynesians, before those dates—or of Polynesians mixed with Melanesians or other races. There is a tradition that on their first arrival in New Zealand the Maori found the land in the possession of a dark-skinned people, ill-favoured, tall, spare, spindle-shanked, with flat faces, overhanging brows, and upward-turning nostrils. They wore little clothing, and built very poor houses, were ignorant and treacherous, and the Maori regarded them with dislike and contempt. Their women, however, looked with favour on the handsome Maori men, and a mixture of the two races was the result. The Maori learned that they were the descendants of the crews of three fishing-canoes that had in times past been driven out to sea by a westerly storm from their homeland, and that their original home was much warmer than New Zealand. The Maori called them Maru-iwi, and the Moriori of the Chatham Islands may have been descendants.

In some of the recitals regarding their early voyages names are given of islands which cannot now be identified; and it is thought that this indicates the disappearance of some islands, formerly used as landmarks, and may account, for instance, for the sudden cessation of voyages between the Hawaiian and the Society Islands. It will be seen, however, that many islands had several names, one or more material and at least one spiritual; the spiritual name may be the one in the recital, while the material name has survived, or *vice versa*. A voyage often made, moreover, could still be made by following direction, even should an intermediate visible point disappear. It is so in bird-migration. The course of the migrations of the Polynesians into the Pacific by way of Indonesia is being studied more

MANGAPIHO ROCK, TOM BOWLING BAY, NORTH ISLAND
Site of an old Maori stronghold.
N.Z. Government Publicity Photo

(See page 32)

SAMOAN ROUND HOUSE

Showing temporary reed curtains let down for protection.

Photo Tattersall, Apia, Samoa

(See page 36)

and more scientifically, and Fornander (1880) and Percy Smith (1921) relied mainly on genealogies and native tradition; but, however reliable these may be up to a certain or uncertain point, calculations based on genealogies cannot be more than approximate, if they are even approximate. In calculating his dates Fornander took the length of a generation as thirty years; Percy Smith, however, after due consideration, and taking the opinion of Polynesian scholars who knew the race well, reduced this to twenty-five years; and it is on the basis of a twenty-five-year generation that the dates are calculated.

Churchill (1911, 1916) used nothing but linguistic data, and from it he gathered that there were two principal streams of Polynesian migration into the Pacific through the Asiatic Archipelago; one, which he calls the Samoan, about 2000 years ago; the other, which he calls the Tonga-fiti, 1000 years ago. The Samoan stream passed from Indonesia down by the north coast of New Guinea, through the Bismarck Archipelago and the Solomon group, finally reaching Samoa, making it later on a starting-point for further migrations to various more remote islands—Tonga, Niue, Hawaii, Mangareva, New Zealand. The Tonga-fiti stream passed from Indonesia along the southern coast of New Guinea, through the Torres Strait, finally reaching Viti Levu, in the Fiji group, and from thence migrating, apparently by way of Samoa to other islands, in the manner of the Samoan stream—to the Marquesas, the Hervey and Society groups, and thence again to other islands scattered over the watery waste of their wandering. It was questioned if the southern stream might not have been, not an independent stream, but a reflex of the Samoan stream, returning along the south side of New Guinea from south to north; but Churchill thinks the evidence favours the two streams at wide intervals of time.

Rivers (1914) has studied the question from quite another aspect—the sociological; and if his conclusions do not altogether agree with Churchill's, they at least agree with them in deriving the Polynesians through Indonesia. He

33

goes back much farther in time than other investigators. He sees in the present Polynesians, as all must see who know their extraordinarily varying characteristics, the descendants of several different peoples, reaching the Pacific at different periods. First, he thinks, there must have been an aboriginal people of Melanesia of whom practically nothing is known. Then came a stream passing through Melanesia and into the Pacific—a people who buried their dead in a sitting posture. They were possibly the original inhabitants of Polynesia; many remained in Melanesia, fusing with the Melanesians and forming a dual or composite people. Then came a stream of *kava*-drinking people, composed of two bodies emigrating at different periods; of these, one mummified their dead, the other buried them in extended position. They came in small successive bodies, were apparently a peaceful people, mostly men, and were well received. They were of a higher culture, and before passing on they introduced new ideas and new beliefs. The earlier dual people dealt in magic, believed in spirits that had never been men, and the spirits of their dead lived underground : the *kava* people, on the other hand, were religious, dealing in religious ceremonies rather than in magic rites; they believed in ghosts, the spirits of dead men, and the spirits of their dead passed to other places upon earth or above it. Then followed a betel-chewing people, and after them a cremation people, but the influence of these two migrations was apparently confined to North-west Melanesia. Rivers finds other cultural distinctions, and while he agrees with Churchill on many points, he finds himself at total variance with him as regards the two streams that passed north and south of New Guinea; they are separated by far too great a period. Williamson (1924) points out, however, that Churchill's dates are purely approximate, as all such surmised dates must be ; and that his two streams, the Samoan and Tongafitian, might well be the two streams of Rivers's *kava* people. It is thought, too, that Percy Smith's migrating stream was the second stream of Rivers's *kava* people.

POLYNESIA AND ITS PEOPLE

Hawaiki, the traditional name of the Polynesian fatherland, Percy Smith thinks originally referred to India; but the Polynesians carried the name with them in their wanderings, applying it to many of their later homes. It appears in many forms, according to the letter-changes of the various branches of the race, as Hawaiki, Havaiki, Hawai'i, Avaiki, Savaiki, Savai'i, Java, Jawa. Another old name often applied to the homeland is Tawhiti, and this Percy Smith identifies with a mountain in Hawaiki itself. This name too has been carried with the wanderers and applied to other homes; as Tafiti (a Samoan name for the Fiji group), Viti Levu, Tahiti (or Society Islands), and Kahiki, an indefinite name, applied by the Hawaiians generally to places outside the Hawaiian group.

There are other less-known names of the fatherland, Atia-te-varinganui being one. Percy Smith thinks its meaning was " Great Atia-covered-with-rice," but the interpretation is dubious. At about the year 450 B.C., according to Percy Smith's conjectured dates, this land of Atia' was governed by Tu-te-rangi-marama. He built a temple, twelve fathoms high, enclosed it with a stone wall, and named it Koro-tuatini. It was very spacious, and was built as a meeting-place for gods and men; and here after death the spirits of the ancients foregathered with the gods. Here originated different kinds of sports, and games, and the *eivas* (dances). Here also originated the *kariei*, or houses of amusement, singing, and dancing, and many other customs; also the sacred games and feasts to the gods Rongo', Tane', Rua-nuku, Tu', Tangaroa, and Tongaiti. Here were meeting-places for the great chiefs of those days, as Tu-te-rangi-marama, and Te Nga-taito-ariki, and Atea, and Kau-kura, and Te Pupu, and Rua-te-atonga, and many others, when appointing rulers, and devising measures for the good of the people. Here, too, originated the wars that caused the people to enter and spread over the Pacific.

The name of the first resting-place in Indonesia was Avaiki-te-varinga, supposed to be Java, it and Indonesia itself being already inhabited by Papuans or Melanesians,

35

who were overcome—the Polynesians being themselves urged onward into the Pacific, not only by internal wars, but by the pressure of Malayans migrating from Asia. At this time, too, they came in contact with the Manahune, Manahua, or Makahua—known in Hawaii as the Mene-hune—mountain-dwellers, and adepts in sorcery.

No certain date can be assigned to the leaving of Indonesia; but Percy Smith conjectures, from the traditions preserved by the Rarotongans and Marquesans, that it was between the first and fifth centuries that the Hawaiian and Rarotongan branches (including the Maori) set out, the Samoans and Tongans probably preceding them. Their route, he considers, was *via* Celebes, Ceram, and Gilolo, and afterward along the shore of New Guinea. Fornander also thinks this was the route of the Samoans, but he considers the Tongans came by way of Torres Strait. Fiji is regarded as the general gathering-ground preparatory to the wider dispersal over the Pacific. By the year 575 all the groups about Fiji were occupied, including Samoa; and in 650 began a period of ocean-voyaging, led by the intrepid Ui-te-rangiora and his brothers Tu-te-rangiatea and Whenua-haere.

The voyage of Kupe to New Zealand is one of the earliest to those islands of which there is fairly clear record. From the genealogies it is surmised that he—that is, one of the four men known to have borne the name Kupe—lived about the year A.D. 950, and he was one of those navigators who lifted the wide horizons of the Pacific. He visited many islands, his home being in Ra'iatea, of the Society group. He was on a visit to Rarotonga, when he was for some reason impelled to set out on a voyage of discovery to the south-west. The course to New Zealand was set out by him, and preserved by his descendants: " In sailing from Rarotonga to New Zealand, let the course be to the left hand of the setting sun, moon, or Venus, in the month of February."

Kupe made the land near the North Cape in his canoe *Mata-hou-rua*, and his companion Ngake in the *Tawiri-*

36

rangi; and from there, after replenishing their stores, they sailed down the east coast to Wellington Harbour; thence by the west coast of the South Island to the extreme south, and passing through Foveaux Strait returned north by the east coast to Cook Strait. After adding again to their stores they passed up the west coast of the North Island to Hokianga Harbour, returning thence to Ra'iatea. The name Hokianga is said to have been given by Kupe because at this point he turned back. He reported the discoveries of large islands, suitable for settlement and without inhabitants—the absence of inhabitants is repeatedly mentioned in the history of the voyage. He mentioned having seen the birds (spoken of as men) *kokako* (New Zealand crow) and *tiwakawaka* (fantail). He also killed a *moa* at Arahura, at which place he found the prized greenstone. Ao-tea-roa was the name given to New Zealand by Kupe from an observation made by his wife when the land was sighted.

Kupe does not hold the honour of discoverer undisputed; for another legend says that Raka-taura first reached the country on the *taniwha Pane-iraira*. He explored the North Island, and part of the South Island, saw no men nor fire, and, returning to Hawaiki, told Kupe of the islands, whereupon Kupe set out on his voyage.

Yet another legend says that Kupe met, near Hokianga, the men of a previous migration, that of Nuku-tawhiti; but while the first discovery by Kupe may be discredited, the more claimants that appear for the honour the more clear it becomes that long voyages were accomplished by the Polynesians even before William of Normandy set foot on English ground, and that the Pacific had been explored centuries before Columbus ventured across the much narrower Atlantic.

On the return of Kupe many people of Tahiti and the adjacent islands were anxious to go at once and occupy this new-found land; but none of the Eastern Polynesians did so for over two hundred years, when Toi-te-huatahi settled in New Zealand.

From other traditions, both in the North and the South

Islands, it is possible that New Zealand was settled in about the tenth century, shortly after the visit of Kupe, but by people having no direct connexion with him. It is conjectured that they were people in whom there was a considerable mixture of Melanesian blood. The later migrations settled in the North Island, the earlier immigrants being either absorbed or expelled. They lingered longer in the South Island, a remnant perhaps persisting in the Chatham Islands until early in the twentieth century, though there is no actual evidence that the Chatham Islanders came from New Zealand. Many words are used by the southern tribes that are not used by the northern, and it may be that through these words the source of these tenth-century immigrants may be yet discovered.

Kupe was by no means the earliest of the Pacific voyagers and explorers. His expeditions set out from Ra'iatea; but about three hundred years earlier, in 650, there flourished a man called Ui-te-rangiora, known to the Maori as Hui-te-rangiora, and in his time voyages with Fiji as headquarters first began. Colonies were already established in the Tongan and Samoan groups, and some of the people were still living in Indonesia.

Ui-te-rangiora decided to build a *pa'i* (*pahi*), or great canoe, named *Te Ivi-o-Atea*, and in this canoe he explored a great part of the Pacific. The relation of his voyages is like the Early English poem *The Traveller's Song*; and it includes the names of the islands of most of the important groups in the Pacific, together with many isolated islands. A large number of the islands cannot now be recognized, but others are easily identified. The voyages extended from New Zealand, then known as Avaiki-tautau, to the Hawaiian Islands, about 3200 miles, from the New Hebrides (probably) to Easter Island, about 4000 miles, besides expeditions back to Avaiki in Melanesia, a yet greater distance. Many of the islands were colonized during this period, among them probably the Hawaiian Islands.

These voyages may cause surprise at their extent; but they were in tropical seas, and the vessels were by no means the insignificant objects usually associated with the name canoe. Even their single canoes, large dug-outs, or vessels made of pieces lashed and sewn together, were more than the equals of the Greek ships at the siege of Troy, or of the dragons of the Norsemen, or even of the vessels of Columbus and other early European voyagers. Their single canoes could carry a hundred men, and were up to 108 feet in length; their double canoes had even greater capacity, the larger of them being up to 150 feet in length, and carrying as many as four hundred men.

There is a part of the voyage of Ui' that will cause even greater surprise. Other adventurers in later days wished to emulate him; and in the history of Te Aru-tanga-nuku, also a great voyager, it is said: " The desire of the *ariki* Te Aru-tanga-nuku and all his people on the completion of the canoe was to behold all the wonderful things seen by those of the vessel *Te Ivi-o-Atea* in former times. These were those wonderful things: the rocks that grow out of the sea in the space beyond Rapa [about 1100 miles south-east of Rarotonga]; the monstrous seas; the female that dwells in those mountainous waves, whose tresses wave about in the waters and on the surface of the sea; and the frozen sea of *pia*, with the deceitful animal of that sea who dives to great depths—a foggy, misty, and dark place not shone on by the sun. Other things are like rocks, whose summits pierce the skies; they are completely bare and without any vegetation on them."

This is a graphic description of the impression made in the Antarctic on men accustomed only to the tropics. The rocks growing from the sea, and the objects piercing the skies, bare of vegetation, are icebergs; the female whose hair waves about is conjectural, but the hair is the long kelp of those seas; the deceitful animal is probably the sea-lion or sea-elephant; *pia* is arrowroot, which when scraped is exactly like snow, and the snowy wastes were compared with the white substance most familiar to them. The Antarctic ice is to be found south of Rapa in the summer, so there are two instances, about three hundred years apart, of Polynesian voyagers sailing into those high latitudes for the sheer love of adventure, and from a desire to see the wonders of the deep.

There was another object that often led the voyagers to distant lands, and that was the search for the red feathers used by them as adornments. Ui-te-rangiora is said to have sailed to Enua-manu, conjectured to be New Guinea, for the purpose of securing such feathers. As the Spanish first, and afterward the English, were lured to the Americas by the actual gold and silver and the fabulous hoards of it, so the Polynesians were lured to the lands of the red feathers ; for to them these feathers were jewels of as great value as gold and precious stones were to the voyagers of the Old World. It must here be noted, as against the above conjecture, however, that Enua-manu was the spirit-name of the island Atiu; and it may be that names of islands preserved in traditions are spirit-names now no longer used, and possibly forgotten.

Many of these voyages must, of course, have extended over years, and the statement is made regarding the voyages of Ui' that when a canoe decayed others were built. An ancestor of the Rarotongans, Tangi'ia, who flourished in the thirteenth century, made known voyages totalling over 18,000 miles, and from this total the longest, the one to Avaiki, is omitted, as it is not known exactly where Avaiki was, though it was somewhere in Indonesia. His longest single voyage was from Fiji to Easter Island, 4200 miles.

Doubts have often been expressed as to whether it was possible for these long voyages to be made, and as to whether reliance can be placed on native traditions. When, however, traditions of one island are corroborated by comparison with traditions of another hundreds of miles away, the two peoples having been separated for hundreds of years, their authenticity must be accepted. Moreover, as the people had no written language, and the utmost importance was attached to their genealogies, these mental records must be kept scrupulously exact. They were subject to as much scrutiny as Debrett, were as exact, contained far more minutiæ, and the slightest variation would at once be detected.

The Maori had preserved the sailing directions from the Sandwich Islands to New Zealand, and they have been recorded, with other matter, in *The Lore of the Whare-wananga*. The words are : " In laying a course for the canoe to Ao-tea-roa from Ahuahu (which is the full name, though some call it Ahu), come straight to the south from Maui-taha and Maui-pae. These are twin islands outside of Ahuahu. The bows of the canoe must be directed straight to the south, and the same course leads on to Hawaiki." This refers to the first part of the voyage from Hawaii to Tahiti (the Hawaiki of these directions, Ao-tea-roa being the North Island of New Zealand). Later on in the narrative the directions from Hawaiki are given as a little to the left of the setting sun.

In a Hawaiian tradition, again, the sailing directions are given for a voyage from that group to Kahiki (Tahiti). Hoku-paa (the North Star) was left directly astern ; in other words, they sailed south. When they arrived at the Piko-o-Wakea (the equator) they lost sight of the North Star, and the guiding star of the south was Newe.

The island Oahu, upon which Honolulu is situated, was originally called Ahu, the ' O ' being prefixed subsequently. A little to the south-east of it is another island, Maui, off whose south-western coast lie two islets, Lanai and Kahoo-lawe. Now the names Maui-taha and Maui-pae both mean " Maui to the Side," a meaning that applies well to Lanai and Kahoolawe. Moreover, according to the Hawaiian tradition, it is stated that the point or channel of departure for Kahiki was a point on the islet Kahoolawe called Ke ala-i-Kahiki (Maori Te ara-i-Tahiti—" the Road to Tahiti "), and this is believed to be a point lying toward Maui, or the channel lying between the two. Wherever the exact point was, the departure was taken from the islet Kahoolawe, the more southerly of the two, and there seems to be little doubt that the islets referred to by the Maori are the same. The Maori sailing directions are attributed to the famous Kupe, who discovered New Zealand in approximately the year 950. There is some significance in the fact that the Maori and Hawaiian sailing directions agree even as closely as they do, especially considering the centuries that the two peoples have been separated by over two thousand miles of ocean; and if they have preserved for this length of time a sailing direction that has been of no use to them, at any rate so far as the Maori are concerned, it strengthens the reliance that may be placed on other of their traditions.

The distance from Hawaii to Tahiti was just on 2000 miles; and while the journey south was fairly simple, the return journey was a different matter; and in connexion with it an ethnological romance has flowered within the last two years. At the season of the return from Tahiti the prevailing wind was south-east, and, the starboard tack being taken, the voyagers were carried too far to the east. The problem was how to know when the latitude of Hawaii had been reached, so that the westerly course for the group might be set. The voyagers held on until Hoku-paa (the North Star) again appeared above the horizon, and until it occupied a position in the heavens as high as it would occupy in Hawaii at that time of the year. The eye was not trusted altogether, but a mechanical check was contrived, and the position was verified by means of the magic calabash. An ordinary calabash had its top cut off level, and some distance below the rim four equidistant holes were bored at the same level. When it was desired to see if the star were at the right elevation, water was poured into the calabash to the level of the holes, and an observation of the star taken through one of the holes. The instrument was 'set' for Hawaii, and when the star took the position over the rim that it occupied in that place, the westerly course was taken, and Hawaii fetched in due time. The magic calabash was no other than a combined sextant and compass. "Of all the Polynesian exploits in the Pacific," says Te Rangi Hiroa, our Maori anthropologist, "none can appeal to us more than the thought of Neolithic man boldly

42

making a voyage of nearly two thousand miles, crossing the line, and finding his position for the run home by taking a shot at the North Star through the holes in a calabash."

Besides this, the Polynesians possessed rude charts; at least two, made of sticks and string, are known. An island sailor might be taken out of sight of land, yet by means of one of these charts he would be able to indicate the direction of any known island, though ignorant of the course the vessel had taken. Their principle is not known except to those who made them and used them. Standing on the deck, the native navigator would adjust his chart, perhaps to the set of the waves, whose roll was regular under the regular trades, perhaps to something the brown eye could see, but the blue cannot; at any rate, he would adjust it to something that enabled him to pick at least his direction. He was able, moreover, to detect the presence of land while it was still below the horizon; the ' heaping up ' of the water, the colour of the sky, the shape of clouds—a thousand signs are so well known to the older natives, have been learned by them so gradually and as a matter of course, that they hardly think of them consciously, and certainly do not think they could be of interest to the sagacious white man. It is a fact that until within the last two years the use of the magic calabash was not known to Europeans; only by accident has its use been discovered. Now it has been examined, and it is found that the angle made at the eye-hole by the artificial horizon and the rim is 19°; the Hawaiian group lies on both sides of the twentieth parallel of latitude. Memory is a never-ending marvel; so many things of apparent inutility are retained by it, and here one of these with a stray gleam throws how pleasing a light on one of the dim places of the past.

It is difficult for people who habitually use writing to record events to conceive of the powers of memory possessed by people who have nothing but the memory to trust to. Yet instances are not uncommon. The tales of the *Morte d'Arthur* were remembered until they were written down by Malory, and printed by Caxton; the German epic *Der*

Nibelungen Noth, the Finnish epic *Kalevala*, the Hindu epic *Mahabharata*, the Greek epic *Iliad*—all were carried in the memory; so too were the Hindu religious books, the *Upanishads*; and we know at least of the last-named that they were unvaried in the many minds in which they were retained.

The Maori started to learn the history of his people from his very cradle; his lullabies were histories. Every chief knew the genealogies of every member of his tribe, knew the history of all the names in the genealogies. He had his regular schools of learning, too, where the tribal history was taught, under scrupulous supervision. Our written histories are generally the work of one man only, who consults such documents as he is able to peruse, documents which may or may not be true, and of which he may or may not render a faithful account. The Maori and other native histories are composite productions of the entire tribe, where the history of one man is known to every other man, and any deviation from fact would have to be by collusion of the whole tribe.

CHAPTER II: 'KOROPANGA AND RUKUTIA

WHEN the Hawaiian Islands were settled in the seventh century a distinguished chief Nana-ula was the first to arrive from the southern islands. As he brought with him his gods, priests, prophets, and a considerable body of retainers, as well as dogs, pigs, fowls, and seeds of useful plants, it is hardly likely that he found the islands by chance, but that the voyage was deliberately made; and it is probable that he found the group without inhabitants.

Other chiefs of less importance also arrived, either from Tahiti or Samoa, coming in large double canoes accommodating from fifty to a hundred persons each. They brought with them, too, the earliest Polynesian traditions, and it is thought that none of these earliest immigrants ever returned to the islands they had left; nor did others immediately follow this first migratory wave.

Traditions regarding these pioneers are meagre, and they lived apparently in uneventful peace until about the end of the tenth century, when a new migration began, probably from the Society group, under the leadership of Nana-maoa, followed by other chiefs. For a century or more there were feuds and wars, but in the end invaders and invaded, both of the same Polynesian race, settled down together, becoming so assimilated through intermarriage that in time most chiefs of note traced their lineage along both lines to Nana-ula and Nana-maoa.

The descendants of the first migration had not, however, lost their old spirit, but were quite as adventurous and skilled in navigation as their southern invaders; and while the latter, continually increasing in numbers by fresh arrivals, were steadily possessing themselves of the lands, a few resolute chiefs of the old line, either in a spirit of retaliation or because the southern islands offered them better scope, boldly set their sails for the abandoned homes of the invaders, and by conquest or other means acquired land and influence in the new home.

45

Olopana and Lu'ukia

About the year 1040 Maweke, a chief of the line of Nana-ula, was *alii-nui* (Maori *ariki-nui* = great chief) of the island of Oahu.   He had three sons, the eldest of whom, Muliele-alii, also had three sons, Kumu-honua, Olopana, and Moikeha, and a daughter, Hainakolo.   The eldest son in due course succeeded to the estates and titles of his father; but the younger brothers, Olopana and Moikeha, not content with the small lots that must have fallen to their share, determined to seek elsewhere.

The Pau-makua family occupied a large part of the eastern side of the island; and, while they were of the second migration, they appeared to live peacefully with the original inhabitants.

Pau-makua was a famous voyager, and tradition claimed for him that he had visited all the foreign lands then known to the Hawaiians, bringing back many strange things and tales of marvellous exploits.   From one of his voyages he returned with two white priests, Keakea and Maliu; at another time he brought back Malela, a noted prophet and sorcerer, and three other persons of a strange race, one of whom was a woman.   They are described as foreigners of large stature, bright, staring, roguish eyes, and reddish faces.   As his voyages were sometimes of many months' duration, and he is said to have ventured in almost every direction, it is not impossible that these foreigners were North American Indians, though it must be noted that, owing to their rosy tinge, the faces of Europeans, to us white, are by the Polynesians called red.

Moikeha, though unmarried, like his brother Olopana, had adopted a young son of Ahukai, great-grandson and successor of this famous Pau-makua.   The name of the boy was Laa, or Laa-mai-kahiki.

Taking leave of their relatives at Oahu, Olopana and Moikeha, with the young chief Laa, embarked for Hawaii, establishing themselves in the beautiful valley of Waipio. But they did not remain here; for a terrible hurricane, followed by storms and floods, completely devastated the

46

valley, compelling them to abandon their homes and seek refuge elsewhere. Moikeha had never been satisfied with Waipio, and now had little difficulty in persuading his brother to set out boldly for the misty and far-off land of Kahiki (Tahiti). Olopana meanwhile had married Lu'ukia, descended, like himself, from the ancient line of Nana-ula.

They set off in five large double canoes, favourable winds taking them to Ra'iatea, of the Society group. Here they established themselves, Olopana being accepted as sovereign of the district, with Moikeha as chief adviser.

They lived in harmony for some years, when trouble was brought about by a chief named Mua. Jealous of the popularity of Moikeha, whose place in the favour of Olopana he wished to take, he drew the attention of Lu'ukia on several occasions to the affluent style of living of Moikeha, suggesting that his intention was to secure the friend-ship of the influential chiefs, and ultimately to wrest the sovereignty from Olopana. Alarmed at last, she repeated the tale to her husband, and being a woman was able to do what Mua himself would have failed in doing ; she aroused his suspicions. A coldness to Moikeha naturally followed ; and, once his attention was called to it, Olopana could not but see that his brother's style of living certainly was lavish, and that his popularity was without doubt increasing. One day he took occasion to rebuke him for his extravagance and love of display, and suggested that a more modest style of living would better suit his position.

Moikeha, who had ever been loyal, was grieved at the suspicion the rebuke implied, and resolved to leave Ra'iatea, and return to the Hawaiian Islands. He had never married, declaring he had a wife in his spear and an heir in Laa, and would not create jealousy by adding another wife to his family. Olopana, feeling he had gone too far, endeavoured to persuade him to remain, but Moikeha had made up his mind, and refused to be persuaded.

He set out with an imposing fleet, the double canoe bearing him, his priests, his astrologer, La'a-maomao, director of the winds, his principal navigator, and personal

47

attendants being the same on which he had sailed to Kahiki. It was nearly a hundred feet in length, was painted red, and at the masthead floated the pennon of a Polynesian *alii*. Laa, as a sign of friendship, he left in the care of Olopana.

The tedium of the voyage of 2000 miles was enlivened with musicians and drummers, and La'a-maomao from his calabash gave them favouring winds; but as the green hills of Kau came into view songs and shouts of joy went up from the canoes. Many leapt into the water and swam beside the canoes. Mookini, the chief priest, burnt incense before the gods, and addressed to them a prayer of thanksgiving; Kama-hua-lele, the astrologer and poet, celebrated the occasion in an inspiring chant.

Some of the early poetic accounts of the first appearance of the islands of Hawaii above the surface of the ocean mention Hawaii as suddenly rising from the great deep and becoming a part of a row or cluster of islands " stretching to the farthest ends of Kahiki," from which it is conjectured that, centuries back, islands now no longer existing marked the way between the Society and Hawaiian groups:

> Rising up is Hawaii-nui-akea!
> Rising up out of the night!
> Appeared has the island, the land,
> And string of islands of Nuuamea,
> The cluster of islands stretching to the
> farthest ends of Kahiki. . . .

Kama-hua-lele began by repeating an ancient story of the origin of the several islands, and concluded hopefully:

> " O Haumea Manukahikele,
> O Moikeha, the chief who is to reside,
> My chief will reside on Hawaii—ah!
> Life, life, O buoyant life!
> Live shall the chief and priest,
> Live shall the seer and the slave,
> Dwell on Hawaii and be at rest,
> And attain old age on Kauai.
> Oh, Kauai is the island!
> Oh, Moikeha is the chief! "

They landed on Hawaii to offer sacrifices on behalf of

the expedition, then, proceeding, touched here and there until they arrived at Kauai, anchoring near Kapaa, where Puna was the governing *alii*. He was one of the most popular rulers of the group; and though strict in the exercise of his prerogatives, he was merciful in dealing with offences thoughtlessly or ignorantly committed. He would pardon the humble labourer who might inadvertently cross his shadow or violate a *tapu*, but never the chief who deliberately trespassed upon his privileges, or withheld a courtesy due to his rank. His disposition was naturally warlike, but as the condition of the island was peaceful, and military force was seldom required except in repelling occasional plundering raids from other islands, he kept alive the martial spirit of his chiefs and subjects by frequent sham fights, marine drill, and the encouragement of athletic games and friendly contests at arms, in which he himself occasionally took part. Feasting and dancing usually followed these warlike pastimes, and the result was that the court of Puna became noted for the chivalry of its chiefs, and the splendour of its entertainments.

The Winning of Ho'o-ipo

Puna had but one child, a daughter named Ho'o-ipo, an attractive maiden, the pride of the court, and much sought by aspiring chiefs; but, flattered by the emulation displayed by the young chiefs, and vain of a face which the unruffled pools assured her was more than ordinarily beautiful, she showed no haste in her choice of a husband.

Her indecision was but gently rebuked by Puna, for she was his only child, and he did not seek their separation; but as time passed the suitors became more persistent; the rivalry assumed so bitter and warlike an aspect that Puna deemed it wise for her to restore harmony by making a speedy choice. But she felt no decided preference; and suggested that, since a choice must be made, she was willing to leave the decision to some contest between the rivals. Puna eagerly accepted the suggestion; and, indeed, it commended itself to all, who had been so accustomed to chivalrous contests for prizes far less valued than the royal Ho'o-ipo.

The difficulty lay in choosing the form the contest should take; for each chief was no doubt master of some special accomplishment, and it would be difficult to select a trial that would seem just to all. Puna appealed to the chief priests; and next day announced that his carved whalebone ornament (*palaoa*) would be sent by a messenger to the little island of Kaula; and that four days thereafter the rival chiefs should, each in his own canoe, and with no more than four assistants, start at the same time and place from Kauai; and the one who returned with the *palaoa*, which the messenger would be instructed to give to the first chief landing, should be the husband of Ho'o-ipo, and the others must remain his friends.

All were well accustomed to the sea and to the sailing of a canoe, and it was admitted that the contest was as fair as any that could be devised. The rival chiefs all agreed, and at once began to prepare for the race by securing suitable canoes and skilful assistants.

After a few days allowed for preparation, the messenger was sent on to Kaula. He had been gone two days (and had probably reached his destination, as the distance was little more than a hundred miles), and the rival chiefs had everything in readiness to bend their sails for Kaula, when Moikeha arrived, anchoring his fleet in the evening off Kapaa.

The next morning, becomingly dressed, and with his double canoe flying the standard of his rank, Moikeha went ashore, where he was cordially received by the chiefs, and escorted to Puna. Without referring to his family connexions, he simply announced that he was a chief from the distant land of Kahiki, and was travelling through the Hawaiian group on a tour of observation and pleasure. He wore a *maro* (apron) fringed with shells, a *kihei* (mantle) of finely woven and decorated cloth, and on his head a *lei-alii* (chief's headdress) of brilliant feathers, while from his neck was suspended by a cord of plaited hair a curious ornament of mother-of-pearl set in ivory. He was of handsome appearance, and his bearing was dignified, courtly, and correct in every way.

During his audience with Puna Moikeha met Ho'o-ipo; and so charmed was he with the brightness of her glances that he did not leave until he had found opportunity to exchange a few pleasant words with her. They seemed mutually attracted, and Moikeha accepted the invitation of Puna to consider himself his guest until the next day, at the same time allowing him to send fresh provisions to his people, whose canoes had been drawn up on the beach.

A brilliant entertainment of feasting, music, and dancing in his honour followed in the evening, and during its progress Moikeha had the pleasure of the company of Ho'o-ipo, who could not fail to tell him of the contest about to take place. Feasting and merrymaking occupied the next day and evening also, for on the morning following the contesting chiefs were to start for Kaula in the presence of Puna.

Morning came, with its throng of eager spectators. The canoes and their crews were examined, and the chiefs made their appearance, followed soon after by Puna and most of his household, including Ho'o-ipo, who was carried to the beach in a palanquin borne on the shoulders of four attendants. She wore an embroidered *pau*—a short skirt of five thicknesses of *kapa*-cloth (*tapa*) reaching to the knees —and a cape or short mantle trimmed with feathers. Her hair was braided in a single strand at the back; her head and neck were adorned with *lei* of flowers and feathers, and her limbs were ornamented with circlets of shells and coloured seeds.

Everything being ready, the contending chiefs, eight in number, appeared before the great chief Puna; and, making obeisance, each in turn as required recited his genealogy, to show in a formal way that he was worthy of alliance with Ho'o-ipo.

The last of them had given his pedigree, retiring respectfully, but with a smile and look of confidence toward the young woman, the terms of the contest had again been announced by a herald, and Puna was about to order the simultaneous launching of the canoes, when Moikeha suddenly presented himself, bowing first to the great chief and then courteously to the lesser chiefs, and said :

" Great chief, as this contest seems to be free to all of noble blood, I too ask permission to present myself as a contestant for the prize."

The chiefs were surprised, and exchanged glances ; and a pleased expression lighted the face of Ho'o-ipo, who till then had shown little interest in what was going on. Puna hesitated a moment, and then graciously replied, " Noble stranger, if your rank is equal to that required, and the chiefs now ready for departure urge no objections, my consent will not be withheld."

A hurried consultation showed that some of the chiefs objected; but as the stranger, with no knowledge of the coast, and apparently with no canoe or crew in readiness, did not seem a competitor to be feared it was finally agreed that, should he be able to establish his rank, he might be admitted to the contest.

Moikeha thanked them, and began to recite his genealogy. Curious to learn the descent of this courteous stranger, the chiefs pressed round him, eagerly listening to every word. He began with Wakea, away in the dim past, when his ancestors were resident in other lands referred to in Hawaiian story. He brought the connexion down to Nana-ula, the pioneer of the first migration into the Hawaiian Islands some hundreds of years before. Thence, generation by generation, naming father, mother, and heir, he traced down a line of sixteen successors to Maweke. Pausing a moment, while covert looks of surprise and wonder were exchanged among the listening chiefs, Moikeha continued:

> " Maweke the husband,
> Naiolaukea the wife;
> Muliele-alii the husband,
> Wehe-lani the wife;
> Moikeha the husband,
> Ho'o-ipo the wife."

'KOROPANGA AND RUKUTIA

Applause followed the announcement by the stranger that he was the son of Muliele-alii, the great chief of Oahu; and the jesting and good-natured manner in which he concluded the genealogy by predicting his success in the coming contest made him no enemies among the rival chiefs. There was another on whom he had made a good impression; and Ho'o-ipo was now sure that she could make a choice without the trouble and excitement of a race to Kaula; but the canoes were ready, and all she could do was to hope and pray that Moikeha would bring back the ornament.

When asked by Puna what his preparations were, he pointed to a small canoe with outrigger drawn up on the beach, and a solitary long-haired man of strange aspect standing beside it with a paddle in his hand. Puna shook his head doubtingly; Ho'o-ipo looked disappointed; others imagined he was treating the contest as a jest; but he announced himself ready, and the signal for departure was given.

The chiefs sprang toward the beach, and in a few minutes had launched their canoes and passed through the heavy surf, when with strong and steady pulling the race began in earnest for the open sea. Moikeha alone seemed to be in no hurry. He took formal leave of Puna, and, noting the look of impatience on the face of Ho'o-ipo, he smilingly said to her as he turned toward the beach, " I shall bring back the ornament!" His assurance contented her; the other canoes were beyond the surf, but she believed him, and her heart was happy.

Satisfying himself that everything necessary was ready, Moikeha and his assistant pushed the canoe into the water, and with a few vigorous strokes of their paddles dashed through the surf. The passage was adroitly made, and as the canoe lay motionless except for its lifting to the waves the sail was spread. This was an unaccountable movement to those on the shore, for the little wind stirring was directly from the west, to which point the canoe was bearing for an offing to round the southern capes of the island.

53

But if they were surprised at the setting of the sail in such circumstances they were astounded when they saw it fill with wind and the canoe suddenly speed out to sea as if driven by a hurricane.

The spectators did not know that the long-haired companion of Moikeha was La'a-maomao, god of the winds, who had accompanied him from Ra'iatea. Behind the sail sat the friendly deity, and from his inexhaustible calabash of imprisoned winds a gale was sent forth which carried the canoe to Kaula before daylight the next morning. When they landed the messenger was found, and he at once delivered the ornament to Moikeha, who with his companion remained on the island for refreshment until past midday. They then started on their return, favoured by the same winds, but proceeding with less haste. Toward night the eight other chiefs landed within a few hours of each other, and great was their astonishment on learning that the ornament had been delivered to a chief claiming it early that morning.

" He must have come on wings," said one. " He was surely helped by the gods," suggested the one who had landed next after Moikeha; " but for that the ornament would have been mine, as you well know. But who can struggle against the gods? Let us not incur their anger by complaint."

As it was easy for the others, who had lost in any event, to reconcile themselves to the success of Moikeha, good-humour was soon restored, and next morning, in company with the messenger, they set out on their return. On the evening of the same day Moikeha landed at Kapaa, and hastened to place in the hands of Puna the ornament that made him the husband of Ho'o-ipo. Puna was gratified at his success, and Ho'o-ipo made no attempt to disguise her joy.

In the course of a few days the chiefs returned, and Moikeha invited them to a feast, in which they forgot their rivalry, and renewed the pledges of friendship with no thought that the conditions of the contest required them to do so. In many ingenious ways they sought to draw

MOIKEHA SAILS OUT AGAINST THE WIND
(See page 54)

from Moikeha the secret of his success, but he baffled their curiosity, and they had to content themselves with the belief that he had been aided by some supernatural power; possibly by Apu-ko-hai, the great fish-god of Kauai, who sometimes seized canoes and bore them through the water with almost incredible speed.

In due time Ho'o-ipo became his wife; and on the death of Puna Moikeha succeeded him as great chief of Kauai, where he remained to the end of his life. He had seven sons, and his court, like that of Puna, was noted for its distinguished chiefs, its priests, its prophets, and its poets.

The Marriage of Laa

As the life of Moikeha was drawing near its close a strong desire possessed him to see again his foster-child Laa, who had become heir-presumptive and successor to Olopana. He ordered a large number of double canoes to be repaired and made ready for the open sea. He had some time before dispatched a large party of hunters to the cliffs along the coast for the feathers of the *mamo*, from which to make a royal mantle for Laa. The choicest feathers only were used, and the garment, representing the labour of a hundred persons for a year, was one of the most elaborate and brilliant ever made on Kauai.

When everything was ready for his departure, however, Moikeha concluded that he was too old to undertake the voyage, and he sent instead his third son, Kila, distinguished for his courage and ability, and especially for his skill as a navigator. He was to invite Laa to revisit the Hawaiian group, so that his foster-father might embrace him before he died.

Kila was delighted with the mission. For several years intercourse with the south had been suspended, but from boyhood he had hoped to visit the misty, far-off Kahiki, of which he had heard his father speak. With energy he pursued the task of getting the canoes ready and storing them with provisions. These, for the long voyages of that period, consisted of dried fish, dried bananas and plantains,

coconuts, yams, potatoes; with the paste of *taro*, called
poi, and *paiai*, which is pounded *taro* for making *poi*, fresh
fruits, cooked fowls, and pigs for early consumption.
Large calabashes of fresh water were also provided, but
frequent bathes largely diminished the craving for water.

Sacrifices were offered, the auguries were favourable,
and the fleet set sail. Kila was accompanied by three of
his brothers, and by the venerable Kama-hua-lele, the friend
and astrologer of Moikeha, who had borne him company
from Ra'iatea more than twenty-five years before. He
went as chief navigator and special counsellor of Kila.

Kila landed at Opoa through the sacred entrance of
Avamoa. His flag and state were recognized by Olopana,
and the son of Moikeha and his personal attendants were
ceremoniously conducted to the royal court, where Kila
made known the purpose of the visit. Olopana was greatly
interested in the story of the successful establishment on
Kauai of Moikeha, and learned with sorrow of the death of
his father Muliele-alii.

With affectionate greetings from Moikeha, Kila presented to Laa the royal mantle, the brilliant *mamo*, but
Olopana strongly objected to the proposed journey, urging
his own advanced years and probable early death; but when
assured by Laa of his speedy return he reluctantly consented; and after a round of hospitable feasts and entertainments Laa, in his own double canoes, and attended by
his priests, astrologer, master of ceremonies, musicians,
and a number of friends, accompanied Kila and his party
back to Hawaii.

The voyage was made in good time, and as the combined
fleet, with canoes of royal yellow and pennons flying, sailed
through the group to Kauai, stopping at several points to
exchange courtesies with ruling chiefs, it attracted unusual
attention; and when Laa landed at Wai-a-lua, on the island
of Oahu, to greet his relatives, and the people learned that
the son of Ahukai, rich in honours and possessions, had
returned, they strewed his path with flowers, and gave him
wild welcome.

Proceeding to Kauai, Laa was affectionately received by his foster-father; and for a month or more the festivals in his honour continued. Then he returned to Oahu, where a large mansion was prepared for him, with accommodation for his friends and retainers, and the chiefs received him without jealousy, knowing he would soon return to Kahiki.

As Laa was direct in descent from the first families in Hawaii, it was not deemed well that the line of Pau-makua should be perpetuated on stranger soil. The chiefs consulted together, then approached Laa on the subject; and as their patriotic desires did not run at all counter to his wishes he expressed willingness to comply with what seemed a general desire. But his agreement did not altogether settle the delicate question, as the chiefs discovered on casting about for a suitable wife for so desirable a husband. Most of them had daughters or sisters of eligible age and rank. Which of them all should they select? Whose family should be so honoured? They were willing to leave the choice to Laa; but though young in heart he was wise, and, sagaciously foreseeing the result, he declined to make his selection.

As usual in momentous cases of doubt, the chief priest was consulted, and the matter was settled in a manner quite satisfactory to Laa. It was agreed that he should marry three wives, all on the same day; and the maidens selected were Hoaka-nui, daughter of Lono-kaehu, of Kualoa; Waolena, daughter of a chief of Kaalaea; and Mano, daughter of a chief of Kane-ohe. The event was celebrated with splendour and enthusiasm. The marriage agreement, as was then the custom among the nobility, was made public by a herald; the brides, richly attired and decked with garlands, were delivered in due form to the bridegroom; and in the evening a feast was served in the grounds to more than a thousand guests, with *hula* dances, songs, and other festive accompaniments.

After his marriage Laa remained a year at Kualoa, and then began to prepare for his return to Ra'iatea, looking

forward to his departure with mingled regret and satisfaction. His brief married life had been happy, and each
wife on the same day had borne him a son, as is said in
an ancient chant:

O Ahukai, O Laa-a, O Laa,
O Laa from Kahiki, the chief;
O Ahukini-a-Laa,
O Kukona-a-Laa,
O Lauli-a-Laa, the father
The triple canoe of Laa-mai-kahiki,
The sacred first-born children of Laa,
Who were born on the selfsame day.

Moikeha died soon afterward, and Laa bade farewell to
the Hawaiian Islands, leaving, as promised, his three wives
and their sons in Oahu. The names of the sons were as
mentioned in the chant, Ahukini-a-Laa, Kukona-a-Laa,
and Lauli-a-Laa, from whom in after generations it was the
pride of governing families in Oahu to trace their lineage.

Laa returned to Ra'iatea in time to receive the dying
blessings of Olopana, and all communication between that
place and Hawaii appears then to have ceased for about
six hundred years—that is, until the arrival of Captain Cook
in 1778; and until that time the Hawaiians learned nothing
of the world outside their archipelago, and knew that other
lands existed only through the mysterious recitals of their
priests.

Tama-nui-a-raki and Rukutia

Two of the persons mentioned in this story, Olopana
and Lu'ukia, are well known in Maori legend, where their
names are 'Koropanga (Tu-te-Koropanga in full) and
Rukutia. Their descendants, said to have come to New
Zealand in the Matiti canoe before the great fleet of 1350,
were the Waitaha people of the South Island of New Zealand, a tribe now long extinct.

The Hawaiian story deals rather with the relatives of
these two people; the Maori story deals more particularly
with the two themselves; and though the surroundings

seem quite different the Maori episode may be one, or a variant of one, about which the Hawaiian is silent.

Tama-nui-a-raki dwelt with his wife Rukutia, his eldest son, Tu-te-hemahema, his daughter Merau, and two other children.

To them came the company and children of Tu-te-Koropanga on a friendly visit. The day after their arrival the dancing and merrymaking began, and as was customary the children of Tama-nui' danced a *haka* (dance with gestures) for the visitors. They wore round their waists belts adorned with dogs' tails; but when the children of 'Koropanga danced their answering *haka* they wore aprons of beautiful red feathers, which gave them a noble appearance. Seeing this, Tama-nui' was overcome with shame on account of the beauty of the feathers and the attractiveness of the *haka*; and he retired to the temple of the priests, to the Huikura.

While he sat in this sacred place 'Koropanga made himself agreeable to Rukutia; and being a man of ready address and pleasing appearance, whereas Tama-nui' was exceedingly ill-favoured, he prevailed on her to depart with him, deserting her husband Tama-nui-a-raki. He made no secret of his intention; and before leaving in this unfriendly manner he said to the children of his wronged host, " Remain ye here with your father; and should he meditate pursuit, this is my word to him: ' All effort to overtake us will be unavailing, whether by sea or by land; for by land there will be prickly hooked vines of *tataramoa*, and thickets of sharp *tumatakuru*, and stiff spines of *taramea*; and by sea there will be foaming waves and monsters of the deep; all these, being subject to my will, will be as obstacles and unsurmountable obstructions.' " Thereupon he departed, and Rukutia willingly accompanied him.

The eldest son came to the place where his father sat, and, looking through the window, he was seen by his father, who chanted this *karakia* (charm, incantation):

" *Tapa-ti, tapa-ta, hui e, tai ki . . . e.*
Haere mai te toki haumi . . . e."

59

" Our mother," said the son, " has departed with your guest, with Tu-te-Koropanga."

Tama-nui' answered with this *karakia*:

> " Rukutia has gone that she may learn to *haka*.
> Not jealousy, so fierce, can stay her now.
> I dreamt a dream of other days——
> > *Tapa-ti, tapa-ta, hui e, tai ki . . . e.*
> > *Haere mai te toki haumi . . . e.*"

He then came out from the Huikura, and going to his children he wept over them, saying, " Why has your mother been forsaken by you? "

" It is indeed she who has forsaken us," they said, " on account of your ill-favouredness and unattractive appearance; she has become enamoured of Tu-te-Koropanga, and with that noble-looking man has she departed."

" Is it indeed so? " said Tama-nui'.

" Yes," they said; " because of your ill-looks she has deserted you."

" Remain ye here with your eldest brother," said he; and therewith he left them.

An unexpressed desire led him toward the mournful Te Reinga, that there he might hold converse with his ancestors, and learn how he might become a *purotu*, a handsome person. On his way he saw a white heron; and, envying the bird its beautiful plumes and graceful shape, he took its appearance upon himself, and as a heron he flapped in heavy flight to Te Reinga, alighting at the margin of a lake in the netherworld.

By the side of the lake walked some of his female ancestors—Tu-maunga and Tu-whenua, and Kohi-wai, the daughter of one of them. They saw the bird walking along the edge of the lake, stretching its long neck and picking up food here and there; and they remarked, " That is something not hitherto seen in this place. The graceful bird! It has twice eight bends in its neck."

Knowing that their descendants still living upon the earth had the power to visit this place, and hold converse with such of their ancestors as had not yet trodden the path

60

leading between the giant-spirits Tua-piko and Tawhaitiri to the yet lower world, the women fancied this bird might be one of those descendants, and said to Kohi-wai, " Let two fish be cooked"; and when this had been done, " Lay them one over the other, and perform the ceremonies customary when offering to the gods and goddesses.   Then from the flax used in the ceremonies prepare nooses; and taking first the noose made from the flax used in offering to the gods, throw it, with the fish, towards the bird. Should it be caught by the neck, it will be your brother Tama-nui-a-raki in disguise."   The name of this charm was *tamatane*.   The girl made the noose, and threw the fish; it was eaten by the bird, which was caught in the noose. She led it toward their home, but on the way the bird was transformed into a man, and they recognized him as Tama-nui'.

Looking at his ancestors, he marvelled at the beauty to which they had attained; they had become tattooed.

Their first greetings over, they asked him what had brought him to the underworld.   " The treasure of your ornaments," said he.   " I also wish to be made handsome as you have become."   They did as he desired, drawing graceful curves and lines over his face and on his body ; but when he bathed the marks were washed off and obliterated ; and this happened, too, a second time.

" How is it," Tama-nui' complained, " that your tattoo lasts, while mine does not ? "

" Ah," said they; " we cannot make the permanent marks here; for them you must go down to your other ancestors, to Taka and to Ha, at the place of the spirits Tua-piko and Tawhaitiri; they have the instruments and the pigments, together with the skill to use them."

Tama-nui' went to that place, and was asked the object of his visit.   " Your ornament," said he.   " I wish to be tattooed."   " Ah," said they, " that is death outright." " It cannot be death," said he, " since you have borne it and live."   " It is as dreadful as death," they answered, " though it may be survived."

61

Tama-nui' persisted in his request, so the instruments and the pigments were made ready. He was laid on the ground, and the tattooing was commenced; but when several of the first lines had been cut the pain caused him to swoon. When he recovered he said faintly, " O Taka, O Ha, I am very bad." Several times he swooned, murmuring on regaining consciousness, " O Taka, O Ha, I am very bad."

Then the operator replied pointedly, and as if to comfort him:

> " We do not cause the pain.
> It is the instruments,
> And blood, and severed flesh.
> Now darkness comes—
> Black darkness covers thee,
> And he is watchful.
> We too are watching now."

And darkness came again; and again painful light; and Tama-nui' murmured:

> " O Taka! O Ha!
> Tua-piko! Tawhaitiri!
> In agony I shall die."

The operator repeated his *karakia*, whose effect was to cause Tama-nui' to faint away, when he was oblivious to pain.

After many days of painful operation the work was at last finished. Tama-nui' was taken to bathe his face and body, and as he bent over the water he murmured:

> " Man near death
> Reels and trembles,
> And beloved ones
> Show their affection."

He lay face downward, and one of the operators knelt on him to cause blood to flow from the incisions; again he swooned, and was carried away on a litter, taken into a *whare* (hut), and laid before a fire. After three days he felt better; the swellings had subsided, so that he could see

ENTRANCE TO GATEWAY

CARVED FRAME OF WINDOW

(See page 62)

CARVED SLAB

MAORI CARVED DOOR-LINTELS

Photos Dominion Museum, Wellington, N.Z.

(See page 66)

things round about him.   Day by day the incisions healed;
the sores began to fall off; he was able to walk about, and to
bathe.   He was now a *rangi-paruhi*, a person fully tattooed;
he bathed, and the marks remained; he looked into the
unruffled water, and beheld a handsome man.

" I will now return to my children on earth," said he to
his ancestors.   They presented him with fine cloaks, with
the sweet flower *rotu*, of great virtue, with *puairuru*, with
pokeka-kiekie, and with these treasures he returned to the
world of life.   Excepting *pokeka-kiekie*, a garment made
from *kiekie* blades, it is not known what these treasures were;
their names only have been remembered, and that only
by the Maori of the southernmost part of New Zealand.
At least, that is the only place where they have been heard
of by Europeans; and Wohlers, who recorded the story,
suggested that *rotu* might be a memory of lotus, the sacred
flower of India, though the usual transliteration does not
support this.

Returning to his welcoming children, Tama-nui' said to
them : "Do you remain here quietly, while I go in search
of your mother."   He adorned himself with the beautiful
cloaks received from his ancestors, and set out on his
journey.

He went by way of the land, through the shady forests;
but the *tataramoa*, and the *tumatakuru*, and the *taramea*,
with their barbs and thorns and spears, obstructed his progress.   Then, to overcome the spell cast upon these by
Tu-te-Koropanga, he chanted this *karakia* :

> " O obstructing mountain!
> Thou, now standing yonder,
> Stand aside,
> That now I may
> With path all clear
> Travel on
> With song resounding.
> That now I may
> With path all clear
> Travel on
> With song resounding,

63

> Along the road
> Which echoes still.
> The path of Tama'
> Still vibrates
> With song resounding."

He cut the obstructing thorns and brambles, and a path was opened before him. Over his fine cloaks he now put on rough and ragged garments, and he smeared his face with dirt and ashes; and falling in with a company of people gathering firewood he was by them taken for a slave of mean condition. " Here is an old man for us," said they. " Do not compel me to bend beneath a burden," said he; and as his appearance led them to suppose that he was weary and in miserable mood they said, " No; we will not load him with firewood; allow him to depart, even as his desires may lead him."

He learned that the firewood was for making bright fires in the *whare* of Rukutia, the wife of Tu-te-Koropanga. She, with others, was that night to dance a *haka* before them, and they wished to make the fires bright so that her excellent grimaces might be seen to advantage.

Tama-nui' accompanied them; and, entering the *whare*, he seated himself at the main post. The fires burnt well, and Rukutia was at last called for. 'Koropanga gave her an ornamented apron to adorn her waist, and this she put on; but as she commenced the distortions that were so much admired Tama-nui' murmured a *karakia*, " The eyes are wet, the eyes are wet," which caused her eyes to run with tears, and she must sit down to wipe them away. Again she rose, and commenced the grimaces that were the chief grace of that *haka*, when Tama-nui' repeated the *karakia*, and the tears flowed a second time. " It was not always so," said the women; " for the first time, O Rukutia, have you stopped because of tearful eyes." But 'Koropanga was offended, and struck her, so that she shed real tears.

The people dispersed to their rest, and the fires were allowed to die down. Tama-nui' remained, and when

64

MAORI MEETING-HOUSE, PARAWAI

Photo Iles, Thames, N.Z.

MAORI DWELLING, SHOWING PAINTED RAFTERS AND CARVED SLAB

(See page 64)

" THERE SAT RUKUTIA, RESTORED TO LIFE "
(See page 68)

those still in the *whare* had fallen asleep he opened a small calabash, containing essence of *rotu* brought from the netherworld, which he had carried under his armpits. Rukutia perceived the sweet odour; and it may have been the fragrance that called 'Tama-nui' to mind, or it may have been that unknown to herself the thought of him had been in her heart as he himself was in the *whare*, causing her tears; but now she murmured, "O thou sweet smell of *rotu*! Dost thou come from my husband, from 'Tama'?" He closed the calabash, and opened another, containing filth, when Rukutia exclaimed, "Oh, how disagreeable! Our *whare* is filled with an evil odour." He closed this calabash, and after a time opened one with *mokimoki* fern. "O thou sweet odour of *mokimoki*," murmured Rukutia. "Dost thou come from my husband, from 'Tama'?"

Tu-te-Koropanga was by this time awakened from his sleep, and he spoke roughly to Rukutia, saying, "How can 'Tama' overcome my obstructions and come hither?" And she answered, "Yet I think by the twinkle of his eyes that the old man who sat by the main post was 'Tama'."

When all were asleep again Tama-nui' stole quietly from the *whare*. He washed the ashes from his face, tied his hair, which after the manner of slaves he had allowed to straggle disorderly about his head, in a knot at the top, and threw aside the old and ragged cloaks. He then returned, and sat beside the door, and murmured a *karakia* instilling in Rukutia a desire to leave the *whare* for a while. She arose, and came outside; and as she passed him he gently pulled her garment. Looking closely at him, in the noble and handsome face she yet recognized her husband Tama-nui-a-raki.

"I will return to our home with you," said she. "No," said he; "you will remain here with that husband of yours." "He is unkind, and beats me," said she; "I will not stay with him, or I shall die." "Remain with the husband you have chosen," said Tama-nui'. "You deserted me because of my ugliness; stay then with 'Koro-

65

panga. But if indeed in your heart you desire to return to me, each morning on arising turn your eyes towards the sea; and when one fine day you see the shining of my distant sail, climb upon the roof and say to the people :

> " ' Shoot up, O rays
> Of coming day!
> And also, moonbeams,
> Shine ye forth,
> To light the path
> Of prow where sits
> My husband Tama'.' "

With these words he left her, and arriving again at his home he prepared for a voyage. He took ashes on board, and a calabash of oil, and shapes of wood. Then on a day he set sail; for as he had once reached the dwelling of Tu-te-Koropanga by land, so now he would, in defiance of his obstructions, reach it by sea. He had not sailed far before the sea became rough with foaming waves, and monsters of the deep appeared in obedience to the commands of 'Koropanga. Tama-nui' was beaten back; but soon it was seen that he had greater *mana* (power, prestige). He threw out the ashes to darken the waters, and the oil to smooth them; he threw out the shapes of wood, and with these the monsters occupied themselves, and he sailed on his way, swiftly and unimpeded.

At early morning they were within sight of the dwelling of 'Koropanga; and Rukutia, watching, saw the sail of Tama' shining on the sea. To the roof she climbed, calling as Tama-nui' had bidden; and to the words she added others :

> " O ye above! descend;
> O ye below! ascend.
> I see the shadow,
> The canoe oncoming
> Of Tama', my husband! "

On hearing this from where he sat within 'Koropanga said, " O women, give no heed. Remain within the *whare*, and be not persuaded to go and see this noble-looking

66

Tama'; for indeed he cannot approach this place either by sea or land because of my enchantments."

Tama-nui' came on until he was close inshore, when one of the crew stood up. "Is that your husband?" asked the women. "He is my brother." Another of the crew stood up. "Perhaps that is your husband?" "He is my father," she answered. "Well, he is noble-looking," said the women; continuing, as another arose, "Is he your husband?" "He is my uncle."

Tama-nui' now called to Rukutia, "Swim this way; swim this way." "O Tu-te-Koropanga," cried the women, who had shown more faith in the words of Rukutia than in his enchantments, "do you sit still while your wife is going to Tama', the handsome man?" But his faith in his own enchantments was greater than his faith in the words of the women, and he did not believe them. "He cannot overcome my obstructions," said he. "And, further-more, Tama' is an ugly man; to him Rukutia will not return."

Rukutia went down, and swam toward the middle of the canoe; but Tama-nui', now standing up, cried, "Swim to me." She swam toward him, and the women in ex-asperation again called out to 'Koropanga, "Do you remain seated in your *whare*, O Tu-te-Koropanga? You ugly man! Come and behold Tama', the *purotu*, the hand-some one!" But he sat unmoved, believing that his spells had *mana*.

Rukutia was now close to Tama-nui'; he seized her and drew her across the gunwale, then severed her body in two, allowed the lower part to sink in the sea for 'Koropanga, but retained the head for himself. "Paddle on," he cried, "and let the prow of the canoe be turned seaward."

They returned; the head was wrapped in cloths of precious red, laid in a box, and buried by the side of the *whare* of Tama-nui'. He dwelt alone in the house of mourning, lamenting for his wife, and murmuring this *tangi* (lament):

67

" Her praise is ever heard—'tis praise of kindness.
I am shorn of all, and live in silence,
Friendless and alone.
I would that I could haste me to the heavens.
Oh that the wanderers from above would come,
That I might weep
In *whare* of the god of crime!
   O heaven outspread!
With fortitude inspire my heart,
That not for ever I with tears
Lament for her my spouse.
Stir up my inmost soul to deeds of daring,
That my calamity may be forgotten.
Has Merau, goddess of extinction, died,
That I for ever still must weep,
While day on day succeeds,
And each the other follows?
Grief on grief; now gathers all my woe,
And floods my heart with weeping.
Yet agony I dread,
And now I shrink with fear
Of ev'n one drop of rain.
At eventide,
As rays of twinkling stars shine forth,
I weep and on them gaze,
And on their shining courses.
   But, oh! for naught in space I float.
Oh! woe is me! who now like Rangi' am,
From Papa' once divided.
Now flows at flood the tide of keen regret;
And severed once, for ever severed is our love."

He dwelt alone until the spring began to warm the
earth ; and when the shoots of the *tutu* were budding forth
he heard a sound, as of a singing fly ; a humming, that
sounded like " *U-u-u-m* ; *u-u-m* ; notwithstanding my head
off, *u-u-m* ; *u-u-m*." He uncovered the box ; he opened
it ; and there sat Rukutia, restored to life ; he saw her
face radiant with smiles, and heard her voice of joyful
greeting.

It must be pointed out that there is some doubt as to
the certainty of the identification of the Hawaiian Olopana
and Lu'ukia with the Maori 'Koropanga and Rukutia.

'KOROPANGA AND RUKUTIA

The Hawaiian legend says nothing of the noted character Tama-nui', nothing of the lapse of Rukutia. Kahiki is usually identified with Tahiti, and often the name does refer to Tahiti; but Fornander also says that it was a general name, designating any or all foreign lands outside the Hawaiian group. There is a fine chant, known as the chant of Kualii, in which both Kahiki and Olopana are mentioned, but they are not necessarily the Kahiki and Olopana of the foregoing stories. The following portion of the chant is of great interest:

> O Kahiki, land of the far-reaching ocean,
> Land where Olopana dwelt!
> Within is the land, outside is the sun;
> Indistinct are the sun and the land when approaching.
>> Perhaps you have seen it?
>> I have seen it.
> I have surely seen Kahiki.
> A land with a strange language is Kahiki.
> The men of Kahiki have ascended up
> The backbone of heaven;
> And up there they trample indeed,
> And look down on below.
> Kanakas [men of our race] are not in Kahiki.
> One kind of man is in Kahiki—the Haole [white man].
>> He is like a god;
>> I am like a man;
>> A man indeed,
> Wandering about, and the only man who got there.
> Passed is the day of Kukahi and the day of Kulua.
> By morsels was the food;
> Picking the food with a noise like a bird!
>> Listen, bird of victory!
>> Hush! with whom the victory?
>> With Ku indeed.

The chant was composed in the middle part of the seventeenth century; and while Kualii speaks of Kahiki, the land of Olopana, it cannot be Tahiti that is referred to, since the people speak a strange language, and the sun and the land are indistinctly seen, as if shrouded in fogs, appearing to elude the view of the approaching voyager. The people, too, are not of his race, but are white men; and

69

the voyage is so long that food becomes scarce. Fornander notes that the only lands bordering on the Pacific in the occupation of white men at this time were the Ladrone Islands, parts of the Philippines, and the western coasts of America. Between these places the regular trade was carried on by Spanish galleons, and there seems to be little doubt that the Hawaiian Islands were discovered by Gaetano, a Spaniard, as early as 1555, though no written evidence of this has been found. It is possible that some passing galleon had picked up Kualii while at sea fishing off Oahu, carried him to Acapulco, and brought him back on a return voyage. Fornander judges the land to have been to the east from the peculiarly Hawaiian expression " Within is the land, outside is the sun," indicating that the land was to the east of the voyager.

La'a-maomao, the friendly god of the winds in the foregoing story of Ho'o-ipo, was known in New Zealand as Raka-maomao. Here too he was connected with the winds, the south wind being called a child of Raka-maomao. At Samoa La'a-maomao represents the rainbow. The keeping of the winds in a calabash is a favourite resort throughout Polynesia, and seems a more convenient way than keeping them imprisoned in a cave.

CHAPTER III: KELEA AND KALAMAKUA

SOMETHING more of the knowledge the Hawaiians had of navigation is learned, with much other pleasant lore, from the story of Kelea, the beautiful but capricious sister of Kawao. She had been humoured and petted by her father, king or highest chief of the island Maui, and the historic songs (*mele*) speak of her as a maiden of uncommon beauty, but wayward, volatile, and capricious; and no consideration of policy, or persuasion of passion, could move her to accept any of the high chiefs who sought her in marriage. She loved the water, and became the most graceful and daring surf-swimmer in the kingdom. Often when the Auau channel surged fiercely under the breath of the south wind Kelea, laughing at the fears of her brother, would plunge into the sea with her surf-board (*onini*), and so audaciously ride the waves that the many who watched and applauded were half inclined to believe that she was the favourite of some water-deity, and could not be drowned.

When her brother spoke to her of marriage she gaily answered that her surf-board was her husband, and she would never embrace any other. The brother frowned, for he hoped to consolidate his kingdom by her marriage.

"Do not frown, Kawao," said Kelea coaxingly. "A smile better becomes your handsome face. I may marry some day, if only to please you; but remember what the voice of the oracle said at the last feast of Lono."

"Yes, I remember," said Kawao; "but I have sometimes believed that when the prophet declared that in riding the surf Kelea would find a husband he was simply repeating an augury imparted to him by Kelea herself."

"You will anger the gods by speaking so lightly of their words," returned Kelea reproachfully; and Kawao smiled as she took her leave with a dignity quite unusual. Had he really touched a secret? Or was the dignity really unassumed?

Kawao loved his sister, and was proud of her beauty; and while he was anxious to see her suitably married, and felt no little annoyance at the importunity of her suitors, he recognized her right, as daughter of a king, to a voice in the selection of her husband.

But the voice from the oracle was truly prophetic; and while Kelea continued to ride the waves at Lahaina a husband from the island of Oahu was in search of her.

There lived at that time at Lihue, on Oahu, a chief named Lo-Lale, a brother of Pili-wale, the great chief or nominal sovereign of the island.

Lo-Lale was an amiable and handsome prince, but had reached the age of thirty-five without marrying. The reason was supposed to be the death by drowning, some years before, of a chiefess of great beauty whom he was about to marry, and to whom he had been greatly attached. He abhorred the sea thereafter, and was content to remain at Lihue, beyond the sound of its ceaseless surges.

Pili-wale had two daughters, but no son, and was anxious that his brother should marry so that the family line might be perpetuated, and the family authority strengthened; and to his and other importunities Lo-Lale finally yielded. As no suitable wife for so high a chief could be found in Oahu, or at least not one who would be personally acceptable to him, it was necessary to seek her among the royal lines on the other islands.

A large canoe was fitted out at Wai-a-lua, and messengers of rank dispatched in search of a wife for Lo-Lale. Among the chiefs selected, the greatest reliance was placed upon the judgment of Kalamakua, a cousin of Lo-Lale. He was a noble of high rank, dwelling on the coast of the Ewa district. He was bold, and adventurous, and readily consented to assist in finding a wife for his royal and romantic relative. Lo-Lale was at Wai-a-lua when the messengers embarked. He took an encouraging interest in the expedition, and when banteringly asked by his cousin if age would be any objection in a bride of unexceptionable birth replied that he had promised to take a wife solely to please his brother, and any age under eighty would answer.

" Not so," said Pili-wale, more than half in earnest. " I

will not become the uncle of a family of monsters. The bride must be worthy in person as in blood."

"Do you hear, Kalamakua?" said Lo-Lale. "Do you hear the words of Pili-wale? She must not only be young, but beautiful. If you bring or give promise to any other, she shall not live at Lihue!"

"Do not fear," replied the cousin gaily. "Whosoever she may be, we will keep her in the family; for if you refuse her, or she you, I will marry her myself!"

"Fairly spoken," said the King. "And I will see that he keeps his promise, Lo-Lale."

Although the object of the voyage was known to few, hundreds gathered at the beach to witness the departure, for the canoe was decorated, and the embarking chiefs appeared in feather capes and other ornaments of their rank. Turning to the chief priest, who was present, Pili-wale asked him if he had observed the auguries.

"I have," replied the priest. "They are more than favourable." Then, turning his face northward, he continued, "There is peace in the clouds, and the listless winging of yonder bird betokens favouring winds."

Amid a chorus of *Aloha! Aloha!* the canoe dashed through the breakers to the open sea, holding a course in the direction of Molokai. Reaching the island next day, they landed at Kalau-papa. The great chief received them well; but inquiry leading to nothing satisfactory, the party proceeded around the island, landing next at Lanai. They remained there one day, and next day proceeded to Hana, Maui, with the intention of crossing to Hawaii. They learned that Kawao had removed his court from Lahaina, for the season, to Hamakuapoko, to enjoy the cool breezes and indulge in surf-bathing. They further learned that a large number of chiefs had accompanied him, and that Kelea, sister of the King, and the most beautiful woman on the island, as well as the most daring and accomplished surf-swimmer, was also there.

This was agreeable news, and the party re-embarked, arriving next morning off Hamakuapoko, just as Kelea

73

and her attendants had gone down to the beach to enjoy a buffeting in the surf. Swimming out beyond the breakers, and oblivious to everything but her own enjoyment, Kelea suddenly found herself within a few yards of the Oahuan chiefs. Presuming that the canoe contained her own people, she swam closer, when she discovered, to her amazement, that all the faces in the canoe were unknown to her. Perceiving her embarrassment, Kalamakua rose to his feet, and addressing her in a courtly and respectful manner invited her to a seat in the canoe, offering to ride the surf with it to the beach—an exciting and often dangerous sport, in which great skill and coolness are required.

The language of the chief was so gentle and suggestive of the manners of the court that the invitation was accepted, and the canoe mounted one of the great waves following two of lighter bulk and force, and was adroitly and safely beached. The achievement was greeted with applause on the shore, and when the proposal was made to repeat the performance Kelea willingly retained her seat. Again the canoe successfully rode the breakers ashore, and then, through the attendants, Kalamakua discovered that the fair and dashing swimmer was none other than Kelea, the sister of the ruler of Maui.

With increased respect he again invited her to join in the pleasure and excitement of a third ride over the breakers. She consented, and the canoe was once more pulled beyond the surf, where it remained for a moment, awaiting a high combing roller on which to be borne to the landing. One passed and was missed, and before another came a squall, known as *mumuku*, suddenly struck the canoe, rendering it utterly unmanageable, and driving it out upon the broad ocean.

Kelea would have leaped into the sea had she not been restrained ; but Kalamakua spoke so kindly to her, assuring her that they would safely ride out the storm and return to Hamakuapoko, that she became calmer, and consented to curl down beside him in the boat to escape the fury of the

74

wind. Her shapely limbs and shoulders were bare, and her hair, braided and bound loosely back, was still wet, and grew chilling in the wind where it fell. Kalamakua took from a covered calabash a handsome mantle, and wrapped it around her shoulders, and then seated her in the shelter of his own burly form. She smiled her thanks for these attentions, and the chief was compelled to admit to himself that her beauty was yet greater than the reports of it. He could recall no maiden on Oahu who was her equal in grace and comeliness, and felt that, could she be secured for his eccentric cousin, his search would be at an end. He even grew indignant at the thought that she might not prove acceptable, and smiled the next moment at his promise to marry the girl himself should she be refused by his cousin.

But the fierce *mumuku* allowed him but little time to indulge such dreams. The sea surged in fury; the canoe was tossed from one huge wave to another. The spray was almost blinding; and while Kalamakua kept the little craft squarely before the wind his companions were earnestly employed in alternately bailing and trimming as emergency demanded.

On sped the canoe, farther and farther out into the open sea, tossed like a calabash by the crested waves, and pelted by the driving spray. The scene was fierce and wild; the southern sky had grown black with wrath, and the long streamers sent from the clouds shot northward as if to surround and cut off the retreat of the scudding craft. All crouched in the bottom of the boat, intent only on keeping it before the wind and preventing it from filling. A frailer craft would have been battered to pieces; but it was hewn from the trunk of a stout *koa*-tree, and buoyantly rode out the storm.

When the wind ceased and the skies cleared, late in the afternoon, however, the canoe was far out to sea and beyond the sight of land. It was turned and headed back; but as there was no wind to assist the paddles, and the waters were still rough and restless, little progress was

75

made ; and when the sun went down Kalamakua was un-
decided which way to proceed, as he was not certain that
the storm had not carried them so far from the coast of
Maui that some point on Molokai or Oahu might not be
more speedily and safely reached than the place from which
they had started. Their supply of *poi* had been lost during
the gale by the breaking of the vessel containing it ; but
they had still left a small quantity of dried fish, raw
potatoes, and bananas, and a calabash of water ; and they
ate their evening meal as cheerfully as if their supplies were
inexhaustible and the green hills of Wai-a-lua smiled on
them in the distance. Such was the Hawaiian of the past ;
such is the Hawaiian of to-day. His joys and griefs are
centred in the present ; and he broods but little over the
past, and borrows no trouble from the future.

The stars came out, and a light wind began to steal
down upon them from the north-west. It was quite chilly,
and felt like the breath of the returning trade-winds, which
start from the frozen shores of North-western America,
gradually growing warmer as they sweep steadily down
over the tropic seas. These winds, continuing, with intervals of pause, eight or nine months in the year, are what
give life, beauty, and a tempered climate to the Hawaiian
group.

As the breeze freshened sails were raised, and then the
course to be taken remained to be determined. Kalamakua expressed his doubts to Kelea, as if inviting a
suggestion from her ; but she was unable to offer any
advice, declaring that she had not noticed the course of
the wind that had driven them so far out on to the ocean.

" I am equally in doubt," said the chief. " We may
have been blown farther towards the rising of the sun than
the headlands of Hana. If so, the course we are now
sailing would take us to Hawaii, if not, indeed, beyond,
while in following the evening star we might even pass
Oahu. I therefore suggest a course between these two
directions, which will certainly bring us to land some time
to-morrow."

76

KELEA AND KALAMAKUA

" Then, since we are all in doubt," replied Kelea, "and
the winds are blowing landward, why not trust to the gods
and follow them ? "

" Your words are an inspiration," returned the chief,
delighted that she had suggested a course that would enable
him to make Oahu direct; for, as may be suspected, he
was an accomplished navigator, and was really in little
or no doubt concerning the direction of the several islands.
" You have spoken wisely," he continued, as if yielding
entirely to her judgment. " We will follow the winds that
are now cooling the shores of Hamakuapoko."

Thus adroitly was Kelea made a consenting party to
her own abduction. Kalamakua took the helm, slightly
changing the course of the canoe, and his companions made
themselves comfortable for the evening. Their wet rolls
of *kapa* had been dried during the afternoon, and there was
room enough to spare for the arranging of a couch for
Kelea in the bottom of the boat. But she was too much
excited over the strange events of the day to sleep, or even
attempt to rest, and therefore sat near Kalamakua in the
stern of the canoe until past midnight, watching the stars
and listening to the story, with which he knew she must
sooner or later become acquainted, of his romantic expedition in search of a wife for his cousin.

It is needless to say that she showed surprise and interest
in the narration ; and when Kalamakua referred to the high
rank of his cousin, to his handsome person, and extensive
estates at Lihue, and begged her to regard with favour the
proposal of marriage which he then made to her on behalf
of Lo-Lale, she frankly replied that, if her royal brother
did not object, she would give the proffer consideration.

As Kalamakua had decided not to take the hazard of
securing the consent of her brother, who doubtless had
some other matrimonial project in view for her, he con-
strued her answer into a modestly expressed willingness
to become the wife of Lo-Lale, and the more resolutely
bent his course toward Oahu. He watched the Pleiades—
the great guide of the early Polynesian navigators—as they

swept up into the heavens, and, bearing still farther to the northward to escape Molokai, announced that he would keep the steering oar for the night, and advised his companions, now that the breeze was steady and the sea smoother, to betake themselves to rest. And Kelea at last curled down upon her couch of *kapa*, and Kalamakua was left alone with his thoughts to watch the wind and the stars.

Although a long and steady run had been made during the night, no land was visible the next morning. Kelea scanned the horizon uneasily, and, without speaking, looked at Kalamakua for an explanation.

" Before the sun goes down we shall see land," said the chief.

" What land? " inquired Kelea.

" Oahu," was the reply; but the chief was not greeted with the look of surprise that he had expected.

" I am not surprised," returned the Princess indifferently. " You seem to have been sailing by the wandering stars last night, for before daylight I looked up and saw by Kao that your course was directly toward the place of sunset."

Five of the planets—Mercury, Mars, Venus, Jupiter, and Saturn—were known to the ancient Hawaiians, and designated *na hoku aea*, or wandering stars. The fixed stars were also grouped by them into constellations, and Kao was their name for Antares.

With a look of genuine surprise Kalamakua replied, " I did not know that so correct a knowledge of navigation was among the accomplishments of the sister of Kawao."

" It required no great knowledge of the skies to discover last night that we were not bearing southwards, and needs still less now to observe that we are sailing directly west," Kelea quietly remarked.

" I will not attempt to deceive one who seems able to instruct me in journeying over the blue waters," said Kalamakua. " Your judgment is correct. We are sailing nearly westwards, and the first land sighted will probably be the headland of Kaawa."

"You have acted treacherously," resumed the Princess, after a pause, as if suddenly struck with the propriety of protesting.

"Possibly," was the brief reply.

"Yes," she continued after another pause, "you have acted treacherously, and my brother will make war upon Oahu unless I am immediately returned to Hamakuapoko."

"He will find work for his spears," was the irritating response.

"Is it a habit with the chiefs of Oahu to steal their wives?" inquired Kelea tauntingly.

"No," Kalamakua promptly replied; "but I would not eat from the same calabash with the chief who would throw back into the face of the generous winds the gift of the rarest flower that ever blossomed on Hawaiian soil!"

The compliment moved Kelea to silence; yet the chief observed that there was a sparkle of pleasure in her eyes, and that the novelty and romance of the situation were not altogether distasteful to her.

Land was sighted late in the afternoon. It was Kaoio Point, on the western side of Oahu. Rounding it, they landed at Mahana, where they procured food and water and passed the night, and the next day had an easy voyage to Wai-a-lua.

Landing, Kalamakua at once communicated with Pili-wale, telling him the high rank of Kelea, as well as the strange circumstances under which she had been brought to Wai-a-lua. The Queen promptly dispatched attendants to the beach with appropriate apparel, and in due time the distinguished visitor was received in a manner consistent with her rank.

The next day a message brought Lo-Lale from Lihue. He was most richly dressed, and brought with him, as an offering to Kelea, a rare necklace of shells and curiously carved mother-of-pearl. He was conducted to the Princess by Kalamakua. They seemed to be mutually pleased with each other; in fact, Lo-Lale was completely charmed, and in his enthusiasm offered to divide his estates with his cousin as evidence of his gratitude.

Kalamakua had himself become very much interested in Kelea, and secretly had hoped that his cousin might find something to object to in her blood or bearing, in which case he felt that she might be induced to regard himself with favour; but Lo-Lale declared her to be perfection, and wooed her with so much earnestness that she finally consented to become his wife without waiting to hear from her brother.

The event was celebrated with games, feasting, dancing, and the commencement of a new temple near Wai-a-lua, which was in time completed and dedicated to Lono, with a large image of La'a-maomao, the Hawaiian Æolus, at the inner entrance, in poetic commemoration of the winds that drove Kelea away from the coast of Maui.

At the conclusion of the festivities at Wai-a-lua Kelea was borne all the way to Lihue in a richly mounted *manele*, with four bearers. There were three hundred attendants in her train, besides thirty-six chiefs as a guard of honour, wearing feather capes and helmets, and armed with javelins festooned with many-coloured *lei* of flowers and tinted feathers. It was a royal procession, and its entrance into Lihue was the beginning of another round of festivities, continuing for many days.

Returning to Hamakuapoko, the King was deeply grieved on learning of the sudden disappearance of Kelea before the tempestuous breath of the *mumuku*. To all the attendants whom he summoned to relate what had occurred it was manifest that the canoe had been blown to sea in spite of the efforts of its occupants; and as the gale continued to increase in violence during the day it was feared that the entire party had perished. As to the strangers, no one seemed to know anything of them; they did not seem to belong to the common people, and one of them, it was believed from his bearing, was a high chief.

Little else could be learned. One man, who had noticed

80

the canoe as it came and went through the surf, thought it was from Hawaii, while another was as certain it was from Oahu; but as the general structure of the canoes on the several islands of the group differed little, their descriptions of the craft gave no real clue to the mystery.

With the cessation of the storm late in the afternoon came a hope to Kawao that the missing canoe had safely ridden out the gale, and would seek the nearest land, favoured by the changing winds. He summoned the chief priest, and instructed him to put his diviners and his magicians to the task of discovering what had become of the Princess Kelea. Pigs and fowls were killed, prayers were offered in the temple, and late in the evening information came through supernatural agencies that Kelea was still living. But the King demanded something more specific, and a prophet of great sanctity was prepared and placed in the *anu*, a wicker enclosure within the inner court, and in due time, in answer to the questions of the chief priest, he announced that the canoe containing the Princess was sailing in safety toward Oahu.

The words of the prophet were repeated to the King, who next day dispatched a well-manned canoe to find and bring back the lost Kelea. Owing to unfavourable winds, or bad management, the canoe did not reach Maka-puu Point, Oahu, until the fourth day. Proceeding along the north-eastern coast of the island, and landing whenever practicable to make inquiries, the messenger did not arrive at Wai-a-lua until two days after the departure of Kelea for Lihue.

Learning that the Princess had become the wife of Lo-Lale, the disappointed messenger did not deem it necessary to communicate with her, but briefly paid his respects to the King, to whom he made known the nature of his errand and his resolution to return at once to report his discoveries.

Appreciating that, in his anxiety to see his brother well married, he had countenanced a proceeding sufficiently discourteous to the King of Maui to warrant a hostile response, Pili-wale treated the messenger, a man of note, with marked kindness and consideration, and insisted upon sending an escort with him back to Maui, including the bearer of a friendly explanatory message from himself to Kawao. For this service none could be found as competent as the courtly Kalamakua, who was well versed in the genealogies and the histories of the various families, and would be able satisfactorily, if not altogether truthfully, to explain why it was that the canoe, when driven out to sea, was headed for Oahu instead of Maui when the storm abated.

Kalamakua was accordingly sent on the mission ; and, being a much better sailor than the messenger, he found no difficulty either in parting company with him off the coast of Eastern Maui or in reaching Hamakuapoko three or four hours in advance of the party he was supposed to be courteously escorting. This enabled him to win the advantage of securing an audience with the King and deliver his message and explanation before the King's own messenger could land and give his version of the story.

The explanation given by Kalamakua of the impossibility, after the storm, of landing in safety anywhere but at Oahu or Molokai seemed to be satisfactory ; and when the chief dwelt on the well-known high rank of Lo-Lale, and referred to his noble bearing, his manly disposition, and the amplitude of his estates, Kawao answered sadly :

" Then so let it be. It is perhaps the will of the gods. I would have had it otherwise ; but be to Kelea and her husband, and to my brother-king of Oahu, the messenger of peace."

Thanking the King for his kindly words, Kalamakua took his leave. As he was about to re-embark in the afternoon for Oahu, the discomfited King's messenger, having just landed, passed him on the beach. Knowing that he had been outwitted, in his wrath he reached for the handle of his dagger. But he did not draw it. Kalamakua stopped, and promptly answered the challenge ; but the messenger passed on, and with a smile the Oahu chief stepped into his canoe, and a few minutes later was on his way with the message of peace from Kawao.

The years came and went, and Lo-Lale in his quiet home at Lihue lost none of his love for Kelea. No wars distracted the group. To gratify his wife Lo-Lale surrounded her with every comfort. The choicest fruits were at her command, and every day fresh fish and other delicacies were brought from the neighbouring coasts. Everything not prohibited to women was at her command. Summer-houses were built for her in the cool recesses of the Waianae Mountains, and a *manele* was always ready for her whenever she desired it. The people were proud of her rank and beauty, and at the season of gifts she received gratifying assurance of this in the abundance of rare and valuable offerings made to her.

Yet, with all this, Kelea became more and more restless and unhappy. Nor did the presence of her three children seem to make her more contented. She longed for the sea. She longed for the bounding surf that had been the sport of her girlhood; for the white-foamed billows which she had so often fearlessly ridden to the shore; for the thunder of the breakers against the cliffs; for the murmur of the reef-bound wavelets sliding up the beach to cool and tickle her feet; and the more she longed for her old-time pleasures, the greater became her dissatisfaction with Lihue and its beautiful surroundings.

Knowing her love for the sea, Lo-Lale made occasional excursions with her to the coast, frequently remaining there for days together. Sometimes they visited the east side of the island, sometimes the south; but the place which seemed to please her above all others was Ewa, where Kalamakua made his home. He too loved the sea, and during her visits there she had every opportunity to indulge her passion for it. Together they had enchanting sails around the Puu-loa lagoon, and gallant rides over the surf at its entrance. There, and there only, did she seem to recover her spirits; there only did see seem to be happy.

This did not escape the notice of Lo-Lale, and a great

grief filled his heart as he sometimes thought, in noting her brightened look in the presence of Kalamakua, that it was less the charms of the surf than of his cousin that made the waters of Ewa so attractive to Kelea.

Life at Lihue finally became so irksome to her, and even the kindness of Lo-Lale so unwelcome, that she announced her determination to leave the home of her husband for ever. This resolution was not altogether unexpected by Lo-Lale, for he had not been blind to her growing restlessness, and was prepared for the worst; and as the prerogatives of her high rank gave her the privilege of separation if she desired it, he reluctantly consented to the divorcement. When asked where it was her purpose to go, she answered, " Probably to Maui, to rejoin my brother."

" More probably not beyond Ewa," was the reply of Lo-Lale. " But no matter where you may go," he continued with dignity, " take your departure from Lihue in a manner consistent with your rank. You were received here as became the sister of a king and the wife of the son of Kalona-iki. So would I have you depart. I reproach you with nothing, myself with nothing; therefore let us part in peace."

" We part in peace," was her only answer, and the next morning she quietly took her departure with four or five attendants. A chant expressive of the grief of Lo-Lale at the separation was recited long afterward, and of this chant a few lines have been preserved :

> Farewell, my partner on the lowland plains,
> On the waters of Pohakeo,
> Above Kane-hoa,
> On the dark mountain-spur of Mauna-una!
> O Lihue, she is gone!
> Snuff the sweet scent of the grass,
> The sweet scent of the wild vines
> That are twisted by Wai-koloa,
> By the winds of Wai-o-pua,
> My flower!
> As though a mote were in my eye,
> The sight of it is troubled;
> My eyes a dimness covers.   Woe is me!

KELEA AND KALAMAKUA

Leaving Lihue, Kelea descended to Ewa; and skirting the head of the lagoon by way of Halawa arrived at the entrance on the afternoon of the second day. There she found a large number of nobles and retainers of Kalamakua, the high chief of the district, amusing themselves in the surf. As she had not seen the sea for some months, Kelea could not resist the temptation to indulge in her old pastime; and, borrowing a surf-board from one of the bathers, she plunged into the sea, and soon joined the party of surf-riders beyond the breakers.

Soon a huge roller appeared, and all mounted it and started for the shore. The race was exciting, for the most expert swimmers in the district were among those present; but in grace, daring, and skill Kelea excelled them all, and was loudly applauded as she reached the shore. Kalamakua was resting in the shade, not far away; and hearing the tumult of voices, he inquired the cause. He was told that a beautiful woman from Lihue had beaten all the chiefs at surf-riding, and the people could not restrain their enthusiasm. Satisfied that there was but one Lihue woman who could do this, he proceeded to the beach, and arrived just as a second trial had resulted in a triumph to the woman no less decided than the first. As she touched the shore Kalamakua dropped his mantle over her shoulders and respectfully greeted her. Kelea then informed him that she had formally separated from her husband, and was about to embark for Maui.

"If that is so," said Kalamakua, gently taking her by the arm as if to restrain her, "you will go no farther than Ewa. When I went in search of a wife for Lo-Lale, I promised that if he objected to the woman I brought, or she to him, I would take her myself—if she so willed. You have objected to him; is Kalamakua more to your liking?"

"I shall remain at Ewa," was the answer.

"Yes; and you should have gone there instead of to Lihue when you landed at Wai-a-lua years ago," continued Kalamakua earnestly.

" My thought is the same," was her frank avowal; and she beckoned to her attendants, and told Kalamakua she was ready to follow him.

They lived happily together. Lo-Lale sent her a present of fruits and a message of peace. They had a daughter, Lai-e-lohelohe, who became the wife of her cousin Piilani, son and successor of Kawao, the King of Maui. And these are far-off things, and happenings of nearly five hundred years ago.

Canoes and Voyages

The foregoing story shows how familiar the Hawaiians were with the seas and the skies, and how the stars and the winds were used as guides for direction in navigation.

Captain Cook bore constant testimony to their knowledge of the stars, noting that they had names for them, that they knew at what parts of the heavens they would appear in every month of the year, and also knew with accuracy the time of their annual appearing and disappearing. Even in his day, when long-distance voyaging had been abandoned by the Polynesians, they were sometimes two weeks or three weeks at sea, and could stay longer if they had more accommodation for provisions. He notes the accuracy with which they were able to foretell the weather and the direction in which the wind was to blow, in the latter respect at least being more accurate than Cook's people. They were guided by the stars at night, the sun by day; and if these were obscured the direction of the wind and of the billows gave some indication. Birds in the air, and sea-weeds in the water, indicated the nearness or absence of land; and there is actual record of one voyager aiming at Rarotonga from the north knowing he had missed it by the coldness of the sea; without delay he about ship, and soon made the island. Cruise, an early writer on New Zealand, notes the keen sense of direction possessed by the Maori. He said that while at sea, if at any hour of the day the Maori on board were asked where their country was situated, they pointed in its direction with the accuracy of

86

THE CANOE-BUILDERS

From a picture by F. and W. Wright.

Reproduced by permission of the Committee of the Auckland Public Library, Art Gallery, and Old Colonists' Museum

(See page 86)

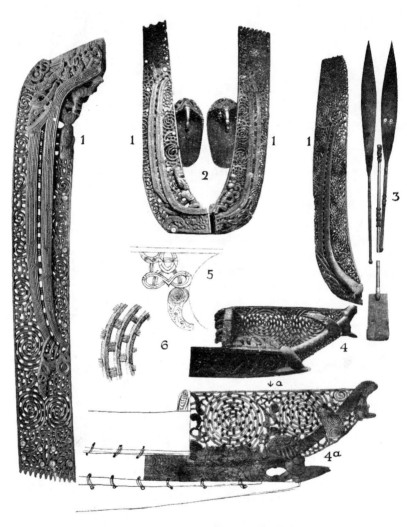

DETAILS OF POLYNESIAN CANOES

1, stern pieces.   2, bailers.   3, paddles.   4, prow.   4a, sketch showing
lashings of top-sides and prow.   5, detail of a part of 4a.
6, detail of part of scroll of 4a.

(See page 88)

a compass; and when the stars appeared in the evening they displayed equal sagacity.

While the big double ocean-going canoes were no longer built once their voyaging was discontinued, Cook saw examples of such craft. He saw one at Tongatabu, in October 1773, each of the two canoes being from sixty to seventy feet long, and four or five feet broad at the middle, each end terminating almost in a point. They were furnished with top-sides, to increase their depth, and the two were lashed together, six or seven feet apart, by strong cross-beams lashed to the top-sides. Over these beams were others, supporting a boarded platform. On this platform a single removable mast was stepped, carrying a triangular sail, point downward, and extended on a long yard. The sails were made of matting, which was no heavier than canvas. On the platform was also built a small shed, or hut, to serve as a shelter from sun and weather. A movable fireplace was carried—a small, shallow trough of wood, filled with stones. The way into the hold of the canoes was from off the platform, down a sort of uncovered hatchway, in which the men stood when bailing. The canoe might be five feet in depth. All the parts were lashed together as firmly as if bolted, and the lashing would be renewed periodically, the whole vessel being taken to pieces and overhauled.

At Tahiti Cook saw, in a naval review, a fleet of 160 large double canoes, and 170 smaller double canoes, each with its little shed on the platform; he estimated that this fleet carried probably 7760 men. He also saw two canoes building, each 108 feet long.

In islands which supplied only small trees the keel, the hull, and the whole body of the canoe might be composed of many pieces, neatly fitted together, and lashed firmly in place. In some islands the separate boards had an edging flange round the inner surface, and through this flange the holes were pierced for the lashing. Ribs were fitted in to support the sides, and the thwarts gave stability and support to the ribs. In New Zealand, where huge trees

87

suitable for vessels were available, the whole hull, up to a hundred feet or more in length and seven feet in width amidships, was hewn from one piece, the top-sides being slabs the full length of the hull dubbed from another tree. In these the lashings passed through the top-sides and the hull, and the junction of the edges was covered with a batten, and all well caulked with *raupo*-bloom.

The Maori gave up the double canoe for the great single canoe of New Zealand; and one of these, with its carved figurehead, its tall, beautifully carved stern-piece fifteen feet high, a festoon of feathers fluttering from its top, was, with its hundred muscular paddlers, a fine sight gliding over the water with a rush of foam. At least one double canoe was seen by Cook off the North Island in New Zealand waters, for on June 3, 1773, he recorded that one of his boats was chased by a large canoe of this kind, full of people. He saw several off the South Island.

An ingenious arrangement was sometimes used in the single canoes with outrigger. The outrigger was a heavy drag, tending to draw the canoe round in a circle. In order to counteract this, and lessen the labour of steering, the keel, when laid down, was forced four inches or so out of line, making a long curve instead of a straight line. The curve was toward the outrigger, so that the two opposing forces would neutralize each other and the vessel keep a fairly direct course. It is said, too, that in order to add buoyancy to the moving hull the sides at the bows would not be made perfectly smooth, but a few vertical strokes would be made with the adze extending from a little above to a little below the water-line, so that the vessel, when cutting through the water, would break it into bubbles, adding something, if only a little, to the buoyancy of the craft.

Cook gives the speed of the canoes at about 7 knots an hour in a gentle gale; but in one place he speaks of double canoes with large sail, carrying from forty to fifty people, sailing around his moving ship as swiftly as if it had been at anchor. He noted that for the natives it was a three days' sail from Tongatabu in the Friendly Islands to Fiji, a distance of about three hundred miles.

The long voyages appear to have grown less frequent after the time of the great migration to New Zealand, which took place about the year 1350. It may be that the branch of the Polynesians who took up their final abode in New Zealand consisted of the most turbulent or restless element of that vigorous race; it may be that on New Zealand becoming occupied there were no islands left undiscovered, none left uncolonized. That the coming to New Zealand was considered final, except perhaps for occasional adventurous voyages, would be indicated by the fact that the voyagers brought with them the *kumara*, the *taro*, the paper-mulberry (*aute*), and other useful plants, also the dog. While the coconut died out, its name has been preserved in a divination ceremony called *niu*—*niu* being an old name for the coconut, which was used in divination. The *kava*-plant was not brought, or did not thrive if brought, but a plant of the same kind was found in New Zealand—the same in leaf and growth, if not in property—and it was named *kawakawa*.

The more rigorous climate of New Zealand made a more vigorous race of the Maori, so that physically and mentally they are, as Cook found them, the finest developed among the Polynesians.

Voyages from New Zealand to Hawaiki

There are records, dim sometimes, it may be, and sometimes fragmentary, of voyages from New Zealand back to Hawaiki and again to New Zealand since the date of the great migration. The clearest record is one of an expedition by the Bay of Plenty tribes for the purpose of obtaining a supply of *kumara*. A chief named Toi' is supposed to have settled in New Zealand before the arrival of the fleet of the migration. He did not bring the *kumara* with him, his people living on one cultivated plant, the *hue*, a gourd, and the wild food provided by fern-root, *mamaku*-fern, berries, young leaves of the *ti* (*Cordyline*), and the tap-root of varieties of *ti*.

89

It happened that one morning a young woman named Kura-whakaata, daughter of Tama-ki-hiku-rangi, a descendant of Toi', was walking at the water's edge below the cliff-set *pa* when she caught sight of two strange men lying on a rock close to the water, and heard them repeat a *karakia* in order to cause the sun to shine brightly and warm their chilled bodies, for they had undergone much hardship and exposure in a long voyage from the islands of Polynesia. The men were two brothers, Taukata and Hoaki, sons of Rongoatau of Hawaiki, and they had made the adventurous journey in a canoe named *Nga-Tai-a-Kupe*.

" From whence do you come? " asked Kura-whakaata. " We come from Hawaiki, from Mata-ora." She conducted them to the *pa*, to Kapu-te-rangi, and as she brought them in she cried, " Visitors are with me ; strangers from a far land."

The people were disturbed, not knowing what this visit might portend ; but food was prepared for the guests— fern-root, *mamaku*, *ti*, roots of the *raupo*, and earthworms. Then was heard the sound of the beating mallets as the women crushed the fibrous fern-root.

" What is the loud sound we hear? " asked Taukata. " It is Haumia-roa," answered Tama'—the name being an emblematic term for, or a personification of, fern-root.

The brothers found the food placed before them unpalatable ; and Taukata said, " The prized food of Hawaiki has arrived in Ao-tea-roa." He asked for a bowl of water, and took from his broad double belt some dried *kumara* (*kao*), which he crumbled into the gourd of water, stirring it up, and presenting the resulting mush to his hosts. They were delighted with the new food, and asked, " How may this food be obtained? " " By means of a canoe," said Taukata.

The building of sea-going canoes seems to have been abandoned by the people of Tama', and the superintendence of the building of a canoe was left to the two strangers. They found a fine *totara* stranded on the banks of the river, near the present town of Whakatane, and out of the bole

THE MAORI FLEET LEAVING HAWAIKI FOR NEW ZEALAND
From a picture by Kenneth Watkins.

Reproduced by permission of the Committee of the Auckland Public Library, Art Gallery, and Old Colonists' Museum

(See page 90)

THE ARRIVAL IN NEW ZEALAND OF THE MAORI FLEET FROM HAWAIKI
From a picture by Kenneth Watkins.

(See page 92)

of this tree they built the canoe *Te Ara-tawhao*, hewing it
and dubbing it with stone tools and fire. " You must go
far across the sea," said the brothers ; "you must go to
Pari-nui-te-ra, and to Ngaruru-kai-whatiwhati, where you
will obtain the best *kumara*-seed, such as *toroa-mahoe*."

Taukata remained at Kakaho-roa (the old name of
Whakatane), Hoaki going with the others to act as guide
on the voyage. There was a proposal to leave Tama-ki-
hiku-rangi behind ; a fear of his magic powers, for he
was a noted *tohunga*, seemed to oppress the people ; but
Tama' heard of it, and declined to be left; and either in
revenge, or in justification of their fears, he caused them
much uneasiness and alarm during the voyage. Some of
the *karakia* used on the voyage have been preserved ; one,
a *rotu*, for calming angry surges and boisterous winds ;
another, a *tata*, for assisting in bailing the canoe; another,
an *awa*, for rendering the course smooth and easy to follow ;
another, a *ruruku*, for binding the vessel and keeping her
seaworthy.

On arriving at Hawaiki, Hoaki visited Maru-tai-ranga-
ranga, greeting him with a song. As the people gathered
round him, Hoaki said to Maru', " Sir, I have a people
with me." " Who are they? " asked Maru'. " They
are the descendants of Toi'." " For what purpose have
they come? " " They tasted the dried *kumara* we took
with us, and have come to obtain seed for planting." So
the seed was obtained, at the two places mentioned.

Te Ara-tawhao did not return to New Zealand; she
was left at Hawaiki, her crew returning in the *Matatua*.
It is said that it was the reports about the land of New
Zealand brought by these voyagers that induced so many
others to leave Hawaiki in the great migration of the period
about the year 1350.

The *Matatua* seems to have been expressly built for the
purpose of taking immigrants as well as the crew of *Te Ara-
tawhao* to New Zealand, and it was not well for Taukata,
who had stayed behind; for when the Whakatane people
obtained the seed-*kumara* their Hawaikian friends said to

them, " When you arrive home, be careful in the storing of your seed ; and when it is placed in the store, then lead our friend Taukata in to the storehouse, and there slay him, so that his blood may be sprinkled within ; and do you also sprinkle his blood upon the door, lest the *mauri* [vitality, or life-principle] of the *kumara* return to Hawaiki." They did as directed, and the bold Taukata fell a sacrifice. For many years afterward his skull was, in the planting season, brought from its repository and set at the edge of the cultivation, a seed-*kumara* in each eye-socket, while the officiating *tohunga* performed rites to ensure a plentiful crop and to prevent the *mauri* of the *kumara* from returning to Hawaiki.

One of the many fine string-figures of the Maori is called Pari-nui-te-ra (Great Cliff of the Sun), and is a representation of one of the places from which the *kumara* was on that occasion brought to New Zealand.

CHAPTER IV: UENUKU

MAORI legend relates that in the dim years following the half-mythical times of Tawhaki there lived a powerful chief, Uenuku, said to be a lineal descendant of Tu-matauenga, the god of war. One record says that he married Pai-hu-tanga, a granddaughter of Rata. Another of his wives was called Taka-rita ; she was a sister of a great chief, Tawheta, who lived at Matiko-tai and Po-rangahau.

Taka-rita committed adultery with two men, Tu-mahu-nuku and Tu-mahu-rangi, and for this offence Uenuku killed her ; and being very powerful killed not only her, but also the two who were partners in her guilt. When she was dead he cut out her heart and broiled it at a sacred fire made at the foot of the carved centre-post in his assembly-house, Te Pokinga-o-te-rangi. While it was cooking at the fire, kindled for the purpose, he recited the following *karakia* :

" My fire is newly kindled by friction;
The land desires it;
Let a fire burn to eat up a great chief;
Let a fire burn to eat up a first-born;
Let a fire burn to eat up an *ariki*; [1]
Let a fire burn to eat up a *tohunga*; [2]
Let it burn; but by whom is the fire?
Let it burn; it is by Hine-i-kuku-te-rangi;
Let it burn; it is by Hine-hehe-i-rangi;
Let it burn through two periods of close-quarter fighting
    of the sky.
Let it burn; on, on, onward.
My sacred fire is verily kindled by friction.
Above, abroad, toward the west;
Toward the west; a vengeful, desolating *ariki*.
Never shall the great chiefs be forgotten by me; never.
Never shall the first-borns be forgotten by me;
Eater of scraps and leavings!
The cooking-oven is baking slowly.
I am wasting away; naked, waiting.
The cooking-oven is baking badly;

---

[1] First-born of a first-born.   [2] Priest, or expert.

Go on, bake away the baking-oven.
The oven baking above.
The oven baking below.
Rush to the fight, O space!
Rush to the fight, O sky!
Show forth valour;
Show forth valour;
Return from the charge—return;
Cause it to return. It is ended."

His *karakia* finished, he fed their son Ira with the cooked heart. Hence arose the saying " Ira, devourer of the rich soft interior," and that saying has descended to his offspring, the tribe Nga-Ira.

When the news of the death of Taka-rita reached her brothers they mourned for their sister. Afterward Tawheta formally inquired the particulars. " Why was she killed by Uenuku? " " Because she committed adultery with two men." " His act is no doubt justifiable," said Tawheta; " nevertheless, he shall be repaid. To-morrow he himself shall be eaten by grasshoppers. Here, near me, are his food-preserves, which in the season will without fail draw his children and his people this way. To-morrow he shall be full of trouble when he shall desire the fruit of the trees to be gathered from the ground where they have fallen; the women shall be as a cliff over which men leap to death! " This saying too became a proverb, meaning that unless women are protected men court death and destruction; and for a time Tawheta dwelt quietly, but brooded on his anger.

Uenuku attached no great importance to his act, nor did he anticipate any consequences; another season came, and he had forgotten about it. He sent his children and his people to collect the fruit of his preserves at Matiko-tai and at Po-rangahau; a large number went, men and women, seventy in all. On their arrival, unarmed and unapprehensive, Tawheta took them unawares and killed them all. Four sons of Uenuku were among those killed—Maputu-ki-te-rangi, Ropa-nui, Mahina-i-te-ata, and Whiwhinga-i-te-rangi; while a fifth, Rongo-ua-roa, barely escaped with his life, being the only survivor of the whole party. He had been severely wounded ; his skull was hacked and broken, and he was left for dead among the others. After this slaughter Tawheta and his people went in and ate food ; and it was then that Rongo-ua-roa revived. Opening his eyes and looking around, he saw his brothers and companions all lying dead on the ground. On seeing this, he summoned up all his remaining strength and crawled away and hid himself among some bushes close by. While there, he heard Tawheta and his people loudly vaunting of their doings ; and Tawheta said, " To-morrow, early, we will all go to the *pa* of Uenuku ; we will deceive him, and kill him also, that he and his may die together." Their meal and talk over, they all came out to drag the bodies of the slain into the *pa*, in order to cut them up for food. When it was night Rongo-ua-roa crept out of his hiding-place and crawled into one of their large canoes, stowing himself snugly away in the forehold, and uttering this *karakia* to ensure his not being discovered:

> " Tu', overspread the face of the sky,
> That I may be hidden;
> Let their eyes be dazzled
> In looking at the stars,
> And at the moon,
> And at the light."

And so, sure enough, he was hidden securely ; and, having uttered his charm, he laid himself quietly down, in confidence awaiting the morrow.

Early in the morning Tawheta and his party set out, to deceive, and if possible to kill, Uenuku. They quickly put their things aboard, and paddled away with vigour. Arriving at the *pa*, they dragged up their canoes and left them on the beach, when they proceeded quietly to the *pa*, amid the waving of garments and the shouting of welcoming cries : " *Haere mai! Haere mai!* Come hither ! Come hither ! Most welcome visitors ! " And so they went into the *pa*, entered the big reception house of Uenuku, and sat down. The people of the place were now busy and bustling in preparing a plentiful meal for their unexpected visitors ;

95

the cooking fires were everywhere lighted, the ovens heated, and great preparations made, for Uenuku and his people supposed them to have come with good intentions, and therefore they were most welcome. A knot in the reed can be seen, but a knot in the mind cannot be seen. And so the minds of the visitors were full of deceit, and their hearts of evil intention.

While the food was preparing, Uenuku arose, in the large open space before the house, to address his visitors. "Come hither; welcome hither," said he. "Art thou indeed Tawheta? Welcome hither! Dost thou come from our children and young people?" To this Tawheta replied : " They are all there enjoying themselves in their usual games of play—spinning tops, flying kites, setting up *whai* [string-figures], darting reeds, and all manner of games." This reply was not to Uenuku, who still spoke in welcome. It was spoken by Tawheta, whose turn for speech would follow, to his companions, as if to amuse them, knowing, as they did, what had really taken place.

Now when those visitors had entered the *pa* it happened that the wounded Rongo-ua-roa managed, though with great difficulty, to leave the canoe in which he had lain hidden, and to crawl a little way to a clump of drooping *toetoe* (*Arundo*), where he lay down in the sun. The food for the visitors having been placed on the leafy covering of the hot stones of the ovens, covered over with leaves and grass and flax mats sprinkled with water, and earthed in, the women went outside to gather green blades of flax with which to plait *kono*, or dishes, on which to place the food when cooked for the visitors ; and so some of them got to the place where Rongo-ua-roa was lying with his wounds and broken head. After seeing him, and hearing in a few faint words his tale, they soon went back to the *pa* ; and, unobserved calling Uenuku aside, they told him, " Master ! Master ! it is all false ; they are come with an altogether different design. The whole of our young people have been killed by Tawheta, and only one has escaped— Rongo-ua-roa ! They are come to cajole and destroy thee!" "Where is that survivor?" "Oh, there he is, lying down outside by the clump of *toetoe*, with his head all broken and smashed with a club." "Fetch him," said Uenuku, "and lead him here into the *pa*." So he was fetched. But first of all he was led to the sacred place close by, where the proper ceremonies were performed over him, including the feeding of the *atua* (deity) with his blood, and the lifting up of his blood before Mua. Then this *karakia* was uttered for him:

> Provoking, irascible sinew, striving to kill!
> Hither is come the one they sought to murder.
> Verily, thy own skilful *tohunga* are here;
> Thou and I together as one.
> Thy wound is sacred;
> The lips of thy wound shall meet,
> Through Hine-i-kuku-te-rangi;
> Through Hine-hehe-i-rangi;
> By the evening, lo! thy wound shall be as
>   nothing.
> The stone axe was verily strong as the tide,
> Rushing on to the shores,
> Tearing up the beds of the shellfish.
> Striving, provoking sinew! eager after food for
>   baking.
> The wounding, indeed, of the man
> Who courageously enraged the *atua*.
> Thy internal parts are open to view,
> Verily, just as the stirring up of the fire
> Burning in the courtyard of the *pa*.
> But lo! thou and I together as one.

This done, Rongo-ua-roa was taken into the *pa*, that he might be shown publicly to Tawheta and his party. Now Uenuku had returned to his oratory, keeping his son Rongo-ua-roa out of sight, on one side behind him; the visiting party, according to custom, being all within the big house, while the chief of the *pa*, Uenuku, was outside making his speech to them. They were tired with their paddling, and wanted their morning meal; and now Uenuku recommenced his speech: "Come hither! Come hither! Thou art indeed Tawheta; yes, thou thyself.

Thou art indeed come hither from our children; but are they living, or are they dead?"

On hearing this, Tawheta bounded out from the house, as if with indignation at the suggestion in the words of Uenuku. He thought that Uenuku might have dreamed a dream, or received some warning omen, but he knew that he could have had no certain word, and he cried, "And who indeed is that *atua* who is able to kill our children?" Then it was that Uenuku said to Tawheta, "Our children are dead, slain by thee! Behold the only survivor!" at the same time bringing forward Rongo-ua-roa, making him stand in the open space before the door of the house, so that he might clearly be seen by all within.

On hearing these words of Uenuku, and on seeing Rongo-ua-roa, the whole party was seized with panic fear, and would instantly have fled, or would have endeavoured to do so. But Uenuku was of noble disposition; and though he could at the time easily have doomed them to destruction, he restrained them and their fear, keeping them until the food for them was properly cooked, served up, and eaten before their departure. "Fear nothing," said he; "remain quietly; let the food which has purposely been prepared for you be well and properly cooked and served; then eat it and depart." Therefore they did so, and when the meal was over they left the *pa* in silence, and dragged their canoes down to the sea.

The people of Uenuku were very anxious to fall upon the visitors and kill them; but Uenuku restrained them, and they escaped without harm. As, however, they were leaving the shore Uenuku called out to Tawheta, "Depart peaceably, O Tawheta! Ere long I also shall go thither to our children; no warrior art thou, but a betrayer under cover of darkness." To this Tawheta replied vauntingly, "By what means canst thou possibly venture thither, to the home of the many, the multitude, the hosts as innumerable as the ants and the Haku-turi?" "Depart," Uenuku rejoined. "Soon shall I be going thither; thou shalt not escape me; slippery is thy bravery in battle;

to-morrow shalt thou be devoured by the grasshoppers!
Depart! Depart!" These were the parting words of
Uenuku, and Tawheta returned to his own place.

After this Uenuku stirred up his people to make ready
his war-canoes; the top-sides were newly lashed to the hull,
all was caulked and got ready, and the canoes launched for
war. Then it was that one of the brave fighting-men of
Uenuku, a chief named Whati-ua, arose and made an
oration. He thought it better that the canoes should not
at once proceed by sea to fight. "This is my opinion,"
said he; "first let the *kumara* and the *karaka*-berry be ripe;
then do thou go by sea, when the waters are calm; but
I and my party will go at once by land, and first engage the
enemy, breaking off only the tips of the branchlets of our
revenge for this our sad loss; to-morrow morning we will
start."

They did so; and as they were leaving the *pa* Uenuku
called out to them, "Listen, friends; this is my word to
you: if you succeed in capturing Pou-matangatanga, the
daughter of Tawheta, let her live, to become a wife for me."
So the war-party, the *taua*, seventy in number, left on their
march. They went away inland, up over the high hills,
and kept on until nightfall, when they halted and slept.
At break of day they recommenced their march, and again,
as before, halted and slept. The third morning, at day-
break, they resumed their march, and kept on until they
came within sight of Rangi-kapiti, when they again halted
until it was dark. In the night they went stealthily forward,
and surrounded the big house of that place, whose people
kept a watch by night, but kept it badly. On arrival there
they found that the *tohunga* had invoked the *atua*, who was
with the people in the house; and the *tohunga*, whose name
was Hapopo, was encouraging his people by questioning
the *atua* as to the expected war-party; and they on the
outside overheard the conversation going on between them.
Said Hapopo, the *tohunga*, to the *atua*, "Speak; tell me; is
the war-party at hand? For we are here dwelling in great
fear, not daring to sleep soundly at night." The *atua*,

whose name was Te Kanawa, replied to him, " No, there is no war-party near ; nothing of the kind ; let us dwell quietly together, even as the ancient ones dwell, away in the skies afar." Those were the words spoken by the *atua* through the medium, whose name was Kahurangi. Hapopo, however, again asked him, " Tell me, sir, is not the war-party at hand ? " " Not a single bit of a war-party, respected sir ; no fighting whatever, great sir, will come hither against you ; rest quietly."

All this conversation between the *tohunga* and the *atua* was heard by those outside, listening in the dark ; and at break of day they assaulted the great house, rushing upon it from all sides. Great was the slaughter of the people of Tawheta. He, however, escaped from the house ; they pursued him, but he got clear off ; whence arose this proverbial saying, " Through flight only was Tawheta saved." The *tohunga*, Hapopo, they dragged outside, and killed him there ; his last words were, " Lying and deceiving *atua*, thou gettest clear off, leaving the trouble with Hapopo." These words have since been handed down as a proverb. There was only one prisoner kept from that great slaughter, the daughter of Tawheta, whose name was then changed from Pou-matangatanga to Pai-mahutanga.[1] The victors feasted on the slain, carrying away with them portions of the bodies to their own *pa*. Thus was avenged the death of the sons and the young people of Uenuku, slaughtered by Tawheta. On the return of the war-party they delivered Pai-mahutanga to Uenuku, and he made her his wife.

The desire of Uenuku for vengeance was not yet satisfied, and he commanded another expedition to be got ready, that he might himself go and fight with Tawheta. The warriors therefore made themselves ready, and the war-canoes were dragged to the beach and fitted up. Uenuku ordered that extra large stones should be taken as anchors, and extra long ropes attached. He took with him two celebrated

---

[1] There is here some confusion of names. One legend says that Rata married Kani-o-wai, their son being Pou-matangatanga. He married Rangi-ahua, and it was their daughter, Pai-hu-tanga, who became the wife of Uenuku.

garments of his ancestor Tu-matauenga, named Te Rangi-tuitui and Te Rangi-kahu-papa.

They set out, and paddled away until they came to Matiko-tai and Po-rangahau, where was the fortified *pa* of Tawheta. The canoes anchored, at the command of Uenuku, just outside the swell of the waves, the stones being dropped and the long ropes paid out as the canoes were paddled toward the shore. Then it was that Tawheta and his people, who were gathered there in great numbers, rushed down to meet the party of Uenuku, even wading out into the sea to fight them and oppose their landing. Putua-ki-te-rangi, one of the warriors of Tawheta, was seized by the party under Uenuku, dragged into the canoe, and carried off, Uenuku giving the order to draw all the canoes outside by their long ropes. There, according to custom, they killed their first prisoner, tore out his heart, and made a sacred fire by friction. When it was blazing well they roasted the heart on the fire, and when it was fully cooked they covered over both the heart and the sacred fire with the two garments.

Then it was that Uenuku, standing up in his canoe, called on the mists from the summits of the mountain Tiri-kawa, saying, " Attend! fall down and encompass; fall down and cover up! " And the day became suddenly dark, and stars were seen in the sky. Uenuku and his people listened, and they heard sounds of warfare; Tawheta and his people were fighting among themselves in the darkness; groans and objurgations were heard, and the dull-sounding blows of clubs crushing skulls. They imagined that the war-party of Uenuku was opposing them; but Uenuku and his men sat listening in their canoes. After a time Uenuku called to the mists, " Clear up! clear up! " and it became bright day. The war-party looked from the canoes, and saw that many of the people of Tawheta were still alive. On this Uenuku again commanded the mists on Tiri-kawa, saying, " Fall down, cover up! "; when, as before, it was again dark as night, and the people of Tawheta began afresh to slay one another, with greater fury than before. By and by Uenuku again called on the mists, "Break up! clear up!" and immediately it was again clear daylight. Then Uenuku, thinking that they had by now destroyed one another, pulled off the garments from the roasted heart and the sacred fire, and lo! on looking at the sea they saw that it was covered with floating corpses, and red with the blood of the slain—deeply red with blood all around them. Three times did Uenuku call on his *atua* before his foes were destroyed. Then Uenuku and his party paddled to the shore, and killed the few who survived. Tawheta was still living, and with these remaining men rallied, and came on, and renewed the fight, which was desperately taken up by Uenuku and his party, by whom Tawheta himself was also killed.

The battle was called "the Day of Two Sunsets"; but on account of the great amount of blood in the sea it was also called "the Sea of Loathsome Water"; and the name given to the last battle, when Tawheta was slain, was "the Rising Tide."

These were the battles of Uenuku, these his desolations; and the murders of his children were fully avenged.

There are other accounts of these doings; and in one of these it is said that when Uenuku called on the mists to settle a second time he sent his dogs ashore to attack the enemy, after some time causing the mists to lift again so that those in the canoes might witness the battle between the dogs and the people of Tawheta—here called Whena. This battle was known as Te Maua-a-te-kararehe, at the Ra-torua (double sunset).

Many years afterward Uenuku caused a large canoe to be built. It was called *Te Huri-purei-ata*, and the name of its skilled builder was Haeora. When finished it was painted red and fully ornamented with pigeons' feathers and other adornments. When after a long time the canoe was fully ready to sail the seas, Uenuku ordered his sons, and the sons of other chiefs, to assemble in order that the hair of their heads might be combed and anointed and neatly fixed in a knot on the crown, and ornamented with a high dress-comb stuck in behind in the manner of chiefs, so that all might look well when they went together to paddle the new canoe to sea. Uenuku himself performed the sacred task of preparing, and dressing, and tying up their hair. The young men were seventy in number all told, and Uenuku finished with Kahutia-te-rangi. All were fine, able young men; there was not a boy among them.

Now by his wife Pai-mahutanga, the daughter of Tawheta, Uenuku had a son named Rua-tapu. When all the young chiefs were ready, this Rua-tapu called to his father, " O honoured sir, see, dress and tie up my hair also ! " Uenuku replied to Rua-tapu, " Where then shall a dress-comb be found for thy hair? " " Why not use one of those combs there by thee? " rejoined Rua-tapu. " Wouldst thou ornament thy hair with one of the combs of thy elder brothers? " asked Uenuku; for indeed the combs were *tapu*, and might not be used by a junior. On hearing that, Rua-tapu cried out, " O noble sir, noble sir, I was supposing that I was truly a son of thine; but now I perceive it is not so." Then his father said to him, " O sir, thou art indeed my own, but a son of little consequence; a son of inferior birth," reminding him in these words that his mother had lost her rank, being degraded to the position of slave-wife through capture in war.

At this saying of Uenuku Rua-tapu was overcome with shame; his whole heart was filled with grief and pain; and, loudly lamenting, he went away to the place where the canoe lay, planning in his mind how he might best murder his elder brothers, the favourite sons of Uenuku. He soon hit upon a plan. With a stone chisel he worked away at the bottom of the new canoe until he had cut a hole through, which he plugged up and hid with wooden chips and scrapings so that it should not be seen. Then he went back into the *pa*, but he would eat no food, for his heart was still deeply grieved at the degradation implied in the words his father had used respecting him. Early the next morning Rua-tapu went and aroused and brought together the men of the place to drag the new canoe down to the sea.

They all came, and she was soon afloat. Then those young chiefs, seventy in number, who had already prepared for that duty, entered on board the canoe, Rua-tapu himself taking care that no boys entered with them, some who came to do so being by him sent off again to their homes. He himself entered, and the canoe being fully manned with smart paddlers, and all being ready, away they went. Rua-tapu kept his heel on the place where he had plugged the hole, and when they had paddled a great distance out to sea he removed his heel, and knocked the plug aside, so that in rushed the water. On seeing the water in the bottom of the canoe, " We shall be upset," cried some; " turn her head to the shore." But Rua-tapu, covering the hole again with his heel and bailing vigorously, gave them assurance, the canoe was soon free of water, and they paddled out still farther. " Let us now return," said some one; " for we have come a great distance." " We will soon return," said Rua-tapu; " let us first go out a little farther." So away they paddled, until they were quite out of sight of land, when he again removed his heel, and the water rushed in. " Where is the bailer? " they called out. " Hasten; bail out the water; we are lost! " But Rua-tapu had hidden the bailer; the canoe filled with water, and was upset. Then, as they swam, Rua-tapu made after one and another of his brothers, and by holding them under the water drowned them. Having done so, and seeing Paikea still swimming, he followed hard after him to drown him also; but Paikea repeatedly eluded him. At last Rua-tapu said to Paikea, " Which of us two shall carry the tidings of our disaster to land? " And Paikea replied, " I will, for I am able to do it; I am a flowering of the union of the male element and the female element; I am a son of the sea." And this was his reason for saying he was a son of the sea, and for his escaping drowning: he was descended from certain sea-deities, from Rongo-maitaha-nui, and from Te Petipeti, and from Te Ranga-hua. Then Rua-tapu cried out, " Go thou, then; swim away to land; and note well, if I am lost here, then am I not descended from our father. Go thou on ; and let the crowded assemblies of the summer season ever remember me that I am also there. When in that season the squid and the jellyfish shall have reached the sandy beaches, then look out, I am but a little way behind them, going also toward the shore. Go on, swim away ; proceed thou to the land ; those who should be survivors from this wreck are become as a pile of slain in the day of deadly battle. This is another word of mine to thee : let Kahu-tuanui have the striking up of the song, so that when ye, the ample broad-chested, may be sitting closely together in a row by the side of the fire it shall be sung in parts, in fruitful seasons and in unfruitful, at the times of assembling together, and at the times of living separately ; through this shall I be ever remembered." Then Paikea said, " The tidings of our calamity shall safely be carried by me, for I am verily descended from the sea, from Te Petipeti, from Te Ranga-hua, from Te Aihu-moana." Here Rua-tapu gave his parting words to Paikea, " Go on, swim away to land, to the loved home " ; and so saying he held up his paddle, still retained in his grasp.

So with strong strokes Paikea proceeded, swimming toward the land, reciting as he went a powerful *karakia* to preserve his strength:

" Now shall be shown, now revealed, the vigour of the trembling
    heart!
Now shall be known the force of the anxious heart!
Now shall be seen the strength of the fluttering weak female heart!
The great fish of the sea swims fast through strenuous exertions,
Blowing forth the spray of sea-water from its nostrils;
The great fish is lifted above the waters.
Space makes it buoyant; Sky upheaves it above the swell of ocean.
Now, rushing forward, a steep descent;
Anon, as if climbing the fence of a fort!
Now a roughening squall of wind comes on;
Anon, as a bird's feather borne before it.
Ha, ha! as my heart is thy heart.
Now the great enduring, courageous heart of the heaven-descended
Shall set itself to emerge through all dangers
To the habitable, to the dwellings of light.

A full deliverance for the son of an *ariki*.
Son above; son abroad;
Son according to the ceremonies duly performed;
Son according to the signs of the breaking away of clouds,
The lightening hitherward from the outermost sides of the far-off
    horizon.
Ha! abroad, far away on the deep,
This is verily the place to exert strength,
To show the straining of sinews.
Here, now, is the skid; I mount on the top of it;
The very skid of Houtaiki;
The skid satisfying the heart; the skid sure and fast.
Ha, ha! the cold wind laughed at; defied;
The wind, icy and cutting to the skin;
The bitter-cold penetrating and numbing vapour;
The faint internal feeling of sickness.
Here is the skid! I mount to the top of it;
Verily, the same skid of Houtaiki, so greatly desired and looked for.
Once, twice, thrice, four times, five times, six times,
Seven times, eight times, nine times, ten times.
Let not the fastening roots of Tane' be unfixed by thee;
Let not the winds hateful and ill-omened to Tane' be set free by
    thee.
Let the swimmings of a man in the ocean finally end;
Let him emerge at the habitable regions, at the lightsome, joyous
    dwellings.
Take up this descendant of *ariki*;
Behold! he lives, he swims bravely.
Lo! he swims on; the man born an *ariki* pursues his course;
He follows on, still swimming away.
Lo! he swims; behold! he swims strongly;
Still swimming onward, enabling, enduring.
An *ariki* follows on, still persistently swimming; lo! he swims.
Behold! he swims away, even Paikea, an *ariki*,
Who goes forward continually, still keeping on swimming.
Lo! he swims; behold! he swims; upborne he swims;
Upborne he continues; he perseveres, swimming onward, toiling
    manfully.
Now above the surface, then below! anon rolling between the billows;
All which ends in the very reaching of the shore by Tane' himself, his
    canoe!
Lo! look out! there it is; coming onward toward me,
A huge rolling wave! strike it down; fell it;
With the famed axe of ancient times, that which overturned the
    land.

UENUKU

Ha, ha! his own mighty *rangatira* [1] appears to aid and succour;
That is, Rongo-maru-a-whatu; therefore it,
The huge and overwhelming wave, fled away, afar off, ha!
The plugging and caulking stand good; the fixing and lashing stand good.
Let it be uplifted and carefully borne;
Let it be raised and supported;
Let it be borne along.
Alas! my distress, causing me to toil laboriously at swimming;
Here, indeed, my distress is now seen.
Make thyself to swim on courageously and well,
As a skilful, knowing one of old:
Truly so! here, indeed, thy courageous swimming is now being shown.
In the midst of the great ocean, here, indeed, it is being seen.
In the midst of the desolate wild, far from man, here, indeed, it is
    shown.
In the ragged first appearings of daylight,
Far off on the horizon, when first seen away there,
Here, such is now being seen.
My bird is verily met above; yes! there it is now returning;
Here indeed it is shown.
Rua-tapu stood upright in the sea grasping his paddle—
His last token! alas! it was evil!
One *rangatira* dies, another succeeds him.
Kahutia-rangi took Te Panipani to wife,
Son of a great *rangatira* was he, highly esteemed at Whangara.
Here am I, still swimming on;
Floating, but alas! going in no certain direction.
The great fish is beaten stiff in the tide of swiftly dashing waves.
Lo! there it comes! the canoe of Paikea is swiftly sailing hither.
O big black-and-white seagull, flying aloft there!
Settle down hither on the sea from the sky.
O Tane', enwrap and involve me
In the garment of carefree insensibility,
That so I may quietly float to the shore.
Lie quietly down, O young *ariki*, upon the sea,
Purposely becalmed for thy safe voyaging.
Let the brave swimming man be safely carried to the shore.
O Hikita! here am I, even as a great fish.
O Hikita! O Hikitaiorea!
I am as a waterlogged canoe of *kahikatea*.[2]
O Hikita! Oh! O Hikitaiorea! Oh!
I am as a whale, basking and rolling in the deep.
O Hikita! Oh! O Hikitaiorea! Oh! O Tu-parara!
Seek me, carry me to the shore.

[1] Chief.   [2] White pine.

O Wehenga-kauki!
Fetch me, carry me to the shore.
Tane'! fetch me, carry me to the shore, to my own land;
To the very shore there; to my father, indeed, on the shore,
Away there—alas! alas! "

Then Paikea warmed, cheered, and consoled himself by
thinking of another of his ancestors, named Matai-ahuru;
and, remembering him, he continued his *karakia*:

" Matai-ahuru! Matai-ahuru!
Through the warm sea, through the warm water-tide,
Let my own skin now become warm;
Let it now become as if I were verily basking
In the heat of the noontide sun, suddenly shining;
Let it now be as if I were by the blaze of the fire brightly kindled,
That it may become hot with a comfortable glow."

And through these last words Paikea caused himself to possess warmth and comfortable feelings, and at last he reached
the shore, at a place called Ahuahu.

This swim of a day and a night is reminiscent of the
swim of Ulysses. The legend does not relate how the story
of the disaster was received; it does not even say that
Paikea reached the home from which he set out; and
in one version the remarkableness of his feat of endurance
is lessened by the fact that he is said to have ridden the
distance on the back of the great fish Rua-mano. The
ancestors mentioned by him in his *karakia*, and in his col-
loquy with Rua-tapu, are creatures of the deep, whales and
jellyfish; and his own name, Paikea, is the name of a species
of whale.

The story illustrates the estimation in which the obtaining of vengeance was held by the Maori; and throughout
Polynesia such stories abound. Nor is Polynesia singular
in this respect; our own civilized histories, religious or
political, can furnish parallels. The vengeance taken by
Rua-tapu was terrible and complete; but it was not undertaken merely to avenge the insult he himself had received
from his father, but also the wrongs of his mother and her
people. He was not afraid to die with the others; he
could no doubt have reached the shore as Paikea did, but

he died holding his paddle, the act of a strong and brave man. His parting allusions to his home and the people, their gatherings, their diversions, his wishing to be with them in spirit, show that his affections were with them ; he too would be remembered with admiration rather than with execration. Vengeance was a duty, even if it entailed death upon the person securing it. In our own heroic poem *Beowulf*, written in the eighth century, at the time when the Polynesians were establishing themselves throughout the Pacific, the same sentiment is expressed :

> Wise man, sorrow. not,
> Better for each to avenge his friend than mourn.

Rua-tapu left a wife, Te Kite-ora, and a son, Hau, from whom some of the tribes of the east coast of the North Island of New Zealand trace their descent.

These feuds of vengeance often led to long and bitter wars, the smouldering fires, fanned to life by some trivial incident or accident, suddenly breaking out though hidden for years and apparently extinguished.

A Broken Betrothal

There had been constant reprisals and counter-reprisals between the Ngai-Tahu and Ngati-Mamoe, two tribes of the South Island of New Zealand, the feud having extended over many years. After a term of peace a chief of the Ngai-Tahu named Manawa attacked a Ngati-Mamoe *pa* at Omihi, though it was partly under the protection of Tuki-auau, a Ngai-Tahu man, and nephew of Te Rangi-whakaputa, friend and companion-in-arms of Manawa. Having approached the *pa* with six companions for the purpose of reconnoitring, Manawa caught sight of the head-ornament of Rakai-momona, father of Tuki-auau, who was sitting outside his house. Judging his position by his headdress, Manawa hurled a spear, which pierced the old man through the heart ; and without being aware of what he had done he returned to rejoin the main body, resolving to attack the *pa* at dawn.

Within the *pa* all was confusion when the death of Rakai-momona was discovered. It was decided to desert the *pa* during the night, but in order to conceal their intentions from the enemy they left fires burning in all the usual places. Manawa, ignorant of all that had happened, cautiously approached at dawn; but seeing no one moving about he sent scouts to the top of a neighbouring overlooking hill, and they soon returned with the intelligence that the place was deserted. Manawa immediately returned to Waipapa and reported to Maru, a chief related to both tribes, what had happened. Maru offered to follow the fugitives and bring them back; his secret reason for doing this being that his Ngati-Mamoe connexions might have an opportunity of avenging the death of Rakai-momona at some future time. He found Tuki-auau at Tutae-putaputa, preserving his father's head. This he intended to keep, according to custom, at one end of his house, where his children could look upon it, surrounded with cloaks, and think the old man still among them. Maru urged Tuki-auau not to go any farther, but to build his *pa* where he was, at Pakihi. This he consented to do, and Maru left him. Not long afterward a circumstance occurred which indicates the existence of such a curious state of things that it is hard to understand how any tribe could survive when subject to such internal disorders, and where its leading members were animated by such different motives.

Rakai-te-kura, daughter of Maru, was in infancy betrothed to Te Rangi-tau-hunga, son of Te Rangi-whakaputa; but, notwithstanding this, she married, with her father's consent, Tuakeka. This so incensed Te Rangi-whakaputa that, on hearing of it, he went directly to the enclosure of Maru, and before his very face killed one of his servants, Tu-manawaru. Such an act could not patiently be borne, and Maru sought the protection of Tuki-auau, with whom he remained till Te Rangi-whakaputa was forced by the Ngai-Tahu, who regretted the absence of a favourite chief, to go and request his return. On his arrival at Pakihi he was presented by Maru with a large *poha*, or kelp-vessel, full of preserved birds, which was called *tohu-raumati*. Te Rangi-whakaputa, while accepting it, refused to allow it to be opened, saying, " It shall be for you, Maru, when you return to us." As soon as Maru did reach Waipapa he proposed that the *poha* should be eaten on the war-path, as they had a death to avenge. Maru could not kill the man who had insulted him, nor any of his people, but he hoped that in fighting the common enemy some of the kin of Te Rangi-whakaputa would be killed, and so *utu* (payment or satisfaction) for his murdered servant and injured honour would be obtained.

The Ngai-Tahu, ever eager for war, responded to his invitation, and followed him to the attack of the *pa* Kura-te-au. It was taken, and among the prisoners was Hine-maka, a woman of rank, who was brought to Maru in order that he might put her to death; but instead of doing so he gave her in marriage to his son, and when asked the reason for his strange act his reply was, " When my descendants, the offspring of this marriage, are taunted with being slaves on the mother's side, the particulars will be inquired into, and it will be found that the mother was taken prisoner when the death of my father was being avenged, so that the memory of my father's death having been avenged will be better preserved by sparing this woman than by killing her."

During the peace which followed the fall of Kura-te-au the most friendly intercourse existed between the various communities; and to such an extent did this prevail that the slumbering fires seemed to be extinguished, and Manawa even ventured to visit Tuki-auau, whose father he had killed a few years before. The object of the visit was to see the far-famed beauty Te Ahua-rangi, daughter of Tu-whakapau, with a view to making a proposal of marriage on behalf of Te Rua-hikihiki, son of Manawa. While such a marriage would probably obliterate all differences between the two tribes, at least for a time, Manawa did not conceal from his own people that he hoped, by means of the marriage, to secure the Ngati-Mamoe, to whom the beauty

belonged, as serfs for his son. The idea pleased the fancy
of his followers; and they, while employed in fastening on
the top-boards of his canoe preparatory to his departure,
could not refrain from joking about the people who were
so soon to become, as it were, vassals to their chief. But
that which is whispered in the *whare* is presently spoken in
the *marae* (village common).

The visit passed off pleasantly, and Manawa was returning home ; the people were flocking to the beach-side of the
pa to speed him on his way, when Te Rangi-whakaputa,
hearing some one sobbing behind him, turned and saw
that it was Tuki-auau. " Are you a woman that you
lament? " said he. " No," was the answer; " I am only
grieving at my brother's departure." " Beware ! " said
Te Rangi-whakaputa. " Do not use green flax, but prepared fibre. Do not take the foremost nor the hindmost,
but the one in the middle, the star of the year himself. Do
not divulge this hint of mine." The treacherous suggestion so enigmatically conveyed to Tuki-auau by the friend
of Manawa was not forgotten.

Having waited an appropriate length of time, Manawa
returned to Pakihi to obtain the formal consent of Tu-
whakapau to his daughter's marriage with his son. Accompanied by a hundred followers, he approached the *pa*, and
was welcomed with the customary greetings in the waving of
garments, and beckoning, and cries of " *Haere mai ! Haere
mai !* " Among the party were the brother of Maru and
several other relations of his. These were led by Hine-
umu-tahi to her house, while the rest were shown into a
large house set aside for their reception. Manawa was
the last to enter the *pa* ; and as he bent his head in passing
through the low gateway Tuki-auau, who was standing just
inside it, struck him a violent blow with a stone axe.
Manawa staggered forward, but before he reached his companions he received a still more violent blow. Immediately
he was within the house the door was closed ; and the old
chief, after wiping the blood from his face, addressed his
men. He told them that their situation was hopeless.

MAORI FOOD-STORE
Photo Iles, Thames, N.Z.

CARVED FRONT OF MAORI FOOD-STORE
Photo Dominion Museum, Wellington, N.Z.

(See page 94)

THE SON OF TAHU MAKES HIS ESCAPE
(See page 112)

Caught in a trap, surrounded by overpowering numbers, they must prepare to die. All he desired was that an attempt should be made to convey to the Ngai-Tahu the tidings of their fate.

Many at once volunteered for the dangerous service. One having been chosen from the number, Manawa, after having smeared his forehead with the blood from his own wound, charged him to be brave, and, committing him to the care of his *atua*, sent him forth. Hundreds of spears were ready, and the messenger fell transfixed before he had advanced more than a few paces. Again and again the attempt was repeated, but in vain. The imprisoned band grew dispirited, and volunteers did not come forward so readily. At length a youth, closely related to Manawa, offered to make a last attempt. The old man was loth to consent; he loved the youth; but he persisted. The moment seemed propitious, for the enemy, certain of the fate of the prisoners, were less vigilant. Smeared with the blood of the dying chief, and charged with his last message to his family and tribe, Tahua sprang forth. Some spears he warded off, some he eluded; he evaded his foes among the houses and enclosures. He reached the outer fence, over which he climbed safely, and turned to rush down the hill. But the only path bristled with spears; his enemies pressed upon him. One only chance for life remained. The *pa* stood on the edge of a cliff; by leaping down upon the beach below he might escape. He made the attempt; and a shout of triumph arose from his foes when they saw his body extended upon the sands; but shouts of triumph turned to cries of rage when he sprang up, and defied them to track the swift feet of the son of Tahu. He fled along the coast, and passed successfully on to Waipapa.

The Ngati-Mamoe now proceeded to kill and eat the remaining victims; and while these abhorred the degradation, they did not fear death, knowing that vengeance was sure. In death itself there was no dishonour, and every warrior would choose death rather than be spared as a slave—" a remnant of the feast."

MYTHS OF THE POLYNESIANS

Maori Contempt for Death

The deliberate choosing of death has been known to take place on many occasions. In one instance a *pa* had been invested, but the besiegers were beaten off, and retreated. During the repulse a leading chief had been wounded so that his movements were hampered, and he threatened to become a danger to his friends. He therefore bade them leave him while they hurried on, returning for him when danger was past. Loth to leave him, unseen by the pursuers they deviated from the line of flight, hid him in a thicket, and passed on.

It happened that among the pursuers was one who, instead of following the direct line of flight, beat about, as odd men will, on this side and on that, not anticipating anything, yet never without expectation. He thought he perceived a slight movement in leaves that should be still; he watched, they were motionless; but now he thought he heard a suppressed groan. Cautiously he approached, and discovered the wounded chief. The elated scout awaited the return of his companions, who were unsuccessful, having slain no one, captured no one. They knew their prisoner to be a chief of note, and his capture was sufficient reward. Then the prisoner inquired, " Is so-and-so slain ? " " No." " Or so-and-so ? " " No." " Or so-and-so ? " naming leading chiefs of the retreating party. " No." " Who then has fallen ? " They could name no name. " Ah," said the prisoner with a smile, " it will then be necessary for you to kill me so that your victory may have a name." They acknowledged the strength of his argument, and reluctantly they slew him; they would have preferred to keep him alive, a slave in degradation; but they had killed no man of note, and their victory would have been a barren victory, a victory without a name.

CHAPTER V : FAIRIES AND TANIWHA

THE parti-coloured, misty Bifroest of tradition is a never-closed pathway to the glimmering, unforgotten events of the past, with its glooms of the forgotten. There are still those who believe we have beings about us of too tenuous a nature to be seen by the physical eye, but not too intangible to be apprehended. In the childhood of man, as in the childhood of the race, the division between the visible and the invisible, the world of reality and the world of the imagination, is not sharply marked ; it is a broad, undefined, undefinable region, the scene of marvels, of wonders, the stage of dreams, the playground of the imagination. Little wonder if, in the dim past, the figures moving like shadows in mists were sometimes in a world of reality, sometimes in a world of the imagination ; sometimes in a world which may be either, or both ; we cannot tell.

Tura and the Fairies (New Zealand)

When Tura ventured forth with Whiro he ventured into such a doubtful world. There are two well-known personages of the name Whiro ; one a human being of comparatively recent times, one a deity. The incidents concerning the two were for a long time seemingly inextricably confused, but they have now been more or less disentangled. The deity Whiro is the personification of darkness and death ; he was the great rival and adversary of Tane', the personification of light and life. The other Whiro was a voyager and adventurer ; and because of certain proclivities he on his death was made the patron of thieves. Guilty of a murder, and wishing to escape its consequences when it was discovered, he invited Tura to accompany him on a voyage.

Tura was a wanderer ; and when Whiro proposed a voyage to the distant Wawau, an early home of the Polynesians, Tura gladly accompanied him. They sailed away, and the sea was full of wonders ; and as a hand may some-

115

times be seen thrust from the ground or from the water with extended fingers, so in mid-ocean a canoe suddenly appeared; coming, as it were, without motion, and arriving without first approaching. In it sat Tu-tata-hau, and he hailed the canoe of Whiro, crying, " Canoe, canoe of whom?" " Canoe of gods," answered one of the crew. Him Tu-tata-hau seized and slew, and again called out, " Canoe, canoe of whom?" " Canoe of gods," answered another of the crew. Him also Tu-tata-hau seized and slew; and, calling a third time, he was answered by Whiro, " Canoe of Whiro; canoe of the ancients who tear and rend"; which answer caused Tu-tata-hau to disappear as he had come, and he was no more seen.

They approached O-tea, where they sailed so swiftly that Tura grew suspicious; he felt certain they were rushing on destruction. When, therefore, the canoe passed close inshore he slipped over the side unobserved, swam in under the overhanging trees, and drew himself ashore as the canoe sped on into the distance.

He travelled inland until sundown, but saw no sign of living being. On the morrow he went on, and not until the sun was again declining did he see any habitation. He then came to the abode of the blind old woman Ruahine-mata-morari, and he would have taken her as wife; but the woman said, " I am the guardian only; there are other females of this people, one of whom you can take as your wife." The blind old woman occurs repeatedly, under many names, throughout Polynesia.

Tura looked this way and that beneath the trees, but he could see no village, nor any other dwelling than the one where Ruahine' sat. Casting his eyes upward, in the leaves of the *kiekie* and *wharawhara* he saw moving forms; and then he perceived that the people of whom the old woman spoke were none other than the Nuku-mai-tore, little folk, unlike human beings, whose home was in the trees with the birds. Tura took one of these, who was a daughter of the old woman, and whose name was Turaki-hau, and dwelt with her, making his home with this little and kindly

116

people. Because of his wandering disposition Tura was known to them as Wairangi.

They offered him food, but it was uncooked ; and by this sign he knew that they were not mortals—they were *atua*, spirits. He had brought with him his fire-sticks, and he kindled fire ; but on the smoke arising, and its pungent smell being perceived by them, the little creatures fled into the forest. Turaki-hau also turned to flee, but Tura detained her, bidding her sit near him while he prepared the oven and cooked the food in the steam from the heated stones. When the steam arose through the coverings and earth heaped over them the food was cooked ; and, the coverings being jerked aside, a savoury smell arose, and was wafted to the nostrils of the affrighted Nuku-mai-tore. One by one they timidly returned, encouraged by the assurances of Turaki-hau ; and having tasted the food, they found it good and sweet.

Wairangi lived quietly and happily with his wife, and the time came when a child should be born. The people knew it, and Turaki-hau grew sorrowful. Wairangi was perplexed that his wife should look to the time of joy as to a time of sorrow, nor could he understand her sighs until on a day her female friends and relations approached her, each with a sharp flake in her hand, and some of them bearing clothing.

" Why do these women come to disturb thee ? " said he.

" They come to give birth to thy child."

" To thine and mine," said Wairangi.

"Not so," she answered; "thine only; for I shall die"; and she drew closer in to his side.

" Why should you die ? " he asked her kindly.

" They will cut the child from my side," said she, her cheeks wet with tears.

" Is it so ? " said Wairangi. " Is that their practice ? "

" Yes," answered Turaki-hau, trembling in her fear.

Wairangi said no more ; but when the women came near wrathfully he forbade them to touch his wife, or to approach her. They obeyed him, afraid of his anger, and wondering. He built a house, and in it fixed two posts for her support in her short time of anguish. One he called Pou-tama-wahine, the Post of the Daughter, and the other Pou-tama-tane, the Post of the Son. "These will assist you," said he, "so that you will not be overcome; but should not the child be born speedily, you must say, ' One to Ao-nui ; one to Ao-roa ; one to Ao-tauira ' ; and should the child still be unborn, then you must add, ' One to Tura.'" It was thus that she first learned the name of him they called Wairangi.

She observed his instructions ; Tura too chanted his *karakia*, and the child was born in the natural way. Tura performed all the ceremonies usual with his own people, and the child they called Tauira-ahua.

When the child was of such an age that he was able to run about alone, Tura one day said to his wife, " Comb my hair."

She did so ; but while combing she murmured words of surprise, saying at last to Tura, " Why, among the black hairs, are there some that are white ? "

" They are the ' weeds of Tura,' the grey hairs of age," said he ; " the signs of decay."

" The decay of what ? " said she.

" The decay of the body," answered Tura ; " there is coming and going ; there is youth and age ; they are the signs of death."

" Are they the signs of very death ? "

" Yes."

" O Tura, is man then subject to two deaths ? "

" Yes," he answered ; and he became downcast, and wept over their little child, over Tauira-ahua, while Turaki-hau wept for him. " *Aue!* " said she. " Alas that we must part ! For in this land there is no decay." And Tura saw that among the gentle fairies there were none afflicted with the infirmities of age, and he knew that he must pass hence with his mortal body.

After two days he spoke to the boy, saying, " Farewell ; live peaceably, and do not practise evil."

Sorrowing, Tura left his wife and child, and the Nuku-mai-tore, and after three days he came to the seashore, where he found a whale stranded. He cut up the huge fish, dried the flesh, and stored it in two storehouses ; one raised up high for present use, the other low for the time of old age. He built a house called Hau-turu-nuku, and in this he lived until he became so aged and feeble that he was unable to move out for any necessity.

Though he became decrepit in body, his mind remained clear ; and as old folk are wont, he thought continually of his younger days. Now a great longing possessed him ; a longing for his wife in the land he had left, a longing for Rau-kura-matua, and for his son by that wife ; so that in the dusk he sat calling the name of his son softly to himself : " O Ira-tu-roto ! O Ira-tu-roto ! " And again in his sleep he murmured, " O Ira-tu-roto ! O Ira-tu-roto ! "

Now his son in the old land one night had a dream ; and in the morning he arose, and said to the people, " I have dreamed a dream in which I heard my father calling, ' Ira-tu-roto ! Ira-tu-roto ! ' "

Again at dusk the thoughts of Tura wandered back, and again, feeling a longing, he called to his son, continuing as before to murmur the name in his sleep. His son dreamed the same dream, and, waking, he related it to the people ; and he said to his mother, " Give me oil that I may anoint my body." He anointed himself, and the next day he set out in search of his father. The longing of the father guided the steps of the son ; for, journeying over strange seas, he came to a strange land, to O-tea, where he found his father, feeble and destitute. He washed the old man, and carrying him to his canoe he took him again to his old home, where he was received with rejoicing.

Since that time of Tura people have had the affliction of grey hairs, and suffer the infirmities of age ; as the proverb says, " The weeds of Tura are near thee."

Ati and Tapairu

Parts of the Tura story appear in Rarotonga, but the names differ. In the village of Ao-rangi, a name famous

in New Zealand as the name of its loftiest snow-peak, Mt
Cook, and of many a lowlier eminence, was the small fountain Vai-tipi.   On the night after full moon a woman and a
man, white of complexion, rose up out of the crystal water.
When the inhabitants of this world were supposed to be
asleep they came up from the world of shades to steal *taro*,
plantains, bananas, and coconuts, taking all these good
things back to eat uncooked in the netherworld.

Little did the two fairies think that they had been seen
by mortals, and that a plan to catch them was being devised.
A large scoop-net of strong sennit was made for this purpose,
and constant watch set at the fountain by night.   On the
first appearance of the new moon up they came again, and,
as before, went off to pillage the plantations.   The net was
now carefully spread out at the bottom of the fountain, and
then they gave chase to those fair beings from the spirit
world.   The fairy girl was the first to reach the fountain.
Down she dived, and was at once caught in the net, and
carried off in triumph. But in replacing the net after the
struggle a small space remained uncovered ; and through
this tiny space the male fairy contrived to escape.

The lovely captive became the cherished wife of the chief
Ati, who now carefully filled up the fountain with great
stones, lest his fairy wife should escape to the netherworld.

They lived happily together.   She was known all over
Rarotonga as Tapairu—the Peerless One of Ati.   She
became reconciled to the ways of mortals, and grew content
with her new life in the world of light.   In the course of
time a child was to be born ; and when the period of birth
arrived she bade her husband cut the child from her side.
" Then bury my dead body," said she, " but cherish tenderly
our child."   Ati refused to do as she wished, allowing
nature to take its course, so that the fairy became the living
mother of a boy.

When at length the boy grew up and became strong, the
mother one day wept bitterly in the presence of her husband.
She told him her tears were caused by her grief at the
destruction of all mothers in the shades upon the birth of

their first-born. Would he consent to accompany her in a return thither, in order that so cruel a custom might be ended? This was agreed to by Ati, and accordingly the great stones were dragged up from the fountain. All kinds of vegetable gums were collected, and the fairy carefully besmeared the body of Ati, so as to facilitate his descent to the world of the fairies.

Holding her human husband by the hand, both dived to the bottom of the fountain, and nearly reached the entrance to the invisible world. But Ati was so exhausted that she returned with him. Five times was the attempt repeated, but in vain! The fairy wept because her husband was not permitted to accompany her; for only the spirits of the dead and immortals may enter.

Sorrowfully embracing each other, they stood at the fountain. "I will go alone, to teach what I have learnt from you," said the Peerless One. At this she again dived down into the clear waters, and was never again seen on earth. Ati went sorrowfully back to his habitation, and thenceforth their boy was called Ati-ve'e—Ati the Forsaken—in memory of his lost fairy mother. He was fairer than mortals, like his mother from Spirit Land, but his descendants are dark, like his mortal father.

It is to this lovely fairy woman that the old song of the Ati tribe alludes:

> She has descended again to Spirit World!
> Men praised the divine being first seen by
> Ati at the fountain.
> But his heart is now filled with grief.

The reversal in the story is noteworthy; in the Maori story the mortal leaves the fairies; in the Rarotongan the fairy leaves the mortal. How powerfully, too, the Rarotongan story recalls the tragic ballad of Agnes and the Merman!

The name of the beautiful fairy wife of Ati, Tapairu, was derived from the name of the daughters of the dreaded Miru, goddess of the netherworld. She, deformed and repulsive, like Hel of the Norse myths, had, like Hel, her home in the netherworld, where she cooked human spirits for her food. Her son Tau-titi presides over the dance called by his name. Besides Tau-titi, the pitiless devourer of spirits had four daughters, called Tapairu, or Peerless Ones, on account of their matchless beauty. They delighted to make their appearance in the upperworld whenever a dance was performed in honour of their brother. These dances were always held by moonlight; and if a dance took place anywhere on the northern half of Rarotonga they would be sure to appear that evening at sunset, bathing at a little shady stream named Au-paru (Soft Dew). These fairies would then climb the almost perpendicular hill overlooking the fountain in order to dry themselves, and to arrange their beautiful tresses in the moonbeams, ere proceeding to witness the performances of mortals. But if the dance were to take place on the southern part of the island these Peerless Ones would appear at two little streams, named Vai-pau and Vai-kaute, and there perform their usual toilet on the crest of the neighbouring hill.

These fairies, always associated with the worship of Tane', would even take part in the dance, provided that one end of the dancing-ground were well covered with freshly cut banana-leaves; and after they had merrily danced over these fragile leaves through the night not a single one would be in the least soiled or bruised. As soon as the morning star throbbed in the east they disappeared, returning to their gloomy home in Avaiki.

The names of these four were Kumu-tonga-i-te-po (Kumu-tonga of the Night), Karaia-i-te-ata (Karaia of the Morn), Te Rau-ara (Pandanus-leaf), and Te Poro (the Point). Throughout the Eastern Pacific Tapairu is a favourite name for girls. In Hawaii, as here in Rarotonga, the test of a fairy is her ability to dance upon fresh leaves and leave no bruise.

In every valley of Rarotonga are crevices in the soil, through which superfluous waters drain, and the fairies of the netherworld avail themselves of these narrow passages from time to time to climb up in order to be present at the dances of mortals.

The festival of Te Rangai, an ancestor of the tribe of Tane, was specially honoured by fairy visitors. This festival was held at Butoa. Te Poro and Te Rau-ara, daughters of Miru, came from the netherworld, and the sound of the great drum, penetrating to the very depths of Spirit Land, induced four other fairies to climb up and witness their favourite dance, *tautiti*. These fairies, also connected with Miru, were males. Oro-iti and Te Au-o-tanga-roa came up at a gorge known as Tua-o-ruku, in the south. Maranga-i-ta'ao ascended through a disagreeable-looking hole in the west, Maranga-i-taiti through a gorge at the north of the island. Guided by the sound of the drum, these four male fairy visitors tripped along different mountain ridges until they all met at the festal-ground, conspicuous by their unearthly beauty. At dawn they disappeared into the depths of Avaiki in the same manner as they had come.

The prologue of the festal-songs of Potiki alludes to this myth. After years of anarchy and bloodshed peace was proclaimed in the name of the gods. At this, the first festival inaugurating the era of peace, it is hoped that the fairies will be present as at the festival of Te Rangai. The greater gods, whose jealousies cause the wars of mortals, should be chained.

PROLOGUE TO THE DRAMATIC FESTIVAL OF POTIKI,
ON HIS ASSUMPTION OF THE TEMPORAL
SOVEREIGNTY, *circa* 1790

SOLO. Open the entrance to Spirit Land,
That Oro-iti and Tane' may come up.
CHORUS. On this merry night
The ghosts are dancing on the smooth sward;
As at the famed festival of Te Rangai of old.
SOLO. Tane' is the patron of dancing.
Karēia ! [*War-dance.*
Down with your burdens,
Down with them and rest.

MYTHS OF THE POLYNESIANS

CHORUS. Spirit Land is stirred to its very depths
At the music of the great drum.
The fairies Te Poro and Te Rau-ara have come up.
Lead off the dance, ye of the left;
And you too, of the right.
At Tua-o-ruku is a fairy dancing-ground
For Oro-iti and Te Au-o-tanga-roa,
Who have dared to come up to this world.

SOLO. Great Rongo shakes his club.

CHORUS. Softly sounds the cloth-beating mallet o'er the sea.
Beat away! Beat away!

SOLO. Whither go ye, fairies?

CHORUS. We go in search of the pleasing dance, so long disused.
Here it is!
Here are the dancers, the torch-bearers,
And the spectators.

SOLO. Whither go ye, fairies?

CHORUS. We follow the merry sounds of dancing;
Therefore have we come.
Here it is!
Here are the torch-bearers, and the spectators.
Chain up the gods, the offspring of Vatea,
That our sport be not spoiled.
Avaunt! Avaunt!
Ha! I hear shouts of dances at Butoa!
Eia iā! Eia iā!
Iā! Iā!   [*War-dance, twice performed.*

SOLO. Open up for Maranga-i-ta'ao an entrance from Avaiki.

CHORUS. Search us out; join our throng!

SOLO. Open up for Maranga-i-taiti the dark gorge.

CHORUS. Search us out; join our throng!
To what distant spot are these fairies bound?
Beat away! Beat away!
Give us a many-stranded, powerful rope,
Waving to and fro in the wind,
Waving to and fro in the wind,
To pull up Tau-titi and his drum out of Avaiki-nui.
Here is the fairy Maranga-i-ta'ao in search of us.
Beat away! Beat away!
Let the fairies pass in front of the drum;
The fairies who once honoured the festal of Te Rangai.
How dazzling! How brave!

SOLO. Now for a war-dance as we beat on this drum.
Karēia!   [*War-dance.*
Let all take a part; toss it aloft.

FAIRIES AND TANIWHA

CHORUS. Those over yonder; those near at hand;
Prepare to lead off our fairy dance.
SOLO. The dance-loving tribe assembled of yore
On the lands of Te Rangai.
CHORUS. Up with the great drum; toss it in the air.
SOLO. The illustrious Mautara fought
And conquered this island for us, his children.
CHORUS. Up with the great drum; toss it in the air,
And close up the mouth of Avaiki.
SOLO. Come forth, ye players of melodious flutes,
CHORUS. In honour of this dance of the gods.
Iā!   [Shouts.
[Call for the dance to lead off.
The kava of Miru grows in Avaiki.
SOLO.   Go on!
CHORUS. The finest and most pleasing drink.
SOLO.   Ay! E!
CHORUS. Tane', god with the yellow teeth, was once expelled Tahiti,
Yellow with devouring mankind.
SOLO. Let the red kava carefully be plucked,
As a draught for dancers in the upperworld.
Let the drink be prepared for the priests.
CHORUS. The sacred bowl of the priests is ready,
To be quaffed by yon sacred men.
SOLO. Is there not yet another sort?
CHORUS. 'Tis too sacred for mortal use.
SOLO. Two shoots only may we strip; the parent stem
Belongs to Miru only, is reserved for the destruction of
souls.

These fairies were all of one family, the fairies of the netherworld. Ngaru the explorer climbed the heavens, and there discovered another family of Tapairu—all fair women. Of these the most celebrated are 'Ina, wife of the moon, and Little Matonga. They are known as fairies of the sky. Like those of the netherworld, the heavenly fairies have great skill and dexterity in ball-throwing, 'Ina being able to keep eight balls in motion at one time. Ngaru learnt the art from the nether-fairies during his long residence in their home. So proficient did he become that he beat them and the sky-fairies at their own accomplishment, which he afterward introduced to this world.

The Maori fairies also were fair-skinned, and had light

125

or reddish hair, and it has been suggested that they are the
memory of a fair people met by the Polynesians during their
migrations, or that they were an earlier race dispossessed
by them when settling on the various islands. But the
belief in fairies is universal. Some still think that they
exist, though unseen by ourselves, and that they may even
be photographed; others think them no more than the
natural efflorescence of the human imagination. The
general name for these little beings among the Maori was
Patu-pai-arehe, or Turehu. They are called Nuku-mai-tore
in the legend of Tura.

Punga-rehu and the Man-eating Bird (New Zealand)

These same fairies were seen by another man, Punga-
rehu, and his companion, Kokomuka-hau-nei. They had
been out in their canoe fishing, when a storm drove them
to a strange land. They sought wood for making fire by
friction, but found none suitable. They therefore took
each a piece of wood from their hooks and put it under
their armpits to dry it, meanwhile exploring the country.
They came on footprints, one of them being that of a club-
footed person who walked with the aid of a stick. Following
the footprints, they came within hearing of the sound of
axes in the forest. They went in the direction of the sound,
and saw men at work on some timber. They observed that
every time one of the men made a chip fly he followed it
with his eyes. " O man," said Punga-rehu to his companion, " the eyes of these people are watchful ! " " It
indicates no harm," answered his friend, " as they have not
yet seen us." They went cautiously, and before the people
had observed them Punga-rehu caught one of them and
held him.

They all sat down on the ground, and one of them asked
Punga-rehu and his companion, " Where have you two
come from ? "

They answered, " We came from the interior; the wind
has carried us here."

" But where do you come from? " he persisted.

"We two came from Hawaiki, from Tawhiti-nui-a-rua. Where is your home?"

"Our homes are yonder," said the men; "come and see them."

They all went together. When they had gone some distance the men said to Punga-rehu and his companion, "If any of our half-witted people come to meet us, and dance for us, and you laugh at them, they will kill you."

When they reached the settlement they saw the people of the Nuku-mai-tore sitting in the *kiekie*. They went into a house, and food was set before them. It consisted of the raw flesh of a whale; and while the people ate of it, Punga-rehu and his companion would not do so. Again in the evening the same food was put before them. There was no fire at this place.

In the evening those came who were to amuse the strangers. They had in their hands weapons made with sharp pieces of flint or sharks' teeth lashed along the edges of pieces of wood, and while they danced they sang:

> "Now you laugh, and now you don't;
> Now you laugh, and now you don't."

Had Punga-rehu and his companion laughed, they would have been cut up with the flint knives of the dancers; but they sat in silence, and the dancers left the house.

On the evening of the following day Punga-rehu said, "Close the door of the house." When that was done, he and Kokomuka' took from their armpits the wood they had been drying, and by friction kindled a fire. When the fumes of the smoke got into the nostrils of the people they exclaimed:

> "Whispering ghosts of the west,
> Who brought you here to our land?
> Arise, arise and depart.
> Whispering ghosts of the west,
> Who brought you here to our land?
> Arise, arise and depart."

Punga-rehu and his companion now made an oven, and when it was heated they put into it some of the flesh of the

127

whale, covered it up, and sat down until it was cooked. As soon as the oven was opened the people were attracted by the savoury smell, and came round Punga-rehu and his companion, saying, " What a sweet smell ! " The flesh was taken out of the oven and conveyed to the house, and then for the first time these people tasted cooked food.

On the following day they heated another oven and cooked some more flesh, and, having partaken of it, said to each other, " Cooked food is sweet. We used to eat it raw." Punga-rehu said, " It is sweet. You are not men, but *atua* ; you eat raw food."

Then they said to Punga-rehu, " There is one thing which is an evil to us ; it is a *pou-kai*—a bird which eats man." Punga-rehu said, " Where do you go, that it is able to eat you? " They answered him, " If we go to fetch water we are caught by it." He asked, " Can you see it coming? " They answered, " Yes."

They built a house having a window as the only opening, and Punga-rehu and his companion sat at this window. They saw the bird flying toward them with its head down, in the act of procuring its prey. Its beak came near to one of them ; but he struck at the bird with his stone axe and broke one of its wings, and with another blow he broke the other wing ; and, having disabled it, they killed it. They went to see what was in the cave where the bird lived, and found the bones of men strewn all around.

After they had returned from this expedition Punga-rehu and his companion began to long for their wives and children, from whom they had been parted when blown out to sea ; so they went back to their canoe, launched it, and paddled away until they arrived at their home. They went up to the settlement, but found that their houses had been deserted, and smelt disagreeable. One said to the other, " Our house has been deserted, and perhaps all the indwellers are dead." They found another house, however, where the people were all fast asleep round a fire.

THE FAREWELL OF THE FAIRY
(See page 118)

THE GIANT BIRD OF FIJI
(See page 130)

They went in, and these Polynesian Enoch Ardens found that their wives had taken other husbands, and were lying asleep beside them.

One of the wives in her dream murmured this song:

> " Just as eventide draws near,
> My old affection comes
> For him I loved.
> Though severed far from me,
> And now at Hawaiki,
> I hear his voice, far distant;
> And though far beyond
> The distant mountain-peak,
> Its echoes speak
> From vale to vale."

When the morning dawned, and the men and their wives arose, there lay Punga-rehu and the other near the fire in the centre of the house. The one woman said to the other, " Why, there are our first husbands, whom we thought dead ! " There was great rejoicing, and each woman thereafter lived with the husband of her youth.

Te Hau-o-tawera and the Bird *poua-kai* (New Zealand)

While the Waitaha tribe of the South Island of New Zealand has long been extinct, one of their legends relating to a man-eating bird survives. This *poua-kai* had its nest on the spur of a mountain called Tawera,[1] from whence it darted down, seizing and carrying off men, women, and children as food for itself and its young. While its wings made a loud noise as it flew through the air, it rushed with such rapidity upon its prey that none could escape. At length a brave man called Te Hau-o-tawera came on a visit to the neighbourhood; and finding that the people were being destroyed, and were so paralysed with fear as to be incapable of doing anything for their own protection, he volunteered to destroy the bird. With the assistance of fifty men he procured a number of *manuka* saplings, and went with the men one night to the foot of the mountain, where there was a pool sixty feet across. This he com-

[1] Mount Torlesse ?

pletely covered with a network made of the saplings, and under the network he placed the fifty men, armed with long spears and thrusting weapons, while he himself, as soon as it was light, went out to lure the *poua-kai* from its nest.

He did not go far before the destroyer spied him, and swooped down with terrifying sound. Te Hau-o-tawera sped for his life, and succeeded in reaching the network just as the bird pounced. In its violent efforts to reach him it forced its legs through the network and became entangled. The fifty men plunged their spears into its body, and after a desperate struggle succeeded in destroying it.

The name of this bird was evidently widely known: *pou-kai* in one legend, *poua-kai* in others; *pou-kai* is probably a misspelling; and it will be remarked that it is almost the same as that of a goblin, Poua-hao-kai, slain by Rata, as related in a later story. It has been suggested that it may be the memory of some extinct giant bird; but if so, then such birds have existed wherever man has dwelt; and the roc of *The Arabian Nights* and the *poua-kai* of Maori tradition are equalled by Ngani-vatu of Fijian fable.

The Giant Bird Ngani-vatu of Fiji

In a land called Nai Thombothombo (which seems to recall our own Mumbo Jumbo) there lived both gods and men. One of the gods, Rokoua, gave his sister in marriage to another god named Okova. The marriage was a happy one, but there must have been an envious fate superior even to the gods; for one day, accompanying her husband to the reef on a fishing excursion, the wife was seized by a huge bird and carried off. This bird was to some known as Ngani-vatu, to others as Ngutu-lei. Okova besought the assistance of Rokoua, and together they set off in a large canoe to rescue the unfortunate Tutu-wathiwathi. On their way they came to an island inhabited by goddesses, where, as the song says, " there existed no man, but they wiled away the time in sports." Rokoua thought to make this their journey's end, saying to Okova, " Let us sail no farther in search of Tutu-wathiwathi; for here is a land

130

abounding in excellent women, and precious cowries as many." But these had no charm for Okova, whose thoughts were still with Tutu-wathiwathi, and he persisted in sailing on. Arriving at the Yasawas, the adventurers inquired where the bird Ngani-vatu could be found, and were directed to Sawai-lau; but the bird was not in the cave. Looking round, they saw one of the little fingers of Tutu-wathiwathi, which Okova took as a precious relic, rightly concluding that his wife had been devoured.

Having rested a while, the two saw the devourer approaching, its foglike shade shutting out the light of the sun. In its beak it carried five large turtles, and in its talons ten porpoises, which on reaching the cave it began to eat, paying no regard as yet to the intruders. Rokoua proposed to spear the monster, but Okova entreated him to pause while he prayed to three other deities to assist them by causing a wind to blow. The prayer was heard, and the wind, blowing into the cave, spread out the bird's tail. Rokoua seized the opportunity, and struck his spear mightily through its vitals. The spear, though very long, was entirely hidden in the body of the bird.

It was now proposed to make a new sail out of one of the wing-feathers; but as its weight would endanger the canoe, a smaller feather was selected, by means of which they sailed safely home. Before starting, however, they took the dead bird and cast it into the sea, thereby causing such a surge as to wash up and " flood the foundations of the sky."

Kahu-kura learns the Art of Netting (New Zealand)

From the Patu-pai-arehe a man named Kahu-kura learned the art of making nets. He had long wished to pay a visit to Rangi-ao-whia, lying to the north of his home, and it was on the way to that place that he met with his adventure. He passed a place on the beach where he saw by the remains scattered about that people had been cleaning mackerel. " This must have been done by some of the people of the district," said he to himself; but on observing the footmarks more closely he saw that they must have been made during the night; and he said to himself, "These are no mortals who have been fishing here; spirits must have done this; had they been men, some of the seeds and grass used in the canoe would be lying about." He felt sure from several circumstances that spirits or fairies had been there, and that night he returned alone to the place, hoping to discover something about which he could speak to his friends.

Just as he reached the spot back had come the fairies too, to haul their net for mackerel; and some of them were shouting out, "The net here! The net here!" Then a canoe paddled off to fetch another one in which the net was folded, and as they dropped the net into the water they began to call, "Drop the net in the sea at Rangi-ao-whia, and haul it at Mamaku." These words were called out by the fairies as an encouragement in their work, and from the joy of their hearts at their sport in fishing.

As the fairies were dragging the net to the shore Kahu-kura managed to mix among them, and hauled away at the rope. He happened to be a very fair man, so that his skin was almost as white as that of the fairies, and because of that he was not observed by them. As the net came close in to the shore the fairies began to cheer and shout out, " Go into the sea, some of you, in front of the rocks, lest the net should be entangled in Tawatawa-uia-a-Tewetewe-uia," for that was the name of a rugged rock standing out from the sandy shore. The main body of the fairies kept hauling at the net, and Kahu-kura hauled away in the midst of them.

When the first fish reached the shore, thrown up in the ripples driven before the net as they hauled it in, the fairies had not yet observed Kahu-kura. It was just at the very first peep of dawn that the fish were all landed, the sound of their flapping and the sight of their sheening exciting them to eager exertion, and the fairies ran hastily to pick them up from the sand, and to haul the net upon the beach. They did not do as men do, dividing them into separate loads for each, but every one took up what fish he liked, and ran a string through their gills; and as they strung the fish they continued calling out, "Make haste, all of you, and finish the work before the sun rises."

Kahu-kura kept on stringing his fish with the rest of them. He had only a very short string; he made a slip-knot at the end of it, and when he had filled the string with fish he lifted them up, but had hardly raised them from the sand when he pulled the knot free, and off fell the fish. Then some of the fairies good-naturedly ran to help him string his fish again; and one of them tied the knot at the end for him, but the fairy had hardly gone after knotting it before Kahu-kura had unfastened it, tied it as before, filled the string with fish, and lifted it, when off they fell again. Once more he began stringing, and once more they fell off as he lifted the bundle. By repeating this trick he delayed the fairies in their work by getting them to knot his string for him, and string his fish too. At last full daylight broke, so that there was light enough to distinguish a man's face, when the fairies saw that Kahu-kura was a mortal. They dispersed in confusion, leaving their fish and their net, and abandoning their canoes, which were nothing but stems of flax. Without delay they started for their own abodes, leaving everything in their hurry. Their net was made of rushes, and now was first discovered by men the knot for meshing a net.

Te Kanawa sees the Forest Elves (New Zealand)

Another young chief, named Te Kanawa, fell in with a troop of these fairies upon the top of Puke-more, a high hill in the Waikato district of the North Island of New Zealand.

He happened one day to go out to catch *kiwi* with his dogs, and when night came on he found himself right on the top of Puke-more. It was very dark, so his party lit a fire to give them light. They had chosen a large tree under which to sleep for the night—a *pukatea*, whose large buttresses and roots formed very convenient lodges for them. They slept between the roots, making up the fire beyond them.

133

As soon as it was dark they heard the sound of voices, as if people were coming that way; there were the voices of men, women, and children, as if there were quite a number. They looked and looked, but could see no one, and Te Kanawa concluded the voices must have been those of fairies. His people were very much afraid, and would have run off if there had been anywhere to run to; but what could they do? For they were in the midst of the forest, on the top of a high mountain, and the night was dark as dark.

For a long time the sound of the voices grew louder and more distinct as the fairies drew nearer and nearer, until there they came, quite close to the fire; and Te Kanawa and his people were half dead with fright. Te Kanawa was a handsome fellow, and little by little the fairies approached to have a look at him; and to do this they kept peeping slily over the large roots where the *kiwi*-hunters were lying, constantly looking at Te Kanawa, whose companions were in the last extremity of fear. Whenever the fire blazed up brightly off went the fairies and hid themselves, peeping out from behind stumps and trees; and when it burnt low back they came again, singing merrily as they moved:

> " Here you come climbing
> Over the mountain,
> The mountain Tirangi,
> To visit the handsome
> Chief of Ngapuhi,
> Whom we have done with."

A sudden thought struck Te Kanawa, that he might induce them to go away if he gave them the jewels he had about him; so he took from his neck a beautiful little greenstone *tiki* that he wore as a charm, and a precious greenstone pendant from his ear. Ah! Te Kanawa was only trying to amuse them and save his life; but all the time he was nearly dead with fear. However, the fairies did not rush at the men to attack them, but came quite close to look at them. As soon as Te Kanawa had taken off his *tiki*, and pulled out his ear-drop, also a second ear-drop made from the white tooth of a shark, he spread them out before the fairies, and offered them to the multitude that were sitting all round about the place; and thinking it better that the fairies should not touch him he took a stick, and fixing it into the ground hung his neck-ornament and ear-drops upon it.

As soon as the fairies had ended their song, of which only a fragment is remembered, they took the jewels, and handed them about from one to the other, until they had passed through the whole party, which then suddenly disappeared, nothing more being seen of them.

It seemed that they had carried off the jewels; but, looking again, there they were on the stick where Te Kanawa had hung them; so he took them back again. The hearts of the fairies were quite contented to take the shadows only, or their *ahua* (appearance), and these they had taken as patterns. They saw, too, that Te Kanawa was an honest, well-dispositioned young fellow; but, however that may be, as soon as the dawning light dispersed the shadows of the forest he hastened down the mountain as fast as he was able, without stopping to hunt longer for *kiwi*.

The Wife of Rua-rangi carried off by Fairies (New Zealand)

The fairies dwelt away in the wooded mountains, where adventurous wanderers might chance to see the supple-jack palisading of their *pa*; the sound of song and of flute-playing might also be heard floating faintly down, especially when mists swathed the mountains mysteriously. No Maori would sing out of doors at night, for that angered the fairies, the Patu-pai-arehe, who thought themselves mocked by the singing. The sleeping-houses of the Maori were warmed with burning charcoal, and it sometimes happened that a person died of the fumes; but it was then said that the spirit had been carried off by the Patu-pai-arehe. Sometimes, however, they carried off the person, spirit and body too; and it happened that a man, Rua-rangi, returning home after an absence, found that his wife had disappeared. He searched in vain; he found her footsteps leading into the hills, so he suspected that she might have been carried off by the fairies; and, consulting the *tohunga*, he found that it was so.

The *tohunga* performed certain ceremonies to cause the love of the woman for her husband to return, and after a time he said to the husband, " Go and meet your wife; and when you see her, be sure to rub her with red ochre." Now the woman had felt the influence of the *karakia* uttered by the *tohunga*, and had felt a returning longing for the home and husband from which she had been taken. The fairies were kind to her, as too was the fairy chief who had carried her off; but what was their love to mortal love? They allowed her to wander about their village, and even beyond its palisades. " She has quite forgotten her mortal husband," said the fairy chief. But it was not so; and when one day she beheld a white-breasted tomtit, a *ngirungiru*, the messenger of love, and heard its plaintive song, then indeed she knew that her love of the fairies was as nothing to the love of her people, and she hastened away.

Soon the fairy chief noted her absence, and set off in pursuit; he found her footmarks, followed them, and saw that they joined those of a man, and in anger he followed with his minions. But the man had rubbed his wife with the red ochre, and when the fairy came to the Maori village the husband and wife were safely within. The posts, too, were all smeared with red, and the air was full of the odour of cooked food, so what could the fairy chief do? He chanted a *karakia*, but the *tohunga* chanted one more powerful, so that, vanquished and disappointed, the fairies returned to their home in the hills.

The occasional albinos that occurred among the Maori were said to be the children of the Patu-pai-arehe by mortal mothers.

The Menehune of Hawaii

The Menehune of Hawaii are the equivalent of the Patu-pai-arehe of the Maori. It was the Menehune who assisted Laka in building his canoe, as it was the Haku-turi who assisted Rata. The Haku-turi are a tribe of the Patu-pai-arehe. The Hawaiian fairies were also small and industrious, and any task undertaken must be finished in a single night. We have parallels in our own folk-tales :

> And he . . .
> Tells how the drudging goblin sweat
> To earn his cream-bowl duly set,
> When in one night, ere glimpse of morn,
> His shadowy flail hath threshed the corn
> That ten day-labourers could not end.

Pi was a mortal living in Waimea, Kauai, who wished to construct a dam across the Waimea river and from it a watercourse to a point near Kiki-aola. Having settled upon the best positions for the proposed work, he went up to the mountains and ordered the Menehune to prepare the stones. They were portioned off for the work; some to gather stones, some to shape them. All the material was ready in no time, and Pi settled upon the night when the work was to be done, and he then went to the place where the dam was to be built, and waited. In the dead of night he heard the hum of the voices of the Menehune, each carrying a stone. The dam was constructed, the watercourse laid, every stone fitting into place; the work was completed before the break of day, and the water of the Waimea river was turned by the dam into the watercourse on the flat land of Waimea.

When the work was finished Pi served out food for the Menehune. This consisted of shrimps, these being the only kind to be had in sufficient quantity to supply each with a fish for himself. They were well satisfied, and returned, singing, to the mountains of Pu'ukapele.

At one time Pi also told them to wall in a fish-pond at the bend of the Hu-leia river. They commenced work toward midnight, but the walls of the pond were not sufficiently finished to meet, so they were left incomplete, and have ever since remained so.

Rua-pupuke and the Ponaturi (New Zealand)

The Ponaturi, or sea-fairies, are a different class; they are rather goblins than fairies, since they seem always to be at enmity with man. They slew Hema, the father of Tawhaki, and many were destroyed by Tawhaki; they slew Wahie-roa, the father of Rata, and Rata in his turn destroyed them in great numbers.

They occur in the story of Rua-pupuke, whose son, when out swimming in the sea with his boy-companions, was drawn down under the water by Tangaroa, who placed him as a *tekoteko* (gable ornament) on his carved house at the bottom of the sea.

When the other boys returned to the village Rua-pupuke asked them where his son was. " He has sunk in the sea," said they. The father bade them show him the spot where he sank; then, throwing off his clothes, he assumed the form of a fish (which may simply mean that he acted like a fish) and plunged to the bottom, where he saw the carved house, and his son fixed to the gable over the doorway as a *tekoteko*.

As he approached the child cried to him; but he did not heed the cries, searching instead for the occupants of the dwelling. He met a woman called Hine-matiko-tai, and questioned her about the people. She told him that they were all away at their work; but if he waited until sundown they would return. She seemed to take it for granted that he wished to destroy the people, and told him to close up all chinks by which light might enter, and then conceal himself. Rua-pupuke did as directed.

By and by the people of the place, with a loud noise, came pouring in, until the house was filled. Rua-pupuke asked Hine-matiko-tai what he was to do. "Do nothing," said she; "the sunlight will kill them. Only stop up all the chinks, that no warning gleam of light may tell them of coming day."

At the usual hour of waking Tangaroa, the chief of the people, said, " Is it not day? " " No," replied the old woman, whose duty it was to watch for the dawn; " it is

138

long night, the dark night of Hine-matiko-tai. Sleep on, sleep soundly." So they slept till the sun was high in the heavens. Then Rua-pupuke let in the light and set fire to the house. All was burnt except the carved front, of which Rua-pupuke brought away the four side-posts, the ridge-post, and the door- and window-frames, and thus introduced the art of carving into this world.

Nothing is said of any difficulty experienced in kindling fire under the water, nothing is said of his rescuing the child.

Pitaka, the Slayer of Monsters (New Zealand)

Tipua (goblins) and *taniwha* (monsters) seem to be the embodiment of the dreaded, the unknown, the unpropitious, and they assume whatever shape may happen to be given to them by fear, and by the indefiniteness of imagination awakened by fear.

It is remarkable the fear the Maori had of animals of the lizard kind. It may have been because they so firmly believed them to be the visible representation of that mysterious power that attacked man from within, causing disease and death—the *atua*, or demon-deity, of mortal sickness—so that the lizard appearing to them was equivalent to a death-call. Or it is possible that, as has been suggested, it may have been the memory, handed down from father to son through many generations, of monsters of the crocodile kind met long ago during the early Polynesian wanderings.

Cook learned from them of " lizards of an enormous size " which burrowed in the ground, and sometimes seized and devoured men. Nicholas, who was in New Zealand with the Rev. Samuel Marsden in 1814, gathered information of a similar kind, the description of the animal corresponding to that of an alligator. Early explorers often had pointed out to them places where these monsters were said to have dwelt. Such creatures have not inhabited New Zealand in recent times ; and it is strange that there should be such definite stories of a creature of which no remains at all have been found, when there are so few and meagre references to the giant *moa*, whose remains are so plentiful throughout the islands.

The name of one of these monsters was Hotu-puku, and it was slain by certain valiant men of Rotorua, whose names were Puraho-kura, Rere-tai, Rongo-haua, Rongo-hape, and Pitaka. The last-named appeared to be specially valiant in the slaying of *taniwha*, and his apparently was no mere lip-valour like that of the second calender of the *Arabian Nights*, who made a habit of slaying *ifrits*.

It appears that people travelling between Rotorua and Taupo used mysteriously to disappear; whole parties would set out, and be heard of no more. One party travelling from Rotorua went by way of the lakes Tara-wera and Roto-mahana; and they arrived at Taupo safely enough. They were asked about people who had left Taupo for Rotorua, but nothing whatever could be learned of them. On hearing this the people of Taupo earnestly inquired of the newly arrived party by what road they came. They replied, " We came by the open plain of Kainga-roa, by the road to Tauhu-nui." Then it was that the people of Taupo and the party from Rotorua put their heads together, and talked, and discussed, and deeply considered, and said, " Surely those missing travellers must have fallen in with a marauding war-party ; for we all know that they have no kinsfolk in those parts."

Upon this the Taupo people determined on revenge, and an army was got together for this purpose. All being ready, they commenced their march. They travelled all day, and slept at night by the wayside ; and the next morning, at daylight, they crossed the river Waikato. Then they went on over the open plain of Kainga-roa, until they came to a place called Kapenga, where, unknown to them, dwelt a *taniwha*, a noxious monster, whose name was Hotu-puku.

When that monster smelt the odour of men wafted toward it from the army by the wind it came out of its cave. At this time the men were travelling onward in the direction of the cave, unseen by the *taniwha*, while the *taniwha* was also coming on toward them, unseen by the

party. Suddenly, however, the men looked up, and lo!
the monster was close upon them; on which they immediately retreated in confusion. In appearance it was like
a moving hill of earth. Then the fear-awakening cry was
heard: " Who is straggling behind? Look out, there!
A *taniwha*, a *taniwha* is coming upon you!"

They fled confusedly in all directions with dismay at
seeing the dreadful spines and spearlike crest of the creature
all moving and waving about in anger, like the spines and
crests of monsters of the ocean deep. In the utter rout
they fell foul of each other through fear; some escaped
alive, some were wounded and died. Then, alas! it was
surely known what had befallen the many people who had
formerly travelled that way.

The news was soon carried to all parts of the Rotorua
district, and brave warriors assembled, one hundred and
seventy all told, and taking up their arms they marched to
Kapenga, and pitched their camp in the plain. They set
to work, some to pull the blades of the cabbage-tree (*ti*),
others to twist them into ropes of all kinds—round, and flat,
and double-twisted, and three-stranded, and four-sided.

Then the several chiefs arose and made orations as the
custom is when going to do battle with the enemy, exhorting
each other to be brave, and circumspect, and behave as
proven warriors. They told off a certain number to go
to the entrance of the cave where the *taniwha* dwelt, while
others were armed with clubs, and spears, and shaped
rib-bones of whales, and short wooden cleavers, and weapons
of all kinds. They carefully laid their ropes and nooses,
and when all was ready the enticers went toward the mouth
of the cave; but lo! the *taniwha* had already smelled the
odour of men, and needed no further enticing.

It arose, and the men heard the rumbling of its tread,
resembling the dreadful noise of thunder. Notwithstanding, they courageously ran toward it, exposing themselves to danger so as to lure it well away from its cave;
and when the *taniwha* beheld the food it craved for it came
ramping forth with open mouth and darting tongue.

The men entered the snares of ropes, and passed on over and through them, the *taniwha* following. Its head appeared on the top of a little hill; the monster came on, head lowered as it came down that hill, following the enticers, who were ascending a second little hill; and when its head was at the top of the second hill its forelegs also were within the snare. " It has entered; it is enclosed," was the cry. " Now pull! Haul away! " The ropes were pulled, the snares closed, and the *taniwha* was caught fast.

It began to lash about with its tail, which was stabbed again and again with spears, and battered with clubs. It reared, and knocked about with its head also, and that was assaulted as the tail had been assaulted. The holders of the ropes made them fast, and they too joined in the assault. Great was the shouting, the running to and fro; now the monster seemed to succumb, now it seemed to break free. Back fell the men when the hideous head was turned toward them, but on they came again, and at length the *taniwha* became less vigorous, though it still raged, for its whole body was fast becoming a mass of wounds and bruises through the unceasing thrusting and beating. Then it yielded quietly, and by the time it was dark it was quite dead. So they left it until the morning.

When the sun appeared they arose to cut it up. As it lay extended, it resembled a large whale; but its general appearance was that of a great lizard, with rigid spiny crest, while the head, legs, feet, and claws, the tail, the scales, the skin, and the general spiny ridges, resembled those of the *tuatara*. After long examination one of the chiefs said, " Let us throw off our clothing, and all hands turn to and cut up this creature, that we may also see its stomach, which has swallowed so many of the children of men."

They began cutting it open with knives of obsidian and flint, and saws made of sharks' teeth, and the sharp shells of mussels. On the outside, beneath the skin, were enormous layers of fat, thick, and in many folds. Cutting still deeper into its great stomach—an amazing sight! Lying in heaps were the whole bodies of men, women, and children. Some other bodies were severed in the middle; some had their heads off; some their arms, some their legs. And with them were also swallowed their greenstone weapons, their clubs of hardwood, their weapons of whales' ribs, their staves, their spears—all were within the belly of the *taniwha*, as if the monster were a stored armoury of war. Here also were found various ornaments of greenstone for both neck and ears, and sharks' teeth in abundance; also a great variety of garments: fine bordered flax cloaks; thick, impervious war-cloaks, some with ornamental borders; chiefs' woven cloaks covered with dogs' tails, with albatross feathers, with *kiwi* feathers; cloaks of white dogskin; of red *kaka* feathers; white, black, and chequered cloaks of woven glossy flax; garments of undressed flax; and many other kinds besides.

All the dead bodies and fragments were taken and buried in a pit which the men dug there. The *taniwha* was then cut up, the oil of its fat was extracted by heat, and the party consumed and devoured in their own stomachs the flesh of their implacable foe.

The fame of this exploit was carried far and wide; and a messenger was sent to these heroes to inform them that another *taniwha* existed at Te Awa-hou, in the district of Waikato and Pa-tetere, and to invite them to come and destroy it as they had destroyed Hotu-puku. This *taniwha*, whose name was Peke-haua, lived in a deep water-hole, Te Waro-uri. As this was a water-monster, they now made water-traps of basket-work, twisting the vines of supple-jacks and tying them with the smaller vines of another climbing plant, twisting ropes as before with which to fix and set the water-traps. As they went along they recited their *karakia*, charms and incantations designed to weaken the enemy and strengthen themselves.

When they reached the water-hole they sought out from among themselves a fearless and courageous man. Pitaka presented himself, and was selected. He seized the water-trap, which was decorated with bunches of pigeons' feathers,

143

and loaded with stones to sink it and keep it steady, and with it he and his companions plunged into the water, boldly diving into the spring which gushed up from the depths of the earth with a roaring noise. While these were diving those above were performing their work, which consisted of the reciting of various charms and spells for the purpose of overcoming the *taniwha*, and the number of the spells was as great as their potency.

This *taniwha* had a nearer resemblance to a fish, because it had its habitation in the water. When the spines of the monster had become flaccid through the power of the *karakia*, Pitaka and his chosen companions descended to the very bottom of the chasm. There they found the monster in his abode, and the brave Pitaka went forward, coaxing and enticing, quite up to it, and bound the rope firmly about it; having done which, lo! in a twinkling the hero had escaped behind it. His companions pulled a rope, and those above knew the sign, and hauled away, and drew up to the top their companions, together with the monster. At the same time they recited other *karakia*, used for the lifting and upbearing of heavy weights, without which they could not have hauled them up owing to their very great weight.

Up they came by degrees, and at last all floated together on the surface. Soon the *taniwha* was dragged ashore on to dry land, where it was assailed with spears and clubs, and the noise of the beating and the shouting brought the people of the tribes to the spot, to gaze on the body of their defeated foe.

It was cut open, and as in the stomach of Hotu-puku, so in the stomach of Peke-haua were seen the men, women, and children, the weapons, ornaments, and garments, that had been devoured.

A third *taniwha* was discovered to infest the district of Tiki-tapu, near Rotorua, and this one too was destroyed. Its name was Kataore, and its home was in a cave; and when its assailants entered the cave they saw the noxious beast sitting staring full at them, its fearful eyes in appearance like the full moon rising up over dark and distant mountains; and when gazed at by the band those hideous eyes glared upon them like strong daylight suddenly flashing into dark recesses of the forest. And anon they were in colour as if clear shining greenstone were gleaming and scintillating in the midst of the black eyeballs.

When the news of the killing of Kataore was carried to the chief Tangaroa-mihi, however, his heart was overcast with gloom, for the *taniwha* was a pet of his, and its death was the occasion of war between him and the slayers of monsters.

These stories are reminiscent of many in Malory's *Morte d'Arthur* and in the old metrical romances that take more modern form in Spenser's *Faerie Queen*, where wandering knights seek adventure, and find it in encounters with dragons, fire-drakes, and questing beasts. In those tales, however, the hero usually engages the monsters single-handed, and not in parties of a hundred and seventy or like mystic number, as in the present stories. Such an encounter is that between St George and the dragon as immortalized on our sovereign—a coin latterly so rare as to be in danger of extinction like the monsters themselves. Pitaka is like Beowulf in that he undertakes the destruction of more than one beast-enemy of man; and, like Beowulf, he attacks one of them in its watery lair, and with the same equanimity as on dry ground.

The stories are no doubt heritages from a distant past, merely localized in New Zealand or wherever the scene may now be laid. The fishing of Maui' is such a story. Again, Elsdon Best collected the legend of a monster, named Te Kai-whakaruaki, whose lair was in the Nelson district of the South Island. This *taniwha* waylaid travellers passing between Takaka and Motueka, two names of Maori settlements adopted by Englishmen when *pakeha* settlements were made there. Twenty years after collecting this legend from a Maori of the Atiawa tribe, Mr Best met a native of Taha'a Isle, one of the Society group in Eastern Polynesia. From him he learned, among other things, of a man-destroying monster named 'Aifa'arua'i

145

that lived on an islet called Motue'a at Taha'a in ancient times, near Motue'a being another islet Ta'a'a. These slight catches between the vowels of a word mean a dropped letter, and Ta'a'a is the equivalent of Takaka, as Motue'a is of Motueka. Allowing, too, for the usual letter-changes in the Pacific, the name 'Aifa'arua'i is the Maori Kai-whakaruaki. These linkings up, which have so often taken place in the past and are constantly taking place even now, are of rare interest, and add a keen zest to the study of these people, already so interesting in themselves.

The word *moko*, or *mo'o*, is of widespread occurrence in the Pacific; usually it means 'lizard,' or *taniwha*, and in the Western Pacific 'crocodile.' In Mangaia Moko was king of lizards; and the names of the many Maori lizard-deities, all evil, begin with the word Moko, as Moko-nui, Moko-titi, and so on.

The Winning of Roanga-rahia (New Zealand)

Stories of *taniwha* often come as surprises in stories dealing with other subjects, as in one that tells of the origin of the *para* (horseshoe-fern) in New Zealand. Roanga-rahia was a young woman of remarkable beauty, and would have been considered so even if she had not been a chiefess of high rank. She was the admiration and the envy of the surrounding tribes, and upon her many a young man had set his desires; she was as the graceful white heron, a bird seen once in a lifetime.

There were certain brothers, the youngest named Ruru-teina, or Ruru the Younger; and the elder brothers not only determined to visit the famous beauty, but each one assured himself that he would win her as his wife. Now such assurances, though made secretly in the heart, are without fail revealed openly with the lips; and so it came to pass that the object of the visit of these young men became known to Roanga' even before they themselves appeared. She therefore remained secluded in her dwelling, leaving the entertainment to her attendants and the other young women of the village.

146

The brothers reached the landing, and drawing their canoe up above the tide-mark they hastened to the *marae*, or common, bidding Ruru' remain to take care of their personal belongings. They were welcomed with joyful cries and waving garments, and food was set before them, the young women carrying the food in green flax baskets, with swaying, graceful steps, singing appropriate songs. The young men ate with decorum, so that it might be seen that they were nobly born. Meanwhile, they looked for Roanga-rahia ; but among so many beautiful young women who could say for certain which was she ? So they made themselves agreeable to those who pressed round them when their meal was ended. One of these young women seated herself at the side of each of the brothers, and secretly gave the elated young chief to understand that she was Roanga-rahia, and that he had already won her heart by his noble appearance ; and thus were the brothers deceived.

As evening approached Ruru' deserted his irksome watch at the canoe ; and, seeing some children amusing themselves spinning tops, he asked them where the house of Roanga-rahia might be. They pointed it out to him, quite close by ; and, strolling toward it, there he saw Roanga' herself, and was kindly received by her and her mother, Hine-te-rangi-ataahua (Daughter of the Beautiful Heaven). Learning that he was the youngest brother, and that he had been left to watch the canoe while the others amused themselves in the *marae*, Roanga', with a perversity natural to young women, conceived a desire for him, the least in rank of them all. Ruru' was not long blind to this, and was delighted with his good fortune, and with the loveliness of her who caused it.

As night deepened, the mother, whose eyes could not be closed to what was going forward, arose and left Ruru' and Roanga' together, saying, as she went, that they should be awakened ere day dawned. The noise of the door as she drew it back was heard by one of the people, who called out, " Who is that opening the door of the house of Roanga-rahia?" "It is I, Hine-te-rangi-ataahua," said the mother; and, closing the door again, she was gone.

At the dawn of day an attendant cried, as was the custom, "Day is dawning!" Ruru' arose and left the house, returning to the place where their canoe was drawn up; and he laid himself down on the mats as if the night had been passed by him at that place.

He was soon joined by his elder brothers, each asserting—for what boaster can keep counsel?—that he had obtained the beautiful Roanga-rahia as his wife, and that she had promised to return with him to his home. Ruru' complimented each one, as he was privately told of it, on deserved success, but in his heart congratulated himself upon having secured the loveliness that they had failed even to see. "She is as beautiful as the rising of Kopu, the morning star," thought he, the old proverb coming to his mind; "and each of my brothers thinks he has held her in his arms—as if there could be more than one Roanga-rahia!"

He acted in a similar way each night of their stay at the village. On the night previous to their return Ruru' said to Roanga' and her mother, "You two must come with me, and I will put you on board the canoe before my brothers come." But Hine' refused to leave her home, sending an attendant in her stead to accompany Roanga'. Ruru' accordingly took the young women, and secreted them in the cabin occupied by him; and his brothers soon coming, together with their graceful wives, whom each of them still believed to be the peerless Roanga-rahia, they set out on their return journey, to many cries of kindly greeting and farewell.

Having gone some distance on their way, they landed to cook food; and seeing smoke arising from a village near at hand, the village of Ngarara-huarau, they sent Ruru' to obtain fire for them. He at first demurred, apprehensive lest they in his absence should discover Roanga' and her attendant. At last, however, he went, and at the village met Kiore-ti and Kiore-ta, of whom Ngarara', hearing his steps, inquired, " O Kiore', who is this coming?" " It is Ruru'." " For what purpose has he come?" " To obtain fire." Ruru' was about to depart, when she came out from her dwelling; and winding her tail around him she detained him. " You must remain and partake of food," said she. Then he heard another name by which she was known—Karara-hu-ara; and she was half fish, half woman.

Food was cooked, and a portion set before Ruru'; but it was smeared with the scales from the body of Ngarara'. They ate, and she left them. Then Ruru' inquired of Kiore-ti and Kiore-ta, " Is the woman always like this?" They answered, " Yes." " Well, the food set before us was all covered with her scales," said Ruru'. " Do you indeed suppose she is a woman?" they asked. " No such thing; she is an *atua*." Ngarara' overheard these words, and called out, " You shall die to-day." Kiore-ti and Kiore-ta then advised Ruru' to hasten away; this too she overheard, and called out, " To-day you shall be slain." She came to attack these two; but Kiore-ti disappeared into a stone, and Kiore-ta hid himself in the carved *tekoteko* at the gable of the house. She went and scratched at the stone, while Ruru' hastened away. Perceiving that he was making his escape, she pursued, but failed to overtake him. " Come back, O Ruru'. Come back!" she cried; but as he continued in his flight she added, " I will not follow you now, but on a misty day I shall be with you."

He ran until he arrived at the place where his elder brothers waited. When he had related his adventure they determined to slay this *atua*, this goblin Ngarara-huarau. They built a house having but a window in it, and no door, made nooses, and adorned the house with the figures of men. In the centre they erected a post, shaped as if it were a man; and Ruru', protected by a wooden covering, lay hidden in a corner of the house. A day came with mist, and through the mist came Ngarara', calling as she approached, " O Ruru', where are you?" " Here I am," he answered. " And you thought indeed that by running away you could escape from me!" said she; and entering the house she put her tail around the figure which she supposed to be Ruru'. Hearing a noise outside, " O Ruru'," said she, " what is that noise? " " It is your brothers-in-law cooking food for us," said he. Again she heard it, and asked what it was, Ruru' answering in a similar manner. But in truth the noise was caused by the heaping of firewood round and against the house. To this the brothers set fire, and the house was soon enveloped in smoke and flames. Ruru' escaped through the window, which he closed after him, when Ngarara' perceived that it was not Ruru' that she held embraced in the folds of her tail. She screamed with fear and heat, till the burning house fell in, when she screamed louder, crying, " O Ruru', thou deceitful one with the flame of fire! *Aue!* "

The people were standing around the leaping flames to see that the *tipua* was entirely burnt; and as the scales jumped from the midst of the fire they were thrown back again, so that all might be destroyed. Two scales eluded them, however, and did escape, fleeing one to Puke-rau-aruhe and the other to Poro-rimu, one of them murmuring this *tangi* as it went:

> " *Aue!* O hill of fern!
> Am I so ill-favoured?
> O beloved! Oh, evil to forget
> Me, in the midst of flame!
> Oh, woe is me! "

Ngarara' thus died, the two scales alone surviving. Ruru' put off the assumed wooden covering, and he and his elder brothers returned to their home.

When the shadows of evening fell the father and mother said to Ruru', " Now here are the wives of your elder brothers, and each one declares that his wife is Roanga-rahia, the heart's desire; have you alone failed in obtaining a wife? " But he said to his mother, " Has any one been to my cabin? " " Who," she answered, " would dare to enter your cabin? " " Can you go there? " said he. She went, in surprise; but was so astonished on beholding the inmates that she ran to her husband, crying to him, " You

cannot imagine the beauty of the wife of our last-born!"
" Is she of high rank?" asked he. But again she ran to
Ruru', who asked her if she had been to his cabin. "Yes,"
she answered. " Did you enter?" he asked.

"No," said she; "I feared the women." "Yet you
should have entered," said Ruru'. She went again, but
tears were in the eyes of the lovely Roanga-rahia; her
attendant too wept quietly. Potted *tui* had been their only
food, and of that they had had but two calabashes.

They were taken to the village, when Ruru' said to his
mother, "When day dawns, do you go and call aloud, ' I
did indeed think that the elder Ruru' had secured the
famous beauty as his wife; but I find that the veritable
Roanga-rahia is the wife of my last-born.'" She did so.
The elder brothers came to see, and found it was as their
mother said. Then their wives found that a name could
estrange affection; that it was a name only that their
husbands had, in their hearts, embraced, the name Roanga-
rahia.

But what of the *para* fern? For thus ends the story.
The two scales that escaped from the burning, these were
changed into that rarely found fern the *para-tawhiti*.

Hau-tupatu and Kurangai-tuku

The ogres and ogresses of the Maori, like the giants of
the Hawaiians, were often quite kindly people, and one
cannot help sympathizing with them in their often un-
deserved fate. Ngarara' seems to have had nothing but
her appearance against her; and who knows but that the
beauty of the young chiefess Roanga-rahia had affected the
vision of Ruru-teina? For love is like the magic mirror
that makes the desired appear beautiful, the undesired
unbeautiful. So with Kurangai-tuku; but the beginning
must come first.

The brothers Ha-nui, Ha-roa, and Hau-tupatu, or Ha-
tupatu, all lived together in the district between lakes
Rotorua and Taupo and the Waikato river; a district which
the earthquake-god keeps in a continual ferment of unrest.

The neighbouring bush was a famous haunt for birds, and the elder brothers went day by day snaring them, following their sport for many a month while yet the *rahui*, or close season, had not been proclaimed.

Hau-tupatu wished to accompany them ; but no, he must stay in the village and take care of their possessions while the brothers were absent enjoying themselves. Furthermore, they did not share with him the rare dainties, but at each meal he received for his share the lean, tough birds ; and, feeling this treatment keenly, he would sit by the fire eating and crying, crying and eating, during their meals.

But the salt of tears is not a relished savour, and mischievous thoughts began to form and make themselves known in his heart ; until one day, when his brothers had gone off as usual, leaving him to himself, he crept into the storehouse where the birds, preserved in their own fat, were kept in calabashes, and took some of the delicious food, setting resolutely to work to eat it, with some fernroot, well beaten and dressed, as a relish.

When he had eaten as much as he was able—and long abstinence from good things had set a keen edge on his appetite—he crept out of the storehouse again, and trampled round about, on this side and on that side, so that his brothers might think that a marauding party had been there, and had eaten up the food in their absence. He ran a spear into himself in one or two places, where he could do no great harm, and gave himself a few inconsiderable bruises, and then went and lay down on the ground near their hut.

When the brothers returned there they found him, apparently badly wounded ; they ran to the storehouse, and their preserved birds were gone. They asked him who had done all this. " A marauding party," said he. They saw the footmarks, and said, " It is true." They poured warm oil on his wounds, but when he revived they treated him as before, giving him the least tasty birds, and letting him sit on the smoky side of the fire, so that when he wept they laughed, saying, " Never mind him ; those are not real tears ; his eyes are only watering from the smoke."

Next day the same thing happened, and the next ; and at last the brothers suspected him, and, apparently setting out as usual, secretly returned and lay in wait for him. He could not resist the birds ; and out came his brothers from their hiding-place, crying, " Aha ! so we have caught you in your thievish tricks ! " But they had not caught him, for he eluded them and escaped into the dense bush.

When all seemed safe he returned for a spear, for he was determined not to live with his brothers any longer, even if they would allow him ; and wandering about he came to a tree where there were birds sitting feeding, and he started to spear them for food. He thrust his spear at a bird, and another spear came from the other side of the tree, striking the same bird. He looked round, as did the other spearer, and there he saw the ogre-woman, Kurangai-tuku. She had no spear in her hands ; but when she wished to impale a bird she shot out her lips and with them speared it and brought it to her hands. Upon seeing this, Hau-tupatu ran off with all speed ; but the woman easily caught him, for wings were on her arms, and though she was so big her feet were light and swift. She took him with her to her dwelling.

She lived in a cave, and he found that she ate only raw food ; the birds she gave him for food, too, were raw, and not dressed in any way. At dawn she went away to spear birds, leaving Hau-tupatu at home in the cave with her other pets. When she had gone he cooked food for himself, and began to look about him, examining the things in the cave : her beautiful cloak of red feathers from the underwing of the *kaka* ; her cloak of thick dogs' fur ; her ornamented cloak of glossy flax ; her *taiaha* (staff and weapon), fit for the hands of a chief ; and he meditated if he could run off with them. Then he looked at the tame lizards ; and the birds ; and all her many curiosities ; and this went on from day to day, until he began to be tired of idleness and plenty.

One day Kura' asked him what birds she should bring him for food; and he expressed a wish for plump wood-pigeon. She prepared to go to meet his wishes, when he declared that he knew a district where the very best birds might be obtained. She asked where it was, and he said, " Not the first range of hills, nor the second, nor the third," and named an extravagant number of ranges over which she must go in order to secure these birds. She observed that it seemed a very great distance, but consented to go, and away she went.

Hau-tupatu remained in the cave, again roasting birds for himself, and continually wondering how far she had gone; and when he thought she was well out of the way he gathered together the cloaks, and seized the *taiaha*. He put on the cloak of red feathers, thinking how well he looked with that over his shoulder and the *taiaha* in his hands; and, feeling the thrill of the weapon, he made passes with it as if he were confronted with an opponent. He made cuts at the lizards, and killed them; and a *ruru*, seated on a perch, blinked and started aside when a pass of the weapon came nearer than seemed safe. The motion of the bird, and its apparent fear, excited yet more ardour in the breast of Hau-tupatu, and he made a pass that cut the *ruru* down, so that it fell to the ground. One death called for more, and he attacked the helpless birds until all were killed but one, a tiny grey *riroriro*. This bird escaped, and flew off over the hills. " O Kurangai-tuku! our home is ruined; our prisoner is gone; gone, gone, gone—*riro, riro, riro*," and from the bird calling in this way it was called the *riroriro*.

At last it reached the ogre-woman, who asked it, " By whom has all this been done?" " By Hau-tupatu; everything is destroyed." Then was seen the speed of Kurangai-tuku. She murmured a *karakia*, " Stretch out, stride along; stretch out, stride along "; and she strode from hill to hill, from crest to crest, and before long Hau-tupatu spied her coming swifter than a wind, more threatening than a tempest. " There you are, O Hau-tupatu! " she said in her *karakia*. "There you are, O Hau-tupatu; stretch out, stride along; stretch out, stride along"; and the words that gave her speed seemed to paralyse Hau-tupatu.

She came, she saw her ruined cave, and her heart was dark; had she not treated him kindly? She pursued, she caught sight of him, and now she was close upon him. Lucky for him that his grandmother had taught him a powerful charm; now was the time to test it. "*Matiti matata*," said he; "open and cleave asunder." It was a kind of 'open sesame,' and the rock parted and swallowed him up just as the ogre-woman thought she had him.

She was surprised; she saw him, and he was gone; she scratched at the rock, but it was hard and unyielding. "I'll catch you there, Hau-tupatu," she cried, "I'll catch you there"; and she kept crying these words as a kind of *karakia* or charm. She grew tired of waiting, however; and when Hau-tupatu could no longer hear her voice as she receded, out he came from the rock, at some distance from where he had entered, and made off, hurrying as fast as might be. Again she saw him, turned in pursuit, almost had him, and again he was gone; and so it went on until he was quite near his home. The last time he came up it was on the far side of a boiling spring, Te Whakarewarewa. Kurangai-tuku saw him, and not knowing the place she came after him in a direct line, was caught in the spring, and died. The name has always been known as Ha-tupatu, but Elsdon Best has learned that the true old Maori form is Hau-tupatu.

By some Ha-tupatu or Hau-tupatu is supposed to represent the young of the New Zealand shining cuckoo, the *pipiwharauroa*. This cuckoo places its egg for preference in the nest of the grey warbler, *riroriro*, a bird not an eighth of its size, but a most devoted foster-mother. The young cuckoo has the same habits as its European cousin, turning out any egg or young bird that may at first share the nest with it. It leaves the nest sooner than the young *riroriro* would leave it, so that one day the foster-bird returns with food and finds the nestling gone, whence the mournful cry *riro, riro, riro, riro*. But the escapee is anon found, seated on a branch, voracious for food; and so kindly a bird is the *riroriro* that not only the foster-parents, but any other bird within hearing will feed the graceless, clamouring young cuckoo. The local form of the name, Ha-tupatu, does not bear out the form Hau-tupatu; the local contraction, too, is Ha', not Hau', and Ha' seems required at least for the names of the brothers.

CHAPTER VI : THE TAWHAKI CYCLE

TAWHAKI was directly descended from Rehua, one of the highest and oldest of the gods, the generations to Whai-tiri, his grandmother, being as follows: Rehua, Ao-nui, Ao-roa, Ao-pouri, Ao-potango, Ao-toto, Ao-whero, Tu-korokio, Mo-uriuri, Mo-rearea, Mo-haki-tua, Mo-haki-aro, Kupa, Wai-hemo, Ika-tau-i-raki, Maroro-ki-tua-raki, Te Uira, Te Kanapu, Turi-whaia, Whai-tiri. These were all heavenly powers, some or all being personifications of heavenly manifestations; the names beginning with Ao signify Great Cloud or World, Long Cloud, Dark Cloud, Intensely Dark Cloud, Cloud of Blood, Red Cloud; Te Uira is a personification of lightning, a deity known in Hawaii as Kahuila-o-ka-lani (Maori Te Uira-o-te-Rangi—the Lightning-flash of Heaven); Te Kanapu is another name for lightning; Whai-tiri, or Whati-tiri, is the personification of thunder.

Whai-tiri seeks Kai-tangata

There are many variants of this story in the Pacific, even in New Zealand itself; the following is the version collected by Wohlers from the portion of the Ngai-Tahu tribe living on Stewart Island. Wai-tiri, or Whai-tiri, heard in her home in the heavens of the fame of Kai-tangata. Kai-tangata dwelt upon earth; but his name, Man-eater, in no wise described his character, though Whai-tiri supposed it did. She descended to earth and sought the house of Kai-tangata, and he took her as his wife.

He went to sea to fish, but returned without having caught any, for his hooks were without barbs. She asked him to let her see his hooks.

" Are these the hooks you fish with?" said she. " Look here." And she showed him her private barb.

" *E !* " said he.

She sent him to catch a *hapuku* (groper); he caught it, and she made of it an offering to the gods, repeating the *karakia* called Hapuku.

Again he went fishing; and while he was away she made a hand-net, taking it to the shore, where on the water she saw two men, Tupeke-ti and Tupeke-ta, also busy at their fishing. She changed her shape, dived into the sea, and swam to their canoe. Tupeke-ti saw her, and stood up, saying, " Is it a man or a bird? " She speared him, he fell into the water, and she put him into her net. Tupeke-ta hastened to the middle of the canoe to spear her, but she struck him with a *koripi*, a knife edged with sharks' teeth, and he too fell into her net.

She swam ashore, resumed her shape, and left the net in the water, ordering the women to haul it up. They saw in it the slain relatives of Kai-tangata.

On the return of Kai-tangata Whai-tiri requested him to chant the *karakia* and perform the usual ceremonies in offering human flesh to the gods.

" I do not know how to perform that ceremony," said he.

" Nay, but offer the sacrifice," said she; " I have obtained it for our child."

" I do not know how to perform the ceremony," he answered.

" But you must perform the ceremony for our child," said she, " as my child is yours."

As he still persisted that he was unable she performed the ceremony, cooked and ate the bodies, and hung the bones in her house.

When the bones were dry Kai-tangata secretly removed them for the purpose of making barbed fish-hooks, and with these he caught more *hapuku*. Whai-tiri unknowingly cooked and ate of these fish, and slowly she lost the sight of her eyes. Brooding over this misfortune, one night as she slept she dreamt that a woman from the spirit world of Te Reinga came to her, and said, " You are blind because the bones of the sacrifice were taken by your husband; with them he made hooks and caught the *hapuku* of which you have eaten; therefore this evil has come upon you."

Thus she lived till her child was born. He was called Hema. The child grew, and could be taken outside; and

158

one sunny day Kai-tangata was sitting with him when men came to see him.

"What like is the woman who lives with you?" said they

"You ask of the woman who lives with me," said he. "Her skin is like the wind; her heart is like the snow."

This was overheard by Whai-tiri, who sat within the *whare*; and when his friends left and Kai-tangata brought the child to her, she asked, "What were you speaking about?"

"Nothing in particular," said Kai-tangata.

"What were you speaking about?" she repeated.

"Only ordinary talk," said he.

"What were you saying about me?" she insisted.

"Oh, Whai-tane inquired about you," said he; "that was all."

She was overcome with shame; she was offended; she said to Hema, "Do not follow me now; but when you have children let them follow me to the heaven of Tama-i-waho."

She climbed the thatch of their *whare* to the ridge-pole; Kai-tangata reached to seize her garment to detain her; but she eluded him, and disappeared to Pu-o-toetoe, where she dwelt thereafter.

Hema grew up, and took to wife Uru-tonga. The name of the wife differs in the various versions, and in some Hema was not a son, but a daughter. In one of the versions Whai-tiri addresses Kai-tangata as she is about to leave him: "You stay here, and call our child Hema, in remembrance of my living with you as your wife; and do you carefully attend to her, and rear her up tenderly. O old man! hearken to my word to you; though our child fret after me, do not let her follow me, lest she should not be able to climb to the upperworld where I dwell; and when we have a grandchild let his name be Tawhaki, in remembrance of my rushing down to you. He too shall be the man to climb to that upperworld." So ended the farewell words of Whai-tiri to her husband, and, clouds descending, by them she was taken upward and away.

Tawhaki appears

The first child of Hema and Uru-tonga was a daughter, Pupu-mai-nono; their second was a son, Karihi; and their third a son, Tawhaki. Hema went on a voyage, and visiting the *kainga* of Paikea, of Kewa, and of Ihu-puku, by some called the tribes of the Ponaturi, he was attacked, made prisoner, and killed, but his wife, also made prisoner, was spared.

Reaching maturity, Tawhaki became enamoured of Hine-piripiri, who had been betrothed by her seniors to one of their own relatives. But she liked none of these relatives; she loved Tawhaki, and her brothers secretly resolved to kill him. This they resolved not only because of their sister, but because he was so attractive to all the young women; not only was he a *purotu* (a man of fine appearance), but he was skilled in the building of beautiful houses, whose floors were spread with fine, well-woven mats.

The brothers went a-fishing, and Tawhaki with them. Two returned, and with them Tawhaki. They lingered at the pool Rangi-tuhi to wash their hair; and as Tawhaki leaned over the pool, wringing his hair, he murmured this *karakia*:

> " Arise, faint light of dawn;
> Give me my comb,
> My head-ornament,
> That I may go to the water of Rangi-tuhi,
> The pool *ē*, ha! *i*."

Then the brothers, seeing him defenceless, attacked him and left him for dead.

Reaching the village, they met their sister, who asked them, " Where is Tawhaki? "

" He is still with the others," they answered.

On the others returning she met them, and asked them, " Where is Tawhaki? "

" Oh, he returned with the others some time since," they answered.

Then she knew that they were deceiving her, and went herself to seek Tawhaki.

She approached the pool, calling softly, " O Tawhaki, where are you? " A *pukeko* answered, " *Ke!* " She went toward the sound, but the bird ran off, and she saw nothing. Again she called, " O Tawhaki, where are you? " when a *moho* answered " *Hu-u!* " She went toward the sound, but again the bird ran off, and she saw nothing. A third time she called, " O Tawhaki, where are you? " and now she heard a low murmur, and hastened toward the sound. Tawhaki had recovered and was murmuring a *karakia* to stanch the flow of blood.

Hine-piripiri carried him home, washed and dressed his wounds, and cared for him. When he had somewhat recovered he asked his wife to fetch some wood to make a fire.

" If you see any tall tree near you," said he, " fell it, and bring that for the fire."

She found a tall tree, felled it, took it on her shoulder, and, bringing it home, put the whole tree without cutting it on the fire. For this reason she called their first-born Wahie-roa (Long Log of Firewood), for Tawhaki said that she should give this name to the child in order that the duty of avenging his father's wrongs might often be called to mind.

When Tawhaki was recovered he left this place, and with his people he built a fortified village on a lofty elevation, easily protected, and there they dwelt. While in this place he called to the gods his ancestors for vengeance, and they sent the floods that destroyed his enemies. One of these had ventured up for the purpose of killing Tawhaki, whom he followed to the summit of the mountain ; but when Tawhaki, standing there, raised his arms, and lightnings flashed from his armpits, the man fled.

Tawhaki avenges the Death of his Father

Tawhaki and his elder brother Karihi next set out to seek revenge for the death of their father. The Ponaturi dwelt under the water by day, and at night came ashore to sleep in their house called Manawa-tane. By the aid of *karakia* taught them by their sister Pupu-mai-nono Tawhaki and Karihi traversed the seas until they came in sight of Manawa-tane, where they found their mother, Uru-tonga, sitting alone by the door. She knew they were coming, for the bones of Hema, hanging under the steeply pitched roof, heard the *karakia* of Tawhaki as the brothers approached, and rattled in recognition. Mother and sons wept together; and when they had wept awhile for joy of the meeting, the mother said, " My children, return home, and hasten, or you will perish; for the people who dwell here are a fierce and savage race."

" How long will the sun have descended when they return? " asked Karihi.

" They will return when the sun sinks beneath the ocean."

" Why did they permit you to live? "

" They spared me that I might watch for the coming of the dawn, sitting at the door of the house; for this reason they called me Tatau [the Door]; and throughout the night they one or another call to me, ' Ho, Tatau, there; is it yet dawn? ' and I call in answer, ' No; it is deep night; it is lasting night; sleep soundly on, sleep on.' "

" Cannot we hide ourselves somewhere? " asked Karihi.

" You had better return," answered the mother; " you cannot hide yourselves here; the scent of you would be perceived by them."

" But we could hide ourselves in the thick thatch of the house," said Karihi.

" It is of no use," their mother answered; " you cannot hide there."

All this time Tawhaki sat silent; but Karihi persisted. " We will hide ourselves here; for we know *karakia* that will make us invisible."

Their mother then consented to their remaining, in order to attempt to avenge the death of their father. So they climbed up on the outside of the roof, and in the thick layers of reeds forming the thatch they made holes into which they crept and covered themselves up.

" When the dawn is near," said the mother, " come

down and stop up every chink in the house, so that no light may shine in."

At last the day closed, and all the troop of Ponaturi left the water for the dry land; and according to custom they sent one of their number before them, so that he might examine the road and see that there were no hidden foes lying in wait. As soon as this scout arrived at the door of the house he perceived the scent of the brothers, and he lifted up his nose, sniffing as he turned about inside the house. He was on the point of discovering the strangers when the rest of the Ponaturi, whom long security had made careless, came hurrying on, crowding into the house in thousands, so that the scent of the strange men was quite lost. They all stowed themselves away until the house was quite full, and little by little they arranged themselves in convenient places, and at length fell fast asleep.

At midnight Tawhaki and Karihi stole down from their hiding-place, and joined their mother, who had come outside the door to meet them, and there they sat whispering together.

" Which is the best way for us to destroy these people ? " asked Karihi; and their mother answered, " You had better let the sun kill them; its rays will destroy them."

She crept into the house again; and presently an old man Ponaturi called out to her, " Ho, Tatau, there; is it dawn yet ? "

" No, no; it is deep night," she answered; " it is lasting night; sleep soundly on, sleep on."

When it was very near dawn Tatau whispered to her children, who were still sitting just outside the door of the house, " See that every chink in the window and doorway is stopped, so that not a ray of light can enter here."

Presently another old man Ponaturi called out, " Ho, Tatau, there; is it not near dawn yet ? " And she answered, " No, no; it is night; it is lasting night; sleep soundly on, sleep on."

At last dawn had broken; the sun shone brightly upon the earth and rose high in the heavens; and the old man

163

again called out, " Ho, Tatau, there; is it not dawn yet?"

And she answered, " Yes "; and she called out to her children, " Be quick; pull out the things with which you have stopped up the window and the door."

They pulled them out, the bright rays of the sun came streaming into the house, and the whole tribe of the Ponaturi perished in the rays of the sun. One, named Kanae, in long leaps made his escape, plunging into the water, and Tonga-hiti, god of headache, escaped by breaking through the wall of reeds. Kanae is a personification of the mullet. Tawhaki and Karihi then took down their father's bones from the roof of the house, and destroyed the house with fire, together with the bodies of those lying dead within it. They returned to their home with their mother, carefully carrying the bones of their father.

Tawhaki is loved by Tangotango, an Immortal

The fame of Tawhaki, both for his courage and for his manly beauty, reached even to the upperworlds, and induced a maiden of the heavenly race to visit him, so that she might judge for herself whether the reports were true or no. She came by night, found him asleep, and after gazing at him for some time she stole to him, raised the covering, and laid herself down beside him. He, disturbed, thought it only some young woman of this world, and slept again; but before dawn she slipped away from his side, once more ascending to the upperworlds. In the early morning Tawhaki awoke, felt with his hands on this side and on that, but in vain; he could nowhere find the young girl.

From that time on the girl, whose name was Tangotango, stole every night to the side of Tawhaki, and every morning was gone, until she found she had conceived a child, afterward named Arahuta; then, full of love for Tawhaki, she revealed herself to him fully, and lived constantly with him in this world, deserting for his sake her friends above; and he discovered that she who so loved him belonged to the race whose home is in the heavens.

TANGOTANGO RETURNS TO THE HEAVENS
(See page 164)

TYPICAL WET BUSH ON THE WEST COAST OF SOUTH ISLAND

N.Z. Government Publicity Photo

(See page 176)

One day she said to Tawhaki, " Should our child soon to be born be a son, I will wash it; but should it be a daughter, then you shall wash it."

The child was born; and as it was a daughter it was taken by Tawhaki; and having washed it he held it from him, saying, " Faugh! the smell of it! "

His words meant nothing; but Tangotango heard them, and she wept. She arose; and holding the little child she began to take flight for the heavens, pausing for a moment with her foot resting on the *tekoteko*, the carved figure at the gable of the house.

" O mother, return," cried Tawhaki.

" I shall not return," answered the young woman.

" Have you no parting word? " he asked.

Then his wife Tangotango said, " This is my parting word: seize with your hands not the vine hanging loosely from above, but seize the vine that is firmly fixed in the earth." So saying she disappeared, and he saw her no more.

Tawhaki seeks his Lost Wife and Daughter

Tawhaki remained there, but his heart was pained because of his love for his wife and his daughter; and after a month had passed by he said to Karihi, his elder brother, " Let us two go and seek my daughter," to which Karihi consented.

They set out, with two slaves; and coming to the path that led by the abode of Tonga-meha Tawhaki warned the slaves not to look toward the *pa* of Tonga-meha, or he with his enchantments would slay them.

One of the slaves either forgot the warning or disregarded it; for when passing the *pa* he looked up toward it, and immediately his eye was torn out by the arts of Tonga-meha, and the brothers continued their journey accompanied by only one slave.

It will be remembered that the grandmother, Whai-tiri, had, like Tangotango, left her husband and returned to her home in the upperworlds. That place, however, was not apparently in an upward direction, but outward, away over the sea; and, indeed, persons passing to a distance

165

over the sea do appear to vanish into the bending heavens. It was to the home of Whai-tiri, then, that the brothers directed their steps.

They found their grandmother. She was quite blind, and sat beating about with her weapon, so that if anything came within her reach she would kill it, and add it to her store of provisions. Before her lay a little heap of ten *taro*-roots, and now and again she would sit on her weapon while she counted her roots.

Her grandchildren, who had come up noiselessly, were watching her movements when she began to count the roots—one, two, three, and so on; but Tawhaki quietly took a piece, and when she came to nine she felt about for the tenth, but it was not to be found. Thinking she might have made a mistake, she began again—one, two, three, and so on. Now Karihi took a piece; and when she came to eight she felt about for the ninth, but that piece was not to be found. Getting impatient, she began again; but finding that every time she counted there was a piece less she suspected that some one was playing tricks on her, and became very angry, scolding and beating about with her weapon, which she took from beneath her. She turned about as she held her weapon extended, but Tawhaki and Karihi bent close to the ground, and she could feel nothing.

When her anger had calmed down, and she had again seated herself, Tawhaki went up to her and quietly struck one of her eyes. She started, with a joyful exclamation; for with the stroke sight seemed to return to her eye. Immediately Karihi gently struck the other eye, and again light seemed to come with the stroke, and her eyesight was restored to her.

When she learned that the two young men were her grandsons she wept over them in a *tangi*, a murmured welcome mingled with tears; and after mutual greeting they told her the object of their coming.

" Stay with me for a while," said she, " and I will show you the way you must take."

She took them to her house near by, but they did not

feel at ease there; for in it lay a heap of human bones, the remains of victims whom she had eaten. They felt they could not trust her; she might kill and eat them also; so they were very watchful. As they could not always keep awake, however, and she might steal on them in their sleep, they determined to deceive her. They went to the seashore, and from the rocks they took some shells which looked like eyes; and when these were placed on the closed eyes they gave them the appearance of being open. Then at night, when they could keep awake no longer, they fastened the shells over their eyes and went to sleep; and when their grandmother looked at them she believed that they were still wide awake, and was therefore afraid to kill them.

The brothers wished to go on their way; the grandmother wished to detain them; so to their questions as to the way they should go she would only answer, " By and by; by and by I will tell you." After much importuning she showed them a path, but it led to one place, to another place, and to another, but it was not the path they sought.

Again they importuned her, and she said, " Look at me; I am the path." " Are you the path? " " Yes."

They saw that attached to her was a vine; the other end was attached to the heavens. She loosened the vine, and gave them instructions as to how to climb and what to do. " The winds will blow you from side to side of the heavens," said she, " and I fear you will loose your hold and fall; yet if you are determined to go, take care how you deal with those whom you may meet on the way: if you meet women whose behaviour and conversation are unseemly, have nothing to do with them; they are descendants of Tangaroa; but if you meet women of modest behaviour, be friendly with them, for they are of your own people."

Karihi began to ascend by the loose vine; but Tawhaki remembered the saying of Tangotango; and having made a present of his slave to Whai-tiri, he began to ascend the vine that had again taken firm root in the earth, and as he climbed he repeated appropriate *karakia*. Soon the winds of Uru-rangi blew, and the loose vine to which Karihi clung was blown from side to side, so that he became giddy, his hold was loosed, and he fell to the earth and was killed as Whai-tiri had feared, or hoped; but Tawhaki climbed on. Karihi fell to the *kainga* of Whai-tiri; but Tawhaki climbed on. The winds of Uru-rangi assailed him, he was buffeted in the heavens; but Tawhaki climbed on.

He met Tuna', who was coming down. He gave him greetings. "You have come," said he; "what is the reason for your coming?" "It is hard up above; it is dry; there is no water." He had been living in the moist places of Puna-kau-ariki; and as these were becoming too dry he had left them, and was going to Muri-wai-o-ata. His ancestors were Uira, and Te Kanapu, and Te Kohara, and Rautoro; and over his forehead he wore the ancient headdresses Te Kawa and Marae-nui.

Tawhaki climbed on, and soon he heard the chatter of Paki-hika-nui, of Korero-ure, of Korero-tara, wives of Tangaroa. He let them pass on with their blandishments and enticings, and later met Hapai-a-maui and Maikuku-makaka, seated in pools, laving their bodies with the gleaming water. Seeing Tawhaki, they fled to their dwelling, and when he neared the place there they sat, wrapped in soft, well-woven cloaks, smiling welcome.

He approached Hapai-a-maui, but Maikuku-makaka came between them, saying, "For this while the *purotu*, this good-looking man, shall be my husband," and he dwelt with her.

She already had one husband, and that husband was Uru-rangi of the winds; and he, coming home one night, perceived that in his *whare*, where he expected his wife, there lay two people. He put in his hand and touched his wife, who awoke with a start. Tawhaki too awoke, and, resenting the action of Uru-rangi, sought to punish him.

Tawhaki and Maru go Warfaring

In the morning he approached the temple of Maru, the god of war, and chanted a *karakia* calling for his aid. It begins:

Collect, O hosts of heaven!
Collect from far.
Collect.   Evil is near.
Overcome and exhausted,
I am in spirit dead.
Oh that the war-girdle
Might expand itself
And grow before Mua,
And flaunt itself
For me—for me!

.   .   .   .   .

Tu', come near to Maru,
And, Maru, come near to Rongo';
And you, O Rongo',
Come near to me—
Come near to my calamity.
But, O my spear of war!
I vainly flourish it
And only smite the air.

This *karakia* was subsequently used in calling the people together for war.

Maru cried aloud to Tawhaki, " Come to me, to me who possess the weapons of war."   Tu-te-ngana-hau also called, " Come also to me."   And Rehua, " To me also, to me who possess the elements of life."

Tawhaki continued his chanting while performing the haircutting ceremony; and having chanted the *karakia* for the gods he chanted the *karakia* making *tapu* every member and part of his body.

Now, too, men were seen gathering together in battle-array; Tawhaki and Maru placed themselves at the head of the army and led it forth to war.

Ceremonies were duly performed, and sacrifices made to the gods.   The war-party divided in two, one going by the inland road, one by the sea.   The latter was led by Maru; and it happened that passing along the beach they came on a large whale, stranded and long dead.   The war-party halted, and Maru commanded that a huge earth-oven be prepared, so that the monster might be cooked entire. The hole was made, wood and stones were gathered, the

MYTHS OF THE POLYNESIANS

stones were laid, and the wood kindled, and soon the glowing oven was ready to receive the food destined for the hungry war-party. But, indeed, what seemed to be a whale was Rongo-mai, god of the whale; and he muttered a *karakia*, so that when the men approached and, hoisting with levers, rolled him toward the heated stones, lo! the whale melted away, and in its place stood Rongo-mai, glaring at them with angry eyes. Stupefied, the warriors looked on him; nor could they resist when he swept them all into the oven prepared for himself; the whole flock of Maru, and Maru himself, were swept into the glowing oven, where all perished. But the spirit of Maru, leaving his body, fled to the upperworld, to Nga-roto. Te Umu-o-Rongo-mai (the Oven of Rongo-mai) is the name given to one of the large lunar craters.

The army of Tawhaki victoriously assaulted the *pa* of Uru-rangi, and entirely overthrew him. Thus was the *mana* of Tawhaki re-established. Returning, however, he learned from Hapai-maui that Tama-i-waho had come from above and carried off Maikuku-makaka. Tama-i-waho had once before offended Tawhaki; for it was he who assisted the Ponaturi who had slain Tawhaki's father, Hema.

Tawhaki pursues Tama-i-waho

Tawhaki made a kite from the bark of the *aute*-tree, and floating on a favouring wind he soared upward, chanting a *karakia* as he ascended.

Tama-i-waho, peering over his palisades, beheld the approach of Tawhaki, and he bade Haku-wai chant a *karakia* to prevent the coming of his enemy. He obeyed, crying, "Haku-wai, Haku-wai, *hu*!" He repeated his *karakia*, and a wing of the kite was broken. Tawhaki murmured a counter-charm to give the kite power to fly, but as it approached the palisading Haku-wai again cried, "Haku-wai, Haku-wai, *hu*!" when the kite was powerless, and Tawhaki fell. He arose, and slowly he climbed the steep, fixing his eyes on the lattice-work of the *pa* and uttering powerful *karakia*. He reached the *pa*, but now

170

he perceived Tama-i-waho going upward, closing the path behind him as he went; but Tawhaki broke it open and followed.

" Why do you follow me? " asked Tama-i-waho.

" Give me your *karakia*, your incantations."

He answered no; but Tawhaki demanded them as payment for the death of his father. Tama-i-waho refused; but Tawhaki seized him, and he taught him the *karakia* Whatu, Ateatea-nuku, Ateatea-rangi, Hurihanga-te-po, Hurihanga-te-ao, Mata, Korue-hinuku, Mata-atea-whaki.

" Are these all your *karakia*? " demanded Tawhaki.

" These are all; but I have kept some back."

" Give them to me," and Tama-i-waho did so.

" Are these all? " asked Tawhaki.

" So end they; but I have ten more."

" Give those also to me," said Tawhaki.

Tama-i-waho taught him others and left him; their names are given, and counting them up it is seen that he taught him only nine of them.

Tawhaki had not yet reached the abode of Tango-tango, and he went on, still repeating *karakia* as he went.

Tawhaki finds Tangotango

Nearing the end of his journey, he disguised himself as an old, ugly man. He followed the path, which ran through a dense forest, until he came to a place where his brothers-in-law, with a party of their people, were shaping canoes from the trunks of trees. They saw him, and, little thinking who he was, called out, " Here's an old fellow will make a nice slave for us." Tawhaki went quietly on, and sat down with the people who were working at the canoes.

The brothers left off work as evening drew near, and called out to Tawhaki, " Ho! Old fellow there! You just carry these axes home for us, will you? " He consented, and they gave him the axes.

" You go on in front," said he; " I am old and heavy laden, and cannot travel fast." So they started off, the old man following slowly behind. When all were out of

171

sight he turned back to the canoe; and taking an axe he adzed the side rapidly from stem to stern, and one side of the canoe was finished; he adzed it rapidly along the other side, and that side too was finished.

He then walked on again toward the village, when he saw two women gathering firewood; and on their seeing him they bade him carry the firewood to the village, laying it on his back so that he carried that as well as the axes. So this powerful *rangatira* was treated as a slave even by female slaves.

When they reached the village the women called out, " An old man for us ! " And Tangotango answered, " For all of us an old man."

Tawhaki saw Tangotango sitting with their daughter at a fireplace near the upper end of the house, and immediately proceeded toward them. All the people tried to stop him. " Take care," they cried; " do not go there; you will become *tapu* from sitting near Tangotango." But the old man went on as if he did not hear them, and carried his bundle of firewood up to the very fire of Tangotango. " There ! The old fellow is *tapu*," they said; " it is his own fault."

Tangotango did not in the least know that it was Tawhaki who sat with her beside the fire.

They all stayed in the house till sunrise the next morning, when the brothers called out, " Hey, old man; you bring along the axes." So Tawhaki followed them, and they went off to the forest, to shape and dub out their canoes.

When the brothers-in-law saw the canoe Tawhaki had shaped they exclaimed, " The canoe appears quite different; who can have been working at it ? " Their wonder somewhat abated, they set to work to hew out another canoe, and, working at it all day, in the evening bade Tawhaki carry home the axes as before.

The same thing happened as on the first day; and when on the third day the brothers came at early morn they were quite astonished, saying, " Why, here again; this canoe is not at all as we left it; who can have been working at it ? "

They set to work and hewed out yet a third canoe,

labouring until the evening; but a thought came to them that they would hide in the forest and see who it was that came every evening to work at their canoe; and Tawhaki heard them arrange their plan.

They started as if they were going home, but when they had gone some distance they turned aside and hid themselves among the trees in such a place that they could see the canoes. Then Tawhaki, going a little way into the forest, threw off his old cloaks, repeated his *karakia* to remove his disguise of age, took again his own noble and handsome appearance, and started work on the canoe.

Then his brothers-in-law, seeing him so employed, said to one another, " Come here; just watch! His appearance is not at all like that of the old man." Ha! a thought struck them. " A deity! "

Off they went, and arriving at the *kainga* they said to Tangotango, " What is the appearance of your husband? " She described him. " Yes! " said the men; " his appearance is such as you describe." Then said she, " Then that man must be your brother-in-law."

Just then Tawhaki appeared, but as an old man in mean garments, for he had resumed his disguise.

Tangotango questioned him, " Who are you? " but he made no reply. " Are you Tawhaki? "

He murmured assent; came to the side of Tangotango; caught up his little daughter and held her fast in his arms.

All the people rushed from the house, for the place had become *tapu* because of Tawhaki; and all were loud in their admiration of his noble presence, so different from that of the old man they had jested with and slighted.

Thereafter he dwelt with his wife Tangotango and his daughter Arahuta in the world Nga-atua, becoming the beneficent deity to whom, with Rehua, invocations for health are addressed; and fluttering downward to earth from these two celestial lovers came a black moth, emblem of the soul of man. Still from that sixth upperworld, too, Tawhaki reveals himself in the flashing lightning and the rolling thunder.

Rata is born, and avenges his Father

It will be remembered that by his first wife Tawhaki had a son who was called Wahie-roa, though one version says that Maikuku-makaka was his mother. When he grew up Wahie-roa took to wife Matoka-rau-tawhiri, and she bore a son, Rata. Before her child was born Matoka' felt a craving for *koko*, a name of the *tui* when fat, and Wahie-roa set off to snare the birds. A second time he went with a slave ; but as he was unable to snare a bird in the accustomed grounds he trespassed on the preserves of Matuku, who surprised and slew him, carrying off the slave as prisoner.

When Rata grew up he naturally inquired about his father, when his mother told him he had been killed when trying to satisfy her desire for *koko*.

" Where is this Matuku now ? " asked Rata.

" Look where the sun rises from out of the sea yonder," said the mother ; "there in that direction he lives. It is far away ; you cannot get there."

He was silent ; but she knew the desires of his heart, the desires of her own ; and when gathering firewood in the forest one day she found a *totara* from which a canoe might be hewn. She brought home some of the branches, showed them to Rata, and told him of the tree. He looked for it and could not find it, but on the third search found it.

" There are the axes of your ancestors," said she ; but Rata found on examining them that they were blunt. Thereupon he made a journey to an ancestress, Hine-tu-a-hoanga (Daughter of the Whetstone), who bent down, and when Rata laid the edge of the axe on her back she repeated a *karakia*, " *Kia koi, kia koi, kia koi* " (" Be sharp, be sharp, be sharp "). Rata returned, fixed a handle to his axe, and went into the forest to fell his tree.

The Canoe is built by the Wood-elves

He felled it, cut off the top, and returned. On the morrow he went out to shape the canoe, and found the tree

174

standing as though it had never been cut down. He was surprised, but cut it down a second time; but when on going out again next day he found the tree standing as before he determined to watch and see who was interfering with his labours. He felled the tree a third time, but now instead of going home he concealed himself in the bushes near by, and watched.

A dimness came in the air, but not the dimness of evening; a rustling, but not a rustling of leaves; there was singing, but not of birds; there were voices, but not of men; yet the song resounded softly:

> " Rata, O Rata, son of Wahie-roa,
> Thou fellest, without ceremony,
> In the sacred grove of Tane',
> Tane's growing tree.
> Now to the stump the chips fly,
> Now they fly to the top,
> They fit, they close,
> The branches spread,
> Now hold the tree, now raise him."

The tree stood upright; the spirits dispersed; but Rata said, " So; they have done with my tree; so; they have undone my labour, and made a fool of me." And he was angry at the thought, and he rushed out and seized some of the spirits, demanding the reason for their interfering.

Then they told him, as they had already told him in their song, that he had not performed the ceremonies due to Tane', lord of the forests. "Return to your home," said they; " perform the ceremonies, and leave the rest to us, your ancestors "; and they left him. Then he perceived that the great ferns drooped their fronds from their lofty heads; the long leaves of the *toetoe* drooped to the ground; the young tips of the supplejacks bent as if in fear; and indeed it was through fear of the anger of Rata when seizing the spirits that these drooped; and so they have drooped ever since, as if the memory of that day still lingers.

Rata returned, and told his mother what had happened.

175

" It is true," said she ; " the ceremonies should have been performed." They were performed, and again Rata went out to fell his tree. Now, however, the tree was not to be found ; but in its place there lay the canoe, properly shaped, and dubbed, and finished ; and the spirits helped in the launching, for without mishap it reached the sea, where it rode the waves as if eager to be away.

Rata destroys the Goblin

The canoe was named *Niwaru*, or *Niwa-reka* ; another version gives it three names, *Riwaru*, *Tui-rangi*, and *Paka-wai*, marking stages in its progress. It was named, and Rata sailed away to Puoro-nuku and Puoro-rangi, places of the abode of Matuku. First they approached the abode of Poua-hao-kai, and the spirit of his men drooped because of the incantations of this goblin.

" What is his incantation, his *karakia*? " asked Rata.

" When we approach he says, ' Little-heads, little-heads,' and our strength fails us."

But Rata said, " I have a *karakia* more powerful " ; and when they neared the shore they saw Poua-hao-kai walking up and down the beach, and soon they heard the *karakia* "Little-heads, little-heads," when their spirits drooped. But they revived when they perceived that on Rata repeating his answering *karakia*, " Quickly, Big-face, spread over the expanse of heaven," the goblin paused, as if in doubt. They hurled ashore, and though Poua' opened his mouth Rata and his men defied him.

While they were hauling up their canoe Poua' went to prepare food for them, and Rata instructed them as to how they were to act ; so that when they approached the house, and Poua' with his call of " Little-heads " invited them to enter at the door, Rata replied with " Big-face," and they broke an entry for themselves through the wall. " Sit on the mats," said Poua'. " Not so," said Rata ; " sit where there are no mats." So Poua' was thwarted in every particular.

The feast was spread, but the warriors only put the food

to their mouths, and did not eat it.   Then Rata asked for water.

Poua' went for the water, but Rata with his *karakia* caused it to recede, so that as Poua' bent to dip it up it was just beyond him, and he went on, and on, until Rata ceased his *karakia*; when, grumbling, he dipped up the water and returned.

Rata took the water, and then said to Poua' that, as he was no doubt hungry—which by this time, indeed, he was —they had prepared food for him during his absence. " Open your mouth," said Rata ; and Poua' opened it wide.

But the food that Rata had prepared was hot stones ; and taking these from the fire with wooden tongs they quickly threw them into the gaping throat of Poua'.   The stones burst within him, and with them Poua' burst also. Then were revealed the many men and canoes and weapons of war that Poua' had devoured in times past.

They now inquired of Tama-uri, formerly the slave of Wahie-roa, and now the vassal of Matuku, as to the retreat of Matuku.

" Deep in the cavern he lurks," said Tama', " and his food is men."

" Cannot he be lured thence ? "

" In the due season he comes to perform ceremonies that the crops of savoury thistles may be plentiful, and to eat men."

" Can you entice him from his cavern? "   " Yes," answered Tama'.

They landed at Kai-whaia, and ascended the mountain at Whiti-kau, where the opening of the cavern appeared whose name was Pu-tawaro-nuku.   Rata set snares around it, cautioning the men not to haul on the ropes until the snare was well about Matuku's middle.   Tama' then stood at the lip of the cavern, and called, " Matuku, *e* !   Matuku, *e* ! "

An indistinct reply arose from below, and Tama' called on him to come up and perform the ceremonies that the thistles might be plentiful.   But Matuku answered that it was not the season.

Rata then stood at the lip of the cavern and called on Matuku, and soon they heard the sound of his ascending. " Thou weariest the patience of Matuku," said he; " soon shalt thou see Matuku! " As he came near the opening they heard him pause, and then murmur another *karakia* :

> " Scent, scent,
> Odour, odour,
> My food is man."

The head of Matuku emerged; he perceived men, and slowly he came forth; he was half-way from the cavern when suddenly the noose was drawn tight.

" You cannot kill me! " said Matuku.

They attacked him, and lopped off an arm. " You cannot kill me," he cried.

He struggled; they lopped off another arm, but he persisted in his cry, " You cannot kill me," even though he lost a leg, and another leg; and when his neck was severed and his head fell so that he could cry no more, still his words were true; for suddenly the body changed to a bird, the bittern, called after him *matuku*; and his voice is still heard in the marshes as it then was in Pu-tawaro-nuku.

Rata then asked Tama' where the bones of his father were kept; and Tama' told him they were hung under the ridge-pole in the house of the *tohunga*, the wise men, of the Ponaturi. Rata' hastened to the place, reaching it at nightfall. Alone he stealthily approached a fire around which sat the *tohunga* beating human bones together while chanting their *karakia*. He listened. The *karakia* was a powerful one, enabling the user to destroy a war-host be it never so well weaponed and powerful. Rata learned the *karakia*, and he discovered, too, that the bones, which seemed to say " *Ta, ta, ta*," were the bones of his father; and, heartened by the words, while his wrath rose against the slayers, he dashed among them, striking right and left and uttering his war-cries. The *tohunga* did not know the number of their assailants, but, fearing the worst, they soon were slain.

Hastily Rata gathered up the bones and returned to his men, and they set out for their home.

In the morning the Ponaturi beheld with dismay their *tohunga* lying dead; and, finding that the bones of Wahie-roa were missing, they concluded that Rata had been there, and they prepared for revenge.

Rata destroys the Ponaturi

Watching from his *pa* on the day following, Rata beheld the coming fleet of the Ponaturi. Swiftly they approached, and rushing on the beach they came on with fury. What availed the palisades against such numbers? Many were beaten back, many slain, but more came on, and gradually the defenders were driven back into the *pa*, where fell many of the best warriors of Rata. The sea-rovers were like their own waves; they could not be driven back.

" Fight on, fight on," cried Rata, bethinking him of the *karakia*. His men fought, and he began his incantation. It was as if it gave strength to his men while it weakened the enemy; for soon the Ponaturi paused, they wavered, they turned. The men of Rata pressed on; the dead warriors sprang to life again; the Ponaturi fled. They sought their canoes, but not one escaped.

It may be noted that there is a superior version of the story of Rata which has been preserved in the original classic Maori. As is usual in superior versions, much of the marvellous disappears. The expedition undertaken by Rata there appears as a simple though adventurous voyage, probably from the region of Indonesia to a Melanesian country—possibly New Guinea, as a large river is mentioned, possibly Fiji. The date is conjectured to be about the middle of the eighth century, when the Northmen were penetrating the Arctic and Atlantic Oceans, shortly before their first attacks upon England.

Tu-whakararo is killed

The death of his father was avenged, and Rata had the big canoe drawn up on shore, and roofed over to protect it from the weather. He took as his wife Kani-o-wai, and she bore a son named Tu-whakararo, who, when he grew up, took Apa-kura as his wife. One day he went on a voyage to the Rae-roa people, where he saw a young woman, Hakiri-maurea, to whom his fancy turned, as hers to him, though she already had an accepted lover.

There were games of all kinds, and Tuwhaka' wrestled with the young men. After a time who should come forward but the rejected lover! And Tuwhaka' wrestled with him also, throwing him twice, so that he was obliged to retire defeated.

The victorious Tuwhaka' sat down to put on his cloak again, having removed it for the wrestling; and as he was putting his cloak over his head the rejected and defeated lover ran forward and threw a handful of dust in his eyes. Smarting with the pain, and blinded for the time, Tuwhaka' was unable to do anything, and his rival struck him with his weapon and slew him.

The people, instead of resenting the act, took the body of Tuwhaka', cut it up, cooked it, and feasted on it, bringing the bones under the roof of the house Te Uru-o-Manono.

The sister of Tuwhaka' had married Poporo-kewa, the chief of the Rae-roa; and when she heard of what had happened she wept. Tuwhaka' had come to see her, and through love of his sister he had met his death.

Whakatau-potiki destroys the House Te Uru-o-Manono

The youngest child of Tuwhaka' and Apa-kura was Whakatau-potiki. He had been adopted by a sea-ancestor, Rongo-taka-whiu, who taught him magic of all kinds, among others the art of walking under the waters of the sea; and there Whakatau' took delight in flying kites. People saw the kites from the shore, but the string disappeared in the sea, and they could not see the kite-flier, till one day Whakatau' ventured from the water. The people tried to catch him, but he eluded them, saying that he would be caught only by Apa-kura. One of them went and told Apa-kura, and she came to see the strange boy who could live under the water as well as on the land, and to her he revealed himself, continuing to live on the land thereafter.

Besides being skilled in magic, he grew to be a renowned warrior; and when he learned of the treacherous death of his father he determined to avenge it.

Canoes, and among them the famous canoe of Rata, were prepared to convey the warriors, each canoe receiving a special name; and while these were preparing Apa-kura and her women beat the fern-root that should form provision for the voyage. Apa-kura, who was famed as an adept in the *tangi*, sang the following to incite the warriors:

> " List, ye stars!   Hearken, O moon!
> My arms, and hands, and feet
> Shall wage a lasting war.
> Wail the dirge of Apa-kura
> To her elder kindred,
> And wake the sleeping heart
> To act, and slake revenge
> For death of him, Tu-whakararo.
> Drink ye, drink deep of bowls—
> Those bowls kept on high.
> In vain do I essay to climb
> The spider's web; my path
> Is less than nought beneath my tread. . . ."

The reference to the spider's web is a reference to the path of Tawhaki' to the upperworld; this *tangi*, too, strengthened the resolution of Whakatau'; and while girding on his war-belt he sang the famous war-song beginning:

> If Tangaroa should inquire,
> " Who is that young warrior
> So daringly girding on my war-belt? "
> I reply, " Nobody, nobody at all;
> Nothing; only me, Whakatau';
> A man of no rank; a man beneath notice;
> One despised; a poor young fellow;
> Eater of vassals' fragments! "
>   But concerning my war-belt—ha!
> My war-belt which was dreaded . . .

They embarked, and set out, the canoe of Whakatau' coming to their destination much in advance of the others.

They landed ; and reaching a place near the house Te Uru-o-Manono they captured a man named Hioi, and from him learned the details of the interior of the house ; the place where the sister of Tuwhaka' sat ; where Poporo-kewa sat ; and other things. Whakatau' then cut out the fellow's tongue, so that he could only mumble indistinctly, and told him to go and warn his aunt of his coming.

The man went, and Whakatau' followed soon after, and met his aunt, and consulted with her as to what they should do. They agreed on a plan ; she cut his hair close, and smeared his face with charcoal, so that he by no means looked the man he was. He then followed her into the house, and when he was observed, "A stranger! A stranger!" was the cry ; and the fires, dim before, were made up so that he might be seen.

They laughed when they saw what an uncouth-looking fellow he seemed to be, and turned again to Hioi, whom they had been interrogating, endeavouring to learn who had cut out his tongue.

Hioi indicated by his actions that he was a short person, with a large face, and great eyes.

"Was he like me?" said one. Hioi indicated dissent. "Or like me ?" said another, and another, Hioi repeating his gestures indicating a short person, with a large face, and great eyes.

Whakatau' had rubbed off much of the charcoal, and now he stood before Hioi and asked, "Was he like me?"

Hioi was growing impatient ; but, seeing Whakatau', his eyes flashed recognition, and he indicated that he was the man. Before the others had recovered from their surprise Whakatau' had extinguished the fires, seized the bones of Tuwhaka', and he and his aunt had escaped, closing the door of the house and setting it on fire. His men had come up, and they slew all who attempted to escape from the burning building.

In one version of the legend Tu-whakararo and Whakatau-potiki are brothers, not father and son, and this somewhat confuses the story.

THE TAWHAKI CYCLE

Variations in the Tawhaki Cycle

The various parts of this long cycle differ among the different peoples where they are found, often to a very great extent. The complete cycle has not been gathered from any one source. It is apparently most complete in New Zealand, where the most consecutive relation comes from the tribe occupying Stewart Island.

Much detail has been omitted in the above, but the varied detail is of value to the anthropologist; so, too, are the many names introduced; these are of the utmost value, for it is often by means of a name that a story gathered in one part of the Pacific is linked up with one gathered in another part. The name Muri-wai-o-ata, to which place Tuna' was going when Tawhaki met him on his way to the upperworld, is a name well known throughout the Pacific. In New Zealand it is Muri-wai-o-whata. Ata is possibly a proper name. Percy Smith was crossing a stream in Samoa when one of his companions mentioned the name Muri-wai'. "Do you know the name Muri-wai-o-ata?" he asked. "That is it," he was told; "you are crossing it now; that is Muri-wai-o-ata."

The names of the people who slew Hema—Paikea, Kewa, and Ihu-puku—are the Maori names of whales; but they are supposed primarily to be the names of savage and ill-favoured peoples with whom the Polynesian Maori came in contact during their wanderings and sojourn in the Pacific. The above are their names in the southern parts of New Zealand; in the northern parts they are known generally as the Ponaturi, a savage sea-folk that remained hidden by day, venturing out at dusk and by night. When it is said that their home was beneath the water, it may simply mean that it lay below the horizon, and a long sea-journey was needed to reach it.

The Fairy Building of the Canoe in Aitutaki

In one version of the well-known story of Rata he obtains from Ngahue the axe with which he fells the tree, and the

183

building of the canoe by the wood-spirits is told quite differently in Aitutaki. In this story Rata, whose home was in Kupolu, when setting out to fell his tree saw a white heron and a sea-snake fighting in the upper part of a fragrant pandanus-tree. They had been fighting all night; and the heron, seeing Rata pass by, called for help. The sea-snake, however, deceitfully said it was merely a trial of strength, and Rata went on, not regarding the renewed cry of the heron. As he walked he heard the bird say reproachfully, " Ah, your canoe will not be finished without my aid." He cut down the tree and returned home; but going next day to dub it out and shape it, he found the tree growing as before. He again felled it, observing as he went that the bird and the snake were still engaged in their struggle. The same thing happened again; the tree was erect when he returned on the third morning. He then remembered what the heron had said, and went to see if the bird was still alive. It was indeed living, but much exhausted; and the sea-snake, certain of victory, was preparing for a final attack when Rata chopped it in pieces with his axe, and saved the life of the heron. He went back to his work, and felled the tree for the third time.

The heron watched his labours through the day, and as soon as he disappeared in the evening the grateful bird called together all the birds of Kupolu, and with their beaks they hollowed out the canoe, and lashed on the side-pieces, the holes being bored with their long bills, and the sennit firmly.lashed by the stronger land-birds. It was almost dawn when the canoe was ready, and they then, completely surrounding it, carried it to the beach near the dwelling of Rata. As they bore it through the air they sang, each with a different note, the following song to Rata:

> " A pathway for the canoe! A pathway for the canoe!
> A path of sweet-scented flowers!
> The entire family of birds of Kupolu
> Honours thee above all mortals! *Oo!* "

Awakened by the song of the birds, unwonted in its volume, Rata arose, intending to return to his labour in the valley, when he caught sight of the beautifully finished canoe, lying on the sand ready to be launched. He guessed this to be the expression of the gratitude of the heron, the king of birds, and he named it *Taraipo* (*Built in a Night* or *Built in the Invisible World*). The canoe was launched, and Rata set out on his adventures, but these are quite different from any of those known to the Maori. There are, however, two or three striking points. He met various monsters of the deep, one of which was a whale; and the names of the enemies against whom Rata set out are, in the Maori, also names of whales. It was not Rata who overcame these monsters, but a man Nganaoa, who had begged to be allowed to accompany him, as an oracle had bidden him seek his parents Ta'iri-tokerau and Vaia-roa (Wahie-roa). On the whale being encountered, their peril was imminent, for one jaw of the enormous gaping mouth was beneath the canoe, the other above it. But Nganaoa, the slayer of monsters, inserted his stakes in the mouth so that the jaws were unable to close; he walked along and peered down the throat, and there in the stomach sat his long-lost father Ta'iri-tokerau and his mother Vaia-roa, who had been swallowed when fishing by this monster of the deep. They were busily engaged in plaiting sennit, and beheld with joy the coming of their son. Nganaoa determined to be avenged. He removed one of the stakes and broke it in two, and while his father held the lower stick he worked the other and so by friction obtained fire. Blowing the charred powder to a flame, he set fire to the fatty portion of the stomach. The whale made for the nearest land, Iti-te-marama, and Nganaoa and his parents walked out, joining Rata and his men, who had landed, drawing up their canoe.

Metamorphosis of a Name

Now the name of the father of Rata was Wahie-roa, and the name of his mother was Matoka-rau-tawhiri; the name of the mother of Nganaoa, Vaia-roa, is evidently the same as Wahie-roa; and the other names, mother in one and father in the other version, have much in common. Omitting the 'Ma' of the Maori name, 'toka-rau' is near 'tokerau' of the Aitutaki name; and the final part of the Maori name, 'tawhiri,' becomes the first part, 'Ta'iri,' of the Aitutaki name, since the region about this island, having a repugnance to the aspirate, drops it and the *w* with which it is combined in the sound *wh*. This is a striking metamorphosis, and shows that a name is of as much or even more importance than a story. In Grey's version of the story of Rata Tongarau-tawhiri is given as the name of one of his wives—most of these ancient heroes had several—and she is there the mother of Tu-whakararo. The sound *ng* of the North Island of New Zealand is often *k* in the South Island; and the name Tongarau-tawhiri is, allowing for inversion of parts and letter-changes, almost identical with the Aitutaki name Ta'iri-tokerau. This emphasizes the importance of preserving all names, however ridiculously long they may appear.

Rata in Samoa

The name of the fairyland Kupolu in which the Aitutaki Rata dwelt connects the story with Samoa. There Rata, who by the obtaining letter-change becomes Lata, is said to have come to Samoa from Fiji; he was the first to build large double canoes connected with a deck. He visited Upolu, one of the Samoan islands, and at Fangaloa (the Maori Whangaroa) built two large canoes, but died before the connecting deck had been completed. The name Tawhaki is Tafa'i in Samoan.

In another Samoan legend Rata, or Lata, has a different standing. There was, according to Samoan native records, a period of vigorous voyaging during five generations, or about a hundred and fifty years, between Te Alutanganuku, who made the first voyages, and Tangi'ia, who made the last. The first canoe spoken of was built on Savai'i, in a forest belonging to Rata, by Atonga and his two brothers, Olo-keu and Olo-i-nano. The two brothers, Olo-keu and Olo-i-nano, first started the building, being impelled to do so by the harsh treatment of Atonga. They went to a forest on Savai'i belonging to Rata, and without his permission cut down a tree for the purpose of making a canoe in which to seek a home in other lands. Having cut down the tree, they returned to the coast, intending to return next day to proceed with the work. Meantime Rata appeared, and resented the tree having been felled without his permission. He repeated a charm causing the branches, bark, chips, and leaves to fly again into their places and join together, so that the tree would stand again where it was. " Stand upright," said Rata; " I am Tutamaotamea "; on which the tree stood upright, and Rata returned to the coast.

The brothers returned in early morning, and found that their tree had disappeared; but they recognized it by the axes left at its butt, and cut it down again, dividing it ready for dragging it to the coast. Then they returned home.

On their way they encountered another marvel: an owl and a snake were engaged in combat. The owl, claiming to be the lord of the forest in disguise, said to them, " Friends, my brothers, come to my assistance, and put an end to this conflict." But the snake said, " Chiefs, proceed, and do not interfere in the quarrel between a snake and an owl"; on which the brothers prepared to go on, not caring to interfere. They paused, however, when the owl continued, " Behold, I am the lord of this forest in which you two cut down the tree; if you do not put an end to this conflict, never shall you paddle in your canoe," and, remembering how their felled tree had been set upright again, they turned back and killed the snake. Thereupon the owl said, " Go, you two; prepare your canoe, a *va'atele* [large canoe; Maori *wakatere*, swift canoe], with its outrigger, and seats, and set of paddles." In due time, when the canoe had been built, they prepared to drag it to the sea; but when they reached the ridge of the mountain they both died.

Atonga, finding that his brothers did not return, sought

them, and found them lying dead on the ridge, where he buried them, and took the canoe for himself. There is a mystery about this Atonga. He had something to do with the building of the canoe. He was a man of two sides, one side spirit, the other human. The human side worked as a servant, the spirit side built the canoe, finishing it in one night, from which it was first called *The Canoe built in a Night.*

The fame of the canoe reached Upolu, and the chief Te Alutanga-nuku longed to possess it. He sent his wife to Atonga, and she apparently wiled the canoe from him, for Atonga sent a message by the wife presenting the canoe to Te Alutanga-nuku, and directing him to prepare a house for its reception. " Summon all Upolu to come and build a house quickly," said he to the wife, " for the canoe shall be taken to him in the morning. Command that none of the people stand upright, but that all sit down and watch the canoe as it is taken, listening to the song of the birds bearing it."

The woman hastened to her husband with the message ; he summoned the people, and the canoe-house was built by daylight of the next day, when the song was heard of the birds approaching with their burden. Atonga had sent his commands to all the birds to carry the canoe, and instructed them what song they should sing in lifting it. " This," said he, " shall be your song when you take the canoe :

> " The thousands of Kupolu ;
> In the early morning assemble and behold !
> [Chorus] *Olo-keu e ; Olo-i-nano e !*
> *Olo-keu e ; Olo-i-nano e !* "

Atonga had changed the name of the canoe to *Manu-a-lele* (*Birds about to Fly*). It was landed and safely housed at Upolu, the chief changing its name to that of his wife *O-le-puta-o-le-peau* (*The Fullness of the Wave*), which was its third name. After this preparations were made for the first voyage of the canoe.

On the first voyage it visited all the lands on the south-

south-west and west side of the heaven, but did not go to the upper side of heaven, or toward Tahiti; and when the year was finished the chief gave the canoe to his son Te Alutanga-langi, who made the second voyage.

On the second voyage the name was again changed to *O-le-folau-loi-i-Fiti* (*The Voyage direct to Fiti*), but it did not go eastward. At the close of that year the chief gave the canoe to his son Kau-kulu.

On this third voyage the canoe visited Fiti and the lands Kau-kulu's father had visited. It also went to another land, called Tonga-leva, which was then known for the first time. After this Kau-kulu returned to Upolu, when he saw that the canoe was opening in the joints. He anchored it beneath the water and named it *Tuna-moe-vai* (*Eel sleeping in the Water*). When a season had passed he gave the canoe to his son Malu, who again changed its name to *Numia-au* (*Confusion of Currents*).

On the fourth voyage, under Malu, the canoe sailed to the upper side of the heavens, east or north-east, whither Malu went with his father Kau-kulu (? Kahu-kura). They discovered a small island named Toku-tea, where Malu left his father. After further sailing he returned to Samoa. On his return to Savai'i Malu married a woman named Ruamano, by whom he had two girls. One of these married a man named Tutapu, and had a son, who was adopted by Malu as he had no son, and by him named Te Uenga. The boy fell sick; but two *aitu* came, who were Tangaloa and Tongaiti, and looked at the boy. Tangaloa said, " Alas, poor boy! " and, addressing his companion, said, " What do you say—suppose we let the boy live? If he lives he will be our rejoicing." On this they called the boy Tangi'ia, which means " Compassionated "—literally " Cried over "—because of the sympathy of the two spirits for the boy when near death. This Tangi'ia became the famous voyager. The canoe made further voyages, but enough of the story has been told to show the similarity, and the difference, between it and the other Rata stories.

The first name given to the canoe has the same meaning

as the name *Taraipo* in the Aitutaki story, and the giving
of several names agrees with the Maori version, though the
names are different. As the names of the Samoan canoe
were changed, so people often changed their own names, and
it is possible that the same person or object may often be
met, in these old stories, under different names.

The four names Hema, Tawhaki, Wahie-roa, and Rata
are well known to the Maori and Rarotonga people, also to
the people of Hawaii. They occur in the genealogies of
all, and at such definite periods, agreeing closely in the
genealogies, that the date of Tawhaki has been fixed by
Percy Smith as in the neighbourhood of A.D. 700. While
the stories all have much of the marvellous, they have not
more of that quality than similar stories of European
peoples of the same culture-level. The Greeks and Trojans
may seem on a higher plane, but that is only because they
are somewhat more akin to ourselves, and lived in natural
environment more similar to our own; moreover, the
Polynesians were still in the Stone Age.

Among most peoples the fabulous creeps into the stories
connected with ancestors remote in time, so that the actors
almost cease to be regarded as human beings, being rather
regarded as demigods.

In both Maori and Rarotongan histories Hema (Ema in
Rarotongan) had two sons, Tawhaki (Ta'aki) and Karihi
(Kari'i); and while as a rule the Maori histories make
Tawhaki the elder, the Rarotongan histories give that
honour to Karihi, one probable reason being that Tawhaki
is in the direct line of the Maori genealogy, Karihi in the
direct line of the Rarotongan. Karihi is the elder in the
southern part of New Zealand.

In Hawaiian Ai-kanaka (Maori Kai-tangata) is also
known, Hema, Kaha'i (Tawhaki), Wahie-loa (Wahie-roa),
and Laka (Rata) following; but while their actual homes
are localized in the islands, it is thought that the names
were inserted in the genealogies after the arrival of the
Southern Polynesians at Hawaii in the twelfth and thirteenth
centuries.

THE TAWHAKI CYCLE

When thinking of these demigods or heroes as historical personages, however, it is also well to remember how many of them appear, from their names, to be the personification of sky-powers. Their origin was Rehua, signifying a star, or planet, as well as a deity, Kai-tangata following after several sky-powers. The ruddy glow sometimes seen in the sky was said to be his blood. Whai-tiri was the thunder, Tawhaki was a lightning deity, Wahie-roa a comet.

CHAPTER VII: MAUI' (MAUI-TIKITIKI-A-TARANGA)

MAUI' the demigod was the sixth generation in descent from Niwa-reka and Mata-ora. His father was Makea-tutara, his mother Taranga, and there were born four sons and a daughter before Maui' appeared. He was born prematurely as Taranga one day walked by the seashore; and she rolled up the unformed being in a wisp of her hair and cast it into the sea, lest it should become a malignant spirit through never having associated with kindly human kindred.

The sea-deities took the immature child, and hiding it among the long sea-tangles they nourished and preserved it; but storms tearing away the kelp, it was cast ashore, the growing child lying as it were swathed in a jellyfish, about which flies and other devouring creatures swarmed. Seeing this, a sea-ancestor, Tama-nui-ki-te-rangi, hastened to see what the thing was about which so many creatures were gathered. He found a man-child, and, taking him home, wakened him to life.

Maui' dwelt with his ancestor, with Tama'rangi, who related tales, and sang songs, whereby he acquainted the child with the lore of his ancestors; he also described to him the dances and games that went on in the meeting-house not far distant. The boy listened, first with wonder, then with curiosity; and he determined to go and see for himself the things of which he had heard.

Maui' makes himself Known

One night, as they were dancing and making merry, the boy Maui' crept in, and seating himself behind one of his brothers watched the dancing and the games. The brothers were to join in the dancing, and stood before their mother. "One, Maui-taha," said she; "two, Maui-roto; three, Maui-pae; four, Maui-waho"; and then, seeing another, she cried, "E! and where does this fifth come from?"

"I belong to you too," said Maui'. "Oh, no," she

said; "there should only be four; this is the first time I have seen you."

But Maui' insisted that she had five sons, not only four, arguing with her in the very ranks of the dancers, so that at last she became indignant, and cried, "Come; be off now; out of the house; you are no child of mine; you must belong to some one else."

Maui' was not at all abashed, but said, "Very well, then, I had better be off; for, if you say so, I suppose I must be the child of some one else; but indeed I did think I was your child when I said so, for I was born prematurely by the seaside," and he went on to relate all that had happened.

His mother's indignation disappeared; she bent, and pressed her nose to his in the greeting *hongi*, murmuring, "Truly you are my own child, Maui-potiki [Maui the Last-born], Maui-tikitiki-a-Taranga [Maui of the Topknot of Taranga]."

Some of the younger brothers resented the preference shown for the lately come brother, and wished to turn him off; but the others counselled more friendly action, advising that he be allowed to remain; it was better to make a friend than an enemy, better to live in peace than at war. "When on friendly terms," said the proverb, "settle disputes in a friendly way; when at war, redress injuries with violence."

He was therefore accepted by the others, joined in the games, and proved expert in all kinds of sports and exercises, also in all manner of tricks and mischievous performances.

Maui' follows his Mother to the Netherworld

When they retired for the night Taranga called him to sleep at her side, and for the first time he slept with his mother. Awaking in the morning, he found she had disappeared. "She has no doubt gone to prepare food," he thought; but the sun mounted high, and she did not return, so he asked his brothers where she was.

"How should we know?" they answered.

Maui' looked on them in surprise. "Has she left us?" he asked.

" She leaves us every morning before the light appears,"
they told him.

" And have you never discovered to what place it is that
she goes? "

" Why should it trouble us if it please her? "

" And her husband, our father : where is he? "

" We know as little as you do ; what does it matter? "

Maui' said no more, but wondered. Had his elder
brothers no desire to know? Here was a secret—and they
did not seem to care to find it out !

He quickly learned that it was as they said ; their mother
came at nightfall, but she was always gone again before
the dawn ; and the father did not come at all. Maui'
could learn nothing from his brothers, and his questioning
only irritated them, so he determined to discover everything
for himself.

Waiting one night until all were soundly asleep, he arose
quietly and closed all chinks through which light might
enter the *whare* (hut or house) where they slept ; and, con-
cealing his mother's clothing, he lay again beside her,
waiting impatiently for the dawn.

The night drawing to a close, but no light appearing,
Taranga stirred in her sleep, but opening her eyes and
finding it still dark, she muttered, " A long night ; a long
night." Soon the sounds of day came faintly ; Taranga
started ; and, sitting up, she listened. " Surely it is day,"
she said ; and hastening to the window she drew it aside,
admitting a flood of light.

" Alas ! Alas ! It is full day," she cried softly, looking
for her clothing, but in vain.

" Some one has been playing tricks on me," said she, but
never suspecting Maui', who still lay apparently fast asleep.
She drew aside the door and hastened out, repeating a
karakia to cause her body to appear covered, while Maui'
quickly arose and peered after her, to see what became of
her.

She had not gone far when to his surprise he saw her lift
a clump of rushes and disappear into the ground, dropping

the clump back into place above her.   Maui' followed, and cautiously lifted the rushes to see what lay below.   He saw an opening leading directly down to the netherworld, and far below he saw the trees moving and the sun shining.

He replaced the rushes, returned to the *whare*, and woke up his brothers, calling out, " Wake up ; wake up ; it is broad day, and our mother has again left us."

Maui' astonishes his Brothers

They awoke, and their surprise was great—not to find that their mother had left them, but to find how far the day was advanced.

Again Maui' said to them, " Do you not know the place where our mother goes every morning, or where our father dwells ? "

" How should we know ? " they cried, exasperated to hear him beginning all over again.   " We the elder Maui' have never discovered that place, and you must not suppose that it will be revealed to you.   Why do you trouble about the matter ?   Cannot you be content to live quietly with us ?   Why should we trouble to find our parents ? "   And Maui' laughed to himself as they talked on : " Do they supply us with food now that we have grown to manhood ? Or clothe us ?   No such thing ; we must do this for ourselves.   Without a doubt Rangi' above is our father ; he sends the soft mists and the rains to nourish the plants, and the gentle breeze to scatter the rains here and there.   He causes our food to grow in plenty—why need we trouble about our parents ? "

" It may be as you say," said Maui' ; " but such speech were less unkind if made by me ; for if instead of having been reared in the foam of the sea I had been privileged, like you, to be nourished at the breast of our mother I should have been fired with desire to find my parents.   As for the food produced by Rangi' and Papa', time was when you were unable to partake of it ; and have you no desire to seek the abode of your mother, that place where you lay on her breast and received nourishment ?   O my brothers,

I did not drink of life at her breast, nor did I in my childhood receive her fondling; yet because she is my mother I wish to see the place where she and my father dwell."

The elder brothers were astonished at his skill in oratory, even more than they had been at his skill in magic. But Maui' could deceive in words as well as in action, and again he laughed to himself to think how his brothers, unimpressed by his art in assuming the forms of various birds, were filled with admiration at his apparent wisdom.

Maui' displays Magic

Maui' now assumed another form—that of the wood-pigeon. "Now indeed you look well," said the brothers, gazing in wonder; "much more beautiful than in any other of the forms assumed by you." It was the belt of his mother, and her apron, that now made him appear so beautiful; for the sheeny feathers on his throat and breast were the apron of burnished hair from the tail of a dog, the white parts of his breast were the belt, and the black feathers at his throat were the fastenings of the belt.

"Wise indeed and skilled in magic is this younger brother of ours," said the elders. The youngest Maui' assented. "Magic and wisdom are needed to accomplish these things," said he; "and now I mean to depart, journeying to distant places, it may be at hazard of my life."

"No need for any such thing," said the brothers, "were you content to live quietly with us. Do you meditate going to war? Then indeed there were danger or death; but what peril lies in the search for those you love?"

"Danger may not be seen until found, and death lurks in unsuspected places; but soon shall you hear of my remarkable deeds; and if I find our parents we shall all dwell peaceably together."

Maui' meets his Father

Maui' left them; and raising unobserved the clump of rushes he disappeared, quickly descending as a wood-pigeon to the sunny world below. He found people

196

reclining in the shade of a clump of *manapau*-trees; among them Taranga his mother, and near her a man, who he soon discovered was her husband Makea-tutara. He sat above them, and picking a berry he dropped it so that it struck the forehead of his father. Makea-tutara paid no attention, supposing it merely to have fallen from the tree; but on another striking him he glanced upward and saw the bird. His companions also saw it, and tried to dislodge it with stones; but with his magic Maui' warded off the missiles, and not until his father threw did he allow himself to be struck; then he fell, as if wounded, to the ground; but before they could seize him, lo! the feathers falling away, the bird was a man. Then they were filled with fear; for his eyes were red as those of Tu' the god of war, and were fixed flaming upon them.

"Such was the youth," declared Taranga, "who up above asserted himself to be a brother of my sons and a son of their mother"; and she related all that had taken place. Turning to him she said, "Whence do you come? From the west? Or from the north?" "No," answered the man. "Then from the east?" "No." "Then from the south?" "No." "Were you wafted hither by the wind blowing on my skin? "Yes," said Maui'.

"Ah," she cried; "this is indeed my son, the same of whom I have but now told you; this is Maui-tikitiki-a-Taranga, reared by the company of winds and breezes that wander about the heavens. Welcome, my son! For thou shalt cross the sacred threshold of Hine-nui-te-po, and through thee shall she die who now in darkness holds all men in awe and fear of her."

His father took him to the running stream, purified and named him; but in reciting the *karakia*, he omitted a name, and through this omission, though none but he himself remarked it, the power of the *karakia* was nullified, and the anger of the gods must fall. But Maui' had no fears, and laughing at the anxiety of his parents off he went in search of further adventures.

He returned to his brothers, and told them of his

success; but unless they too were able, like him, to assume the forms of birds they would be unable to reach the land where their mother and father dwelt. They seemed to have no desire to emulate Maui' in that, but they gladly learned from him the arts of cultivation. He taught them the best method of using the *ko*, or Maori digging implement, taught them the *karakia* to be chanted to ensure plenteous crops, taught them the best season of the year for planting, so that the crops of his brothers flourished.

Maui' destroys the Crops of their Neighbour Maru'

Now the crops of Maru-i-te-whare-aitu flourished even more, as if he too had received benefit from the *karakia* of the Maui' brothers, or as if he had even more potent *karakia*—at which thought Maui' was vexed. He therefore by magic caused frosts to blacken and wither the tops of the crops of Maru', so that the leaves and young shoots were destroyed. Maru' by diligence saved a portion; and perceiving it to be the work of *makutu*, of magic, he too chanted *karakia*; so that Maui', visiting his young crops in the morning, found them overrun and almost devoured by innumerable caterpillars that seemed to have been showered down in the night. He at once recognized this as the work of Maru', and in anger he visited him, and slew him as he was ascending the hill to his temple to make offerings to his gods. Thereafter he carried off his daughter.

Maui' secures the Jawbone of his Ancestress

He again descended to the home of his parents. Here he saw that every day food was carried out of the village, but saw no person for whom it might be intended. He therefore asked the carriers for whom they carried the food. And they told him, " For an ancestress of yours; for Muri-ranga-whenua." " Where is she? " " Yonder," they answered him. " Your labours may cease," said he; " I myself will henceforth take the food to her." This he said as he wished to discover who it was who dwelt thus apart, away from the *kainga* (village).

He found an old woman ; but instead of giving her the food he left it at a distance. This he did for several days, and the ancient one became eager for food. One day when he took the food as usual her sharpened senses detected the odour of a man ; and, being blind, she arose, sniffing this way and that to discover him. The odour was lost until she turned to the west ; then it was borne to her, and she asked, " Are you from the wind that touches my skin ? " Maui' modestly coughed assent, and she at once knew it was her grandson. " Are you Maui' ? " she asked. " Yes," said he. " Why do you practise your tricks on me ? " " That your jawbone might be given to me," he answered. " Take it," said Muri' ; and thereupon she gave him what he desired, and with this treasure he returned to his brothers.

Maui' snares the Sun

For some time it had seemed to him that the sun hastened too quickly across the sky, so that man's labour was scarcely begun ere night was upon him. " Let us bind 'Ra," said he to his brothers, " so that he may not go so swiftly over the heavens, and man may have a longer day for cultivating and preparing food."

" Man cannot approach that son of Rangi'," said they, " because of his fierce heat." " You have seen many acts successfully performed by me," said Maui'. " I can do even that which I propose, and greater things than this will I do hereafter."

The Maui-wareware, so called from their foolishness, consented—consent was easier than argument—and they commenced to plait ropes, while deeming it all a folly. They took the ropes and journeyed till they reached Rua-o-te-ra, the cave from which the sun emerges. Here they made snares, and set them so that 'Ra might be caught on emerging in the morning.

Maui' instructed his brothers how to act, bidding them not to startle the sun till he was well within the noose. " Indeed," said he, " do not haul on the lines until I give the word." They lay waiting; soon the light appeared, and suddenly 'Ra emerged. His head, his shoulders passed the noose, Maui' gave the word, and the brothers hauled on the ropes. 'Ra closed his limbs with a twitch; Maui' rushed in to attack him, when—snap!—the noose was burnt asunder, and away leapt 'Ra into the sky, swiftly as ever, Maui' gazing after him in anger and exasperation.

"As we said, he is too hot," said the elder brothers; and as Maui-potiki stood silent one or other of the brothers offered some disparaging remark.

"Hu!" at length exclaimed Maui'; "not to have thought of that!" "Of what?" asked the brothers. "The dryness of the ropes," said Maui'; "had they been twice the thickness they could not have held him." "Our word from the first," cried the others. "But ropes of green flax will make a difference," said Maui'.

Therewith they twisted ropes of green flax, and it was at this snaring that the brothers learned the art of making ropes of various kinds—flat, round, square, ropes of three strands, of five strands—in fact, all manner of ropes.

Again the noose was set, again the sun entered it, expecting to leap upward as before; but no, the ropes held him prisoned close to the ground, and Maui' assailed him, beating him with the jawbone of Muri-ranga-whenua. "O man," cried 'Ra, "what is it you do?" And he continued, "Would you cause the death of Tama-nui-te-ra?" And thus for the first time his full name was made known to man. Still Maui' beat him, until he promised to move more slowly along the heavenly path, so that man might have a longer day for labour. So the sun departed, and ever since then he has moved more slowly.

Maui' was thirsty through his labour, and called to a bird, the *tieke* (saddle-back), to bring him water; but the bird took no notice, and Maui' seized it and flung it from him. Now where he touched its back the feathers were all singed with the heat of his hand, and to this day the bird bears the mark of the displeasure of Maui'. He called a *hihi* (stitch-bird); but it disregarded his call, and Maui'

cast it into the flames; and ever since this bird has been
timid, and its breast has borne a yellow hue as of fire. A
toutouwai (robin) next disregarded his wishes, so he set a
white mark at the root of its bill. A tuneful *kokako* (Maori
crow) flew by, and hearing Maui' call for water it brought
it in its ears. As a reward Maui' pulled its legs, so that
they were long, as they remain to this day.

Maui' goes a-fishing

That adventure ended, the brothers returned to their
home. They went a-fishing, but Maui' always caught
many more fish than his brothers—their hooks were without
barbs; nor were they successful until they learned how to
put barbs on the hooks. So, too, with spears for spearing
birds and fish. They speared them, but the prey slipped
off till Maui' taught them how to barb them.

Maui' was one day full of energy, on another day idle;
and on an idle day his wives and children reproached him
for not bringing fish like his brothers, leaving them without
food while others had plenty.

"Now, O mothers and children," he was heard to
mutter, "many great deeds have I accomplished; and
shall the procuring of food prove too arduous? You cannot
imagine the abundance upon which the sun before long
shall shine."

On his offering to accompany his brothers they refused
to give him a place in their canoe. "No, no," said they;
"you may play more of your tricks," and away they went
without him. Early on the following morning, however,
he made himself small and hid in the bilge of the canoe,
and the brothers launched their canoe and paddled to sea,
congratulating themselves that they were free of him for
yet another day. But presently he arose, assumed his own
form, and laughing was among them. "Why, here's this
fellow after all!" said they in disgust. "We had better
paddle to land again, lest he cause trouble."

But Maui' with his magic caused the land to recede.
"Better let me remain," said he. "I will bail out the water

while you go on with your fishing." To this they at length agreed, and were about to cast their lines when Maui' desired them to paddle farther out. They did so, but on their preparing to start fishing he again desired them to paddle farther, and again they did as he desired.

They fished, and soon the canoe was laden. They prepared to return, when Maui' asked that he might cast a line. "You have no hook," said they, "and shall have none of ours." "I have my own hook," said he, producing the jawbone of Muri'. They refused to give him bait; so taking a tangled hank of flax he struck his nose, saturated the flax with the flowing blood, and fixing this on his hook cast it into the sea, murmuring a *karakia* commencing, "Blow gently, Whakarua, blow gently, Mawake," the name of the *karakia* being Hirihiri-mo-te-hutinga-o-te-ao.

The hook sank, and presently the line, whose name was Tiritiri-ki-matangi, grew taut, and Maui' commenced to haul, chanting yet another *karakia*:

> "Why, O Tonga-nui,
> Art thou sulkily biting below there?
> On thee has come the *mana*
> Of 'Ranga-whenua,
> To bind thee together.
> The foam and the noise
> Gathering into small space
> Draw to the surface.
> Shout my triumph
> Over the grandson
> Of Tangaroa-meha."

Slowly he hauled the huge fish to the surface; and when it emerged from the waters it was seen that the hook had caught in the gable of the house of Tonga-nui, the grandson of Tangaroa. There were fires burning and people walking about on the back of the fish.

"My fish is called the fish of what?" cried Maui', but the terrified brothers could not answer; and again Maui' cried, "My fish is called the fish of what?" Still they were mute. "Its name is Hahau-whenua," said he; "that is,

MAUI' HAULS UP THE LAND
(See page 202)

THE MAORI MAKING FIRE

From a picture by G. Lindauer.

Reproduced by permission of the Committee of the Auckland Public Library, Art Gallery, and Old Colonists' Museum

(See page 206)

the Searching for Land." But his brothers cried "*Aue!*
Alas! Our canoe is grounded," and so it was, though so
soon before it had been rocking in mid-ocean.

Maui' arose and returned, that he might make offerings
to Tangaroa for thus drawing up one of his children, and
secure a *tohunga* (priest) to free them from the *tapu* brought
upon them by this deed. "Do not you eat food or touch
the fish until I return from performing the necessary rites
and ceremonies," said he to the Maui-wareware, and with
these words he left them.

No sooner was he gone, however, than out stepped the
elder brothers; and, having eaten food, they thoughtlessly
began cutting and crimping the fish. Then it turned its
head this way and that; it lashed the seas with its tail and
fins; it struggled, and its back was thrown into ridges and
wrinkles. "Well done, Tangaroa!" cried the brothers.
"As briskly the fish skips about on dry land as if it were
still in the sea."

That is the reason why this land, Te Ika-a-Maui' (the
Fish of Maui') is covered with valleys and mountain-
chains, ridges and deep ravines: had the brothers obeyed
the words of Maui' it would have remained perfectly flat.
The first part of the fish to emerge was that where stands
the mountain Hiku-rangi, and it was upon its side that the
canoe grounded; indeed, the canoe, the sail, and the broken
bailer may still be seen there. The part now called
Rongorongo was the upper jaw of the fish, Rimu-rapa its
lower jaw; Whanga-nui-a-Tara (Great Bay of Tara—
Wellington Harbour) was its salt-water eye, Wai-rarapa its
fresh-water eye; Turaki-rae was its head; Taupo and
Tonga-riro its belly; Te Reinga its tail. Upon the eastern
side, forming the point Matau-a-Maui', lies the fish-hook
with which it was hauled from the deep.

Maui' was incensed with his brothers for thus destroying
the flatness of the land, but soon forgot it in meditating
further adventures, for which he again descended to the
home of his parents.

Maui' secures Fire

He had heard of another old ancestress, Mahuika, who was the guardian of fire. " Why," thought Maui', " should we be compelled to guard our fires so carefully lest they be extinguished, and she only have the means for lighting them again?" Thus Maui' justified, at least to himself, his every action, and hence it was that he received many names, each one given on account of some distinguishing characteristic. Such names were Maui-tinihanga (Maui of Many Devices), Maui-nukarau (Maui the Deceitful), Maui-wharekino (Maui of the Evil House), Maui-i-toa (Maui the Valiant), Maui-i-atamai (Maui the Kind-hearted).

No excuse presenting itself to enable him to pay a visit to Mahuika, Maui' determined to invent one. Early one morning he arose ; and after secretly extinguishing all the fires in the village he called for food, pretending anger at the delay of the slaves in preparing it, though they declared that there was no vestige of fire in the whole village.

Taranga, hearing the protestations and chattering of the astonished slaves, and the angry abuse of Maui', inquired the reason ; and, learning the cause, she ordered the neglectful slaves to fetch a fresh supply from Mahuika. But they refused, declaring that she devoured any who approached her ; nor would any one of them obey the order of Taranga.

" What talk is this ? " said Maui'. " Where is the peril in requesting an old ancestress to give some fire ? " " Ha ! " they cried in disgust ; " she devours all who approach her, even as her fire devours the dry brushwood." " I will brave her fieriness and defy her fierceness," said Maui' ; " do but show me the way to her abode." " Be sure you play no tricks on her," said his mother, " or you may bring destruction on yourself and all of us." " It is my desire to bring the fire needed by you," said her son dutifully. " We have heard of your doings," continued his mother ; " your cunning too has been revealed to us, and we know that you are favoured above other men ; but Mahuika will surely take vengeance if you attempt to deceive her."

Maui' proceeded along the way pointed out to him, and soon came to the place where the aged woman sat in the sun. For some time he stood silently regarding her; and at last said, " O old woman, where do you keep your fire? I have come to beg some of you."

She arose, saying, " *Aue!* Alas! Who can this mortal be? " " It is I," said Maui'. " Whence do you come? " said she. " I belong to this place." " Not so," she answered; " your appearance is not like that of the people of these parts. Do you come from the north-east? " " No." " From the south-east? " " No." " From the south? " " No." " From the west? " " No." " Do you come, then, from the direction of the wind that blows upon me? " And he answered, " I do." " Oh, then," she cried, " you are my grandchild. What do you want of me? " " I am come to beg fire of you." " Welcome; welcome; here is fire for you." To his surprise she pulled the nail from one of her fingers, and it burned with the fire that flowed after it. This she gave to Maui', and he departed with it, wondering.

" Does, then, fire lodge in her every finger? " thought our hero, attempting to blow out the fire he had obtained; but still it burned, and was not quenched until he threw it into the water. Back he went, and told the old woman it had gone out. She gave him a second fingernail. This too was quenched, and she gave him a third, and so on until the tenth. " The aged one seems full of fire indeed," thought he; " but where will she now obtain it? " And again he returned, complaining again of the fire going out. At once she gave him a nail from one of her toes. One must suppose that her confidence in Maui' was as unbounded as his impudence, for again and again he returned, till she had but one nail left.

" This fellow is surely playing tricks on me," she thought when he came for the last one. " There! You have it all now," she cried as she pulled it out and dashed it on the ground, which at once took fire and burned like the dry hills in the heat of summer. Maui' retreated before the flames;

at first slowly, but as they augmented with more speed, till soon he was flying in hot haste with the flames at his back.

Behind him he heard the ancient one laughing, but the flames gave him no pause, and it seemed as if they would envelop him. He was angry with pain and mortification; by his magic he changed himself into a hawk, and flew high into the air; but the flames leaped higher, and burned his feathers, and the feathers of the hawk are to this day brown as with fire. In desperation he changed himself into a fish and plunged headlong into the sea. No better! For the sea was almost boiling with the heat; and Maui' leaped upward to regain the land, and brought with him the island Whakaari,[1] which smoulders with fires till this day.

He called aloud to his ancestors; he called to Ua, the rain-god, and to Nganga, the god of sleet, to come and extinguish the fires; they came, but the fires raged on. He called to Apu-hau, to Apu-matangi, the storm-gods; to Whatu, the god of hail-storms; and not until their deluges mixed with those of the others were the raging fires lessened. Soon they were quenched, and the waters rose in floods. But now it was Maui' who laughed; for he saw Mahuika in the waters, which played about her shoulders as the fires had played about his own. To save the remnant of her fire she threw it into the *totara*, but it would not burn; into the *matai* (black pine), but it would not burn; into the *mahoe* (white-wood), where it burned but little; into the *kaikomako* (Maori-fire), where it burned well; and fire was saved from destruction.

Maui' returned to the *kainga*, but met with dark looks and angry words. " A fine thing is this you have done! " cried his parents. " You first cause us to be almost devoured in flames, then drowned in floods; and now fire is quenched and altogether lost to us! How shall we now build fires to warm us or cook our food? Evil enough it was to be beholden to Mahuika; but is it better now? Do not think that because you yourself have escaped

---

[1] Whakaari is White Island, Bay of Plenty.

destruction it will always be so. In spite of all your magic and your *mana* evil will befall you."

" Is this a thing to daunt me? " said Maui'. " And shall I cease doing as I please because of this adventure? Neither flames nor floods shall prevent me ; and as for fire, Mahuika gave you a little, it is true ; but of what do you complain when it is now in your midst to take as you may desire? "

" We have no fire, as you well know," they answered.

Maui' was silent ; but from a *kaikomako* he broke dry branches, and from them he fashioned fire-sticks. While at his request a man held one stick firmly on the ground with his foot, Maui' rubbed the second, sharpened to a point, briskly to and fro on the one so held. First it heated, and formed a little ball of black powder ; then the powder smoked ; then it glowed. Maui' took dry moss ; wrapped the powder in it ; waved it in the air ; when lo ! a flame ! The people did likewise. Then indeed blame and abuse turned to praise, and anger to admiration. This was truly a hero, though disaster seemed the firstfruits of his actions, and though he himself was of unprepossessing appearance.

Maui' exchanges Faces with Rohe

Passing by a quiet pool, Maui' saw his own features reflected therein ; and coming on his beautiful wife Rohe, he thought by his magic to exchange faces. She indignantly refused when he proposed it, but he gained his object by enchantment while she lay asleep. Then she refused to live any longer in this world, and fled to the netherworlds, to the fifth, Uranga-o-te-ra, where she became a goddess ruling over the worlds Uranga-o-te-ra, Hiku-toia, and Pou-ture. She was said to beat the spirits of mortals who had journeyed thither after leaving the world of life.

The name Rohe is probably the one that occurs in a long *karakia* recited by Tawhaki and Maru when preparing for battle against Tama-i-waho :

Give these . . .
For me to cook them
In my oven.
The oven of whom?
The oven of Rohe-ahua-te-rangi.

Maui' and Tuna-roa

Maui' had another beautiful wife, named Rau-kura.
One day she related to him how, while she was dipping
water from the stream, Tuna-roa, a water-monster, half eel
and half man, had appeared. He struck her into the water
and with his tail proceeded to assault her. No need to
urge Maui' to action; he was ever eager for further
adventure. Tuna', who was a son of Manga-wai-roa, lived
in a water-hole called Muri-wai-o-ata. When Maui' came
to the stream he saw Tuna-roa on the opposite bank,
coming toward him. He took two skids, called Rongo-
mua and Rongo-roto, and laid them down for Tuna-roa
to cross over; and as he came along Maui' struck him with
his axe Ma-toritori, and killed him. He took the head
and threw it into the sea, where it became conger and salt-
water eels; the tail end of the body he threw into the stream,
where it became fresh-water eels, the sinews of the tail
becoming *aka* vines. Some of the blood fell on the *kakariki*
(parakeet), some on the *pukeko* (swamp hen), and it caused
the red colour seen on those birds to this day; some fell on
the *toatoa* (celery-topped pine), the *rimu* (red pine), *matai*
(black pine), and *tawai*, so that the timber of these trees is
still reddish in colour. The tail itself became the *kareao*
(supplejack vine), whose leaves are still in appearance
greasy with the fat of the monster. In one version the
wife was named Hine-a-te-repo, a sister of Ira-waru, and
it must be noted that nearly all the stories have very many
variants, which cannot here be even referred to.

After this Maui' made *hinaki* (eel-pots) for catching the
eels in the rivers. His brothers too made *hinaki*, but did
not know of the inner trap contrived by Maui', so that while
his eels were caught theirs escaped. This Tuna-roa was
the same that Tawhaki had encountered on his climbing

to the upperworlds. The skids vary in number in the different versions—two, nine, ten. The number is nine in one version which seems to connect Tuna-roa with Ira, the eel-god of India. In this version, as the eel crossed each skid Maui' repeated the charm:

> " Slay Tuna' on the first skid.
> 'Tis Ira, ah ! 'Tis Ira, ah ! 'Tis Ira of the waters."

Maui' changes Ira-waru into a Dog

Because his brothers, never knowing where his pranks might lead them, would not suffer him to accompany them on their fishing excursions, he proposed one day to accompany Ira-waru, the husband of his sister Hina-uri. Ira-waru consented, and they set out. But this day Maui' was not able to hook a fish ; his brother-in-law hauled them in one after another, and Maui' wondered how he was able to do this when he himself had never a bite. The day wore on, and Ira-waru, with plenty of fish, proposed that they should return. Maui' refused. " But the sun has already tilted over," said Ira-waru ; " it is past noon." Maui' fished on. " Besides," said Ira-waru after a pause, " you cannot catch a fish." But Maui' fished on. Again he wondered why his brother-in-law had all the luck ; and just as he thought this Ira-waru had another bite, and up he hauled his line ; but it had got entangled with that of Maui', and Maui', thinking he had a fish at his line at last, pulled it up quite delighted. When they had hauled up a good deal, however, there were the two pulling in opposite directions, one to the bow, the other to the stern.

Maui', provoked no less at the good luck of Ira-waru than at his own bad luck, called out quite angrily, " Come ; let go my line ; the fish is on my hook." But Ira-waru answered, " No, it is not ; it is on mine " ; and he said so confidently, which angered Maui' the more. " Come ; let go," he cried ; " I tell you it is on mine."

Ira-waru said nothing, but slackened his line ; Maui' hauled in the fish, when he saw that his brother-in-law was

209

right. " What did I say? " said Ira-waru exultingly. " Come now; let go my line."

" Cannot you wait until I take off the fish? " asked Maui' impatiently.

He removed the fish; then, " Why, my bait is all gone! " said he, looking at his unbaited hook. Ira-waru laughed. Maui' looked about for bait, but there was no bait to be seen. " What has become of the bait? " he cried. And after a pause Ira-waru said, " I ate it."

" Ate it? Ate the bait? " cried Maui'. " *Ae*, ate the bait," Ira-waru answered, in the high-pitched voice of his angry kinsman. " Am I a lover that I need no food? Can I live on air like a *moa*? "

" You are a greedy dog," said Maui', and they paddled ashore. Even Maui' would not desecrate the fishing-ground by cutting up the newly caught fish for bait.

Reaching the shore, " Do you get under the outrigger while I shove," said Maui'. Ira-waru did so, but his kinsman jumped with all his weight on the outrigger, crushing him beneath it.

" *Aue!* " cried Ira-waru. " Alas! My back is broken."

" This will teach the greedy dog a lesson—for a dog you shall be, " said Maui', and he chanted a *karakia* over his prostrate brother-in-law, who little by little changed his human form for that of a dog, his speech going till all he could say was " *Ao! Ao!* "

Maui' returning alone to the village, Hina-uri asked him where her husband was.

" Oh, he is down by the canoe sorting fish," answered Maui'.

She went, but could not see her husband, and came back, telling Maui' he was nowhere to be seen.

" He is there," persisted Maui'; " but if you cannot see him, just call ' *Moi! Moi!* ' when he will come to you."

She went; and, not seeing him, she called as Maui' had told her; and on the cry " *Moi! Moi!* " the dog came frisking about her, answering " *Ao! Ao!* " She recognized her husband transformed; and again going to the village she asked her brother why her husband had been treated so. " Why have you turned Ira-waru into a dog? " said she.

" Because he ate the bait like one," said Maui', and turned and entered his *whare* ; and Ira-waru became the deity of dogs.

Hina-uri in her sorrow went to the seashore ; and removing her clothing she put on her magic girdle, chanting a *tangi* to the sound of the lamenting sea.

> " I weep, and to the ocean billows call,
>   And him, the great, the ocean-god,
>   And monsters, hidden in the sea,
>   To come, entombing me,
>   Who now am wrapped in mourning garb.
>   Let, too, the waves their mourning wear,
>   And sleep as sleeps the dead.
>   I weep, I call to monster forms of ocean deep,
>   And thou, great wave of endless roar,
>   To come, engulfing me,
>   Yes, me, who now implore a mighty throng
>   To come and gratify my keen desire.
>   Let, too, the heavens their mourning wear,
>   And sleep as sleeps the dead.
>   The tide of life glides swiftly past,
>   And mingles all in one great eddying foam.
>   Thou heaven, now sleeping, rouse thee, rise to power,
>   And thou, O earth, awake, exert thy power for me,
>   And open wide the door to my last home,
>   Where calm and quiet rest await me in the sky.
>   The sun declines, and hides in dusky eve,
>   And I to Motu-tapu will depart, the sacred isle.
>   Oh, stay, thou voice of mine own heavenly bird—
>   The one bird far in arching skies, whose voice
>   With double sound now weeps, now sings on ocean coast,
>   Close by my Wai-rarawa home !
>   Smite me and thrust me into blackest night,
>   And endless gloom,
>   Where I may stay upon the border-land,
>   And rest submissive to my fate."

She then cast herself into the sea, resigning herself to the monsters of the deep. Her story may be resumed later, when the Maui' episodes have been completed.

Maui' and the Winds

Maui' had control over all the winds but the west wind.
The others he caught and confined in caves, but the west
wind eluded him ; and while he pursued it, riding in chase
on the south and the north winds especially, he was unable
to capture it, so that it blows whether he will or no.

Maui' attempts to overcome Death

Death appeared to Maui' to be a degradation to man ;
he wished that man might not die, but live for ever. He
wished that the death of man might be like that of the moon,
which bathes in Wai-ora-a-Tane' (the Life-giving Waters
of Tane') and is renewed; or like that of the sun, which,
setting every night in Te Po (Darkness), rises with renewed
strength in the morning. Maui' said to his sister Hina',
" Let death be of short duration ; and as the moon dies and
revives, so let man die and revive." But Hina' answered,
" Not so. Let death be long, and when man dies let him
go into darkness and become as earth, that those he leaves
may weep and wail in lamentation." Some versions say
that it was with Hine-nui-te-po, the personification of
death, that Maui' argued, not Hina' his sister, the personification of the moon.

Descending again to the abode of his parents, Maui'
walked with his father, who spoke to him of the reports of
his doings that had come to them. " I have heard of your
jests and your achievements," said his father; " but here
you will find that things are not so easily accomplished,
and without doubt you must in the end be overcome."
" What power is it that threatens me? " asked Maui'.
" Hine-nui-te-po, the Great Mother of Night, my son ; she
who brought death into the world." " We shall see," said
Maui', " if man is henceforth to die or live for ever." " But
the omen at your naming," said the father, " the omission
in the ceremony is a certain omen of death." " Death to
him who made the omission ! " said Maui'. " May it be
so," answered the father. " If punishment must fall upon

212

one of us, may you, my son, go free." "What like is this ancestress of mine?" asked Maui'.

"Fix your eyes upon the far horizon," said his father. "The flashing yonder, the opening and shutting, as it were, is the flashing of her eyes, whose pupils are of greenstone. Her hair is as the writhing masses of sea-tangles; her mouth is as the mouth of the shark."

Maui' referred to his other deeds, and to the success of all his undertakings. Now he desired to subdue the Great Woman of Night, so that man might no more be subject to death.

"Go, then; seek thine ancestress, flashing so fiercely out yonder where heaven and earth appear to meet"; and Maui' set out, with his thoughts going before.

Men were not the companions he sought in this last adventure; his companions were the small birds of the forests of Tane'.

"My little friends," said our hero, "my heart rejoices to hear your cheerful songs and merry twittering; but let your joyousness be hushed while I am creeping into the womb of the sleeping Mother of Death."

"O son," said the birds, "you will be killed outright"; and they were silent in fear.

"Not so," answered Maui', "unless, indeed, you should awaken her before I have crept through her body: if you do that, I shall die; but if you do not, then it is she who will suffer death, and man thereafter shall live for ever."

The tiny things were cheerful again; and merrily their songs sounded in the ears of our hero as he strode to the abode of Hine'. Reaching the place where she lay sleeping, they were silent; and, indeed, the sight of her, and the knowledge of her dread power, might well lay silence on more than birds. Maui' stood before her, and again enjoining silence on his companions he prepared to enter the Mother of Death and destroy her power for ever. Some say that he transformed himself into a lizard in order to be able to cross the strait threshold of Tiki. Howbeit, he entered, and the birds watched him. The threshold was

crossed, almost the entry was won, when the irrepressible
fantail, overcome by the wriggling of the hero, burst into
merry laughter. The Woman of Night awoke; she caught
sight of Maui'; her lips closed, Maui' was nipped in two,
and evermore man was subject to death. As the proverb
says, " Man may procreate, but Hine-nui-te-po strangles his
offspring."

> In vain I look within myself
> To know the cause of death to thee,
> And why the gods swept thee away
> When gifts to them were burnt
> In sacrifices to thine ancestor, Pa-whai-tiri.
> Death does not come from herbs.
> Of old death came by Maui',
> When *patatai* [1] forgot and laughed,
> And caused him to be cut in two;
> Then mist arose, and *tiwaiwaka* [2] flew,
> And rested where heaped up the refuse lay.

The foregoing episodes are from Maori traditions, and
it is among the Maori that most details of the episodes are
preserved. There are all manner of variants among the
different Maori tribes, but the main incidents are the same.
The incidents are not equally spread over the various parts
of the Polynesian Pacific; some are known in one part,
some in another, some in one locality only.

Maui' introduces Cooked Food

Apparently it was not until Maui' followed his mother
to her netherworld home that cooked food was known
among men. This is made clear in the Mangaian legend,
where Ru and Bua-taranga were the father and mother of
Maui'. When she came to visit her children the mother
ate her food apart, from a basket she brought with her. One
day Maui' peeped into her basket while she lay asleep, saw
the food, and tasted it. It was cooked, and appeared to
him a decided improvement upon the raw food to which
he was accustomed. The mother evidently did not pay
the regard to day and night that she did in the Maori
legend, and when one day she went on her way to the

---

[1] The banded rail.　　　　　　[2] The fantail.

netherworld Maui', unperceived by her, followed and watched. He saw her stand opposite to a black rock, to which she spoke in an ' open sesame ' manner :

> " Bua-taranga, descend thou through this chasm.
> The rainbow-like must be obeyed.
> As Opipiri and Oeretue at dawn are parted,
> Open, open up my road to the netherworld, ye fierce ones."

At these words the rock divided, and Bua-taranga descended. Maui' remembered the words, borrowed a red pigeon called Akaotu (Fearless) from Tane', and returning to the rock repeated the words he had heard his mother utter. The rock opened, and, entering the pigeon, he descended. The pigeon alighted first on an oven-house and later on a breadfruit-tree. Then follow the events leading up to Maui's learning the secret of fire.

An interesting point, showing the importance of preserving names, occurs in this part of the story. In the Maori version the pigeon alighted on a *manapau*—a tree unknown as a New Zealand tree, but known in Samoa. If the name does not occur elsewhere, it would seem to locate the origin of the Maori story in Samoa, the name of the tree persisting among the Maori through the hundreds of years that they and the Samoans have been apart.

Maui' snaring the Sun (Manihiki)

The story of the snaring of the sun is widely distributed. Of particular interest is the variant occurring in Manihiki, an island about 650 miles north of Rarotonga and the same distance north-east of Samoa. Here Maui' had two elder brothers, and an elder sister, 'Ina-ika (Hina-ika—Hina of the Fish). When he attempted the noosing of the sun all his ropes were burnt by the fierce heat, and he was unsuccessful until he plaited ropes from the tresses of his sister 'Ina'. In Mangaia the rays of the sun, known to English children as " the sun drawing up water," are called the ropes of Maui'. These ropes may still be seen hanging from the sun at dawn and sundown, for Maui' refused to remove them. By their means the sun was thereafter gently let down into the netherworld, Avaiki, in the evening, and drawn up from the shades in the morning.

Maui's Fishing in other Parts of the Pacific

Even more widely distributed is the story of his fishing up the land. This episode has become localized to a greater extent than any of the others, most versions accounting for certain peculiarities in their land as having been occasioned by some act of Maui'. In Manihiki the islands Rakaanga and Manihiki were separated by Maui's stamping his foot in anger, the separating gap being twenty-five miles wide. The fish-hook he used was thrown into the skies, where it still hangs, making the tail of the Scorpion. So Mangaia was drawn up from the sea; also the Tongan Islands, Ata first appearing, then Tonga, then Lofaga and the other Hapai Islands, then Vavau, and the Hawaiian Islands, which Maui' unsuccessfully attempted to draw together into one, and Mangareva, where also Maui' tied the sun with tresses of hair. In New Zealand it was only the North Island that was pulled from the depths, and the resemblance of its shape to that of a fish was noted by those excellent navigators the Maori.

Maui' and Mahuika in Samoa

In Samoa Maui' is known as Ti'iti'i-a-Talaga (Tikitiki-a-Taranga). He was sometimes known simply as Talaga,[1] the Maori name of his mother (Taranga). Earthquakes were attributed to a god Mafui'e (Mahuika), who was an inhabitant of the lower regions Sa-le-Fe'e. One day Talaga determined to visit Sa-le-Fe'e. He went to Vailele, and standing upon a rock uttered a *karakia*, saying, " Rock, rock, I am Talaga; open to me. I wish to go below." On this the rock parted, and Talaga descended. At this time there was no fire upon earth; but there was fire at the abode of Mafui'e. The fire-deity inquired who it was who came disturbing him. Talaga did not answer his question, but remarked that here was Mafui'e with an ever-burning

---

[1] The *g* in Samoan represents the same sound as *ng* in Maori.

fire, eating cooked food, while those above were compelled to eat their food raw. Mafui'e took this as a challenge, and bade Talaga choose whether they should engage in wrestling, or boxing, or fighting with spears and stones, or twisting of arms. "Let us two twist," said Talaga. They immediately closed, and the right arm of Mafui'e was soon twisted off by Talaga, who then seized the left arm and began twisting that off also. "Enough; let me live," cried Mafui'e; "leave me one arm, that I may be able to take hold of things."

Talaga demanded some acknowledgment of defeat, and Mafui'e said, "Take some fire, this burning brand of *toa*, with these *taro*-tops; thus will your people be able to eat cooked food." On this Talaga left the lower regions; and coming to the place where he had descended he struck various kinds of trees with his burning brand, which caused their wood to yield fire thereafter.

Maui' and Mahuika : the Superior Version

The superior version of Maui's securing fire is very different from the fireside version—or the oven-side, as the Maori would say. In this version the sun, Tama-nui-te-ra, wishing to confer a boon upon mankind, sent down his son, Auahi-turoa, who carried with him the seed of fire. On reaching this world Auahi-turoa took to wife Mahuika, the personification of fire, and from them sprang the five fire-children, Konui, Koroa, Mapere, Manawa, and Koiti, which names are also the names of the five fingers of the hand. Auahi-turoa was a personification of the comet, another name being Upoko-roa (Long-head). In kindling fire the charred and glowing dust gathering at the end of the friction-groove is placed in dry fibrous material and waved to and fro, soon bursting into a flame; and when the flame blazes up the Maori has a saying, "The child of Upoko-roa appears." It was the five fire-children that Maui' destroyed when he quenched the fires from the fingers of Mahuika. Of the trees in which the fire took refuge the *kaikomako* was the chief, hence it was personified as the woman or goddess Hine-kaikomako, the Fire-maid; and when man desires fire he applies to the Fire-maid—that is, he takes a portion of her body wherewith to generate the fire. The term for generating it is the same as the term for generating offspring, *hika*, the means being similar. This idea is also carried out in the act of producing fire; a woman steadies the under piece of wood with her foot while the man rubs the pointed piece along the groove. Hine-kaikomako was taken to wife by Ira-whaki, the Fire-revealer, who is referred to in an ancient song :

> *E, Ira', e! Whakina mai te ahi.*
> [O Ira', thou ! reveal to us the fire.]

Now a sister of Mahuika was Hine-i-tapeka, the personification of subterranean fire. She was a relative of Hine-nui-te-po, and it was because Maui' slew the fire-children that Hine-nui-te-po determined on the subjugation and death of Maui'.

Maui' and the Winds in Samoa

From Samoa, too, comes a fuller account of Maui' imprisoning the winds. He went for a sail in his canoe; and when the south wind, Tuauoloa, blew he said, " Bring hither that wind, and put it in my receptacle; it is a bad wind." This was followed by the north, Matu. " This wind is an annoyance," said he ; " it is too full of tempests," and it was confined. Shortly afterward the east wind, Mata-Upolu, sprang up ; it too was objectionable, as it would be accompanied by rain, and would be unpleasant. This also was confined. The trades, To'elau, came next, but were considered disagreeable because of their strength, and they joined the others. They were followed by the Lau-fala, the Faati'u, and the Piipapa, but as none gave satisfaction they too " came into the sack." The south-south-west wind, Tonga, shared the same fate, because it brought rain and induced drowsiness. At last came a gentle, pleasant wind, the Fisaga ; and Ti'iti'i said, " Let this remain, to sweeten land and sea, and gently fan my flowing hair." ' Receptacle ' has generally been translated ' canoe '; but

218

MAUI'

the word, *va'a*, means, as does the Maori *waka*, not only a canoe, but a receptacle, perhaps canoe-shaped, or long. It is another expression for the wind-calabash.

Maui-kijikiji of Tonga

The confusion and jumble of person and incident are at times extraordinary. No doubt where people were few, and saw many changes, the stories were certain to suffer changes also, from lapses of memory, or through preservers of lore being brought low. One legend from Tonga tells of four Maui'—Maui-motua, Maui-loa, Maui-buku, and Maui-atalanga. There was also a son of the last-named, Maui-kijikiji (Maui the Mischievous). They lived together in the netherworlds, until 'Atalanga wished to live on the surface of the earth. He departed with his son, promising his brothers that he would often return to see them and attend to his garden, or do any other work that might be necessary. They settled at Koloa, the oldest part of Vavau, in the north of the Tonga group, and in his frequent visits to the netherworld 'Atalanga did not take his son with him; he was so mischievous that the father did not wish to be annoyed by his company. He usually stole off before daylight; and 'Kijikiji must have been very young when they came to the earth, for he did not know where his father went, but he determined to watch and follow him. One night, happening to wake, he saw his father take his digging implement and steal quietly away without waking anyone. 'Kijikiji followed unseen, and saw the father raise a clump of reeds, and disappear by a hole in the ground, reaching up and replacing the reeds as he disappeared.

'Kijikiji followed, throwing aside the reeds instead of replacing them, and found his father working in the garden; but he himself climbed up into a *nonu*-tree, from which he picked one of the fruits, bit it, and threw it at his father. 'Atalanga picked it up, looked at it, and thought he recognized the tooth-marks; but looking around, and seeing no one, he went on with his work. A second time he was disturbed by a fruit, and seeing the same marks on this one his doubts vanished, and he remarked, " This is in truth the tooth-mark of that imp of a boy." 'Kijikiji no longer attempted concealment, calling out, " Here I am, Father."

Questioned by his father as to how he had come there, he replied that he had followed him ; and when asked if he had covered up the opening again he untruthfully replied that he had. 'Atalanga called him to come and cut the weeds with him, warning him not to look round while he worked. Needless to say, the youth did look round, whereupon the weeds sprang up again as quickly as he cut them down. His father did the work over again, and the boy, regardless of the *tapu*, continued to look behind, so that at last the father in disgust bade him go and build a fire to prepare food.

'Kijikiji had never seen fire, and went to the house of Maui-motua for it. Maui-motua was an old man whom he did not know ; he was his grandfather, the father of 'Atalanga. He asked for fire, and received it, but going out with it extinguished it. He returned for more, and again extinguished it ; and on his returning a third time the old man was angry ; only one brand was left—a great casuarina log. Maui-motua jestingly told the boy that if he could carry it he could have it, never supposing that he would be able to do so, as 'Atalanga only could even lift it. 'Kijikiji, however, picked it up and started to carry it off with one hand. Maui-motua at once called out to him to put down the fire, and challenged him to wrestle. He did not know his grandson, or he would have hesitated to make that challenge. 'Kijikiji dashed him to the ground again and again, and leaving him for dead picked up the log and carried off the fire.

'Atalanga asked him what mischief he had been doing to Maui-motua since he had been so long away ; but 'Kijikiji replied that the fire kept going out, so that he had to return for more. Further questioning, however, elicited information about the wrestling-match and its result, whereupon 'Atalanga felled his son with his digging implement, and covered his body with the grass *mohuku vai*.

MAUI'

It is said that owing to the body of 'Kijikiji having been thus covered this grass does not die when cut.

'Atalanga then went to see his father, who, he found, had revived ; and when the old man learned that it was with his grandson that he had quarrelled he told 'Atalanga to place *nonu* leaves on the body to bring it to life again.   This tree does not grow upon the surface of the earth, but only in the netherworld and in the upperworld.   This was done, and 'Kijikiji recovered, when the two of them ate food, and prepared to return to the earth.

'Atalanga, always suspicious of his son, requested him to lead the way ; but 'Kijikiji persisted in following, and on they went.   As they set out 'Kijikiji seized a burning brand to take with him, hiding it behind his back.   Presently his father came to a standstill, saying, " Where is that smell of burning?   Are you taking any fire with you? "

" No," answered the boy ; " it is probably the smell from the place where we cooked our food."

The father seemed unconvinced, but they resumed their journey.   Presently he turned round again.   " Boy, where is this smell of fire from? "   The boy did not know. " Have you brought some fire with you? " again asked the father ; and seeing smoke arising from the concealed brand he rushed and seized it, upbraiding 'Kijikiji for his deceit.

They ascended to the surface of the earth, but unknown to 'Atalanga the end of the loincloth of 'Kijikiji was afire, trailing behind him out of sight.   On reaching the surface 'Atalanga hid to see if 'Kijikiji brought anything up from below, and when the son emerged the father saw the smoke from the burning loincloth.   At once he called on the rain to fall ; but although the rain obeyed and there was a downpour the boy was not to be outdone, for he cried to the fire to flee to the coconut-tree, the breadfruit, the hibiscus, the *tou*, and to all trees.

This is the way in which fire was introduced among men, who had previously eaten their food uncooked ; and because fire resides in the trees it may be obtained by rubbing one stick upon another.

Maui-atalanga and his son then returned to their home. One day Maui-atalanga was out walking, and in the road met a woman named Fuiloa, who was crawling along with water from the well called Tofoa. 'Atalanga stopped her and asked for a drink, a request which she refused. He again asked her, saying that in return he would push the sky so high that she would be able to stand upright; for at that time the sky was so close to the earth that man was obliged to crawl about on all fours.

Fuiloa was at first sceptical of the good faith of 'Atalanga —'Kijikiji was evidently the son of his father—but on his repeating his assurances she gave the desired drink. 'Atalanga then gave a great push to the sky, and asked the woman how that would suit. " Farther yet," she replied. He pushed again, and on his repeating his question, " Farther yet; put your strength into it, and get it a long way up," she said. So he pushed again with all his might, and got the sky into its present position. From that time man has been able to stand and walk upright. The name of the road where this was done was Te Kena-ki-lagi.

This story is a curious blending of Maori, Samoan, and Mangaian, the Maori name Maui-tikitiki-a-Taranga becoming two names applied to two persons; and in it the feat of lifting the sky, attributed to the son in Mangaia and elsewhere, is attributed to the father.

Maui' lifts the Sky (Mangaia)

In Mangaia the story says that the sky is built of solid blue stone. When it lay almost upon the earth it rested on the broad leaves of the *teve*, a tree about six feet high, and of the arrowroot, three feet high, the flattening out of these leaves, like millions of outspread hands pressing upward, being the result of their having to support this enormous weight.

In this narrow space the inhabitants of the world moved about. Ru, whose residence was in Avaiki, the netherworld, had come up for a time to this world, and pitying the inhabitants in their cramped home he endeavoured to raise the sky a little, which he did by propping it up with a number of strong stakes, firmly planted at Rangi-motia, the centre of the island and of the world.

One day, when the old man was surveying his work, his graceless son Maui' contemptuously asked him what he was doing. " Who bade you speak? " asked the old man. " Take care of yourself, or I will hurl you out of existence." " Do it, then," said Maui', who took it as a challenge. Ru seized Maui', who was of small stature, and hurled him to a great height. In falling, however, Maui' assumed the form of a bird, and lightly reached the ground, quite unharmed. In a moment he resumed his natural form, but extended to gigantic proportions ; and he hurled Ru, sky and all, to a tremendous height—so high that the sky could never get back again ; and the head and shoulders of Ru got entangled among the stars, where he was held prisoner, struggling, until he perished. As his body decayed his bones came tumbling down from time to time, and were shivered into countless fragments. These fragments are pumice-stone, and that stone is known as the bones of Ru.

It is significant that Maui' plays the part of Tane' in separating the heaven and the earth, this giving colour to the suggestion made later on that the story of Maui' is largely a sun-myth, Maui' representing the sun as Tane' represents sunlight, if he does not also represent the sun. Tane' and Maui' may simply be the superior and fireside names of the same personage.

Maui' and Ro (Rohe) in Pukapuka

The strange story of the exchange of faces between Maui' and Rohe has been found in only one restricted area in New Zealand, and it might be supposed to have been of local origin were it not for the fact that there is a much longer story on the same theme in Pukapuka (Danger Island). The gods Tongaiti, Tangaroa, and many others discussed the question of sending for Maui', who was then living in Avaiki, the netherworld. They decided on sending Ro, also known as Roe (Ro'e, Rohe), to fetch him. Ro descended to Avaiki, where she was seen by Maui',

who knew she had been sent to fetch him. He therefore
said, " What have you come for? " Ro replied, " I have
been sent by the gods in the heavens to fetch you." " Very
well," said Maui' ; " I knew that ; you go ahead—I will
follow." " You, O sir, go first," said Ro ; " I will follow
behind." " No," exclaimed Maui' ; " you shall go first ;
I will follow behind."

Ro went on ahead, Maui' following, and thus they left
Avaiki. While they were coming along the road Ro
suddenly ran and hid in the trees—under the very roots.
Ro thought she would not be seen by Maui'. She also
knew that Maui' intended to do her some mischief ; therefore she hid. Maui' then chanted this spell :

> " O Ro O! of the tribe of tens of thousands—
> The way has been cut off—the path has ended—
> By which way shall I go—where shall I next step?
> O Ro O! thou artful one—now where is 'Ina,
> The goddess daughter of Tangaroa? "

When Ro heard this she laughed, for she knew that
Maui' could see her. She therefore came out, and they
proceeded on their way. They walked on for some distance
until they came to a certain place, when Maui' said to Ro,
" Let us exchange heads." Ro would not consent—she
did not want to give her head ; she knew that Maui'
intended to do her mischief. She said to him, " O Maui',
my head cannot be removed." Maui' then took off his
own head, and when Ro saw this she became very much
afraid. They walked on again for a long distance, when
Maui' removed the head of Ro and fixed it on his own body.
He then cast the body of Ro to the side of the heavens ;
thus she perished.

Maui' now ascended to the upperworlds, and when the
gods saw him coming they saw that he was changed, and
they recited this *karakia* :

> " Mauled and maltreated—ripped and torn—
> Come to the initiation, to the cult of the shades.
> Auriki-toma, now disclose it—now disclose—
> In prophetic vein, prophesy."

MAUI'

Then Maui' uttered his prophecy :

> " Twice the challenge was uttered
> By the will of the gods—
> Through the medium of man—
> Disclosed from the sacred *maire*-tree
> That stands on the sacred [courtyard] Ara-akaako.
> Therefore will I disclose it—
> 'Twas Rongo-ma-Tane, who shall bind it on."

When the gods heard this prediction uttered by Maui', they exclaimed one to the other, " Oh, Maui' is a man who cannot be fooled ! "

The 'Ina referred to in the first spell is the one who came from the upperworlds and taught certain games to men, such as juggling *tiporo*-fruit, also mat-plaiting, net-making, and beating out *tapa* cloth. She led a fish with her when she came, named the *koriro* (conger-eel). This was the monster that Maui' fished up with his hook. That fish is now in the heavens.

No doubt the gods, being wise, could see the meaning of the prophecy of Maui' in this extraordinary story ; it eludes mere mortals. The fish now in the heavens is probably the Milky Way, one of the names of which in Maori is Mango-roa-i-ata (the Long Shark of the Dawn), or Ika-roa (the Long Fish), or Ika-o-te-rangi (the Fish of the Heaven). The fruit of the *tiporo* was evidently used instead of balls for juggling.

The strange fancy of this story also appears in the Norse mythology, for when Skirner was to set out to woo the beautiful giantess Gerda for his master Frey he stole the reflection of Frey's face from the crystal water beside which he was seated, and imprisoned it in his drinking-horn, intending to pour it out in Gerda's cup and with its beauty win her. Like Maui', Frey was the sun-god ; his sword was the sunbeam ; his ship *Skidbladner*, which could grow small or great at his pleasure, was the clouds ; his golden-bristled boar on which he rode was the sun itself ; his gift at his tooth-cutting was Fairyland, the beautiful Alfheim. Gerda is said to be the personification of the frozen, wintry north.

Skirner won her, but not until he had inspired her with terror—for at first she refused the golden apples and gold ring brought by him—and she consented to meet Frey in nine days. The nine days are the nine winter months; her refusal of the gifts is the refusal of the North to yield to the adornments of spring; her howling watch-dogs are the wintry blasts; and the flaming barrier surrounding her home is the array of the Northern Lights.

In one version of Maui' and Tuna-roa the monster emerged from the stream over nine skids laid down by Maui'; and it is supposed that these nine skids may represent the nine months of a gestation-period.

The Identity of Maui'

The manner in which the story of the exploits of the great hero of Polynesia has been preserved throughout the Pacific is remarkable. Dialects have arisen, and people who can no longer understand one another have yet preserved the tales, sometimes altered, sometimes added to, but recognizable as the same. Names have undergone changes owing to unaccountable dialectic transformation, yet are still recognizable. Religions have arisen, have completely changed, but have no more than changed the dress of the stories. New homes have been sought and founded, hundreds or thousands of miles distant, often under entirely different conditions; still the stories have persisted, localized, it may be, yet integrally the same.

Maui' is generally regarded as a demigod, or deified man; often he is regarded merely as a man; sometimes he is regarded as a god. It has been suggested that he was one of the leaders of the Polynesians in their entry into the Pacific; but Fornander supposes that some of the tales originated in times yet more remote, when the Polynesians were dwellers on some continental area.

The earliest mention of Maui' is at a time when the Polynesians were still in Indonesia. He is said to have been the son of Tangaroa by the wife of Ataranga, named Vaine-uenga. This Tangaroa was a man, not the god of that name, though the attributes of the two may have been confused, and probably have been confused. Percy Smith supposes this Tangaroa to have been one of the adventurers and voyagers of the Indonesian sojourn, and he is said to have discovered a new kind of food, called *ui-ara-kakano*. It was found on the beach, was white in colour, and became a common food of the people, almost to the exclusion of rice (*vari*), the common food up till that time. The new food is conjectured to be the egg of the *maleo*, one of the Megapodidæ. The names of lands visited by Tangaroa are mentioned in the old traditions, and some of his adventures are related. He married Ina, the daughter of Vai-takere, who, according to genealogical tables preserved by the Rarotongans, from whom the stories are derived, lived about the first century. Vai-takere, too, is said to have introduced the breadfruit to his people, and his wife the *i'i* (*ifi*, *ihi*—chestnut); and these two foods being discovered in Avaiki, the use of rice, so troublesome to cultivate, was abandoned. The breadfruit is a native of Java, and it was taken with them by the Polynesians in their wanderings. The varieties now growing in Polynesia—of which there are a great many—are seedless, so that the plant is evidently not indigenous to those parts. That the Maori was long ago familiar with breadfruit is shown by the word *kuru*, an old name for breadfruit in the Pacific, occurring in old *karakia* and in place-names; the word was retained, though its meaning had been forgotten.

Maui', the son of Tangaroa, was a voyager like his father, the names of many of the lands visited by him also being preserved in the Rarotongan recitals, including Manihiki, the Marquesas, Tuamotu, Tahiti, Mangaia, Rarotonga. It was in Avaiki-runga, which in one account includes the Hawaiian Islands, that he visited Mauike, the lord of fire, one of whose daughters was Pere (the Hawaiian fire-goddess Pele). The entry of the body of the Polynesians into the Pacific is conjectured as between the first and fifth centuries.

Some of the Maui' stories are evidently much older than

others. The efforts of Maui' to lengthen the daylight may refer to a time when the people were living in a northern land where the winter days were very short, and migration to the south secured the longer days. To this period may be referred the very brief reference to the destruction of the crops of Maru' by frosts. Of great antiquity, too, is the story of his attempting to overcome death. His acquisition of fire may also be a story of very ancient date. In one of the teachings of the Maori college of learning it is said that the fire obtained was *ahi-komau,* or volcanic fire; so it may mean that the Polynesians first obtained fire from the glowing lava; and the subsequent conflagration may refer to the volcanic outbursts, when the vegetation is frequently set ablaze.

There have been many men of the name of Maui', and doubtless the tales regarding them have, as is a common occurrence, been transferred to one outstanding Maui', this accounting for many inconsistencies. The general agreement, however, indicates that the stories are very ancient; that they were, most of them, known to the Polynesians before their scattering among the islands of the Pacific.

Maui' and Cat's-cradles

Maui' was also credited with being an expert in games and exercises of various kinds. He could not be excelled in throwing *niti,* a small dart, as his brothers discovered. He was also an adept in kite-flying. He or his elder brother Maui-mua invented the game called *whai,* a kind of cat's-cradle, played with a loop of string. In the European game it is played by two persons; in the Polynesian game usually by one, or two in competition. Complicated figures, however, require two, three, or more persons for their display, and in some of the figures two loops are used intertwisted in various ways. Until quite recently nothing but a number of names of these figures of the Maori had been recorded; now over fifty have been collected, and their method of construction described. Some of the figures have parallels in islands of the Pacific, some in other parts

228

of the world, including Europe and America. Some appear,

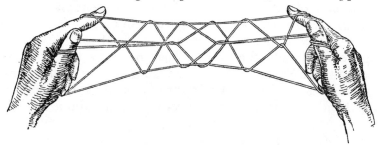

ONE FIGURE OF TE KURI RUARANGI

Represents the fire at which the heart of a certain person was roasted. The central diamond is the heart, and the double strings leading right and left are the spits on which the heart was impaled.

so far, to be purely Maori. One very complicated figure represents the ascent of Tawhaki to the upperworlds,

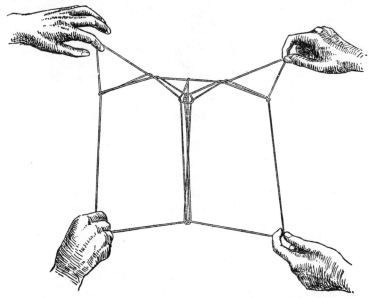

REPRESENTING THE BEGINNING OF TAWHAKI'S ASCENT TO THE UPPERWORLD

different movements in the figure showing progressive stages of the ascent; one represents the four Maui' brothers.

One is named Tawhiti-nui, an ancient place-name in Maori tradition ; one is Pari-nui-te-ra, another ancient place-name. One, Rerenga-wairua, is of particular interest. The words *rerenga wairua* mean " the leaping-place of souls," and the figure represents the cliff of that name at the northern extremity of New Zealand, where the soul leaps to the realms of the netherworlds. The figure is extended between the two hands : a small triangle near the right palm is the first

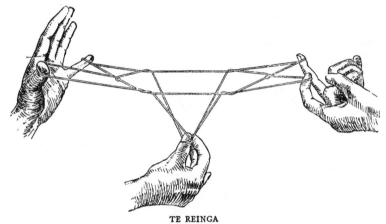

TE REINGA

Representing the underworld from the canoe of Tama-rereti.

rock on which the spirit stands ; it leaps to a second and lower rock, represented by a similar triangle at the left palm ; and thence downward to the wide opening of Te Reinga. In Rarotonga the place of departure for Spirit Land was known as Reinga-vaerua, or Rerenga-vaerua ; it faced the setting sun, as did three such places on Mangaia. The spirit stood on one bluff rock, leaped to a second, smaller block of stone resting on the inner edge of the reef, on which the surf ceaselessly beats, and from this point the final departure to the shades was taken in the track of the sun. There are many other remarkable parallels in these apparently unimportant string-figures, but reference has been made here only to such as touch the mythology or history of the Polynesians.

230

TUHOE FOLK (AND AUTHOR) SETTING UP TAWHAKI

The figure is Ru-mokomoko, the earthquake-god.

(See page 230)

MAUI'

Mythological Parallels

The many parallels between the Maui' stories and stories in other mythologies may or may not have significance as regards the origin of the peoples. It would be remarkable if there were no such parallels, seeing that it is the common mind of man that has throughout been working on the same or similar natural phenomena, and the common heart of man expressing the same or similar desires and aspirations. The love of a goddess for a mortal, as in the Tawhaki myth, is an extremely common incident, and is no more than the love of a person of high rank for one of low rank carried a little further. There is therefore no need to see in Tawhaki a counterpart of Endymion. So in the transformations of Maui' there is no need to point out parallels, since such transformations occur in all mythologies, all folk-tales. Bird-disguises play an important part, and mortals continually move from place to place *incognito* by their means. It is, of course, the natural means of levitation, and is more picturesque, as well as more easily understood, than the magic carpet or the flying horse of *The Arabian Nights' Entertainments*. Belief in the transformation to flying creatures, in the shape of angels, persists to the present day.

Maui' and Thor

A connexion between the Polynesians and the Norsemen has been suggested in the similar forms of the canoes and ships of these two peoples. But surely such similarity of construction need not imply even contact ; races of men are not altogether singular in their conceptions, and what may be evolved by one may equally well be evolved by another. One rather curious parallel to the story of Maui' fishing up the land occurs in Norse mythology. The god Thor visited a giant Hymer, and finding that he was about to go out fishing proposed to accompany him. He asked what bait was used, and was told that he must provide that for himself. Thereupon Thor went and took the head from one of Hymer's giant oxen. The giant was scornful of Thor and his rowing powers until they took their place in the

231

boat and Thor rowed the giant out of breath, the latter admitting that the boat went at a great rate—so great that they were very soon over the fishing-ground. On Hymer observing this, Thor expressed a wish that they might row out farther. They did so, and soon the giant said that if they rowed much farther they would be in dangerous ground on account of Iörmungandr, the serpent encircling the world. Thor desired to row just a little farther; and they did so.

Thor now produced his line and hook, baited with the ox-head. In brief, the serpent took the bait, as was Thor's design; and feeling the hook in its jaw made off, so that the sudden jerk knocked Thor's fists against the gunwale. This angered him, and he immediately leaned against the pull of the serpent, and so powerfully that his feet went through the side of the boat and he stood on the bottom of the sea. "He drew the serpent to the surface, and certain it is that never was seen a more fearful sight than when Thor glared angrily at the serpent, and it in turn glowered and spat poison at Thor." So speaks the Younger Edda. Hymer was greatly afraid; the water streamed into the boat; and just as Thor raised his hammer to make an end of the serpent Hymer cut the line and Iörmungandr sank again to the bottom of the ocean. Thor, incensed, struck the giant so that he fell backward into the water, his legs in the air. Thor then strode ashore.

There are several points of resemblance in the two stories, even to the walking ashore, although the boat was out on the deep ocean; but these parallels need not imply that the stories were derived from a common source other than the human imagination.

While Maui' was mischievous, he was not evil, like Loke of the Norse mythology, so that his tricks had not the tragic effects of those of Loke. His mischief was more like that of the Greek Hermes—Mercury of the Romans; it generally resulted in some benefit for the human race. On the whole, indeed, Maui' was a benéficent being; and, considering the barbaric times in which he lived, his pranks do not

232

inspire the aversion they would in a being nearer our own times.   In his having been cast up by the sea, a babe coming who knew whence, he touches King Arthur, cast up by a ninth wave, as related by his sister Bellicent.

Maui' as a Solar Deity

Again, remembering the fondness of primitive man for personification of the powers of nature, there is a possibility that at least part of the composite Maui' myth may be a personification of this kind.

There is much, in at least some of the stories, to suggest that he represents the sun, or light.   In the fishing up of the land he appears in his two characters ; there is a combination of Maui' the voyager and Maui' the solar deity.   He persuades his brothers to paddle farther and farther out to sea, possibly in a direction in which he had a suspicion land might lie, the source of his suspicion being perhaps hinted at in the earlier story of his securing the jaw of his ancestress as a fish-hook.   The name of the fish was Hahau-whenua (Land Long-sought), and the part really played by the jaw-bone was probably in the imparting of information.   The very name of this ancestress, Muri-ranga-whenua (Breeze that encircles the Land, as it is interpreted by White), contains a suggestion of this kind.

Here, then, is the adumbrated picture.   The brothers go on a voyage, unwilling, but urged by Maui' ; they are riding at sea, out of sight of land, when the sun rises, the mists part, and the first rays fall on the gable of the house of Tangaroa.   Fires are seen, and people moving about. Maui' is the sun, his rays are the line, his blood used as bait is the morning glow.   If the brothers are afraid until reassured by Maui' it is because they have come upon an unknown land, and, the stranger being an enemy, they fear for their lives.

It has further been suggested that Maui' is also an earth-quake-god, and that the appearing of the land was due to a volcanic disturbance ; but then there could not have been houses, and fires, and people seen upon it.   It may have

233

been a volcanic island, and the brothers may have experienced an earthquake during their sojourn there—hence the jumping about of the fish. In the Samoan story Mafui'e is possibly an earthquake-god as well as a fire-god; and Ru, whose bones formed pumice-stone in the story from Mangaia, was there the father of Maui'; and in New Zealand Ru', or Ruau-moko, the still unborn son of Papa', was god of earthquakes. Argument may swing almost at pleasure when an interpretation of these old myths is attempted.

Again, it will be remembered that in one story of the snaring of the sun Maui' was unable to hold that deity until he plaited ropes from the tresses of his sister 'Ina'. Now Hina', known throughout Polynesia as Hina, Ina, or Sina, is the personification of the moon. As Hina-keha (Pale Hina) she is the moon in its bright phases; as Hina-uri (Dark Hina) the moon in its dark phases. Here the sun and the moon are brother and sister, as they are in Greek mythology, Apollo the sun-god and Diana the moon-goddess being the twin children of Latona by Jupiter. The ever-jealous Juno sent the serpent Python to torment Latona, and she found no rest until Jupiter raised from the bottom of the sea the island Delos, where Latona found refuge and gave birth to the two children. Apollo afterward attacked and slew Python, and this again is reminiscent of Maui's slaying Tuna-roa. Tuna-roa came down from above because of the drying up of the marshes; and in the interpretation of the Greek myth of the destruction of Python by Apollo it is said that the meaning is the drying up by the sun of the marshes where serpents and other monsters harboured. The poetic imagination ever has its prosaic bandog followers. In Norse mythology the sun and moon are sister and brother, not brother and sister.

In mythology, folklore, the old ballads and romances, the same idea or phrase may be used over and over; and the figure of fishing up the land has no doubt been applied to the act of discovery again and again. So, too, his " lifting up of the heavens," told as a literal deed in Manihiki

234

and Mangaia, is no doubt a metaphor used to explain his onward course beyond the apparent horizon, " where the sky hangs down." It is a picturesque way of speaking, as was that of the Maori in later times when they spoke of " felling with an axe " the storms and difficulties they met on the voyage to New Zealand. Among the Polynesians, as among more advanced peoples, poetic expressions such as these puzzled prosaic minds, and many of the seeming ridiculous stories no doubt originated in prosaic attempts to explain what needed no explanation to imaginative minds, but was incomprehensible to unimaginative ones. Many stories were no doubt intended to be ridiculous.

Rohe was said to be a sister of the sun, and for her beauty was likened to the rays of the sun; she was probably the personification of some form of light—it may be the dawn, though the Dawn-maid was the daughter and wife of Tane'; but as she is said to have returned from the netherworlds and caused the death of Maui' it may be that she was a personification of the evening light.

There is little doubt that the last great adventure of Maui' is a story of the attempt of the sun, or sunlight, to overcome darkness. The very choosing of his companions by Maui' is an indication, for the small birds always accompany the setting sun with song, as they hail his rising with song. The laughing note of the fantail, too, is one of the last among the notes of the more familiar birds to be heard as the shades of evening close in. The sun stoops to enter the Great Woman of Night, the Mother of Death, but meets his own death, his blood suffusing the evening sky; and when darkness lays its silence over the earth the flashing of the eyes of Hine' is seen in the flashing of the summer lightning low on the horizon.

CHAPTER VIII: HINA', SISTER OF MAUI'

Hina' at Motu-tapu

TO return now to Hina-uri, who had cast herself into the sea because of the treatment of her husband Ira-waru by Maui'. She drifted in the sea for many moons, finally coming ashore at Wai-rarawa, where she was seen lying on the sand by Ihu-atamai and Ihu-wareware. She was covered with weedy growth, and at first they thought it a log only; but perceiving that it had a human shape they parted the weeds, and saw the body of a woman.

They carried her to their house, laid her before the fire, and little by little removed the weed and growth, and she awoke to life again. They saw how beautiful she was, and Ihu' took her to wife; she told them her name was Ihu-ngaru-paea.

Soon afterward Ihu-wareware went to Tini-rau and told him about her. He came to their home to see her, and took her away to be his wife. He took her to his home Motu-tapu, but his two wives, Hara-taunga and Horo-tata, were angry when they saw Hina-uri in the company of Tini-rau, and cursed her, intending to kill her. But Hina' was more skilled in witchcraft than they were, and as she uttered the *karakia* "Let the booming blows of the axe be heard," their bodies lay stretched on the ground, and Hina-uri was without rivals.

The story is told differently and more in detail in another part of New Zealand. Here Hina' is known as Hine-i-te-iwaiwa; and Tini-rau was a chief of islands in the north, who was famous for his fine form and beauty of face. Several clear pools of water were set aside for his use, and in them he would, like Narcissus of old, admire his face and form. He also kept several whales as pets, among them a special favourite named Tutu-nui.

The fame of Tini-rau reached Hina', or Hine-i-te-iwaiwa, and her desire to see for herself if fame spoke truly or no became so great that she determined to pay a visit to Motu-tapu, the home of Tini-rau. One day, therefore, when out with her women gathering mussels in the sea, she dived unperceived and swam under water, coming up on a rock some distance from the shore. She was able to transform herself into a being which was half fish and half woman, and in this form she swam to the home of Tini-rau. She sat on the shore for some time, thinking of the adventures she had had on the way, and of her conversations with various fish that she met, and considering how she should introduce herself to the man of whose fame she had heard so much. She determined to get into his pools and muddy the water. He would be sure to be told of this act by the bird Ruru-atamai, which acted as guardian to the pools.

It was so; the bird saw what Hina' had done, and it at once called to Tini-rau, who was seated sunning himself on an elevated stage. He came to see what was the matter, and, seeing Hina', fell in love with her; but as he had other wives, for fear of them he kept Hina' in a secret place. This he did until the time came when the child should be born; then the other wives learned of it, and in jealous anger came to kill Hina'. As before, however, she overcame them with her *karakia*.

Resenting her treatment, she determined to return to her people, which she did after the birth of her child. His birth being difficult, she composed and murmured a *karakia* rendering it easier, and this *karakia* has subsequently been used in cases of difficult labour. She became the goddess presiding over childbirth. One version relates how she called to her elder brother, Rupe, to come and carry her away. This Rupe, according to a version from the south of New Zealand, was a fifth brother of Maui' and Hina', Maui-mua. Like Maui-tikitiki-a-Taranga, he too had the power of transforming himself into a pigeon, whence probably his name Rupe. The word *rupe* is the name for a pigeon in the Pacific—*lupe* in Samoa, *lube* in Tonga, *rupe* in Tahiti, Rarotonga, and other islands—but in New Zealand it is no longer used, its place having been taken by *kereru*, *kuku*, or *kukupa*. Rupe had lamented the loss of his

237

sister Hina', and sought her everywhere, ascending as far
as to the tenth upperworld, where he learnt from Rehua
that she was at Motu-tapu. Assuming the form of a
pigeon, he flew to her at the time she was calling to him,
and carried off both her and her new-born baby. Until he
heard her brother call her Hine-te-iwaiwa Tini-rau had
known her as Hine-te-ngaru-moana (Daughter of the Sea-
wave). It was under the name Hine-te-iwaiwa or Hina-te-
iwaiwa that she was patroness of women and domestic arts;
and as *iwa* means nine, it is possible that here again the
number nine has significance.

Tini-rau, missing her society, followed her after she had
been away for a time. When he approached the *kainga*
where she lived he saw some children playing in a swamp
near by, among the tall clumps of *toetoe*. He hid himself,
and made a noise that attracted their attention. He
recognized his son among them by a mark he had on his
body, had a talk with the child, and sent him to his mother
with a sachet of sweet-smelling moss hid round his neck.
This sachet had been a present from Hina' in the days of
their first love, and Tini-rau had constantly worn it round
his neck. The child took it to his mother, who at once
recognized it, and came presently to see Tini-rau, taking
him into the *kainga*, where he was received with every mark
of distinction.

By and by the people suffered from want of food; and
Tini-rau promised them a plentiful supply of fish provided
they all remained in their houses, and kept the doors shut
fast until he gave the word for them to come out. They
agreed, and he uttered a powerful *karakia*. The people
heard a sound as of a rushing wind, which continued all
through the night. When morning came, and the word
to come out was given, they were amazed to find the village
filled, up to the raised storehouses, with all kinds of fish.

The Decoying of Kae

After a time Hina' returned with Tini-rau to Motu-tapu,
in order that the ceremony of naming their child might be

performed. With them came a noted *tohunga* named Kae to perform the ceremony. The son was given the name Tu-huruhuru.

When about to return Kae asked that he might be carried home by Tutu-nui, the pet whale of Tini-rau. Tini-rau was loth to give his consent, but remembering the obligation he was under to Kae he agreed. " When on nearing the shore Tutu-nui shakes himself," said he to Kae, " you must dismount, and wade ashore, as the water will be shallow." Kae promised to comply, but forgot his promise; and on Tutu-nui shaking himself he did not dismount, but urged him into shallower water, where he stranded, and died.

Kae thought it a waste of good food to leave the dead whale thus stranded, so he built a huge oven, made a fire of *koromiko* shrub, and roasted it; and because of the fat of Tutu-nui the leaves of the *koromiko* have ever since been greasy; so that if the leaves are put on a fire, and the greasiness appears, the proverb says, " There's some of the savouriness of Tutu-nui."

Tini-rau awaited the return of his pet. It failed to appear; but a fragrance was borne to his nostrils, and he guessed what had taken place. The act must be avenged; and Tini-rau sent Hina' his wife with other young women to catch Kae and bring him back to punishment. None but young women went, so that his suspicions might not be aroused. Kae might be known to them by the fact that he had two front teeth missing; and he rarely laughed because of his sensitiveness on this point; he feared ridicule on account of his missing teeth.

The young women set out by canoe, accompanied by their pet birds. These flew over the land, uttering a short cry over each village on the way, and passing on. The young women knew by this that Kae was not there; so having performed a *haka* for the entertainment of the villagers they passed on after the birds. At length the birds arrived at a village where they cried, but flew no farther; this was the village of the old *tohunga*, of Kae.

239

They entered, and the bones of Tutu-nui rattled in recognition and anticipation. They danced a *haka*, and in the evening they entered the *whare-matoro* (the house of games), where they played games and sang songs to their delighted hosts. They played on the *koauau* (flute) and on the *putorino*, singing the accompanying songs; they played and sang to the resonant beaten *pakuru*. They played at motions with the fingers and hands; they sang to the trembling grotesques of the jumping-jack, to the humming whiz-gigs.

Through all these performances the man they supposed to be Kae had refused to laugh; so now they danced one *haka* after another, with motion and posture and grimace, but not until they danced the *haka* Wai-toremi did Kae throw back his head and laugh heartily, when his open mouth betrayed him; for not only was it seen that the two teeth were missing, but between the others pieces of the flesh of Tutu-nui were still adhering. Kae laughed at the drollery of the performers; and since that time when any ill-natured person is seen to smile this proverb slips from the tongue, " Kae laughs ! "

Having discovered him, the young women ceased their exertions, and the fires were allowed to die down, so that all might seek repose. Kae watched warily, for despite his laughing he suspected them; but soon all were asleep, even Kae himself, and from their nostrils came a sound like the flood tide. And how could it be otherwise? For with soft voices the young women murmured a *karakia*, called *rotu*, which induces sleep.

All slept, and Kae with them. The young women arose, and lifting Kae in his enchanted sleep they bore him to their canoe and returned to Motu-tapu.

Kae had built a new *whare* for himself, and of this the young women had taken the design and sent it to Tini-rau. He had caused a similar one to be built; and when Kae, still sleeping, was brought to Motu-tapu he was laid in this *whare*.

On awaking in the morning he heard cries of " Here comes Tini-rau ! Here comes Tini-rau ! " He sat up drowsily, thinking it was Tini-rau come to visit him. Approaching, and seating himself at the door of the *whare*, Tini-rau said, " Salutations to you, O Kae! How come you here?"

"Nay," replied Kae; "but, rather, how come *you* here?"

" Is this, then, your *whare*?" " It is my very *whare*," said Kae, looking around at the walls, and finding them as in the *whare* built for him.

" Is it so?" said Tini-rau, and laughed. Kae, seeing none of his own people, grew suspicious. He glanced out, and beheld a different scenery, and the people of Tini-rau and Hina', when he knew that he had been trapped, and began to lament his falling on evil days.

" Did Tutu-nui wail when his skin was severed by you?" asked Tini-rau, and Kae knew that his end had come.

Tu-huruhuru, the son of Tini-rau and Hina', whose naming it was that caused all the trouble with Kae, is said to have taken Apa-kura to wife, she giving birth to a son Tu-whakararo, a daughter Maira-tea, and several other children, the last two being Whakatau-potiki, a son, and Rei-matua. Poporo-kewa took Maira-tea to wife, and on Tu-whakararo's paying a visit to the Ati-Hapai, the tribe of Poporo-kewa, for the purpose of seeing his sister, he fell in love with Maurea, the youngest sister of Poporo-kewa, and for his sake she jilted an already accepted lover. This led to the cowardly killing of Tu-whakararo, and the subsequent vengeance taken under Whakatau' on the Ati-Hapai tribe, when their famous *wharekura*, known as Te Uru-o-Manono, was burnt, as already related in another version of this story.

Tini-rau in Samoa

There are at any rate fragments of the story of Kae (as 'Ae) in Tonga. He for a time attached himself to a chief Tinilau, who travelled from place to place on two turtles. 'Ae wished to visit Tonga, and begged from Tinilau the loan of his turtles. Tinilau consented, cautioning 'Ae to be very careful with them. 'Ae promised, but no sooner did

241

he reach Tonga than he called his friends to get the turtles ashore. They did so, killed them, and enjoyed a feast.

Tinilau, after waiting some time for the return of his turtles, suspected they had been killed, and suspicion turned to certainty when a wave tinged with blood ran up the beach where he stood. He called together the avenging gods of Savai'i; a party was dispatched to Tonga to capture 'Ae; he was found, and in a sound sleep brought back to Samoa and laid in the house of Tinilau.

At cockcrow 'Ae woke; and seeming to recognize the clarion said aloud, " Why, you cock! you crow like the one belonging to the pig I lived with." It was thus he referred to Tinilau, who had bestowed favours upon him. Tinilau called out, " Had the fellow you lived with such a fowl? " " Yes," answered 'Ae, not recognizing the voice; " the pig had one just like it." " Tell us more about him." So 'Ae went on chattering, still using the abusive epithet 'pig' when speaking of Tinilau; and he talked about the turtles, and what a fine feast that was; and he went on, until it grew lighter, when he looked up toward the roof, and said, " This, too, is just like the house the pig lived in." By and by, as it grew quite light, he began to realize that somehow or other he was again in the very house of Tinilau, and that that cannibal chief was not far away. He was dumb and panic-stricken. Orders were given to kill him; he was dispatched accordingly, and his body prepared for the oven.

A Samoan variant gives the full name of Tini-rau as Tigilau-ma'olo. The name is a combination. Tinilau, or Tigilau, as a boy went out fishing with 'Olo, whom he displeased, and to avoid punishment ran off to his parents Tigi and Lau. They named him Tigilau, combining their two names; but when 'Olo heard of it he wished that his name too might be given to the boy, who was thereupon called Tigilau-ma'olo (Tigi, Lau, and 'Olo). It was to him that 'Ae came from Tonga, and the names of the turtles were Utuutu and Toga, the first of which may be a remembrance of Tutu-nui, or *vice versa*, or both may be the remembrance of another name.

HINA', SISTER OF MAUI'

There is often a difference in the rendering of a story when collected by two different people. So much depends upon the collector's standpoint. Some think the literal telling of a story may give offence; some refuse to put on record what they personally consider improper. It is therefore often a matter of difficulty, if not impossibility, to say if variants are actual variants among the people where the stories are current or if they are due to the collector. The value of all stories would be enormously increased if they were recorded in the actual words of the story-tellers and in the original as well as translation.

'Ina in Mangaia

Hina' was a personage very widely known throughout Polynesia. She becomes 'Ina in Mangaia, and the story in part closely resembles the one from New Zealand. She was the only daughter of Vai-tooringa and Ngaetua, her brothers being Tangi-kuku and Rupe, in which two names enter the old Maori words for the pigeon, *kuku* and *rupe*. The word *tangi* means ' to sound ' as well as ' to lament,' so *tangi-kuku* means ' to sound *kuku* '—that is, to utter the call of the pigeon. Her parents were the wealthiest in the land of Nukutere, owning a rich breast-ornament, an abundance of finely braided hair, beautiful white shells worn on the arms, and a gorgeous headdress ornamented with scarlet and black feathers, with a frontlet of berries of the brightest red.

One morning the parents for the first time left their home in the care of 'Ina. The mother bade her put the treasures out to air, but to be sure to take them back into the house should the sun be clouded; for she knew that the arch-thief Ngana would not dare to come in the bright sunlight, daring to venture only on a lowering, cloudy day.

The sun shone brightly, and 'Ina spread out the treasures on a piece of purest white native cloth. But Ngana was on the watch. Cautiously he approached through the neighbouring bushes to get a good sight of the coveted treasures. He uttered an incantation, so that the sun

243

suddenly became obscured, when he fearlessly emerged from the thicket and endeavoured to seize the longed-for ornaments. But 'Ina was too quick for him, and secured them.

Now with affected humility he begged to be allowed only to try on the various adornments, for her to see how he would look in them. 'Ina was loth, but Ngana was persuasive, and at last she consented that he might put them on inside the house. Ngana entered, and to prevent the possibility of his taking any of them away she closed all means of exit. Ngana arrayed himself in the gorgeous adornments, all but the headdress, which 'Ina held in her hand. Ngana with soft words at length induced her to give up that too. Thus completely arrayed he began to dance with delight, round and about the house, keenly looking for some loophole of escape. At last he espied a little hole at the gable end, a few inches wide, through which at a bound he took his flight, and disappeared with the treasures. 'Ina at first had been delighted with the dancing of her visitor; but was in utter despair as she witnessed his flight, and heard his parting words:

> " Beware of listening to vain words,
> O 'Ina, the fair and well-meaning."

Not long afterward the parents of 'Ina came back in great haste, for they had seen the arch-thief, magnificently attired, pass proudly and swiftly through the sky, and a fear crept over them that all might not be right with their own treasures. From the weeping girl they learned of their loss. " But is nothing left? " they demanded. " Nothing whatever," said the downcast 'Ina.

Cruelly they beat her, both the mother and the father, until a divine power entered into her, and the astonished father heard the words :

> " Most sacred is my person;
> Untouched has been my person;
> I will go to Motu-tapu,
> That Tini-rau alone may strike me."

HINA', SISTER OF MAUI'

Her younger brother Rupe cried over his beloved sister. After a while 'Ina arose, moving about as if aimlessly; but no sooner did she elude the eyes of her parents than she ran to the sandy beach. She met her elder brother, Tangi-kuku; and on his asking her where she was going she gave an evasive answer; but fearing he might inform her parents of her flight she snatched his bamboo fishing-rod, broke it in pieces with her foot, and selected one of the fragments as a knife. With this she cut off the tip of his tongue; and after fondling her brother she pressed on to the shore, where she gazed long and wistfully toward the setting sun, where lay Motu-tapu, the sacred isle.

Looking about for some means of traversing the ocean, at her feet she saw a small fish named the *avini*; and, knowing that all fishes are subjects of Tini-rau, she thus addressed the little fish that gazed at her :

> " Little fish! art thou a shore-loving *avini*?
> Little fish! art thou an ocean-loving *avini*?
> Come, bear me on thy back
> To my royal husband Tini-rau,
> With him to live and die."

The little fish at once intimated its willingness by touching her feet. 'Ina mounted on its narrow back; but when only half-way to the reef, unable any longer to bear so unaccustomed a burden, it turned over, and 'Ina fell in the shallow water. Angry at this wetting, she repeatedly struck the *avini*; hence the beautiful stripes on its back to this day, called the tattooing of 'Ina.

The disappointed girl returned to the beach, to seek for some other means of reaching Motu-tapu. A fish named the *paoro*, larger than the *avini*, approached her. She addressed this as she had addressed the *avini*, and, mounted on its back, started a second time on her voyage. But, like the *avini*, the *paoro* was not long able to bear the burden, and dropped her in the shallow water. She struck it in her anger, producing the beautiful blue marks with which that fish has ever since been adorned.

'Ina next tried the *api*, which was originally white, but was made intensely black for upsetting her a third time, though this time the outer edge of the reef was reached. She tried the sole, and was borne to the edge of the breakers, when she experienced a fourth wetting. Growing more and more angry, she stamped with rage on the head of the unfortunate fish, until the underneath eye was removed to the upper side, so that ever afterward it was constrained to swim flatwise, one side of its face having no eye.

At the margin of the ocean a shark came in sight; and when she addressed it as she had the others to her delight it came to her feet, and she mounted on its broad back, carrying two coconuts with her as food. When half-way to Motu-tapu 'Ina became thirsty. She told the shark so, and it immediately erected its dorsal fin, on which she pierced the eye of one of her nuts. Again becoming thirsty, she again asked the shark for help. This time it lifted its head, and 'Ina forthwith cracked the hard shell on its forehead. This was apparently unexpected; for the shark, smarting from the blow, immediately dived, leaving the girl to float as best she could. From that day there has been a protuberance on the forehead of all sharks, known as " the bump of 'Ina."

'Ina, however, was favoured; for now appeared Takea the great, the king of sharks, and on his back, after adventures with other sharks, she reached the long-sought island Motu-tapu.

Upon going ashore she was astonished at the salt-water ponds, full of all kinds of fish, everywhere to be seen. Entering the dwelling of Tini-rau, the lord of all fish, she found one noble pond inside, but Tini-rau himself was nowhere to be seen. In another part of the house she was pleased to find a great wooden drum, and sticks for beating it at its side. Wishing to test her skill, she gently beat the drum, when to her astonishment the sweet sound filled all the land, and reached even to Pa-enua-kore (No Land at All), where Tini-rau was that day staying. He returned to Motu-tapu to discover who was beating the drum, but 'Ina saw him approaching, and ran and hid herself behind a hanging.

He entered, but could not discover the drummer; left the house; and set out to return to Pa-enua-kore. Then the shy girl, unwilling to lose so noble a husband, again beat the wonderful drum. Tini-rau returned, and, finding 'Ina, he made her his wife.

She gave birth to the famous Koro-mau-ariki, usually known as Koro', and a daughter, Ature. One morning she noticed on a bush near her dwelling a pretty linnet, such as she used to see in her old home. Gazing on it with pleasure, she was surprised to see the bird change into a human form. It was her brother Rupe, who, very desirous of seeing his sister 'Ina again, had asked a *karaurau* (a bird of the linnet species) to let him know where she lived. The bird consented; and Rupe, entering into it, had flown over the blue ocean to Motu-tapu. After a short stay Rupe returned to their parents, and told them of the welfare of 'Ina. They were rejoiced to hear of her, for though they had beaten her they had grieved for her when lost to them. A feast was made ready, and finest cloth prepared for 'Ina and her children. Mother and son now entered two *karaurau*, and laden with good things flew off in search of 'Ina. They arrived at the isle, mother and daughter embraced, the past was forgiven. For three days there were festivities in honour of Koro' and Ature; then the visitors returned to their home, and 'Ina was left happy with Tini-rau and her children.

The Dancing of Tini-rau and Koro'

It appears that Tini-rau and his son Koro' occasionally lived in the northern part of Mangaia. The son repeatedly noticed that his father disappeared at night, remaining away from their home two or three days at a time. Where he went was a mystery; but one thing greatly attracted the admiration of Koro'; whenever his father came back he was adorned with a fresh necklace of fragrant pandanus seeds, yellow and red. Determined to solve the mystery,

one night Koro' hid the girdle of Tini-rau, and then lay down
to sleep. Not long afterward his father sought everywhere
for the girdle, but in vain. He woke the boy, who found it
and gave it to him. Koro' pretended to go to sleep again,
but lay watching his father, who, adjusting his royal girdle,
went outside. Koro' silently followed him, and saw him
going through certain strange ceremonies: climbing a
coconut-tree in the usual fashion, but using his right hand
only, and never allowing his chest to touch the tree, selecting
nuts, descending in the same odd manner, and carefully
grating up the kernels. With this grated food wrapped
up in a leaf he set off toward the sea. On reaching the
beach he stood on a point of rock, still known as Aka-tangi,
or the Calling-place, and from it scattered the grated
coconut over the waters, while chanting a long incantation
to the fishes of the sea. Koro' listened attentively as he
had watched attentively, learning all, actions and words,
for future use if necessary. To the delight of the son, the
smaller fish of the reef immediately responded to the call
of Tini-rau, and came to taste of the food. Before long
the sound of the incantation was heard by the larger fish
in the ocean, who hurried to the shore, and ere the incantation was ended Motu-tapu itself came from afar and lay
at the edge of the reef. Thus the entire throng of the
subjects of Tini-rau assembled on the moving isle; and,
changing their forms into a partial resemblance of human
beings, came dancing to meet their lord. He joined them
in the dance, which was of the famous sort called *tautiti*,
in which hands and feet move at the same time. All were
arrayed in necklaces of sweet-scented pandanus seeds, which
grow plentifully in the home of Tini-rau. Motu-tapu,
Tini-rau, subjects and all, started off, dancing, and were
quickly lost to sight in the distance of ocean. Koro'
returned home, satisfied now that he knew the reason of
his father's disappearances.

A day or two afterward Tini-rau returned to his son,
fragrant as before, with a pandanus necklace, but quite
ignorant that Koro' had witnessed the proceedings on his

KORO' AND THE DANCERS BY MOONLIGHT
(See page 248)

last visit to Motu-tapu. It was some time before he went again; but he did not escape the vigilance of Koro', who was anxious to learn all the necessary invocations. All happened as before, and away went the merry Tini-rau, enjoying with his subjects their favourite pastime of dancing in the moonlight.

On the following night Koro' climbed the tree as his father had done, gathered the nuts, prepared the food, and proceeded to the calling-place. Reciting the incantation, he scattered the food on the waters; when, to his delight, the fish obeyed the summons, swimming in shoals to his feet. Motu-tapu too, with all its ponds and all its fish, appeared, and among the merry dancers Koro' had the joy of seeing his own father, dancing in the moonlight. He at once joined them, when his father greeted him thus: " Son, this, then, is why you hid away my girdle ! "

Arrayed like the rest in beautiful necklaces of fragrant pandanus seeds, father and son that night, and ever after when so inclined, enjoyed the pleasure of the midnight dance. It was Koro' who first planted the pandanus close to Aka-tangi, and it was he who taught the inhabitants of Mangaia the art of dancing. He divided his time between Motu-tapu and the northern shore of Mangaia, which was thence named Atua-Koro.

Festal Song of the Journey of 'Ina

Festal songs have been composed on the journeying of the lovely 'Ina, on the gathering of the fishes, on the dancing in the moonlight. The following is that on the dance *tautiti*, composed a hundred years ago—a hundred years and ten :

> *Call for the dance to begin.* I am Tau-titi.
>> The fragrant pandanus of the beach is mine, O 'Tane'.
> SOLO. Go on!
> CHORUS. That fragrant tree was first planted by the divine Koro'.
> SOLO. Ay!
> CHORUS. In yon gullies grow the favourite wreaths of Tau-titi.
> SOLO. Yes, in those gullies grow the red pandanus berries to adorn the dance.

249

MYTHS OF THE POLYNESIANS

SOLO. Groves of pandanus cover yon sandy beach.
CHORUS. Yes, groves of fragrant pandanus
For Tau-titi, whenever he may come.
SOLO. Ay!
CHORUS. This famous tree came from some other isle
To grace the sacred sandstone.
SOLO. Yes, to grace the sacred sandstone.
The fragrant pandanus on the beach is mine, O Tane'.
CHORUS. Go on!
That fragrant tree was first planted by the divine Koro'.
SOLO. Ay!
CHORUS. In yon gullies grow the favourite wreaths of Tau-titi.
SOLO. Yes, in those gullies grow the red pandanus berries to adorn
the dance.

Second Offshoot [1]

SOLO. Entwine sweet-scented fern-leaves.
CHORUS. What is going on yonder?
SOLO. At the margin of the sea?
CHORUS. Ay! Ay!
SOLO. Himself the god reveals!
CHORUS. Up from the netherworld has come Tau-titi.
SOLO. He stands revealed, O Tane'.
CHORUS. Through my body thrills the pleasure.
SOLO. Would I were a dragonfly
In the sun's beam exulting!

Sina and her Eel in Samoa

The foregoing story of 'Ina appears in many Polynesian variants. In Samoa the name 'Ina is Sina, the dropped *h* being restored, but replaced by *s*. In the Samoan variant Sina was the daughter of a couple, both apparently called Pai, dwelling at Mata-faga-tele. One day Sina found a young eel, which she kept and reared in a coconut shell. The eel grew, so that the coconut shell grew too small, and she changed it for a *kava*-bowl. The bowl growing too small, she kept the eel in a spring at Maata'a. It filled this spring, so she kept it in a bigger, and a bigger, and yet a bigger. At the side of the last spring grew a beautiful tree, the fruit of which was called *pua*. Sina

[1] Literal translation of original, evidently equivalent to "First Theme," "Second Theme," or something similar.

picked the fruit and threw it into the water, and herself entered the spring, swimming and gathering the fruit together. While she was so doing the eel struck her and pierced her with its tail. Sina was angry, and in displeasure went to Savai'i; but the eel left the water and followed her; and through all the land, where Sina went, there too went the eel. It followed to Upolu, coming there as the sun was sinking in the west. Its shadow was cast eastward, and the district that lay under the shadow was called Laloata.

The people of Fuata, as the whole of the district was called, determined to kill the eel. Poisonous leaves of the *lalago*-tree were gathered, bruised, and mixed with water in a bowl. When the eel saw that his death was meditated he called Sina, and said to her, " I know that poisoned drink will be brought to me. Therefore, O Sina, if you love me you will, on my death, claim my head as your share. Bury it by a Tonga stone wall, and from it a coconut-palm will grow for you. O Sina, you will have leaves for the plaiting of mats and fans with which to ensnare the monsoon and show your love for me." Thereupon the eel drank the prepared drink and died. Of Sina, since she had been pierced by the eel, this song was sung :

> Maiden Sina, daughter of Pai,
> Thou hast plucked the *pua*-fruit and flung it in the water.
> Swimming thou hast gathered it,
> And by the tail of the eel hast been shamed.

It is difficult to understand how she was to ensnare the monsoon with her fan—assuming that the story has been correctly recorded; it no doubt means that she catches the wind with her fan as a serf to cool her, as the sail of the canoe catches the wind to propel it.

This again has a variant. The mother of Sina went down to the sea to draw salt water for cooking purposes. A small sea-eel adhered to her coconut-shell water-bottle, and she took it home as a plaything for her daughter Sina. She fed it, keeping it in a cup; but the eel grew, and they dug a pond for it. One day Pai and his wife returned from some plantation work, and found Sina crying, as the eel had bitten her. Fearing it must have become the incarnation of some cruel deity, they determined to leave that place.

Away the three went eastward; but when they looked round, there was the eel, out of the water and following after them. "You make your escape," said the father to his wife and Sina; "I will remain here and raise mountains to keep it back." Sina and her mother went on, but when they looked over their shoulder, there was the eel again, still following after them. Then the mother said to her daughter, "You make your escape alone; I will remain here and raise mountains in the way of the creature." Sina went on alone, but the eel followed just as before. As she passed through the villages the people called her in to rest and have a little food; and she agreed to do so provided that they would try to deliver her from the pursuing eel. When they heard that, and saw the creature, they said, "Oh, no; you had better pass on; we are afraid of that thing."

She thought escape impossible, and gave it up, turning again toward her home. As she passed through one of the villages east of Apia the people called the attention of the chief to the young woman passing, followed by an eel. He told them to call her in to have something to drink. She said she would gladly do so if they would only get rid of the eel. "Yes, come in; we can do that," the chief called to her. She went into the house; the eel remained outside. The chief gave orders for the preparation of a cup of 'ava (kava) for the strangers, and quietly whispered to the young men to bring from the bush all the poisonous things they could find to mix with the drink. Soon the 'ava was declared ready to hand round.

"Give the first cup to the stranger outside," said the chief to the young men; and out went one of them with the cup for the eel, which drank it eagerly. But immediately the creature called to Sina to come outside; and when she went out it said to her, "Since I am dying, let us part in peace. When you hear that they have cooked me, ask the head as

252

your share. Take it and bury it near the stone wall, and it will grow up into a coconut-tree for you. In the nuts you will see my eyes and mouth, and so we shall still be able to look at each other face to face. The leaves of the tree will be a shade for you, and you will be able to plait them into mats and fans."

Saying this, the creature died, and was soon in the oven; and when it was served up Sina begged the head, took it home with her, and buried it near the stone wall. It grew up into a coconut-tree, and she got her leaves, and mats, and fans, and nuts; and the nuts were marked with the eyes and mouth of her departed eel, whose face she could still touch with hers. There, too, she had a shade—and hence the introduction of coconuts. The dying words of the eel are here more easily understood than in the former version, where Sina is told to ensnare the monsoon.

Origin of the Coconut in New Guinea

Now while New Guinea forms no part of Polynesia, the story of Hina and the eel is there so extraordinarily transformed that it is of more than passing interest. The men of Kulawa were out hunting, found a snake, and killed it. Returning home they smoked it, and would have eaten it at their evening meal, but a girl who was near asked for a portion to taste, and they gave her the tail. She found it so agreeable that she asked for more, and they gave her the middle; and more, and they gave her more, and so on until she had all, including the head.

After a time she gave birth to a son who had the form of a snake, and she feared him. She therefore left him, and crossed the sea to the island of Iriwavo. Rain fell, and thunder sounded, but the snake swam after, so as to be with his mother. She fled farther, to Bolanai; but she knew she would not even here be safe from her son, so she said to the men of Bolonai, " Cut many sharp stakes. Presently a snake will come to the village. Spare him not, but cut him in pieces." They did so, cut the snake in pieces and boiled them. " We have done well to obey

the voice of the woman," said they, " for the eating is good."
Then said an old woman to them, " It were a pity for the
memory of this good food to fade. Give me some to plant
in my garden, that we may see if perchance it will live there."

They gave the old woman some of the flesh, and she
planted it in her garden. After many days it sprouted and
grew above the earth ; and many people came and broke off
shoots from the strange plant, and planted them in their
own gardens ; and they ate the roots, the name of the plant
being *taro*. Thus it was that the *taro* was introduced to
the people of Bolonai.

Thinking of Hina, one had expected the plant to be a
coconut ; but there is another story. In a certain village
the men went every morning to catch fish, each man
bringing home his string full ; but one man, who always
went alone, brought enough to fill a basket.

The others wondered how it was that he always brought
so many more than they did, and why he always persisted in
going alone. A boy, hearing them consulting together,
thought of a plan, and said, " When he sets out to-morrow
I will creep behind him, and will watch from the long grass
to see what he does." " It is well said," said the men.

On the morrow the boy did as he proposed, following
through the grass as the man went along the path. Sometimes in his eagerness he crept too near, the rustling causing
the man to look round, and even to cast a spear to kill the
animal making the rustling sound. But the boy, seeing the
spear coming, moved to one side, and went more warily.
When the man reached the seashore the boy hid behind
a *tioba* (corkwood-tree), when he saw this strange thing.
The man set down his basket, and putting both hands to
his head he pulled, and the head came off in his hands.
He laid his head beside the basket on the beach, and walked
into the sea until the water reached about his middle. There
he stood, and bowed himself, and a multitude of fishes
rushed down his throat, which was open to the water, the
head being on the beach. After a short time he stood up,
turned, and walked slowly to the shore. There he shook

out the fish, and feeling for his head he lifted it up and placed it on his neck, and it was part of him once more. Then he sat down and sorted out the fish he had caught, filling his basket with the largest and throwing the others away.   All this the boy saw from behind the *tioba*, and having seen he fled, for he feared the man who did such things.

At supper-time all except the boy ate of the fish which had been thus caught; and though asked why he did not eat, he would not say, but refused even to touch the fish that the man had caught.

After supper certain of the men went apart with the boy and inquired of him the reason for his refusing to eat the fish, and he told them all that he had seen, and they too were filled with loathing.   They determined to punish the man, and next day they secretly followed him to the beach; and when he laid his head beside the basket not one but many were watching him.   When he bowed himself and the fish swam into his throat a man rose up, ran to the head, seized it, and flung it far into the bush.   Then all waited to see what would happen.

Having fish enough, the man turned and came slowly back to the shore.   There he shook out the fish as was his custom, and then with his hands he felt for his head, but lo! it was not there.   He crawled over the pebbles with hands outstretched, searching and seeking, but in vain. Suddenly he arose and rushed into the sea again; and there before their eyes he became a huge fish and dived out of sight.   Having taken their vengeance, the men returned to the village.

After many days the boy who had first spied upon the man sought the head, to see what had befallen it; but when he reached the spot where it had been thrown it was no longer there.   In its stead had grown up a slender palm, with spreading leaves.   None knew what plant it might be; and when it bore fruit men feared to eat of it lest it might harm them.   But at last a woman boldly ate of the nuts, and anointed herself with the milky juice, and they saw that she was none the worse for it, but rather better.   Thus did

255

men come to know the coconut, and from that time it became their fruit and drink. If, too, the husk be taken from the nut there may be seen the face of the man from whose head the tree first sprang.

Origin of the Coconut in Pukapuka

There is a peculiar variant in Danger Island (Pukapuka), about 350 miles north-east of Samoa, which refers only to the origin of the coconut-tree, making no mention of Hina. There was a man, Avie-ure, and a woman, Avie-poto, who had long lived together happily. The woman had not yet conceived, and she would eat of any of the fish caught and brought to her by her husband. When at last she became pregnant, however, she grew fastidious, and would not eat of the fish brought by him. He went fishing every day, and brought a great variety of fish, but she had no desire for them. He went again and again to the seashore, as he was anxious to discover some fish his wife would care for.

On one of his expeditions he caught a very great variety, and quite filled his basket; he took them to his wife, who emptied them out to examine them, but found none such as she desired. On striking the bottom of the basket, however, there fell out one of the particular fish for which the woman had a desire. It was a very tiny fish, but as soon as she saw it she called to her husband, " Here it is ! " She then asked whence it came, to which he answered, " There are more." She ate it; and when the husband saw this he prepared a fish-hook, which was made of *toa*-wood, and twisted a line, afterward placing on the hook bait consisting of sweet-scented flowers of plants, such as *tiare*, *maire*, *nau*, *vavai*, and many other flowers, even the flowers of the *tamanu*. He placed these in a basket, and proceeded to the shore to a place of which he knew, to fish for that particular fish, whose name was *tuna* (eel). It was not a fresh-water eel, but a sea-eel.

He fished with one of those baits, but the fish would not take it; then with several others, but without success, until the man almost despaired of catching any, and all his bait

256

was exhausted. He struck the basket, and out fell the flower of the *tamanu*-tree, and at last he was successful; he caught the fish, and carried it to his wife.

Now when they proceeded to cut up the *tuna* it spoke to them, saying, "Salutations to you two! When you eat me, first cut off my head and bury it in front of the door of your house, and when it begins to grow do not shake it, nor when it grows big, nor when its leaves appear, nor when it grows tall, nor when it *taume* [meaning unknown], nor when the food is cooked, nor when the food is ripe, nor when the nut is large, nor when it falls ripe to the ground; but when you see the coconuts are very numerous, then you must distribute them to all the people."

When the *tuna* had finished his directions they cut off his head, buried it in front of their door, and waited for the fulfilment of the directions of their fish. The tree grew, until it bore coconuts, great coconuts, of the *nu-katea* kind; the fruit fell to the ground; but they carefully guarded the tree until the fruit was plentiful, and then they distributed it to all the islands of this world. But Pukapuka was without it, so the two people searched and found a *nu-ponga* (a kind of coconut) and distributed this among the people there. Hence these people say it is from that *nu-ponga* that all their coconuts are *ponga*. This is a cryptic saying that may be clear enough to the people themselves; it is part of the story, so the story is incomplete without it, be its interpretation what it may. Furthermore, it is evident, since they had to bring the coconut to Pukapuka, that the man and woman of the story did not live on Pukapuka, though the story does not say so; as in many of these legends, the hearer is already supposed to know enough to render explanations unnecessary.

Origin of the Coconut in the Tuamotu Group

Away on Napuka (Disappointment Island), on the northeast margin of the Tuamotu group, Maui' enters into the story of Hina and the eel. The story, once widely known in the archipelago, is in the form of a dialogue:

SCENE I

TUNA. Who art thou?
MAUI'. I am Maui'.
TUNA. Whence comest thou?
MAUI'. I come from below.
TUNA. Look hither, then; wait, and leap thou into the jaws of Tuna.
MAUI'. Open then.

> [*Maui' leaps into Tuna, and with a shark's tooth begins to saw vigorously and with long strokes. Anon he reappears outside.*

SCENE II

Tuna persists.

TUNA. Who, then, art thou?
MAUI'. It is I, Maui'.
TUNA. Look hither, then; wait a little, and then leap into the jaws of Tuna.
MAUI'. If thou openest.

> [*Again Maui' enters into Tuna; he saws and saws, until he has made an end. He then emerges.*

SCENE III

The same interrogations, the same replies. It was not until Maui' had entered the third time that he killed Tuna. Maui' then cried out.

MAUI'. Tuna, Tuna.
Thou thyself hast invited me to wait and enter thy jaws.

> [*With his adze Maui' saws, cuts, and detaches the head of Tuna, and carries it down into the earth. Arriving there, he calls to Hina his wife, saying, "Tuna is slain, and here is the head of him." Hina hastens to see. Each takes a jawbone, and buries it. Both jawbones germinate and grow, becoming the first coconut-trees of the Tuamotu group.*

In this story, where Hina is the wife of Maui', not his sister, are linked up many of the variants of the stories of Maui' and Tuna-roa, Hina and the eel.

'Ina' and the Eel in Mangaia

Besides the 'Ina above (page 243), there were four other women of this name known in Mangaia. These were daughters of Kui the blind; but while they are unrelated so far as parentage is concerned to the 'Ina whose story has been told, one of them at least is related to 'Ina the voyager in another way. While *kui* is the word for an old woman, Kui seems also to have been used as a proper name; and the name Kui appears, often in a shadowy fashion, far and wide in Polynesia. The incidents in the Mangaian story of Kui the blind relate her to Whai-tiri of the Tawhaki cycle. It is the god Tane' who steals her roots in the Mangaian story, while it is Maui' in Manihiki, and Ta-whaki in Tahiti and New Zealand.

One daughter of Kui, 'Ina-moe-aitu ('Ina who had a Divine Lover), dwelt at Tamarua, near a sluggish stream abounding in eels. At dawn and sunset 'Ina' loved to bathe in that stream near a clump of trees. On one occasion a great eel crept up the stream, and startled her with its touch. This occurred again and again, until 'Ina' became accustomed to its presence. To her surprise, one day as she sat watching her companion its form changed, and the fish assumed the appearance of a handsome youth, who said to her, " I am Tuna, the god and protector of all fresh-water eels. Your beauty induced me to leave my gloomy home to win your love." She gave her love, and in his human form he became her admirer, always resuming his eel-shape to return to his haunts in the sluggish stream. Some time after he said to 'Ina', " We must part; but in memory of our attachment I will bestow on you a boon. To-morrow there will be a great rain, flooding all the valley; but do not fear it. It will enable me to approach your house on yon rising ground in my eel-form. I shall lay head upon your wooden threshold; at once cut off my head and bury it; then visit the spot daily and see what will come of it."

'Ina' saw no more of her lover, but was that night roused from sleep by the rain falling in torrents. Remembering the words of Tuna, she remained quietly in her dwelling until daylight, when she found that the water, streaming from the hills, had risen close to the entrance to her hut. A great eel approached her and laid its head upon the threshold. 'Ina' fetched her axe, cut off the head, and buried it on the hillside at the back of her hut. The rain ceased, and the waters subsided.

'Ina' daily visited the place where the head was buried, and after many days she was delighted to see a stout green shoot piercing the soil. Next day the shoot had divided into two. The shoots, gradually unfolding, were quite different from other plants. They grew to maturity, sending forth great leaves, and in the course of years flowers and fruit appeared. They were coconut-trees; and of the twin trees, sprung from the two halves of the brain of Tuna, one was red in stem, branches, and fruit, while the other was deep green. Thus the two varieties of coconut came into existence, the red being sacred to Tangaroa, the green to Rongo. The white kernel of the nut is called the brain of Tuna; and when the nuts are husked, on each one is seen the eyes and the mouth of the lover of 'Ina'. No woman will eat of the flesh of the fish whose protector was, before his death, that lover of 'Ina'.

This story of the girl with an eel for a lover was also collected from an old blind man at a Whanga-nui village, in New Zealand, by Elsdon Best in 1922. The old man could recall no names, but the main facts were the same; and I remember Elsdon Best's smile that night as he came away from the old man. "A curious and interesting old folk-tale," said he as he went to his note-book.

'Ina in the Moon

The eldest of the attractive daughters of Kui the blind was simply called 'Ina. Marama the moon had long admired her from afar, and at last he became so enamoured of her that one night he descended from his place in the heavens to take her to be his wife. She became a pattern wife, always busy, and on a clear night may easily be discerned the pile of leaves for her never-failing oven of food, also her tongs of a split coconut branch, to enable her to move the hot coals without burning her fingers.

'Ina is indefatigable in the preparation of splendid cloth —that is, the white clouds of the sky. As soon as her bark-cloth (*tapa*) is well beaten and brought to the desired shape she stretches it out to dry on the upper part of the blue sky, the edges all round being secured with large stones. Smoothing out the creases, she leaves it there to bleach.

INA AND THE EEL TRANSFORMED INTO A YOUTH

(See page 260)

THE PARTING OF THE MOON-GODDESS AND THE MORTAL
(See page 262)

The manufacture of the *tapa* being on a grander scale than on earth, the stones are of much greater size ; and when the operation is completed 'Ina takes up these stones and casts them aside. They roll violently crashing against the upper surface of the solid blue vault, producing what mortals call thunder. Occasionally she first removes the stones from the portion nearest herself ; then, hastily rising, shakes off the others, emptying out, as it were, the lot at once, when the great stones, all falling together, produce a terrific thunderclap. The cloth glistens like the sun ; hence it is that when she hastily gathers up her many rolls of *tapa* flashes of light seem to fall on the earth, which are called lightning.

In Norse mythology, Frigga, the wife of Odin, was said to delight in sitting in Fensaler, her hall of mists, spinning her long webs of coloured clouds. The jewelled distaff then used by her was what is known to us as the belt of Orion.

Throughout the Hervey group of islands the only names for moonlight and moonless refer to 'Ina. Moonlight is 'Ina-motea (the Brightness of 'Ina) ; no moon is 'Ina-poiri ('Ina Invisible) ; these names correspond to the Maori Hina-keha and Hina-uri, where again 'Ina is connected with the sister of Maui' and through her with 'Ina the voyager.

The Sorrow of the Moon-loved Mortal

At Atiu, 100 miles north of Mangaia, it is said that Ina of the moon took to her celestial abode a mortal as a husband. After living together happily for many years she said to him, " You are bending to age and infirmity ; soon death will claim you, for you are a native of earth. This home of mine must not know the defilement of death ; we must embrace and part. Return to earth, and there end your days." At that moment 'Ina caused a beautiful rainbow to span the heavens, by which her aged and disconsolate husband descended to the earth to die. *Aue !*

Hina-tu-moana reaches the Moon

Another linking up of the stories comes from Tahiti, where Hina-tu-moana was beaten by her parents because

261

she lost the family treasures in a freshet. She voyaged to
Motu-tapu on a ray-fish with her brother Ru, no doubt the
same as Rupe. She went on farther in her canoe, aimed
at the moon, reached it, and became goddess of the moon,
leaving Ru as master of the earth. Many places in the
Society Islands are named after her—the opening of the
reef through which she sailed, the place where she beat out
her *tapa*, the site of her breadfruit-tree, and others.

The names 'Ina, Hina, and Sina link up yet more closely
when it is known that the aspirate in Maori was sometimes
accompanied by a sibilant, so that the well-known name
Hongi was heard, and written, Shongi, and Hauraki
Shouraki. With that sound Hina would be Shina (the *i*
with the sound of *ee*), and, the aspirate dropped, Shina
would become the Sina of Samoa. The intentional omission
of the *s* sound from the Maori alphabet, together with the
omission of the once-heard *d* and *l*, has caused those sounds
to be quite lost in Maori; they are now rarely heard at all.

Sina in the Moon

In Samoa Sina is connected with the moon. It may, of
course, be a different Sina who was, during a time of famine,
sitting with her child in the twilight beating out bark for
cloth. The moon was just rising, and its appearance
reminded her of a great breadfruit. Looking toward it
she said, " Why cannot you come down and let my child
have a bit of you? " The moon was indignant at the idea
of being eaten, came down forthwith, and took up Sina, her
child, mallet and all. People looking up say, " Yonder is
Sina, and her child, and her beater and board."

Rona in the Moon

The preceding story is the parallel of the Maori story of
Rona, who one bright moonlight night went to fetch water
from the stream for her children. In her hand was the
basket containing the calabash to hold the water. On her
way the moon suddenly disappeared behind a cloud; and,
the track being narrow, with projecting roots of trees and

bushes, she kicked her foot against a root. In her momentary anger she cursed the moon, saying, "You cooked-headed moon, not to come forth and shine!" These words displeased the moon, who came down to earth and seized her. Rona caught hold of a *ngaio*-tree that was growing on the bank of the stream; but the moon tore the tree up by the roots, and flew away, taking Rona, the tree, and the gourd and basket far up into the sky. Her friends and children, thinking she was a long time away, went to look for her. Not finding any traces of her, they called, "Rona, O Rona, where are you?" She answered from the sky, "Here I am, mounting aloft with the moon and the stars."

When it is a clear night, especially when the moon is full, Rona may be seen reclining against the rocks, her calabash at her side, and the *ngaio*-tree close by.

This is, of course, the fireside version; in the superior, Rona and Tangaroa between them control the tides, whence their secondary names, Whakamau-tai.

Lono of the Moon

The sex both of Rona and the moon is different in different versions; and in a Hawaiian version the sex of the one person changes. There Hina was the wife of Ai-kanaka (Maori Kai-tangata); and being disgusted with the uncleanness of her children Puna and Hema, she left them and went up to the moon to live. As she was going her husband seized her to detain her, and in the struggle he broke her leg and maimed her, on which account she was called Lono-moku (Rongo-motu), the Maimed (or Crippled) Lono. Lono was a male—the god of light.

The Legend of Hina' in Hawaii

The legend appears to have undergone great change in Hawaii, where the story of Hina' is mixed up with the fishing of Maui' and his slaying of Tuna-roa. Ku-ula (Tu-kura) was the Hawaiian god of fishermen, his wife, goddess of fishes, being Hina', or Hina-hele, known also

263

as La-ea (Rakea) and Hina-ulu-ohia (Hina-uru-ohia). Their home, strangely enough, was on the island Maui, one of the Hawaiian group.

While living at Leho-ula (Reho-kura) he devoted all his time to fishing, and near his dwelling he constructed a fishpond on the surf-beaten shore which he stocked with all kinds of fish. The fish knew him, and would always come to call. A son was born to Ku-ula and Hina', and named Aiai-a-Ku-ula (Akiaki-a-Tu-kura).

A large eel called Koona (Tuna) lived at Wai-lau (Wairau), on the island Molokai, but it left this haunt and came to live in a cave Kapukaulua (Taputaurua), on purpose to rob the pond of Ku-ula.

Ku-ula caught the eel committing its depredations, and meditated its destruction, but his wife persuaded him to leave that to their son Aiai'. He ordered the preparation of long ropes, and when they were ready two canoes set out laden with the ropes and two large stones, which Aiai' placed in the canoe in which he went; and he held in his hands a fisherman's gourd containing a large hook called Manaia-akalani (Manaia-atarangi).

The canoes went far out to sea, and when he had located his position by certain landmarks, and by looking down into the depths of the water, he gave the order to cease paddling. Taking one of the stones in his hands, he dived into the sea, rapidly reaching the bottom, where he saw the opening of a great cave, with *ulua* and other deep-sea fishes darting about the entrance. He rose to the surface, and took out the hook Manaia-akalani, and tied it to two lengths of rope. He also took a long stick, at the end of which he fixed the hook, baited with a preparation of coconut and other substances. He picked up the other stone and again dived down, and on reaching the cave thrust the hook into it, while murmuring incantations in the name of his parents. When he knew the eel was hooked he signalled, as had been arranged, to those above.

He returned to the surface, and the canoes were paddled ashore, each to its own landing, and on a signal from Aiai'

the ropes were hauled and Koona dragged ashore. The bones
of its jaws and its backbone may still be seen in the rocks.

The second part of this story is here omitted, as it is in
the first part that the parallels with other stories occur.
Hina' appears and Tuna-roa, and the fishing and eel-slaying
of Maui' are combined. In a Maori version of the fishing
Aki was a man used as bait by Maui'. It is curious, too,
though perhaps without significance, that a famous chief,
Manaia, who fought two battles in Hawaiki owned a weapon
called Rakea; and while one meaning of *atarangi* is ' a
heavenly shadow,' it almost corresponds to part of the name
Maui-tikitiki-a-Taranga. Some of these parallels are
significant; some perhaps merely curious. The descent of
Aiai' in the sea to the cave of Koona is reminiscent of the
descent of Beowulf in the mere to the cave of the mother
of Grendel. In the long chant of Kualii of Oahu, given
by Fornander, the hook Manaiakalani (? Manaia-akalani) is
the hook of Maui' :

> A messenger sent by Maui' to bring,
> To bring Kane and his company,
> And Kanaloa, and Kauakahi,
> And Maliu.
>> To praise and to offer, to offer up prayer,
>> To offer and decree the fortune of the chief.
> The great fish-hook of Maui',
> Manaiakalani,
> Its line, naturally twisted is the string that ties his hook.
>> Engulfed is the lofty Kauwiki,
>> Where Hina-i-ka-malama dwelt.
> The bait was the Alae of Hina',
> Let down upon Hawaii,
> The sacred tangle, the painful death,
> Seizing upon the foundations of the earth,
> Floating it up to the surface of the sea.
> Hina' hid the wing of the *alae*,
> Broken up was the table of Laka,
> Carried away below [was the bait] to Kea;
> The fish ate it, the *ulua* of the deep muddy places.

The *alae* was the mud-hen, sacred to Hina', the wife or
daughter of Kanaloa (Tangaroa and Tini-rau sometimes

change places in the myths), who hid one of the wings of the bird, and defeated the purpose of Maui', so that the bottom of the sea, called the table of Laka (Rata), was broken up, and came to the surface only in the shape of islands. Kauwiki refers to a prominent hill in Hana, a district in Maui, where Hina-i-ka-malama (Hina-i-te-marama—Hina of the Moon), mother of the Hawaiian Maui', dwelt.

The stories of Hina', or 'Ina, appear to be as ancient as the stories of Maui'. In some legends Hina' was the mother of Maui', in some his wife, in some his sister. The very many variants seem to point to the fact that both Maui' and Hina' were known to the Polynesians before their separation on entering the Pacific, and that while the names have been preserved among the various branches of the race, and the stories in great part, the latter have undergone considerable change; parts have been lost, and new incidents have been added.

CHAPTER IX: PELE THE FIRE-GODDESS

ONE of the strangest figures in the Hawaiian pantheon is Pele, goddess of volcanoes, more especially of Kilauea. She appeared to enter more closely into the lives of the people than any of the gods or demigods, perhaps because her origin as goddess was almost within historical times. She was fiery and impetuous as her own volcano, and almost as elemental in her passions; it was dangerous to cross her; it was almost as dangerous to be loved by her. Kahawali, chief of Puna, and a favourite companion one day went to amuse themselves with a *holua* (sled or toboggan) on the side of a hill. Numbers of people gathered at the bottom of the hill to view the sport, and a company of musicians and dancers enlivened the scene. They began their dance, and amid the sound of the drums and the singing the sledding of Kahawali went on.

The merriment that echoed from the spot attracted the attention of Pele, who came down from Kilauea to witness the sport. Standing on the summit of the hill as a woman, she challenged Kahawali to slide with her. He accepted the challenge, and off they went together, flying down the hill. Pele, less expert than Kahawali in the art of balancing on the narrow sled, was beaten, and Kahawali was applauded as he returned up the side of the hill.

Before starting again, Pele wished to exchange sleds, thinking perhaps that the virtue of speed was in the sled rather than in the guider; but Kahawali, supposing her from her appearance to be no more than a native woman, said, " *Aole!* [*Kahore*—No!] Are you my wife that you should have my sled? " And as if impatient of delay he ran a few yards to take a spring, and then with vigour he threw himself on his sled and shot down the hill.

Pele, incensed at his answer and action, stamped her foot on the ground, and an earthquake followed which rent the hill asunder. She called, and fire and liquid lava arose; and, assuming her supernatural form, with these irresistible ministers of vengeance she followed down the hill. When

Kahawali reached the bottom he arose, and on looking up the hill he saw Pele, accompanied by thunder and lightning, earthquake, and streams of burning, steaming lava, closely pursuing him.

He took up his broad spear and fled for his life. On came the lava, Pele riding its advancing crest, and overwhelmed musicians, dancers, spectators. Kahawali reached the house of his mother. "Compassion great to you," said he. "Close here, perhaps, is your death; Pele comes devouring." Thus he met relative and wife, and with farewell sped on. He came to a chasm; he laid his spear across it, and walked over in safety, the lava rolling near. He reached the sea, he leaped into a canoe, and paddled for the open sea. Pele, perceiving his escape, stood on the shore and hurled after him, like a female Polyphemus, great stones and cliffy fragments of rock, which fell thickly around him, but did not strike his canoe. When he had paddled a little distance an east wind sprang up; he fixed his broad spear upright in the canoe to act as mast and sail, and soon reached the island of Maui. A perilous adventure; a bare deliverance.

At one time Pele fell in love with a mortal; and this is the story of the fiery wooing. Pele, her brothers, and sisters one day, to amuse themselves with a taste of mortal enjoyments, left their lurid caves in the crater of Kilauea, and went down to the coast of Puna to bathe, surf-ride, sport in the sands, and gather squid, limpets, edible seaweed, and like delicacies. As they had assumed human forms for the time, so for the time they experienced human appetites.

While the others were amusing themselves in various ways Pele, in the guise of an old woman, sought repose and sleep in the shade of a *hala*-tree. Her favourite sister was Hiiaka', her full name being Hiiaka-i-ka-pali-o-Pele. She was younger than Pele, and they frequently occupied the same grotto under the burning lake of Kilauea.

Hiiaka' accompanied her sister, and, sitting beside her, kept her cool with a *kahili* (feather plume). Her eyelids

PELE AND HER ANGER OF FIRE
(See page 268)

growing heavy, Pele settled herself to sleep, instructing Hiiaka' to allow her under no circumstances to be disturbed, no matter how long she might sleep, be it for hours or be it for days; she then fell into a sound sleep.

Hardly was she lapped in the silence of forgetfulness when the sound of a beaten drum fell on her ear; a distant beating, but regular as if to the impulse of music. Before leaving the crater she had heard the same sound, but had paid little attention to it. Now in her dreams, however, her curiosity was awakened, and assuming her spiritual form she set off in the direction from which the sound seemed to come. Leaving her slumbering body in the care of Hiiaka', Pele followed the sound all over Hawaii; and always it seemed just before her, but never there, so that she could not overtake it. At Upolu it came to her from over the sea, and she followed it to the island of Maui. It was still beyond, and she followed to Molokai; still beyond, and she followed to Oahu; still beyond, and she followed to Kauai. She stood on the peak of Haupu, when she saw at last that the sound came from the beach at Kaena.

Hovering unseen over the place, she observed that the sound she had so long followed was that of the *pahu-hula*, or *hula* drum, beaten by Lohiau, the young and handsome Prince of Kauai, who was noted not only for the splendour of his *hula* entertainments, where danced the most beautiful women of the island, but also for his own personal graces as dancer and musician. The favourite deity of Lohiau was Laka-kane, the god of the *hula* and similar sport, and it was this god who, in a spirit of mischief, had conveyed the sound to Pele, awaking in her the curiosity that urged her on and on.

The beach was thronged with dancers, musicians, and spectators, all enjoying themselves under the shade of the *hala-* and coconut-trees, with the Prince as leader and the centre of attraction. Assuming the form of a beautiful woman, Pele suddenly appeared among them. Displaying every imaginable charm of form and feature, her presence was at once noted; and, a way being opened for her to the

Prince, he received her graciously and invited her to a seat near him, where she could best witness the entertainment.

Glancing at the beautiful stranger from time to time in the midst of his performances, Lohiau at length became so fascinated that he failed to follow the music, when he yielded the instrument to another, and seated himself beside the enchantress. In answer to his inquiry she informed the Prince that she was a stranger in Kauai, and had come from the direction of the rising sun.

" You are most welcome," said Lohiau, adding, after a pause, " but I cannot rejoice that you have come."

" And why, since I do not come as your enemy ? " asked Pele, increasing, with her glances, the turmoil within him.

" Because until now," answered the Prince " my thought has been that there are beautiful women in Kauai."

" I see you know how to shape your speech to suit the fancies of women," said Pele provocatively.

" Not better than I know how to love them," answered Lohiau. " Would you be convinced ? "

" Lohiau is in his own kingdom, and has but to command," was her reply ; and her play of modesty completed the enthralment of the Prince.

Thus Pele became the wife of Lohiau. He knew nothing of her but what delighted him, nor did he care to inquire about that which he could not discover without inquiry. He saw that she was beautiful above all women, and for a few days they lived so happily together that life seemed a dream to him, as it was a dream to her. But the time had to come when she must return to Hawaii ; and, pledging him to remain true to her, she left him with protestations of affection and the promise of a speedy return ; and on the wings of the wind she was wafted back to the shores of Puna, where her sister was still patiently watching and waiting in the shade of the *hala*.

Lohiau was inconsolable. As each day passed, he thought she would be with him the next, until more than a month went by, when he refused food, and died in grief at her absence. The strange death of the Prince caused much comment, for he was physically strong, and suffered from no malady. Some declared that he had been prayed to death by enemies; some that he had been poisoned; but an old *kaula* (prophet), who had seen Pele at Kaena and noted her actions, advised against further inquiry concerning the cause of death, offering as a reason the opinion that the strangely beautiful and unknown woman he had taken as wife was an immortal, who had become attached to her earthly husband and called his spirit to her.

The Prince was much loved by his people; and his body, wrapped in many folds of *tapa*, was kept in state for some time in the royal house. It was guarded by the high chiefs of the kingdom, and every night funeral hymns were chanted round it, and *mele* recited of the deeds of the dead prince and his ancestors.

Let us return now to Pele. Her body had been carefully watched by her brothers and sisters, who had not dared to disturb it; and her return was greeted with joy, for the fires of Kilauea had almost died out with neglect. Pele rose to her feet in the form of the old woman she had assumed when falling asleep in the care of Hiiaka'; and without referring to her adventures in Kauai, or to the cause of her long slumber, she returned with the others to Kilauea, and with a breath renewed the dying fires of the crater. Hiiaka' asked and received from Pele permission to remain for a few days at the beach with her loved friend Hopoe, a young woman of Puna, who had lost both her parents in an eruption of Kilauea.

It is probable that Pele, on leaving Kauai, notwithstanding her fervent words to the contrary, never expected, or particularly desired, to see Lohiau again; but he had so endeared himself to her during their brief union that she found it difficult to forget him; and, after struggling against the feeling for some time, she resolved to send for him. But to whom could she entrust the important mission? She applied to her sisters at the crater one after another; but the way was beset with evil spirits, and one after another refused to go.

In this dilemma Pele sent her brother Lono-i-ka-onolii to bring Hiiaka' from the beach, well knowing that she would not refuse to undertake the journey, however hazardous. Hiiaka' accepted the mission, with the understanding that during her absence her friend Hopoe should remain in the guardianship of Pele.

Arrangements were made for her immediate departure. Pele conferred upon her some of her own powers, and for a companion servant gave her Pauo-palae, a woman of proved sagacity and prudence.

With a farewell from the relatives of Hiiaka' and many an admonition from Pele they took their departure; and, travelling as mortals, they were subject to the fatigues and perils of mortals. They met a woman, whose name was Omeo, and who was leading a hog to the volcano as a sacrifice to Pele. She desired to accompany them; and, they agreeing, she hastened to the crater with her offering, returned, and followed Hiiaka' and her companion. Proceeding through the forests toward the coast of Hilo, they were impeded by a hideous demon, who threw himself across their path in a narrow defile and attempted to destroy them; but Pele was aware of their danger, and ordered her brothers to protect them with a rain of fire and thunder, which drove the monster to his den and enabled them to escape.

The forests abounded in mischievous gnomes and fairies, nymphs and monsters guarded the streams; the air was peopled with spirits, for a thin veil only separated the living from the dead, the natural from the supernatural.

Again they had not gone far when they encountered a man of fierce appearance who was either insane or possessed of demons; but he lacked the power or the disposition to injure them, and they passed on unharmed. Coming to a small stream, they found the waters dammed by a huge *mo'o*, or lizard (*moko*), lying in the bed. He was more than a hundred paces in length, with eyes the size of great calabashes. He glared viciously, and opened his mouth as if to devour the travellers; but Hiiaka' tossed a stone into his mouth which on touching his throat became red-hot, and with a roar of pain that made the trees tremble he disappeared down the stream.

After many adventures with monsters and evil spirits they reached the coast at Honoipo, where they found a number of men and women engaged in the sport of surf-riding. As they were about to start on another trial Hiiaka' in a spirit of mischief turned their surf-boards into stone, and they fled from the beach in terror, fearing that some sea-god was preparing to devour them.

Observing a fisherman drawing in a line, Hiiaka' caused a human head to be fastened to the submerged hook. The man raised it to the surface, stared at it in horror for a moment, then dropped the line and paddled swiftly away, to the great amusement of Hiiaka' and her companions.

Embarking in a canoe, the travellers reached Maui, crossed it with further adventures, then sailed with a fisherman for Oahu. They landed at Maka-puu, journeyed overland to Kou—now Honolulu—and from Haena made sail for Kauai. Arriving at Kaena, Hiiaka' saw the spirit hand of Lohiau beckoning to her from the mouth of a cave up in the cliffs. Turning to her companion she said, " We have failed ; the lover of Pele is dead ! I see his spirit beckoning from the *pali* [cliff] where it is held and hidden by the lizard-women Kilioa and Kalamainu."

Instructing her companions to proceed to the *puoa* where the body of Lohiau was lying in state, Hiiaka' started at once up the *pali*, to give battle to the demons and rescue the spirit of the dead prince. Ascending the cliff and entering the cave, she waved her *pau*, and with angry hisses the demons disappeared. She searched for the spirit of Lohiau, and at last found it in a niche of the rocks where it had been imprisoned by a moonbeam. Taking it tenderly in her hand, she folded it in her *pau* and in an invisible form floated down with it to the *puoa*.

Waiting until after nightfall, Hiiaka' entered the chamber of death unseen, and restored the spirit to the body of Lohiau. Recovering life and consciousness, the bewildered Prince looked about him. The guards were filled with fear when he raised his head, and would have fled in alarm had they not been prevented by Hiiaka', who that instant appeared before them in mortal form. Holding up her hand to command obedience, she said, " Fear nothing ; say nothing of this to anyone living, and do nothing except as you may be ordered. The Prince has returned to life, and may recover if properly cared for. His body is weak and wasted. Let him at once be secretly removed to the seashore. The night is dark, and this may be done without observation."

Not doubting that these instructions were from the gods, the guards obeyed, and Lohiau was soon comfortably resting in a hut by the seashore, with Hiiaka' and her companion attending to his wants.

The return of the Prince to health and strength was rapid, and in a few days he reappeared among his friends, to their amazement and great joy. In answer to their inquiries he told them that he owed to the gods his restoration to life. This did not altogether satisfy them, but no other explanation was offered.

After celebrating his recovery with feasts and sacrifices to the gods, Lohiau announced to the chiefs of his kingdom that he was about to visit his wife, whose home was on Hawaii, and that he should leave the government of the island in the hands of his friend, the high chief Paoa, to whom he enjoined the fealty and respect of all during his absence.

In a magnificent double canoe, bearing the royal standard, and suitably equipped, Lohiau set sail for Hawaii, accompanied by Hiiaka' and her companions, his high priest, chief navigator, and the customary staff of personal attendants.

Touching at Oahu, Hiiaka' ascended the Kaala Mountains, and saw that her beautiful *lehua* and *hala* groves near the beach of Puna, on the distant island of Hawaii, had been destroyed by a lava-flow. Impatient at the long absence of Hiiaka', and unreasoningly jealous, Pele in a paroxysm of rage had destroyed the beautiful shore-retreat of her faithful sister. She had little doubt that Hiiaka' had dared to love Lohiau, and in her caves of fire chafed impatiently for her return.

274

After bewailing her loss, Hiiaka' rejoined her companions, and Lohiau embarked for Hawaii. Landing at Kohala, the Prince ordered his attendants to remain there until his return, and started overland for Kilauea with Hiiaka' and her companions. Before reaching the volcano Hiiaka' learned yet more of the jealous rage of Pele, and finally from an eminence saw her dear friend Hopoe suffering, near the beach of Puna, the cruel tortures of volcanic fire, which ended in her being turned into stone.

Approaching the crater with apprehension, Hiiaka' sent Pauo-palae and Omeo in advance to announce to Pele her return with Lohiau; but Pele in her wrath ordered the messengers to be slain at once, and resolved to treat her lover in the same manner. Aware of this heartless resolution, but unable to avert his fate, on their arriving at the verge of the crater Hiiaka' threw her arms round the neck of the Prince, whom she had learned to love, yet without wrong to her sister, and, telling him of his impending fate, bade him a tender farewell. On the fiery brink, in the open view of the court of Pele, Hiiaka', in resentment of the broken faith of her sister, and in defiance of her power, invited and received from Lohiau the kisses and dalliance which till that time both had repelled.

This scene was witnessed by Pele, and it did not serve to soften her resolution. Enraged beyond measure, she caused a gulf of molten lava to open between Hiiaka' and the Prince, and then ordered the instant destruction of Lohiau by fire. While the sisters of Pele were ascending the walls of the crater to carry out her command Lohiau chanted a song to the goddess, avowing his innocence and praying for mercy; but the sound of his voice added to her rage, and she was deaf to his entreaties.

Approaching Lohiau, and pitying him in their hearts, the sisters merely touched the palms of his hands, and turned them into lava, and retired. Observing this, Pele ordered them to return at once and consume the body of her lover. Lohiau again appealed to her, but her only answer was an impatient signal to her sisters to complete their work

275

of destruction. In his despair he turned to Hiiaka', but she answered in agony that she could do nothing.

The sisters returned to Lohiau, and reluctantly touched his feet, which became stone; then his knees, his thighs, his breast. Hiiaka' could at least render the body of the Prince insensible to pain, and this she did; and it was therefore without suffering that he felt his joints hardening to stone under the touch of the sympathizing sisters.

Before he was quite turned to lava, Hiiaka' said to Lohiau, "Listen! When you die, go to leeward, and I shall find you!" The next moment he was a lifeless pillar of stone.

Seeing that all that now remained of Lohiau was a black mass of lava, Hiiaka' caused the earth to open at her feet, and started downward at once for the shadowy realms of Milu, to overtake the soul of Lohiau and with the consent of the god of death to restore it to its body.

The god welcomed her, and, answering her inquiry, said that the soul of Lohiau had not yet reached the realm of spirits. Having no desire to return to earth without him, Hiiaka' accepted the invitation of Milu, and, waiting and watching for Lohiau, remained awhile in the land of shades.

The attendants of Lohiau remained in Kohala until they learned of his fate at the hands of Pele, when they returned to Kauai and related the story of his death.

Enraged and desperate, Paoa, the faithful and manly chief to whom Lohiau had confided the government of his kingdom, started at once for Hawaii with a small body of retainers, determined, even at the risk of his life, to denounce the powers that had slain his friend.

Landing on the coast of Puna, he ascended the crater of Kilauea, and, standing upon the brink of the seething lake of fire, denounced the cruelty of Pele and defied her power. He contemptuously threw to her offerings unfit for sacrifice, and stigmatized all the volcanic deities as evil spirits who had been driven with Kanaloa from the presence of Kane and the society of the gods.

Paoa expected instant destruction, and recklessly courted and awaited death. The brothers and sisters of

Pele were momentarily expecting a command from the goddess to consume the audacious mortal. Never before had such words of reproach and defiance been uttered by human tongue, and they could not doubt that swift vengeance would overtake the offender.

But Pele, in one of her sudden and unpredictable revulsions of feeling, refused to harm the desperate champion of Lohiau. Convinced of the innocence of the gentle Hiiaka' and the fidelity of the Prince, instead of punishing the brave Paoa Pele and her relatives received him with friendship, chided him for his words of insult and defiance, but disarmed his anger by forgiving the offence. It is said, too, that Paoa, who was a skilful actor, by his dancing and his prayer-song, both of which were used in the *hula* named after the goddess, not only appeased her, but won her.

Satisfied that she had wronged her sister, and longing for her quiet presence again in the caves of the crater, Pele restored Pauo-palae and Omeo to life, and sent Omeo down to the realm of shades to induce Hiiaka' to return to earth. Milu, however, did not wish that his visitor should depart, and gave no assistance in the search of Omeo for Hiiaka'; indeed, he attempted to deceive her by saying that Hiiaka' had already returned and was on a visit to relatives in Kahiki.

Omeo was about to return, disappointed, to earth, when she discovered Hiiaka' as she was listlessly emerging from a thick grove of trees where she had spent most of her time since her arrival in quest of the soul of Lohiau. Their greeting was most friendly; and when Omeo informed her of what had occurred at the volcano since her departure she consented to leave the land of death and rejoin her relatives in the crater. Her brothers and sisters were overjoyed at her return, and Pele herself welcomed her with assurances of restored affection. Paoa was still there. He was recognized by Hiiaka', and next day she descended from Kilauea and embarked with him for Kauai in search of the soul of Lohiau.

The canoe of Paoa had barely left the shores of Puna when a strange craft swung in on the sweep of the ocean, and was beached at the spot at which Paoa and Hiiaka' had embarked. It was a huge cowrie-shell, dazzling in the brilliancy of its colours, and capable of indefinite expansion or contraction. Its masts were of ivory; its sails and mats were white as milk. Both seemed rather for ornament than for use, since the shell moved as quickly through the water without wind as with it.

The sole occupant of this strange but beautiful vessel was the god Kane-milohai, a relative of the Pele family, who had come from Kahiki on a visit to the volcanic gods of Hawaii. It appears that Pele had been expelled from her native land Honua-mea, in Kahiki, because of her insubordination and disrespect. She voyaged north. Her first stop was at the little island of Kaula, in the Hawaiian group. She tunnelled into the earth, but the ocean poured in and put a stop to her work. The same occurred on Lehua, on Niihau, and on the large island Kauai. She then moved on to Oahu, hoping for better results; but though she tried both sides of the island, first Mount Kaala, the fragrant, and then Kona-hua-nui, she still found conditions unsatisfactory. She passed on to Molokai, thence to Lanai, to West Maui, digging at the last place the immense pit of Hale-a-ka-la; but everywhere she was unsuccessful. Still journeying east and south, she crossed the wide Ale-nui-haha channel and came to Hawaii, and, after exploring in all directions, was satisfied to make her home in Kilauea. Here is the navel of the earth (*ka piko o ka honua*), a name also applied to Rapanui (Easter Island).

This seeking of a habitation is related in a long song in a *hula pa-ipu*,[1] a *hula* of dignified character, dealing, apparently, with an historical period of migration:

> A pit lies far to the east,
> Pit pierced by the fire-queen Pele.
> Heaven's dawn is lifted awry,
> One edge tilts up, one down, in the sky;
> The thud of the pick is heard in the ground.

[1] This, and the *hula* song on pp. 284–285, are from Nathaniel B. Emerson's excellent *Unwritten Literature of Hawaii* (Smithsonian Institution, Washington, 1909).

278

PELE THE FIRE-GODDESS

The question is asked by Wakea,
" What god's this a-digging? "
" It is I, it is Pele,
Who dug Niihau deep down till it burned,
Dug fire-pit red-heated by Pele."

Night's curtains are drawn to one side,
One lifts, one hangs in the tide.
Crunch of spade resounds in the earth.
Wakea reurges the query,
" What god plies the spade in the ground ? "
Quoth Pele, " 'Tis I;
I mined to the fire 'neath Kauai,
On Kauai I dug deep a pit,
A fire-well flame-fed by Pele."

The heavens are lifted aslant,
One border moves up and one down;
There's a stroke of *o-o* 'neath the ground.
Wakea in earnest would know
" What demon is grubbing below? "
" I am the worker," says Pele;
" Oahu I pierced to the quick,
A crater white-heated by Pele."

Now morn lights one edge of the sky;
Streams the light up, and shadows fall down;
Deep below there's a clatter of tools.
Wakea in passion demands,
" What god's this who digs 'neath the ground? "
It is Pele, whose answers resound;
Hers the toil to dig down to the fire,
To dig Molokai to the fire.

.   .   .   .   .

The morning looks landward aslant;
Heaven's curtains roll up and roll down;
There's a ring of *o-o* 'neath the sod.
" Who," asks Wakea the god,
" Who is this demon a-digging? "
" It is I, it is Pele; I who
Dug on Maui the pit to the fire:
Aha, the crater of Maui,
Red-glowing with Pele-won fire."

.   .   .   .   .

Now day climbs up in the east,
Morn folds the dark curtains of night;
The spade of the sapper resounds 'neath the plain;
The goddess is at it again!

Proceeding in a direct route, when about midway between the two islands the god Kane-milohai caught the soul of Lohiau, which had misunderstood the final instructions of Hiiaka', and was on its way to Kauai. Not having gone to the land of spirits, it had been searching and searching for Hiiaka', and at last was taking flight for Kauai when intercepted by the god. He returned to the crater with the captured spirit, and, finding the pillar of stone which was once the body of Lohiau, he restored the Prince to life. As he recovered his consciousness he recognized Pele, who stood before him ; and not knowing all that had taken place in the meantime, and apprehensive of further persecution, he was about to appeal again for mercy, when she said in a tone as tender as that in which she had first replied to his welcome on the beach at Kaena :

" Fear me no longer. I have been unjust to you and to Hiiaka'. After what I have done I cannot expect you to love me. She loves you, and knows better than myself how to be kind to a mortal."

Lohiau would have thanked the goddess, but she was gone, and where she had stood now stood Kane-milohai, who bade him take the shell vessel he would find on the beach below, and proceed to Kauai, where he would probably meet Hiiaka' and his friend Paoa.

Lohiau hesitated, for there was something in the presence of Kane-milohai that inspired a feeling of awe.

" Go, and fear nothing," said the god, who knew the thoughts of the Prince ; " the shell was not fashioned in the sea or by human hands, but it will bear you safely on your journey, no matter how rough the seas or how great its burden."

" The coast of Puna is a day's journey in length," said Lohiau. " Where and how shall I find the shell ? "

280

"Hasten to the shore at Keauhou," rejoined the god. "You will see me there."

Arrived at the beach, the Prince found the god already there; and his wonder was great when the god took from a crevice in the rocks a shell that could lie in the palm of his hand, and passed it to him, saying that it was the vessel in which he was to sail to Kauai.

The god bade him place the shell at the edge of the water. He did so, and was surprised when he saw before him the beautiful craft in which the god had made his journey from Kahiki. To the Prince was given the power of causing the boat to expand or contract at pleasure; he entered, and directing its course simply by pointing with his finger he set out, and was borne swiftly forward on the ocean.

Rounding the southern cape of Hawaii, Lohiau thought of proceeding directly to Kauai; but he pointed too far northward, and the next morning sighted Oahu. Passing the headland of Leahi, he turned and entered the harbour of Hou. Landing, he reduced his boat to the size of a limpet, and hid it in the rocks. He went to the village, where he learned to his great joy that Hiiaka' and Paoa were there on a visit. Hou was at the time the scene of great merriment and feasting. It had become the temporary residence of the high chiefs, the wise men, and adventurers and noted surf-riders and *hula* performers had gathered there from all parts of the island. Ascertaining that an entertainment of great magnificence was that evening to be given by a distinguished chiefess in honour of Hiiaka' and Paoa, Lohiau resolved to be present. Had he made himself known he would have been entitled to the highest consideration; would have been the guest of the *alii-nui* (high chief), with the right of entry anywhere; but fancy induced him to conceal his rank and appear among the revellers in disguise.

Early in the evening the grounds of the chiefess were lighted with hundreds of torches; and under a broad pavilion, festooned and scented with fragrant vines and flowers, the favoured guests, enwreathed and crowned with leaf and blossom, were entertained with all the delicacies the sea and land produced. After the feast came song and music, and bands of gaily decked dancers kept step among the flaring torches, while around the doors of the mansion bards chanted wild legends of the past and sang *mele-inoa* (name-songs) of the hostess and her guests.

In the midst of this inspiring revelry the guests divided into groups, some strolling among the dancers, others listening to the bards; and one party, including Hiiaka', Paoa, and their hostess, entered to engage in the game of *kilu*. It was a pastime in which singing or chanting formed a part, and the chiefess was noted for her excellence in this amusement.

Lohiau entered the grounds toward the close of the feast, and stood watching when the party of *kilu*-players retired. He had turned inward the feathers of his royal yellow mantle, and with his long hair falling over his face and shoulders was readily mistaken for a *kahuna* (*tohunga*, wise man, priest).

A number of people thronged round the *kilu*-players to see the game, and Lohiau entered with them, standing concealed behind two old chiefs who were watching like himself.

The game went on, until the *kilu* fell to Hiiaka'; and as she threw it she chanted a song of her own composing, in which she mentioned the name of Lohiau with tenderness. The song ceased, and from among the onlookers came the answering·song of the Prince. As he sang he brushed back the hair from his face, and turned outward the yellow feathers of his mantle. The throng divided before him, the singer advanced, and before the players stood Lohiau, the Prince of Kauai.

He was recognized at once. Hiiaka' threw herself into his arms, and the faithful Paoa wept with joy. The guests vied with each other in showing him honour. The festivities were renewed and carried far into the night. Learning of his presence, the *alii-nui* wished to entertain him in a befitting manner ; but Lohiau was anxious to return to his people, and set sail for Kauai at once in the shell boat of Kane-milohai, expanded flower-like so as to accommodate Hiiaka' and Paoa.

Although Hiiaka' soon after returned to Hawaii and effected a complete reconciliation with her sister, while Lohiau lived she spent much of her time in Kauai.   Hopoe her friend was restored to life, and Omeo, because of what she had done, was given an immortal form, and thereafter became a mediator between the volcanic deities.

Pele as a Water-goddess

Pele appears as a water-goddess as well as a fire-goddess. In one legend she is said to have caused the ocean to encircle the Hawaiian Islands.   She lived in Kahiki, which may have been Tahiti, since she is said to have told her brother, " I am going to Bolabola ; to Kuai-he-lani ; to Kane-huna-moku ; to Moku-manamana ; then to see a queen, Kaoahi her name and Niihau her island."   Her mother's name was Kahinalii, her father's Kane-hoalani.   Her mother's name is also given as Houmea, or Honua-mea, or Papa.   When she grew up she married Wahia-loa, giving birth to a daughter, Laka, and a son, Menehune.   Here there seems to be a confusion with the Wahie-roa and Rata of Maori myth.   After a while her husband was enticed from her by Pele-kumulani, or Pele-kumukalani ; and she left her home, either because of this incident, or because she was expelled by her brothers on account of her turbulence and insubordination.

At that time there was no ocean around the Hawaiian Islands, nor was there any fresh water.   When Pele set out her mother gave her the ocean to go with her and bear onward her canoes.   From her head she poured out the seas as she went, and the waters rose until only the highest points of the mountains Hale-a-ka-la, Mauna-kea, and Mauna-loa were visible ; but afterward they receded until they reached their present level.   This event was called the Kai a Kahinalii, as it was from her mother that she received the gift of the ocean.   (*Kai* is the Maori *tai*, the sea.)

MYTHS OF THE POLYNESIANS

Her going from island to island with fire has already been told.

Pele has been compared with the Samoan Fe'e, a war-god; there is a suggestion of similarity in certain of their attributes, but the word Fe'e is not the transliteral equivalent of Pele, but of Wheke. Fe'e, the octopus, was said to have been created by Tagaloa at the time he caused the habitable world to appear, and was ordered to live underground or underseas. He gave birth to rocks, and, fighting with fire, was overcome; but fire, fighting with the rocks, was in turn overcome.

There is a legend saying that Fe'e was brought from Fiji by Tapuaau, who swam thence to Samoa on his octopus. Fe'e was adopted as a war-god, and there are various legends concerning him. In one he married the daughter of a chief on Upolu, and for convenience in coming and going he made a hole in the reef, whence the harbour of Apia has its origin. He went up the river at that place, and built a stone house inland, whose ruins still remain, being known as the House of Fe'e. His subterranean or subaqueous home was known as Sa-le-Fe'e, which name is sometimes spoken of as equivalent to Pulotu. Being on one occasion disturbed by a company of women visiting the home built by him up the river, he fled to the mountains, and lived there for a time, returning subsequently to the house first built. The voice of his prophecy was thunder. If he thundered toward the peaks it was an evil omen, and any war projects in hand would be deferred; if toward the sea it was a good omen, and preparations for war, if begun, were eagerly continued. To be sure, this thunder may be the subterranean rumbling of portended earthquakes, which is at times heard coming as if from the sea under the reef.

In the *hula* dance of Pele occurs a song relating her coming on the billows of water as later on the billows of fire:

> From Kahiki came the woman Pele,
> From the island of Polapola,
> From the red cloud of Kane,
> Cloud blazing in the heavens,
> Fiery cloud-pile in Kahiki.

PELE THE FIRE-GODDESS

Eager desire for Hawaii seized the woman Pele,
She carved the canoe *Honua-i-akea*,
Your canoe, O Ka-moho-alii.
They push the work on the craft to completion,
The lashings of the god's canoe are done,
The canoe of Kane, the world-maker.

The tides swirl, Pele-honua-mea o'ermounts them,
The god rides the waves, sails about the island;
The hosts of little gods ride the billows;
Malu takes his seat;
One bails out the bilge of the craft.
Who shall sit astern, be steersman, O princes?
Pele of the yellow earth.
The splash of the paddles dashes o'er the canoe.

Ku and his fellow, Lono,
Disembark on solid land;
They alight on a shoal.
Hiiaka', the wise one, a god,
Stands up, goes to stay at the house of Pele.

Lo, an eruption in Kahiki!
A flashing of lightning, O Pele!
Belch forth, O Pele!

In this song Pele is given the name Pele-honua-mea, a combination of her name with that of her mother. This name is almost a parallel of the Maori Para-whenua-mea, a personification of water, and daughter of Tane' by Hine-tu-pari-maunga, the Mountain-maid. There is some confusion with this minor goddess. She is said to have been the first wife of Kiwa, who had for second wife Hine-moana, the Ocean-maid, whose offspring were shellfish and seaweed. It would almost seem as if Para-whenua-mea were the personification of fresh water, while Hine-moana was the personification of salt water. The former was a daughter of the Mountain-maid, and she could not move abroad were it not for Rakahore, the personification of rock, across whose back she escapes from the confines of her mother, as is said in the song concerning the Water of Kane:

> One question I put to you:
> Where is the Water of Kane?

> Yonder on mountain peak,
> On the ridges steep,
> In the valleys deep,
> Where the rivers sweep,
> There is the Water of Kane.

Pele, too, was connected with the fresh water from the hills, as a song in the *hula* shows :

> To Kauai, lifted in ether,
> A floating flower at sea off Wailua—
> That way Pele turns her gaze,
> She is bidding adieu to Oahu,
> Loved land of new wine of the palm.
> There comes a perfumed waft—*mokihana*—
> The bath of the maid Hiiaka'.
> Scene it was once of contention by Pele,
> Put by for a future renewal.
> Her foot now spurns the long-backed wave;
> The phosphor burns like the eye of Pele,
> Or a meteor-flash in the sky.
> Finished the prayer; enter, possess!

This incident belongs to the story of her journey in search of Lohiau, and the words describe her as about to take flight from Oahu to Kauai. The bath of Hiiaka', the gentle younger sister, which was the subject of contention, was a spring of pure water which Pele had set at Hu-leia on her arrival from Kahiki. The ones with whom Pele had the angry contention were Kukui-lau-manienie and Kukui-lau-hanahana, daughters of Lima-loa, god of the mirage. The spring had been removed by Kama-puaa, the lover of these women, from the rocky bed where Pele had set it to a neigh-bouring hill. Pele was angry, and her eye was as the phosphorescence which her footstep on the wave caused to glow in the sea ; and were it not that she was eager to meet Lohiau, the lover of her dream, she would have stayed to answer the temerity of the women in her usual fiery fashion ; but she would not forget.

Para-whenua-mea is also said to be a man, son of Tane' and Tupari-maunga, and he was one of those whose prayers caused the deluge sent because of men's wickedness and disbelief in the teachings concerning Tane'. These deluge myths, however, show so many traces of missionary influence that it is almost certain that they are no more than perversions of water-legends such as those of Pele and Para-whenua-mea.

Pele is a goddess still to be reckoned with. True, a vulcanological observatory has been established in her very crater, not far from her molten, living sea of lava ; but while all the Hawaiians are now professed Christians, old beliefs die hard—and in any case there can be no harm in being sure ; so offerings, perhaps surreptitious, perhaps open and avowed, are still occasionally made to her. As recently as June 1925 such an offering was made, and Pele expressed her appreciation at the very time of offering by a rumbling and a shaking, an intimation that she still lingered, and had not altogether laid her former power aside.

CHAPTER X : THE SPIRIT WORLDS

Mata-ora and Niwa-reka

THERE appear to have been two kinds of nether-worlds; one to which mortals might go and return during life, one to which they went only after death. The Patu-pai-arehe, or people akin to them, were sometimes said to be denizens of a netherworld, which may mean no more than an unknown land, mysterious because unknown. Such a land was Raro-henga, where dwelt the Turehu, a race of fairies or supernatural beings related to the Patu-pai-arehe.

As Mata-ora one day lay asleep upon earth a party of Turehu young women came upon him, and paused to look at him, for he was well-knit and of an attractive appearance. The chiefess among them was Niwa-reka, whose father, Ue-tonga, was said to be the grandson of Ruau-moko, god of earthquakes. When Mata-ora awoke he was as surprised at seeing the fairies as they had been at seeing him—they were fair-haired and fair-skinned, as was usual with those of the fairy tribes.

Mata-ora invited them into his house, but they would neither enter his house nor partake of the cooked food which he offered them; they were ignorant of the art of cooking, and deemed the food so prepared to be putrid; but they enjoyed the raw food he thereupon procured for them. When they had been satisfied Mata-ora took his *maipi*, a weapon like a *taiaha* (staff and two-edged, tongue-pointed weapon in one), but ending in a point instead of a carved head and tongue, and danced before them the dance known as *tuone*, wherein are displayed agility and command of the weapon. This he did for their entertainment; and when he sat down the Turehu arose and performed a posture-dance before Mata-ora as a return *tuone*. As they danced one of them came forward and danced before the others as a leader, while the others kept repeating her name, " Niwa-reka! Niwa-reka! " She was fair, and graceful; slimly built, with well-formed body. Their long, light-coloured hair hung to their waists, and they wore aprons of seaweed. As they moved hand in hand, sometimes posturing, sometimes tripping and skipping before him, they caused flutterings in the heart of Mata-ora, and his fancy turned to their graceful leader, to Niwa-reka.

She too was by her fancy led to Mata-ora, and for some time they dwelt happily together. One day, for some reason apparently known to no one but Mata-ora himself, in a moment of jealousy and anger he struck the unoffending Niwa-reka, and in surprise and dread she left him, returning to her home in Raro-henga.

Mata-ora was disconsolate; and in grief and dejection he went in search of her. He went to Tahua-roa, at far Irihia, coming to Pou-tere-rangi, where dwelt Ku-watawata, the guardian of the entrance to the spirit world; and of him Mata-ora inquired, " Have you seen a woman passing this way? " " What is the token? " inquired the guardian. " Her long fair hair," answered Mata-ora. " She has passed on, weeping as she went," was the reply; and Kuwatawata permitted Mata-ora to proceed to the netherworld like another Orpheus seeking his beloved. Soon he came to Ti-wai-waka, and inquired of the doings of the folk in the netherworld. " They are busy attending to the *kumara* crops," he told them; " some are building houses; some are tattooing; some are fishing; some are kite-flying; some are top-spinning." Mata-ora inquired after Niwa-reka. " She has passed on," was the reply, " her eyes swollen with weeping, her lips trembling with sorrow, and from her breast a sound of sobbing."

With desire augmented Mata-ora hastened on, until he came to the home of Ue-tonga, father of Niwa-reka. Uetonga was engaged in tattooing a man, and Mata-ora noticed that the blood was flowing freely from the wounds. This surprised him; for at that time tattooing by incision was not known in the upperworld, where designs were merely painted on the body with coloured clays.

" Your mode of tattooing is wrong," said he to Ue-tonga; " it is not done so in the upperworld." But Ue-tonga

replied, " This is the true tattooing ; your mode of decoration is for the adornment of houses only." He stretched
out his hand, rubbed the face of Mata-ora, and effaced the
designs. The people laughed to see them so easily removed.
" You have spoilt my adornment," said Mata-ora ; " you
must now tattoo me in the proper manner."

Ue-tonga called upon those who traced the designs to
prepare Mata-ora for the ordeal ; and, when this was done,
he took his tattooing instrument and began to incise the
lines. As Mata-ora lay there enduring the pain of the
operation he murmured a *karakia* to assuage the poignancy
of his suffering :

> Niwa-reka!
> Niwa-reka, great delight!
> Who hast caused me
> To come to darkness—
> To utter darkness.
> Speak of the pain
> Of the beloved one
> Who is at Ahuahu,
> And at Ranga-tira,
> And at Nuku-moana-ariki.
> Yes, the bloom of red
> Which has swiftly passed
> Along the road to Taranaki—
> Yes, at Taranaki
> Is the beloved one,
> To whom your nimble feet
> Sped swiftly.

Niwa-reka was engaged in weaving cloaks at Taranaki,
—one story says at Aroaro-tea ; and a younger sister, hearing the words of the song of Mata-ora, ran and said to her
sister, " A certain person yonder, a handsome man, is being
tattooed ; and he murmurs a song in which your name is
mentioned."

Niwa-reka arose, and with her attendants went to the
place where Mata-ora was being tattooed. Her father bade
her go away ; but she asked the man to repeat his song ;
and she listened, especially to the closing portion, which
was this :

THE SPIRIT WORLDS

Tell it to the west,
Tell it to the south,
Also to the north.
Look at the stars above,
Glance at the glimmering moon.
I am as the tattooed tree.
Say who is thy beloved,
And let the fragrant breath
Of *mokimoki* fern
Give forth its sweetness,
And foster those desires,
That in the midst of waving plumes
I may a listener be.

From his song she gathered that it was Mata-ora; and when the tattooing was finished she took him, and tended his wounds, and those two were happy again.

When the scarred face of Mata-ora had quite healed, then the lines and curves of the tattooed design looked well; and he proposed that they should return to the upperworld. But Niwa-reka said, " The ways of the upperworld are evil; to both realms has come a knowledge of our trouble; I must consult my people." Then came Ue-tonga; and he said, " It may be you think of returning to the upperworld; if so, return; but let Niwa-reka remain here. Is it a custom in the upperworld to beat women? " And Mata-ora was overcome with shame.

" Mata-ora! " said Tau-wehe, the brother of Niwa-reka. " Abandon the upperworld, the home of evil. Observe how the denizens of the upperworld are compelled by violence and other evils to descend to the netherworld. Let us all dwell here below, in the realm of harmony." And Ue-tonga added, "Mata-ora! Let us hear no tidings of a second evil act of thine in the upperworld! Widely sundered is that upperworld, with its deeds of darkness, from the netherworld, the realm of light and peace."

Yet Mata-ora wished to return; and when at last he was allowed to take Niwa-reka with him Ue-tonga said, " Mata-ora, farewell! Return to Taiao, the upperworld, but let us not again be afflicted with its works of evil." " By the

token of the tattooing with which you have adorned me,"
answered Mata-ora, " the ways of the netherworld shall be
my ways." And they turned to ascend to the upperworld.

As a parting gift Ue-tonga gave to Mata-ora the famous
cloak called Rangi-haupapa, which was the original after
which the cloaks of this world were fashioned ; and the belt
that was intended to confine it was the original pattern of
the belts of this world. On their way the two were stopped
by Ti-wai-waka, the guardian at the base of the ascent, who
detained them until the proper season. They then passed
on ; passed, too, the place of Ku-watawata, but left no
garment or other acknowledgment for being allowed to pass
over the path of the netherworld, for which reason Ku-
watawata called after them, " Go, Mata-ora, and close the
door to the netherworld ; for hereafter man shall not repass
the path leading thither."

This story indicates that the arts of tattooing and of cloak-
plaiting were learned by the Maori from some people
differing at least in appearance and disposition from the
Polynesians. There is some similarity in the feather cloaks
of the Hawaiians and the Maori, but their construction is
different ; and there is no resemblance whatever in their
tattooing. The Maori is alone in possessing the elaborate
decoration of exquisitely symmetrical curves and scrolls
with which the face was covered, deep lines whose incisions
at times perforated the cheeks. Other of the Polynesians
tattooed the limbs and the body, but rarely the face ; the
Maori tattooed the limbs and the body as well as the face,
but the designs of greatest closeness and intricacy were reserved for the face. With the Hawaiians the incisions were
not deep—" so as just not to fetch blood," says Cook ; with
the Maori the blood flowed freely. The Hawaiian designs
were squares, circles, crescents, or ill-designed representations of men, birds, dogs, or other devices.

The Feather Cloak of Hawaii

The Hawaiians have a story of the feather cloak that
served as the first known pattern. Eleio was a *kukini*, or

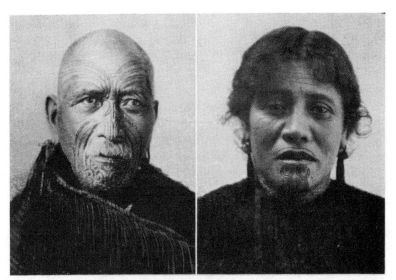

OLD MAORI MAN AND ELDERLY MAORI WOMAN

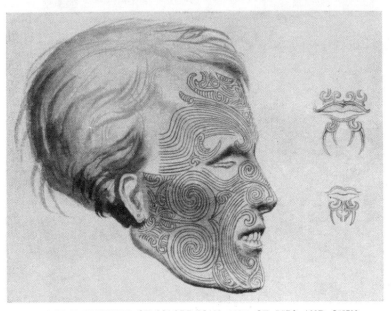

FACE-TATTOOING OF MAORI MAN AND OF LIPS AND CHIN
OF A WOMAN
(See page 290)

TWO YOUNG MAORI WOMEN

One is wearing a fine flax cloak; the cloak of the other is set with kiwi feathers.

Photos Iles, Thames, N.Z.

(See page 292)

trained runner, in the service of Kakaalaneo, chief of Maui. He was not only a swift and tireless runner, but was also a *kahuna* (*tohunga*), initiated into the observances that enabled him to see spirits, that made him skilled in medicine, and able to return a wandering spirit to its dead body if the work of dissolution had not begun.

Eleio had been sent to Hana to fetch *awa* (*kava*) root for the chief, and was expected to be back so that the chief might have his prepared drink for supper. Soon after leaving Olowalu Eleio saw a beautiful young woman ahead of him. He hastened his steps, but, exert himself as he would, she kept the same distance between them. Being the fleetest *kukini* of his time, it piqued him that a woman should be able to prevent his overtaking her, so he determined to capture her, and devoted all his energies to that object. She led him a long chase over rocks, hills, mountains, deep ravines, precipices, and gloomy streams, till they came to the cape of Hana-manu-loa at Kahiki-nui, beyond Kaupo, where he caught her just at the entrance to a *puoa*—a kind of tower, made of bamboo, with a platform half-way up, where the dead bodies of persons of distinction were exposed to the elements.

When he caught her she turned to him and said, " Let me live ! I am not human, but a spirit, and in this enclosure is my dwelling." He answered; " I have thought for some time that you were a spirit ; no human being could have so outrun me."

She then said, " Let us be friends. In yonder house live my parents and relatives. Go to them and ask for a hog, rolls of *kapa* [*tapa*], some fine mats, and a feather cloak. Describe me to them, and tell them that I give all those things to you. The feather cloak is not finished ; it is now only a fathom and a half square, and was intended to be two fathoms. There are in the house enough feathers and netting to finish it. Tell them to finish it for you." The spirit then disappeared.

Eleio entered the *puoa*, climbed on to the platform, and saw the dead body of the girl. She was in every way as

293

beautiful as the spirit, and had apparently been dead but a short time. He left the *puoa* and hurried to the house pointed out as the home of her parents, and he saw a woman wailing, whom he recognized, from her resemblance, as the mother of the girl. He saluted her with an *aloha*. " I am a stranger here," said he, " but I had a travelling companion who guided me to yonder *puoa* and then disappeared." At these words the woman ceased her wailing and called to her husband, to whom she repeated what the stranger had said. "Does this house belong to you?" asked Eleio. " It does," they answered.

" Then," said Eleio, " my message is to you." He repeated to them the message of the young girl, and they willingly agreed to give up all the things which their loved daughter had herself thus given away. But when they spoke of killing the hog, and making a feast for him, he said, " Wait a little, and let me ask if all these people round about me are your friends? "

They answered, " They are our relatives, the uncles, aunts, and cousins of the spirit who seems to have chosen you either as husband or as brother." " Will they do your bidding in everything? " he asked.

The parents answered that they could be relied on. He directed them to build a large arbour, to be entirely covered with ferns, ginger, *maile*, *ieie*—sweet and odorous foliage of the islands. An altar was to be erected at one end of the arbour and appropriately decorated. The order was willingly carried out, men, women, and children working with a will, so that in a couple of hours the whole structure was finished. He then directed the hog to be cooked, also red and white fish, red, white, and black cocks, and varieties of banana called *lele* and *maoli* to be placed on the altar. He directed all women and children to enter their houses and assist with their prayers, all pigs, chickens, and dogs to be hidden in dark houses to keep them quiet, and that strict silence be kept. The men at work were asked to remember the gods, and to invoke their assistance for Eleio.

He then started for Hana, pulled up a couple of bushes

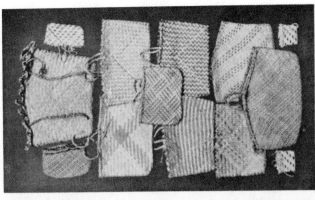

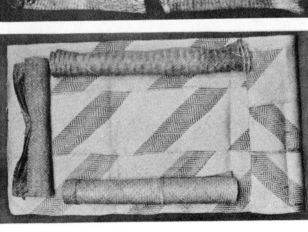

MAORI WOVEN FLOOR-MATTING, FLAX KILTS, AND BASKETS

(See page 294)

"TAKE AS WIFE THE WOMAN YOU HAVE RESTORED"
(See page 296)

of *awa* of Kaeleku, famous for its medicinal virtue, and was back again before the hog was cooked. The *awa* was prepared, and when everything was ready for the feast he offered all to the gods and prayed for their assistance in what he was about to perform.

The spirit of the girl had been lingering near him all the time, seeming to be attracted to him, but of course invisible to every one else. When he had finished his invocation he turned and caught the spirit, and holding his breath and invoking the gods he hurried to the *puoa*, followed by the parents, who now began to understand that he was about to attempt the *kapuku*, or restoration of the dead to life. Arrived at the *puoa*, he placed the spirit against the insteps of the girl and pressed it firmly in, meanwhile continuing his invocation. The spirit entered its former body kindly enough until it came to the knees, when it refused to go farther, fearing pollution, but Eleio by the strength of his prayers induced it to go farther, and farther, the father, mother, and male relatives assisting with their prayers, and at length the spirit was persuaded to take entire possession of the body, and the girl came to life again.

She was submitted to the usual ceremonies of purification by the priest, after which she was led to the prepared arbour, where there was a happy reunion. They feasted on the food prepared for the gods, whose guests they were, enjoying the material essence of the food after its spiritual essence had been accepted by the gods.

After the feast the feather cloak, the rolls of fine *kapa*, the beautiful mats, were brought and displayed to Eleio; and the father said to him, " Take as wife the woman you have restored, and remain here with us; you shall be our son, sharing equally in the love we have for her."

But Eleio, thinking of his chief, said, " No, I accept her as a charge; but, for wife, she is worthy to be one for a higher in rank. If you will trust her to my care, I will take her to my master; for her beauty and her charms make her worthy to be his wife and our queen."

" She is yours to do with as you will," said the father.

" It is as if you had created her; for without you where would she be now? We ask only this, that you will always remember that you have parents and relatives here, and a home whenever you may wish it."

Eleio then requested that the feather cloak be finished for him before he returned to the chief. All who could work feathers set about it at once, including the girl herself, whose name, Eleio now learned, was Kanikani-aula. When it was finished he set out on his return, accompanied by the girl, and taking the feather cloak and the *awa* that remained after a portion had been used during his incantations. They travelled slowly, according to the strength of Kanikani-aula, who now, in the body, could not equal the speed she had possessed as a spirit.

Arriving at Launi-upoko, Eleio turned to her and said, " You wait here, hidden in the bushes, while I go on alone. If by sundown I do not return, I shall be dead. You know the road by which we came; return then to your people. But if all goes well I shall be back in a little while."

He then went on, and when he reached Makila, on the confines of Lahaina, he saw a number of people heating an *imu*, or ground oven. On perceiving him they seized and started to bind him, saying it was the order of the chief that he should be roasted alive; but he ordered them away with the request, " Let me die at the feet of my master," and went on.

When at last he stood before Kakaalaneo the chief said to him, " How is this? Why are you not cooked alive as I ordered? How came you to pass my guards?"

The runner answered, " It was the wish of the slave to die, if die he must, at the feet of his master; but if so, it would be an irreparable loss to you, my master; for I have that with me which will add to your fame, now and to posterity." " And what is that?" asked the King.

Eleio unrolled his bundle, and displayed to the astonished chief the glories of the feather cloak, a garment unknown till then. Needless to say, he was pardoned and restored to favour, the *awa* he had brought from Hana being reserved

THE SPIRIT WORLDS

for the chief's special use in his offerings to the gods that evening.

When the chief heard the whole story of the reason for the absence of Eleio he ordered the girl to be brought, that he might see her, and express gratitude for the wonderful garment. When she arrived he was so charmed with her appearance, with her manner and conversation, that he asked her to become his queen.

This feather cloak, known as the Ahu o Kakaalaneo, is said to be preserved in the Bernice P. Bishop Museum at Honolulu. The Hawaiian name of the feather cloak is *ahuula*. The doubled vowel signifies the dropping of a consonant, usually *k*; the equivalent word, and the equivalent garment in Maori, is *kahukura*. The Hawaiian garment was made of red or yellow feathers on a netted foundation, and was a gorgeous object; the Maori cloak was made of red feathers from the underwing of the *kaka*, on a plaited foundation of silky flax-fibre. There were other feather cloaks, an especially valuable one being the *kahukiwi*, made from feathers of the *kiwi*, fixed on upside down, or quill pointing downward, so that the droop of the hairlike feather gave the appearance of a full fur.

Pare and Hutu

The girl Kanikani-aula of the Hawaiian story—who should have been the wife of Eleio, not of the chief!—had not yet departed to the underworld; but in the Maori story of Pare and Hutu the girl had departed to the land of spirits.

It might happen that if a child were the offspring of a father and mother both of pure and illustrious lineage, that child was of higher rank than either father or mother. Such a child was Pare; she was of such *tapu* (sacredness[1]), and of such high descent, that no man of her tribe was her equal. Such a young woman would not join in the usual free intercourse of young people, but was kept apart as a *puhi*, a high-born virgin, till such time as a man of rank sufficiently worthy might be found to marry her.

[1] *Tapu* may mean ' sacred,' but oftener simply means ' forbidden,' or ' set apart.'

Pare dwelt with her attendants in a beautiful house, set apart for her sole use, and surrounded by three sets of palisades. Her food was given to an attendant, who, taking it to the first enclosure, gave it to one of higher rank ; she, going to the second enclosure, gave it to a third of yet higher rank ; she gave it to one who was even her superior, who placed it before the young *puhi*, before Pare.

Her house, besides being beautiful to the eye, was furnished with the finest plaited floor-mats of flax, rendered white by boiling, and plaited plain or with chequered patterns of various kinds, black and white ; her garments consisted of the finest cloaks, such as *kaitaka*, with broad *taniko* border at the lower edge and narrower borders at the sides, and *korowai*, ornamented with long black thrums, and *topuni*, made from skins of dogs, the long hair of the tails being plaited into the thickened selvage of the upper border. The house was also scented with fragrant *kopuru* moss, *karetu* grass, and gum from the *taramea*, and scent from the *raukawa*, the *kawakawa*, and the *tarata*.

During the season of games a young chief of high rank, named Hutu, came to the village in order to join with her people in throwing the dart, spinning whip-tops, and suchlike games. He was a skilful player, and his dart flew farther than all the others, for which reason the people were pleased, and were loud in their praises. The village common rang with their applause, and this made Pare more restless as she chafed in her house, with its beauty and its three sets of palisades. As if these could ever confine the desires of a *puhi*, or even a maiden of lower birth !

She came to the door of her house to learn the cause of the cries, and, sitting down, watched the games. Hutu, besides being a skilful player, was a fine-looking young man. She took a note of both characteristics, and as she watched him love stole through the palisades and into her heart, eluding the vigilance of her attendants.

They again threw their darts, and Hutu threw his so far that it dropped close to the gate of the outer palisade, to which Pare had wandered. She seized it, and took it

MAORI CLOAKS OF FINE FLAX
One set with *kiwi* feathers, both with *taniko* border.
Photos Dominion Museum, Wellington, N.Z.

MAORI CLOAKS OF FINE FLAX
Two with thrum ornamentation, two set with pigeon and other feathers.
Photos Dominion Museum, Wellington, N.Z.

(See page 298)

within. Hutu came to the gate and asked for his dart, but she refused to part with it. He repeated his request; but she answered, " You, Hutu, come into my house, for I wish to speak to you; in my heart I have conceived an admiration for you ! "

Hutu was troubled by these words of the high-born young woman, and replied, " I have no desire to enter your house. I am alone in the midst of your tribe, a great people. I am a stranger, nor would it accord with custom that I, a man of low birth, should enter the house of my superior in rank. At my home, too, a wife and children await me."

Though Hutu was of high rank, yet he demeaned himself before Pare, and some joy was in the pain with which she heard his words.

" Your words have no effect upon me," said she, " nor is my admiration lessened by what you say. You are master in all the games; your dart flies the farthest, your top hums the loudest; great is my desire for you, O Hutu ! " Still he refused to enter, and, though she pleaded, yet he remained unmoved. He stood unmoved, yet unable to resist; for taking hold of him she led him into her house.

Did Hutu now yield to this beautiful *puhi*? Not so; and Pare's heart grew sorrowful as he said, " I have entered your house, and now I request that you allow me to depart." *Aue!* he left the house, she following. He turned and said, " Remain in your home; in a short time I will return to you." With these words he fled, nor did he once look back toward her.

" Go, O Hutu ! " she cried, " return to your own home," but sobs prevented her speaking and tears dimmed her eyes. She returned to her house, now no longer a beautiful place. She ordered her attendants to arrange all things neatly, and when this was done she sat alone, weeping in her grief. After her *tangi*, her murmured lamentation, she arose, and took her own life for sorrow.

Great was the grief of her people on hearing of her death; and, learning the cause from her attendants, " Hutu must die," said they, " as *utu* [payment] for the death of

Pare." They sent after Hutu, who had departed, seized him, and took him to where her dead body lay; and, being told of his fate, he said, " It is well; but do not yet bury the body. Allow me to depart, leaving the body where it now lies until my return. Three days will pass, or it may be four, and I shall be with you again; for it is right that I should be slain, that your sorrow for the death of your *puhi* may be assuaged." To this the people agreed.

Hutu left them; and when at a distance from the house of Pare he sat down and chanted the *karakia* which *tohunga* chant over themselves when they think of death and of Te Reinga, the abode of spirits. He arose, and journeyed to Te Reinga, and when he came to the region where Hine-nui-te-po sits as guardian he asked her the road leading to the netherworld. She pointed to the path along which the spirits of dogs go to Te Reinga. He presented to her his valuable *mere* of greenstone, and she revealed to him the path by which the souls of men descend. This was her custom, so that men might make presents, and her house be filled with treasure. She prepared food for Hutu, and putting it into a small basket she gave it to him, saying, " When you reach the netherworld, eat sparingly of this food, so that it may last a length of time; for should you eat of the food presented to you by the spirits you will be unable to return to the world of life." He heeded her warnings. Again she said, " When you float from this world, bow your head as you descend; when you are near that place, a wind from beneath will blow upon you, raising your head up again, when you will be in the right position for alighting on your feet."

Hutu took his flight to the world below; and, reaching it, searched for Pare. " She is in the village," the people answered, in reply to his inquiries. Pare heard that Hutu was come, and that he was asking for her, but she would not appear. He wished to take her away again to the land of life, but she steadfastly refused to reveal herself. Hutu, therefore, remembering days not long past, requested the people to join him in games. They threw darts, they spun

whip-tops, they indulged in all the games they had known
in the upperworld. But Pare would not appear, nor could
she be induced to witness the games. The people shouted
for joy, but what pleasure was it for Hutu, when his one
object was to attract Pare, the only one who refused to be
attracted? With a heavy heart, therefore, he amused the
people.

Hutu was dejected; but he cast about for other means of
encompassing his desire. "Bring a long tree," said he to
the people; "a very long tree, with its branches lopped
away." It was brought. "Plait ropes as long as the tree,"
said he. They were plaited. "Fasten the ropes to the
top of the tree, and erect it in an open space." It was done.

He caused the people to pull on the ropes until the tree
bent over, its top toward the ground. He climbed and
sat on the top, requesting a man to sit on his back.
"Let go the ropes," he then cried. They let go; the
tree flew up, throwing Hutu and the man far into the
air. The people laughed and shouted their approval, and
eagerly joined in this new game. Pare too, though at first
she paid no attention to the shouting, yet, suddenly seeing
the body of a man, legs and arms outstretched, flying upward through the air, was unable to resist a desire to see how
this thing was done. First she inquired of her attendants;
and, hearing of the wonderful new swing, she emerged from
her place of retirement. The irresistible Hutu rejoiced to
see her again; the more so when she approached him,
saying, "Let me also swing; and let me too be borne upon
your shoulders."

"Pull the top of the tree down, even to the ground,"
cried Hutu; and as he and Pare seated themselves on the
top, "Keep hold of my neck, Pare," said he. "Let it go,"
he then cried.

They did so; but so great was the swing of the tree that
the ropes were flicked high up, and became entangled in
the roots of the trees growing in the upperworld. Hutu
and Pare being also flung thither, up they scrambled, past
the roots, to the surface of the delightful earth, issuing as

one might issue from a cave on a hillside. They returned to the village where the body of Pare lay, and her spirit, entering it again, took up its abode in its accustomed place.

The people rejoiced to see Pare step out alive and smiling, and they cried welcome to their dear-loved *puhi*. " Hutu is a man of power," said they ; " he has repeated his *karakia* and restored her to life ; he must take her as a second wife." " And what shall I do with the wife and children I now have ? " said Hutu. " You are a man of *mana*," said they, " and two wives you must have." And from that day they called him Parehutu.

Hiku and Kawelu, of Hawaii

This story has a close parallel from Hawaii. Not far from the summit of Hualalai, on that island, in a cave on the southern side of the ridge, lived Hina and her son Hiku, a *kupua*, or demigod, the same as the Maori *tupua*, or *tipua*. During the whole of his childhood and youth Hiku had lived alone with his mother on the summit of the mountain, and had never once been permitted to descend to the plains below to see the abodes of men or to learn their ways. From time to time his ear had caught the sound of the distant *hula* (drum) and the voices of the merrymakers, and he had often wished to see those who danced and sang in those far-off coconut-groves. But his mother, experienced in the ways of the world, had always refused her consent. Now at length he felt that he was a man ; and as the sounds of mirth arose to his ears again he asked his mother that he might go and mingle with the people on the shore. His mother, seeing that his mind was made up, reluctantly gave her consent, warning him not to linger, but to return in good time. So, taking in his hand his faithful arrow, Pua-ne, which he always carried, off he started.

This arrow was possessed of supernatural powers, being able to answer his call, and by its flight to direct his steps.

He descended over the rough lava, and through the groves of *koa* that cover the south-western slopes of the mountain, until, nearing its base, he stood on a distant hill ;

and, consulting his arrow by shooting it far into the air, he watched its flight until it struck on a distant hill above Kailua. To this hill he directed his steps, and picked up his arrow in due time, again shooting it into the air. The second flight landed the arrow near the coast of Holualoa, six or eight miles south of Kailua. It struck on a barren waste of lava beside the water-hole of Wai-kalai, known also as the Wai-a-Hiku (Water of Hiku), used by the people to this day.

Here he quenched his thirst; and nearing the village of Holualoa he again shot the arrow, which entered the court-yard of the *alii* (chief) of Kona, and from the women it singled out the chiefess Kawelu, and landed at her feet. Seeing the noble air of Hiku as he approached to claim his arrow, she stealthily hid it, and challenged him to find it. Then Hiku called to the arrow, " Pua-ne! Pua-ne! " and the arrow answered, " Ne," thus revealing its hiding-place.

This incident of the arrow, and the grace and manliness of Hiku, won the heart of the young chiefess, and she was soon possessed by a strong passion for him, and determined to make him her husband. With her arts she detained him for several days at her home, and when he at last was de-termined to set out for the mountains she shut him up in the house and detained him by force. But the words of his mother came to his mind, and he sought means of break-ing away from his prison. He climbed to the roof, and, removing a portion of the thatch, made his escape.

When his flight was discovered by Kawelu she was dis-tracted with grief; she refused to be comforted, refused all food, and before many days had passed she died. Messen-gers were dispatched, who brought back the unhappy Hiku, the cause of all the sorrow. He had loved her though he had fled, and now, when it was too late, he wept over her. The spirit had departed to the netherworld of Milu, but, stung by the reproaches of her kindred and friends, and urged by his real love for Kawelu, Hiku resolved to attempt the perilous descent into the netherworld, and if possible bring back her spirit to the world it had left.

With the assistance of his friends he collected from the

mountains great lengths of *kowali* (convolvulus-vine). He also prepared a coconut-shell, splitting it into two closely fitting parts. Then, anointing himself with a mixture of rancid coconut oil and *kukui* (candle-nut) oil, which gave him a strong, corpse-like odour, he started with his companions in canoes for the point on the sea where the sky hangs down to meet the water.

Arrived at the spot, he directed his comrades to lower him into the abyss called the Lua-o-Milu (Cave of Milu). Taking with him his coconut-shell, and seating himself on the cross-stick of the swing, he was quickly lowered down by the long rope of vines held by his friends in the canoe above.

Soon he entered the great cavern where the spirits of the dead were gathered together. As he came among them their curiosity was aroused to learn who he was; and he heard many remarks such as, " Whew ! what an odour this corpse has ! " and " He must have been dead a long time ! " Even Milu himself, as he sat on the bank watching the spirits, was deceived, or he would never have permitted the entry of the living man into the regions ruled by him.

Hiku and his swing, which was like the one with one rope only used in Hawaii, attracted considerable attention. One spirit in particular watched him most intently—the spirit of Kawelu. There was mutual recognition, and with the permission of Milu she darted up to him, and swung with him on the *kowali*. As they were enjoying together this favourite Hawaiian pastime the friends above were informed of the success of the ruse by means of a preconcerted signal, and rapidly drew them upward. At first Kawelu was too much absorbed in the sport to notice this; but when at length her attention was aroused by seeing the great distance of those beneath her she was about to flit away like a butterfly. Hiku, however, quickly clapped the coconut-shells together, imprisoning her within them, and both were soon drawn up to the canoes above.

They returned to the shores of Holualoa, where Hiku landed at once and hastened to the house where the body of

Kawelu still lay. Kneeling by its side, he made an incision in the great toe of the left foot, and into this with great difficulty he forced the reluctant spirit, binding up the wound so that it could not escape from the cold and clammy flesh in which it was now imprisoned. Then he began to rub and chafe the foot, working the spirit farther and farther up the limb. Gradually, as the heart was reached, the blood began to flow through the body; the breast began gently to heave, and soon the eyes opened, and the spirit gazed out from them as if just awakened from sleep. Kawelu was restored to consciousness, and seeing the beloved Hiku bending tenderly over her she said, " How could you be so cruel as to leave me ? "

All remembrance of the Lua-o-Milu and what had taken place there had disappeared, and she took up the thread of consciousness just where she had left it a few days before. Great joy filled the hearts of the people of Holualoa as they welcomed back to their midst the loved Kawelu and the hero Hiku, who from that day was not separated from her.

In this myth the entrance to the Lua-o-Milu (in Maori Rua-o-Miru, or Cave of Miru) is placed out to sea ; but the more usual accounts place it at the mouth of the great valley of Waipio, in a place called Keoni, where the sands have long since covered up and concealed this passage to the netherworld.

Every year, it is told, the procession of ghosts marches silently down the Mahiki road, and at this point enters the Lua-o-Milu. This company of the dead is said to have been seen in quite recent times. A man, walking in the evening, saw the company appear in the distance ; and, knowing that should they encounter him his death was certain, he hid himself behind a tree, and, trembling with fear, gazed at the dread sight. There was Kamehameha the conqueror, with all his chiefs and warriors in battle array, thousands of heroes who had won renown in the olden time. They kept perfect step as they marched along in utter silence, and, passing through the woods down to Waipio, disappeared from his view.

The resemblances between the Maori story and the Hawaiian are as remarkable as their differences; in most of the parallel or similar stories the names agree more or less nearly; here the only names at all similar are those of the man—Hutu in the Maori, and Hiku in the Hawaiian (the *k* being equivalent to the Maori *t*). Miru is the ruler of the lowest netherworlds of the Maori, but is there a woman. There is a point of resemblance to the Greek myths in the instruction of Hine-nui-te-po to Hutu to eat none of the food offered by the spirits—if he ate of it he would be unable to return; it was because Persephone had eaten seven pomegranate seeds in the abode of Hades that she was compelled to spend half of the year in his realm. The simplicity of these stories is rather childlike innocence than childish ignorance.

The Return of Patito (New Zealand)

In the story of Mata-ora it is said that the doings in the upperworld are known to the dwellers in Spirit Land; other stories infer this. A man called Patito, having died, left a son who became a very brave man and a noted warrior; and a report of his bravery being carried to the spirits by some of the departed, the martial ardour of the father was roused. In his time he had been considered a most expert spearman, and he revisited the earth with the determination of testing the ability of his son by a contest with him. They met, but the son was unable to ward off the thrusts of his father, who, satisfied that he was still paramount, returned to the netherworld.

The Maori believed that, had the son proved the better spearman, the father could have continued to dwell upon earth, and that man would then not have been subject to death.

The old man had a granddaughter, who followed him to the point where spirits leave this world; and, seeing the old man descend, she called upon him to return to earth. He looked round, and through this look she was turned to stone.

Te Atarahi tells of Te Reinga (New Zealand)

The netherworld was by no means a place to be dreaded. There are various accounts of different people who spent some time there and then came back to earth. There was a man Te Atarahi, who remained there five days and nights, and then returned to life. On the fifth day after this man died two women went out to cut flax blades. While so employed they observed the flower-stalks of the flax springing up every now and then at a little distance from them. One woman remarked to her companion, " There is some one sucking the juice of the *korari* flowers." By degrees this person came nearer, and was seen by the woman, who said, " The man is like Te Atarahi. Why, it surely is Te Atarahi ! " " It cannot be Te Atarahi," replied her companion, " for he is dead." They both looked carefully, and saw that the skin of the man was wrinkled and hanging loose about his back and shoulders, and that the hair of his head was all gone.

They returned to the *pa*, and told the people that they had seen Te Atarahi. " Are you quite sure it was Te Atarahi? " said the men ; and the women answered, " His appearance was like Te Atarahi, but the hair of his head had all gone, and his skin hung loose in folds about his back." A man was sent to look at the grave where Te Atarahi had been buried. He found the grave undisturbed, so he returned and said, " Sirs, the body is well buried ; it has not been disturbed." Then the men went and examined the place carefully, and found an opening on one side, a little way off. They went to the place where Te Atarahi had been seen by the women, and there they found the man seated on a *ti* (*Cordyline*, cabbage-tree). They at once knew him to be Te Atarahi; so they sent for the *tohunga*. He came, and repeated a *karakia*, after which the man was removed to the sacred place, the *tohunga* remaining with him, constantly repeating *karakia*, while the people of the *pa* stood at a distance, looking on. There the man remained many days, food being brought to him, and as time passed he began to have again the appearance of a normal man. He recovered, and became quite well. Then he told how he had been in Te Reinga ; how his relations came about him, and bade him not to touch the food, and sent him back to the land of light. He spoke also of the excellence of the state in which the people of Te Reinga dwelt, of their food, of their choice delicacy the *ngaro*, of the numbers of their *pa*, and the multitude of the dwellers there, all of which agrees with what the *atua* have said when visiting men upon earth.

The conclusion has a touch of innocence ; it would have been surprising had Te Atarahi found it different from orthodox expectations. Nevertheless, it shows that thoughts of the spirit world gave rise to no great dread or apprehension. The choice delicacy *ngaro* is one that has not been identified ; for though *ngaro*, a transposed form of *rango*, a blowfly, is a food of the lizard, and the lizard is a dweller in the lowest of the netherworlds, it is not known that it ever formed a food for spirits, and it could hardly be called a delicacy. Thought and fancy take strange paths, however, and a Hawaiian myth gives the food of the spirits of the netherworld as lizards and butterflies.

The Death of Veetini (Mangaia)

The Mangaian death ceremonies were particularly beautiful, and a number of the songs sung on the occasion of the mourning for a lost loved one have been preserved by the Rev. W. Wyatt Gill.

Veetini was the first who died a natural death in Mangaia. He was the only and much-loved son of Tueva and his wife Manga, and when in the prime of early manhood he sickened and died. The grieving parents instituted those signs of mourning and the funeral games that were ever afterward observed on that island. The chief mourners were Tueva, Manga, and the lovely Tiki, the affectionate sister of Veetini. These three, together with the more distant relatives, blackened their faces, cut off their hair, gashed their bodies with sharks' teeth, and wore only *pakoko* (native cloth died red in the sap of the candle-nut-tree, and then dipped in the black mud of a *taro*-patch, the offensive smell thus imparted to the garment being symbolical of the decaying state of the dead). Their heads were encircled with common fern, singed with fire to give it a red appearance. It was in memory of Veetini that the *eva*, or dirge, in its four varieties and the mourning dance were invented and performed by the sorrowing relatives day by day.

The ceremonies occupied from ten to fifteen days, according to the age and rank of the deceased; and during the entire period no beating of bark for native cloth was permitted in the district where the death took place. This must be done on another part of the island, the object being to avoid giving offence to the female spirit Mueu, who introduced cloth-beating to the world. She herself beats out cloth of a very different texture; her cloth-flail is the stroke of death. So long as the mourning and funeral games were going on Mueu was supposed to be present; when all was over she returned to her home in Avaiki, the shades. Hence the saying when a person dies: " Ah, the flail of Mueu is once more at work! "

The last resting-place of Veetini is at Rangi-kapua, a green spot about half a mile from the sea. The rays of the setting sun fall upon the hill, about a hundred feet above the level of the sea. On the evening he was buried the dirges and dances that had been composed in his honour were performed. The parents and the sister looked wistfully toward the north, hoping for his return, but in vain.

The day following they walked in sad procession, slowly chanting dirges expressive of their passionate desire again to embrace the departed, along the western shore of the island. At night, exhausted with grief and weariness, they slept in one of the rugged caves near the sea, having in vain strained their eyes over the ocean path where the spirit of Veetini had so recently disappeared.

The mourning band next sought the lost one on the southern, almost inaccessible shore; still there was no response to the loud entreaties of the disconsolate parents or the lovely Tiki.

At last they arrived at the eastern coast, and gazed over the vast ocean swept by the life-giving trade-winds, but the life so desired was denied, and once more the lamentation and funeral dances were performed. At night they occupied Ana-kura, the red cave whose wide entrance is washed by the surf. Ere dawn Tueva arose from his stony resting-place to watch the rising of the sun. The shadows of night were fast passing away; in a few minutes the sun rose in all its glory. Tueva noticed a tiny dark speck beyond on the ocean which grew larger as it drew nearer, passing over the ocean in the bright trail of the sun. As it arrived still nearer they saw that there, lightly skimming over the crests of the waves, came their own lost Veetini.

The rejoicing parents rushed to greet him, to embrace him; he was indeed Veetini, yet not altogether like his former self. He said to the joyful throng that he had been permitted to visit the upperworld in consequence of the passionate lamentations of his parents, and to comfort their sorrowing hearts. He also came to show to mortals the manner of making offerings of food to please the dead. He had come, but must again depart on the bright track of the sun, being himself now a denizen of Spirit Land. To gratify his parents and friends, however, Veetini prayed great Tangaroa to detain the sun in its course for a short time, in order that they might rest and converse together. The prayer was granted, and the sun paused while Veetini and his friends rested happily on the spot known as Karanga-iti.

At length he arose, and led the half-joyful, half-sorrowful procession along the beach toward the west, the sun now moving on as usual. They reached Vai-rorongo, directly facing the place of the setting sun. Here they rested a few minutes only, so fast the day was fading away. As the sun disappeared beneath the horizon, and the broad ocean was covered with the golden light, Veetini said the time had come for parting. The weeping parents begged him to remain with them. " I cannot," the son replied; " I do not now belong to this world," and then impatiently he cried:

VEETINI DISAPPEARING OVER THE GLOWING TRACK OF THE SUN
(See page 310)

THE SPIRIT WORLDS

" Thrust down the sun,
That to the netherworld I may descend."

The parents would detain him by force, but, lo! they embraced a shadow. They watched him gliding swiftly over the western ocean in what the Maori called *te ara whanui a Tane'*, the glowing track of the sun, and, with its last rays, Veetini disappeared for ever.

THE DIRGE OF VAIPO FOR VEETINI

Call for the music and dance to begin. The news has sped to
Avaiki
Of Veetini about to die.
Sad day of death.
SOLO. Go on!
CHORUS. A house is built for him at Karanga-iti
To face the rising sun.
SOLO. 'Tis done!
CHORUS. Veetini has gained the drooping sky,
Has fled!
O all-dividing Avaiki!
SOLO. Whence came he?
CHORUS. He came up out of Avaiki,
Stepping lightly on his path
Over the treacherous waves.
Veetini again is trembling on the wing.
He skims, he skims the sea!
SOLO. Alas! he follows thy track, O sun!
CHORUS. Yes, he follows thy dazzling light,
As thou gently settest in the ocean.
Thrust down the sun,
That to the netherland he may descend.

It is in reference to the sad journeyings of the beautiful Tiki with her parents that at the breaking up of a funeral party it is commonly said, " The weary travels of Tiki are over; we part."

When the body of a dead person was committed to its last resting-place the mourners took five old coconuts, which were opened, one after another, and the water poured upon the ground. The nuts were then wrapped up in leaves and native cloth, and thrown toward the grave; or if the corpse were let down with cords into the deep chasm

311

of Auraka the nuts and other food would be thrown after it, the name of the dead being called loudly each time, with the words, " Here is thy food; eat of it." When the fifth nut and the accompanying food *raroi* were thrown the mourners cried, " Farewell ! We come back to thee no more ! "

The Dirge for Vera (Mangaia)

A few years previous to the discovery of Mangaia by Captain Cook in 1777 the priest Ngara was paramount chief of the island. His nephew Vera died in consequence, it was believed, of his having offended the deity Motoro. Imposing funeral rites were performed ; and, as in the case of Veetini, the parents are said to have traversed the island in the vain hope of the return of Vera. The body was conveyed to Tamarua and thrown down a deep chasm, Raupa, having communication with the sea. The mourning parents slept in a cave, in the hope that Vera would return in answer to their laments and entreaties. But he did not return, and the next day the disappointed parents, and a long train of mourners, returned to their dwellings.

The two dirges, or death-talks, following were composed by Uanuku about the year 1770. Their beauty is enhanced by the covert allusions to the myth of Veetini, and in the original the name Manga, the mother of Veetini, occurs instead of the name of the mother of Vera.

DIRGE FOR VERA

INTRODUCTION

SOLO. At Vai-rorongo, toward the setting sun—
Tarry with us this evening.
I go far away, Mother,
CHORUS. By a perilous path to Spirit Land.

FOUNDATION

SOLO. Halt, Vera, on thy journey:
Turn thine eyes toward Mangaia.
Look again upon thy parents,
Whose days are spent in tears,
CHORUS. Resting in Ana-kura by the way.

THE SPIRIT WORLDS

FIRST OFFSHOOT

SOLO. Toward the setting sun
CHORUS.   his home is!
A home, and food in plenty for Vera.
Tueva, encircled with red leaves, is mourning.
SOLO. Tueva, encircled with red leaves, is mourning.
Alas! the death-flail of Mueu is beating.
Weeping we follow thee, beloved Vera.
I go far away, Mother,
CHORUS. By a perilous path to Spirit Land.

FOUNDATION

SOLO. Halt, Vera, on thy journey:
Turn thine eyes toward Mangaia.
Look again upon thy parents,
Whose days are spent in tears,
CHORUS. Resting in Ana-kura by the way.

SECOND OFFSHOOT

SOLO. Rush forth,
CHORUS.   O north-west wind!
Bear him gently on his way.
Awake, O south-west,
SOLO.   O south-west.
Vera will perchance return.
Even Mautara weeps for thee.
How desolate is our home!
I go far away, Mother,
CHORUS. By a perilous path to Spirit Land.

FOUNDATION

SOLO. Halt, Vera, on thy journey:
Turn thine eyes toward Mangaia;
Look again upon thy parents,
Whose days are spent in tears,
CHORUS. Resting in Ana-kura by the way.

THIRD OFFSHOOT

SOLO. Skim,
CHORUS.   Vera, the surface of the ocean,
The ocean path once traversed by Ngakē.
SOLO. Torrents of rain obstruct thy journey,
Yet aided by a mighty god
The band by Vera led shall safely reach
Their home beneath the glowing tide.
I go far away, Mother,
CHORUS. By a perilous path to Spirit Land.

313

MYTHS OF THE POLYNESIANS

FOUNDATION

SOLO.   Halt, Vera, on thy journey:
         Turn thine eyes toward Mangaia.
         Look again upon thy parents,
         Whose days are spent in tears,
CHORUS.   Resting in Ana-kura by the way.

FOURTH OFFSHOOT

SOLO.   Slowly
CHORUS.   traverse these rugged shores,
         Ere Vera gain the western skies.
         Veetini once returned to earth.
SOLO.   Oh that Vera might revisit earth,
         Gliding over the shimmering sea!
         I go far away, Mother,
CHORUS.   By a perilous path to Spirit Land.

FOUNDATION

SOLO.   Halt, Vera, on thy journey:
         Turn thine eyes toward Mangaia.
         Look again upon thy parents,
         Whose days are spent in tears,
CHORUS.   Resting in Ana-kura by the way.

FIFTH OFFSHOOT

SOLO.   Lash firmly
CHORUS.   the outrigger of thy canoe,
         Ere starting on thy voyage far.
         Linger upon the shore awhile, O Vera,
SOLO.   Upon the beach where billows beat;
         Near this rough path.   And must thou go
         To regions of the sunset, oh, how far?
         I go far away, Mother,
CHORUS.   By a perilous path to Spirit Land.

LAST FOUNDATION

SOLO.   Halt, Vera, on thy journey:
         Turn thine eyes toward Mangaia.
         Look again upon thy parents,
         Whose days are spent in tears,
CHORUS.   Resting in Ana-kura by the way.

FINALE
Ai e ruaoo ē!   E rangai ē!

314

THE SPIRIT WORLDS

THE GHOSTS LED BY VERA PREPARING FOR THEIR FINAL DEPARTURE

INTRODUCTION

SOLO.   List, Vera, to the music of the sea.
Beyond yon dwarfed pandanus grove
The billows o'er the rocks are dashing.
'Tis time, friends, to depart.

CHORUS.   Our garments are mourning weeds and flowers.

FOUNDATION

SOLO.   Advance to yonder level rock,
There to await the favouring wind
To bear thee o'er the sea.
Thy father watches thee in sorrow.

CHORUS.   By thee is led the band departing.

FIRST OFFSHOOT

SOLO.   List, dear Vera,

CHORUS.   to the music of the sea.
A wretched wanderer art thou,
Almost arrived at Iva.

SOLO.   Yes, at Iva;
Once from Tahiti, and from Tonga once,
Now to the land of spirits bound,
Whose entrance is the open grave.
'Tis time, friends, to depart.

CHORUS.   Our garments are mourning weeds and flowers.

SECOND OFFSHOOT

SOLO.   I turn my eyes

CHORUS.   to another land.
In other regions may my spirit rest.
Upon this trembling stone I stand,
The chasm's edge——

SOLO.   Yes, at the lip

CHORUS.   of this dark chasm.
My path is o'er yon black rocks near the sea.
Over the roughest and the sharpest stones
This feeble troop of spirits I lead.
Whence come we? Here we stand and wait
The so-long-hoped-for

SOLO.   south-east

CHORUS.   breeze
To waft us over the far-reaching ocean.
Hither and thither we have wandered,

Lightly stepping on the sea-washed stones,
Over the rocks encrusted have we come.
By darkness overtaken, sit we down to weep.

SOLO. A tearful band by Vera guided.
Now from the view a drizzling shower
The heights of yonder mountain hides;
Now we are sprent with ocean spray,
'Tis time, friends, to depart.

CHORUS. Our garments are mourning weeds and flowers.

THIRD OFFSHOOT

SOLO. Press forward,
CHORUS.   on our journey;
Nor let us wander from the way.
SOLO. Yonder the landing-place,
CHORUS.   at Auveo,
Whose entrance is so hard to find.
There, too, my father is
SOLO.   to watch our course.
The sun is low; rest we a little while.
CHORUS. Our feet are weary with these stones;
Yonder the gloomy cave of Raupa is—
Let us move slowly on our way.
We, friendless spirits, have reached Auneke.
Look eastward, and look westward;
Gaze at the setting sun.
SOLO. My father follows hard behind,
Beckoning my return.
Here halt awhile.
'Tis time, friends, to depart.
CHORUS. Our garments are mourning weeds and flowers.

FOURTH OFFSHOOT

SOLO. Thy feet, Vera,
CHORUS.   with wild vines are entangled.
Art thou for Vavau bound, the spirit-home?
Over
SOLO.   the foaming billows
CHORUS.   wilt thou voyage?
Thread thy way, through the pandanus groves,
The favourite haunt of spirits disembodied,
Near where the royal Utakea landed.
SOLO. A level beach, laved by the sea.
The cricket-god chirps to direct thy path
Through thickets to the shore
Where wander spirits of the dead.

THE SPIRIT WORLDS

> O Vera, bathe thy streaming locks—
> Grant a new life to me, O morning light!
> 'Tis time, friends, to depart.

CHORUS. Our garments are mourning weeds and flowers.

FIFTH OFFSHOOT

SOLO.   Descendant of the kings
CHORUS.   of Mauke,
> The favoured one, led by propitious winds
> From sea-drowned skies to these clear shores,
> Ere taking now a long farewell, turn back!
> Thou idol of my dwelling, stay awhile,

SOLO.   Decked with the buds of sweetest-scented flowers,
> And fragrant leaves brought from Tutuila.
> 'Tis time, friends, to depart.

CHORUS. Our garments are mourning weeds and flowers.

FINALE

Ai e ruaoo ē!   E rangai ē!

One other example of these highly poetical, semi-dramatic songs may be given:

DEATH-LAMENT FOR VARENGA, DAUGHTER OF ARO-KAPITI

INTRODUCTION

> Varenga, who came from the sun-rising [Tahiti],
> In Spirit Land [Avaiki] now is wed.
> She was wooed by a shadow!
> Such was my dream on the mountain.

FOUNDATION

> My dream was of thee at the sun-rising—
> Thy form as the lightning dazzling.
> Thou for the dawn wast watching,
> When from my sleep I awoke
> On the steep mountainside.

FIRST OFFSHOOT

> Varenga, who came from the sun-rising;
> Yes, my Varenga!
> In thy maidenhood will Miru cherish thee,
> Thy lovely maidenhood!

317

The admired of all wast thou,
Wherever thy light step wandered.
Now thou art wooed by a shadow!
Such was my dream on the mountain.

SECOND OFFSHOOT

In the ancestral *marae* wast thou buried,
On the side of the steep Maunga-roa,
By the tall fern hidden,
Ay, by the tall fern hidden.
Thy spirit, perchance, is revisiting the spot,
Among the wild rocks hovering.
Now thou art wooed by a shadow!
Such was my dream on the mountain.

THIRD OFFSHOOT

Decayed is thy house in the west.
This home, at Kauava, gathering-place of ghosts,
Built by thine ancestors, where spirits rest
And chatter quietly at eventide,
Or at the cliff-edge wander,
Or on the stones sit still, and inland gaze.
Now thou art wooed by a shadow!
Such was my dream on the mountain.

FINALE

Ai e ruaoo ē! E rangai ē!

Ngaru the Valiant (Mangaia)

In Marua lived the brave Ngaru, his mother Vaiare,
and his grandfather, who was no other than Moko, or Great
Lizard, the king of all lizards. Tonga-tea, the youthful
wife of Ngaru, was the envy of all Marua on account of her
fairness. Longing for fame, Ngaru resolved to try his
strength against some of the numerous monsters and evil
spirits of his time. He learned of two enemies of mankind
who had their home in the ocean—Tiko-kura (the Storm-
wave) and Tumu-i-te-are-toka (the Great Shark), who fed
exclusively upon human flesh. These two always went
together in company, but Ngaru determined to meet them
both—an enterprise seemingly hopeless; for who had ever
escaped their anger?

318

THE SPIRIT WORLDS

His first care was to provide himself with a surf-board of the lightest description, which he named Orua (the Two), in allusion to the two he was about to encounter. Now he appeared on the inner edge of the reef, carrying his surf-board; but the wide coral surface was perfectly dry. Moko sat on a projecting crag of rock to watch over the safety of his grandson, who advanced to the outer edge of the reef, where the surf beats ceaselessly, and loudly cursed the sea-monsters by name. Smarting under the unprovoked insult, the monsters resolved on vengeance without delay. Suddenly the dead calm which left the reef dry changed to a furious tempest. Long breakers rushed inland far beyond the accustomed bounds of the sea, and spent themselves against the gnarled roots of the *utu*-trees. Moko kept his place on the rocky eminence while his grandson daringly floated out to sea on the crest of a retreating billow.

The shark-god, perceiving his opportunity, stealthily glided behind his intended victim, and was preparing for the leap when the quick eye of Moko caught sight of his dark outline, and Moko shouted to the boy, " The shark is under you." Ngaru, hearing this, instantly leaped high into the air, so that this first attempt failed. The monster leaped into the air after Ngaru; but Ngaru dived under the water, and again escaped. The disappointed monster was enraged, so that Ngaru must exert all his strength and skill to avoid the fearful open jaws. Tumu-i-te-are-toka became crafty, but Ngaru was craftier still, Moko often giving his grandson timely warning. For eight weary days and nights the contest went on, until the exhausted Ngaru put an end to it by throwing his surf-board to the monsters, who gladly retired to their ancient haunts in the blue ocean deeps.

Great was the delight of the old grandfather and of his countrymen at the exploit of Ngaru, the first who had dared the monsters in their own domain and yet escaped with life. But the hero was bruised and battered, and his skin lacerated with the coral. He made his way home; but on the way he fell in with his fair wife, Tonga-tea. Arrived at a fountain, they wished to bathe, but a friendly dispute took

319

place as to who should bathe first. Once in, he was in no hurry to get out; and when at sunset he did so his wife was horrified to find that his skin had become almost black through long exposure during the mighty contest with the monsters of the deep. Reviling him for his blackness, she ran off to her friends.

When Ngaru reached home Moko inquired what had become of the fair Tonga-tea; and learned that, disgusted with the appearance of her husband, she had fled to Te Au-tapu. " Nothing blackens the skin so quickly as the sea and the sun," said Moko. The grandson inquired how his skin could be blanched. " The only way to blanch your skin," said Moko, " is to treat you as green bananas are treated when they are to be blanched or ripened." Ngaru agreed that this should be tried. Accordingly, they dug a deep hole, and lined it with layers of sweet-scented fern-leaves. Ngaru descended into this hole, and was duly covered with leaves, the whole being covered with a thin layer of earth. On the eighth day flashes of lightning proceeded from the spot where Ngaru had lain so long, increasing in intensity until earth and leaves were riven away, permitting him to emerge, like a moth from its chrysalis. It then became evident that these flashes of light had come from the face and body of Ngaru, being in reality the dazzling fairness of his skin. But there was one objection—the steam of the blanching pit had left Ngaru perfectly bald. Moko sent his mother Vaiare to great Tangaroa, to ask for some new hair. It was given; but when Moko examined it it proved to be frizzy. Moko was resolved not to spoil the head of his grandson with such a mop, and bade Vaiare take it back and ask for some better hair. Tangaroa put her off with some of the detestable colour light yellow. " This will never do," said Moko; " I must have the best." Vaiare trudged away again; and Tangaroa, finding there was no escape from the importunity of the grandfather, gave a profusion of wavy, smooth raven locks. Moko was delighted, and secured them to the head of his grandson.

320

The dazzling flashes of light from Ngaru reached even to the distant abode of Tonga-tea, so that every one said, " Behold the dazzling fairness of Ngaru ! " Said the runaway wife, " This Ngaru you praise must be a different person from the Ngaru I knew." The people asserted that it was her despised husband ; but Tonga-tea remained incredulous.

Now Tonga-tea had got up a reed-throwing match for women ; but men were invited from all parts to decide upon the merits of the throwers, and to applaud those who should be successful. At the time appointed the young women, gaily attired and covered with fragrant garlands, stood ready to begin, each with a long reed in her hand. Tonga-tea, as mistress of the day, was about to make the first throw when Ngaru appeared, and was at once recognized by her. Her arm dropped powerless to her side. She struggled to conceal her emotion and proceed with the game, but could not.

All was confusion ; there was no further thought of sport ; the visitors disappeared. Tonga-tea, love-smitten, weeping, repentant, followed Ngaru, entreating him to return to her. Ngaru, in whose heart still rankled the bitterness of her reference to his blackness, in the moment of triumph said to the penitent, " Never will I return to thee." Hearing this the despairing Tonga-tea set off in search of some poisonous *kokii kura*, chewed it, and died.

There lived in Avaiki, the netherworld, a fierce she-demon named Miru, whose favourite repast was the spirits of the unfortunate dead, whom she first stupefied with *kava*, then cooked in her oven and devoured. Envious of the great fame of Ngaru, she resolved to destroy him in her never-extinguished oven. There seemed to be no difficulty in decoying him to her realm, and she directed two of her daughters, Tapairu (the Peerless Ones), to ascend to the upperworld and induce Ngaru to marry them both. They, Kumu-tonga-i-te-po and Karaia-i-te-ata, were then to induce him to visit, with them, the netherworld their home ; and,

once there, Miru felt that she could control his fate. On
their entering the dwelling of Moko Ngaru feigned sleep,
while the grandfather tried to discover their real intent.
They said that their mother, Miru, had sent them to escort
Ngaru to Avaiki; and on their arrival he was to be united
to both these Peerless Ones, with whom no mortals could
compare.

Moko, suspecting the real object of their visit, sought to
gain time by showing the utmost hospitality to his unusual
guests. While these fairy women were enjoying themselves,
Moko, the king of the lizards, sent his servants on a secret
mission to the domain of Miru to ascertain what dangerous
means were at her disposal, and what were her usual avoca-
tions. These servants were little lizards, and off they
glided in all directions. On arriving at Avaiki, unperceived by Miru, they noticed that the old, deformed, and
inexpressibly ugly demon had a house full of *kava*, kept exclusively for the purpose of stupefying her intended victims,
who were eventually cooked in her unappeasable oven, and
eaten by herself, her fair children, and her servants. These
keen-sighted little lizards returned to the upperworld, and
reported what they had discovered. Moko privately told
this to his grandson, and bade him exercise the greatest care,
or he would infallibly perish, as multitudes had perished
before him.

As evening drew on the three started off for the land of
Miru. The Peerless Ones had with them rolls of the finest
tapa, in which they insisted on wrapping their future husband, as though he were already dead; they then secured
the bundle well with cords, and, slinging him on a long pole,
carried him off in triumph. After some time Kumu-tonga'
and Karaia' began to ascend a mountain, when the imprisoned Ngaru became conscious of a steep and sudden
movement, and prayed thus:

> " Put me down, put me down,
> Set me free, set me free.
> Oh that I had liberty
> To gaze upon this mountain!

THE SPIRIT WORLDS

'Tis surely the mountain spoken of
By my grandfather Moko-roa,
And by my mother Vaiare,
And by my wife Tonga-tea."

To this Kumu-tonga' and Karaia', temporarily releasing him, responded :

" Devoured forthwith thou shalt be!
Thy corpse shall decay on the mountain,
Thy spirit be borne to Avaiki
To make a repast for Miru."

" 'Tis thus you treat your intended husband!" said Ngaru, as they again wrapped him up, corded the bundle, and proceeded. They bore him to another spur of the range, and when he prayed as before to be released they replied as before, and again he said, " 'Tis thus you treat your intended husband!" Once more they wrapped him in the folds of the *tapa*, secured him with cords, and bore him along until, reaching a shady grove of chestnut-trees, they set him down and unfastened the cords. They hastened to fetch some *kava*, known as " Miru's own," and gave it to him to chew. He chewed the whole, and still, to their amazement, remained wakeful and active ; on him alone of the children of men the powerful narcotic had failed to produce its usual effects. The glowing oven of Miru was ready for its victim, and the pitiless voice of Miru was heard, " Kumu-tonga-i-te-po and Karaia-i-te-ata, bring along your husband ; for him the oven of Miru is waiting." At these words Ngaru put on the girdle his grandfather had wisely provided. With it about him, the dauntless visitor from the upperworld proceeded in search of Miru and her dread oven.

Now was heard the voice of the anxious Moko, sounding from the upperworld in the world of shades ," Return, Ngaru ; yonder is the oven to which you have been destined by her." Heedless of the warning, the brave visitor went on his way ; and finding the red-hot stones raked ready for the victim he asked the mistress of the

323

netherworld what she intended to do with this glowing oven.

" Cook you," she promptly replied. Ngaru reproached her, saying, " Ah, Miru, my grandfather Moko did not prepare an oven for your daughters, but gave them food to eat, coconut-water to drink, and sent them away in peace! You cook and devour your visitors! "

At these words the heavens darkened, Ngaru walked to the edge of the oven, and placed one foot upon the red-hot stones. At this moment the clouds, which had been gathering since he had entered Avaiki, burst suddenly, and a great deluge of water extinguished the glowing oven, and swept away Miru herself, her younger fairy daughters, and all her servants. Ngaru was saved by clutching hold of the stem of the *nono*, and the beautiful Tapairu girls who had allured him held tightly to him and so escaped the fate of their mother and sisters. These fairies taught Ngaru the art of ball-throwing.

After a time the waters abated; and Ngaru, wearying of the company of these attractive but dangerous fairy women, succeeded in finding a dark, winding passage to a land called Taumareva, where fruits and flowers grew profusely, and whose inhabitants excelled at nose-flute-playing. Here he married a girl who had been kept by her parents confined in a house in order to whiten her skin. Time passed pleasantly, until one day two pretty little birds, known as *karakerake*, perched upon the ledge of a pile of rocks. Ngaru recognized them as belonging to Moko, and asked them if they came at his grandfather's bidding. They nodded assent, and Ngaru, shedding tears of joy, prayed them :

> " Ye little birds, pray drop a cord,
> Ay, the cord used for the imperious
> Oraka,[1] the all-devouring.
> Drop it, delay not."

At these words two cords fell, one from the feet of each bird. Securing himself to the double rope, Ngaru gave

---

[1] Chasm down which the dead were thrown.

a signal to the birds, and without a word of farewell to his wife or her musical people he was borne aloft to the upper-world. He safely reached Moko, who had long been ill, pining for the presence of the brave Ngaru, so long a prisoner in the underworld.

There was still another foe to be overcome, another adventure for the intrepid Ngaru. One day the people were astonished at the sight of a great basket let down from the sky. Two or three who were curious to see the wonders of that upperworld, hitherto unexplored, entered the basket, and were speedily drawn up out of sight. Not many days after the basket again appeared, and as before returned to the sky with curious adventurers; but it was remarked that none returned to report what they had seen.

The truth was that a sky-demon named Amai-te-rangi had taken a fancy to feed on human flesh, and had devised the basket and rope as a means of securing food for appeasing his hunger. Hearing from his victims of the prowess of Ngaru, he resolved to entrap and devour him. The basket itself was a very attractive object; and on the day of the return of Ngaru from the netherworld it was let down close to the dwelling of Moko. Ngaru regarded this as a challenge, and determined to ascend and engage the owner in combat. The more wily Moko detained his grandson until his faithful little lizard subjects should have gone up to find out what was going on above there.

The word having been given by Moko, a number of them entered the basket, which was speedily pulled up by Amai-te-rangi. On discovering that he had caught nothing but a number of miserable reptiles he was greatly chagrined. Meanwhile, these active little subjects of Moko overran the place, and when next the basket was let down they were permitted to go down with it. They reported to Moko what they had seen—the gigantic size of Amai-te-rangi, beautiful women engaged in ball-throwing, a huge chisel and mallet in the hands of the sky-demon, and piles of human bones.

Ngaru fearlessly got into the basket, and was at once

drawn up by the delighted Amai', who anticipated a good feast, as the intended victim was unusually heavy. Upon touching the paving of blue stone Ngaru found the demon fully extended, chisel and mallet in hand, ready to deal the fatal blow. At this moment the hero gave a sudden jerk, which precipitated him and the basket down to earth again. The disappointed demon hastily drew them up a second time, resolving now not to permit Ngaru to escape him. But the grandson of Moko was more nimble-witted than the demon, and as soon as the basket touched the solid vault he once more jerked it back to earth. Eight times Amai' pulled, until his strength was nearly exhausted; but at last, to his satisfaction, Ngaru stepped out of the basket and confronted him, and he prepared to deal the fatal blow with his chisel from which no mortal had yet escaped.

All this had been foreseen by Moko; and to ensure the safety of Ngaru, every time the basket touched the earth he had sent up in it a number of lizards, who glided out as soon as the basket touched the blue floor of heaven. To them the monster paid no attention, all his thoughts being concentrated on the destruction of his fearless human adversary. At the moment his giant arms were uplifted to encompass the death of Ngaru all the lizards crept up the legs of Amai', covering his body, neck, arms, and face, but particularly clustering about his armpits, tickling him to such a degree that it was impossible for him to strike with precision. Again and again he endeavoured to brush off the little tormentors, but they were persistent, and so distracted him that he dropped both chisel and mallet. Then Ngaru, seizing the weapons, succeeded in killing the monster, and let himself down to earth again, accompanied by his little four-footed allies, and taking with him the chisel and mallet of the dead Amai'. Before leaving, however, he tried ball-throwing with 'Ina and Matonga, and succeeded in beating them, though they were able to keep eight balls going at a time.

Upon the story of Ngaru was composed a lyric drama, by Tuka, about the year 1815.

326

THE SPIRIT WORLDS

THE DRAMA OF NGARU

*A Reed-throwing Match for Women, in Honour of
Patiki-poro*

TWO WOMEN. Strip branches from the *kava* of Miru
To stupefy the wonder-working Ngaru,
Victorious over monsters,
Pet grandson of Moko,
Descended from Vari-Origin-of-All.

CHORUS. The natives of the sky
Let down a trap to catch Ngaru,
Who then on high ascended.

TWO WOMEN. To save him, the golden lizards
Climbed up the limbs, the body,
Baffling Amai-te-rangi.
'Twas Ngaru, blackened by diving.

CHORUS. Ngaru, blackened in the billows,
Repellent to Tonga-tea,
Whose haunt is Iti-kau.

TWO WOMEN. Whose haunt is Iti-kau, ay!

CHORUS. Refresh yourselves in Marua, ye fair ones,
Like those celestial experts at ball-throwing.

FIRST OFFSHOOT

TWO WOMEN. The wondrous skill of Ngaru, ay!

CHORUS. List to yonder voice!
The voice that calls to Ngaru!
Lightning from him leaps
And flashes all around,
The might of Ngaru-of-the-Sea.
Whence is this power?
From yonder deep Avaiki,
From Vari-Origin-of-All,
Who sends him back to earth.
This is for him, the *kava*.
What have you come for, Miru?
I come to devour mankind.

TWO WOMEN. Do thy worst, Miru of Avaiki!

CHORUS. Provoke no lightnings from thy love—

TWO WOMEN. Thy love whose haunt is Iti-kau!

CHORUS. Ay, Ngaru-of-the-Sea.

TWO WOMEN. Strip branches from the *kava* of Miru
To stupefy the wonder-working Ngaru,
Victorious over monsters,

Pet grandson of Moko,
Descended from Vari-Origin-of-All.

CHORUS. The natives of the sky
Let down a trap to catch Ngaru,
Who then on high ascended.

TWO WOMEN. To save him, the golden lizards
Climbed up the limbs, the body,
Baffling Amai-te-rangi.
'Twas Ngaru, blackened by diving.

CHORUS. Ngaru, blackened by the billows,
Repellent to Tonga-tea,
Whose haunt is Iti-kau.

TWO WOMEN. Whose haunt is Iti-kau, ay!
Refresh yourselves in Marua, ye fair ones,
Like those celestial experts at ball-throwing.

SECOND OFFSHOOT

TWO WOMEN. In Marua is thy home.

CHORUS. Lift up Ngaru-of-the-Sea;
Kumu-tonga' shall upbear thee,
Upbear thee to Avaiki
As food for red-hued Miru,
Loved Ngaru-of-the-Sea.
Strip branches from the *kava*
To stupefy thy senses.
Heaven darkens—down pour torrents.
But Ngaru onward passes
To Taumareva, country
Of red and costly garments,
There at the far horizon.
What have you come for, Miru?
I come to devour mankind.

TWO WOMEN. Do thy worst, Miru of Avaiki!

CHORUS. Provoke no lightnings from thy love—

TWO WOMEN. Thy love whose haunt is Iti-kau.

CHORUS. Ay, Ngaru-of-the-Sea.

TWO WOMEN. Strip branches from the *kava* of Miru,
To stupefy the wonder-working Ngaru,
Victorious over monsters.

CHORUS. Put me down, put me down,
Set me free, set me free.
Oh that I had liberty
To gaze upon this mountain!
'Tis surely the mountain spoken of
By my grandfather Moko-roa,

THE SPIRIT WORLDS

And by my mother Vaiare,
And by my wife Tonga-tea.

Devoured forthwith thou shalt be!
Thy corpse shall decay on the mountain,
Thy spirit be borne to Avaiki
To make a repast for Miru.

Hist, Kumu-tonga'! Hist, Karaia'!
Bring your intended husband;
For the oven of Miru is waiting!

I will not part with my grandson.
Ye fairies thus treat Ngaru!

To the Red Land drop some cords down,
Great ropes, and many-stranded,
Swayed in the breeze, yet able
To bear me, Ngaru the climber,
Resolved to explore all nature.

To the Red Land drop some cords down.
    Seize hold!   [*Great emphasis.*

Seize hold, ye spirits and shadows,
Of the ends of the ropes down-hanging,
To rescue our favourite hero
From all-devouring Auraka.
Delay not; drop them, delay not!

    Hasten hence, O Ngaru!
Yon oven will else consume thee!

This drama is very like an old miracle- or mystery-play. It was performed at Tama-rua by daylight, at the base of the hill Vivi-taunoa. One woman was named Miru for the occasion; a second Moko; a third Ngaru; two others represented the daughters of Miru, Kumu-tonga' and Karaia'. All the performers of this drama were women; men might be onlookers, but not participants. The daughters of Miru, at the proper time, carried over the crest of the hill a bundle made to look like a corpse, ready to be thrown down Auraka, the last resting-place of the dead. An oven was made, but no fire lighted. Two cords were fastened to the woman who played Ngaru, and she was dragged to the edge of the supposed oven. The part from "Put me down . . ." to ". . . a repast for Miru" is taken

329

from the myth, which is known to be of great antiquity. Gill believes it to have been brought by the original settlers from Avaiki, or Savai'i (Hawaiki), and there is a place Manono mentioned in the myth which is believed to refer to the island Manono in the Samoan group.

There is another of these fine lyrical dramas that sings of Ngaru excelling the fairies at the ball-throwing: it was composed about the year 1790.

THE BALL-THROWERS' SONG

Or, The Fairies beaten by Ngaru

Call for the dance to lead off. Keep the balls all going;
        two are left.
    In all Spirit Land thou hast no equal.

SOLO.   Go on!

CHORUS. Here are the fairy players from Avaiki,
    As well as natives of the sky.

SOLO.   Ay!

CHORUS. 'Ina alone keeps seven, ay, eight balls in motion.
    Little Matonga is beaten, utterly beaten.

SOLO.   Ah! Matonga, thou art beaten—
    At the outset a ball has fallen to the ground.

First Offshoot

SOLO.   Give me the balls.

CHORUS. This art was taught me by the gods,
      By Teiiri and Teraranga.
    Encircled with chaplets of laurel,
      I select round scarlet fruits
      To serve as balls for our game,
    For fairy women who once and again
    Have come from Spirit Land to dance at Kaputai.
    Of these fairies the most strangely fascinating
    And expert at our game is 'Ina.
    Lovely blossom, whose home is in the sky,
    Beloved wife of Marama, I have beaten thee!

SOLO.   Go on!

CHORUS. Here are fairy players from Avaiki,
    As well as natives of the sky.

SOLO.   Ay!

CHORUS. 'Ina alone keeps seven, ay, eight balls in motion.
    Little Matonga is beaten—utterly beaten,

THE SPIRIT WORLDS

SOLO.   Ah! Matonga, thou art beaten—
At the outset a ball has fallen to the ground.

SECOND OFFSHOOT

SOLO.   How high!
CHORUS. All the balls in the air; how dextrous the hand!
The balls are all red, and greatly admired.
Thanks to the divinities who taught thee,
Catch them, throw them in succession.
    All eyes are fixed on thee,
    Women and men in wonder
    Gaze on thy face and form.
With these balls I again challenge you fairies.
    I have beaten thee too, Matonga!
Call the second.   Keep the balls all going; two are left.
In all Spirit Land thou hast no equal.
SOLO.   Go on!
CHORUS. Here are fairy players from Avaiki,
As well as natives of the sky.
SOLO.   Ay!
CHORUS. 'Ina alone keeps seven, ay, eight balls in motion.
Little Matonga is beaten—utterly beaten.
SOLO.   Ah! Matonga, thou art beaten.
At the outset a ball has fallen to the ground.

THIRD OFFSHOOT

SOLO.   Again!
CHORUS. One, two, three, four, five, six, seven, eight balls!
Pai and the royal Manoinoi admire.
    The crowd is astonished.
Akaina, though skilled in all arts,
    Surpassing the men of his day,
The bravest and wisest of men,
    Never could equal thee.
Let perfect silence now be observed.
    Again I have beaten thee, 'Ina!
SOLO.   Go on!
CHORUS. Here are fairy players from Avaiki,
As well as natives of the sky.
SOLO.   Ay!
CHORUS. 'Ina alone keeps seven, ay, eight balls in motion.
Little Matonga is beaten—utterly beaten.
SOLO.   Ah! Matonga, thou art beaten.
At the outset a ball has fallen to the ground.

MYTHS OF THE POLYNESIANS

Fourth Offshoot

SOLO.   Avaunt!
Avaunt, avaunt, thou of the scraggy back!
CHORUS.   Avaunt, avaunt, thou of the long spine—
Tall to deformity and ready to die.
Give me my grand scarlet balls
Like young turtle in the palm of Vatea.
Beaten once, twice, thrice, ay, four times;
Beaten again, again, and again;
Beaten times innumerable, all of you.
Pack up your traps, one and all,
Ye sweet-scented ball-players from the skies
And from the netherworld, and be off!
Again I have beaten thee, Matonga.
Call the third.   Keep the balls all going; two are left.
In all Spirit Land thou hast no equal.
SOLO.   Go on!
CHORUS.   Here are fairy players from Avaiki,
As well as natives of the sky.
SOLO.   Ay!
CHORUS.   'Ina alone keeps seven, ay, eight balls in motion.
Little Matonga is beaten—utterly beaten.
SOLO.   Ah! Matonga, thou art beaten.
At the outset a ball has fallen to the ground.

Conclusion

Call the fourth.   And now a game of ball-throwing with
Kumu-tonga',
With Karaia-i-te-ata from Avaiki.
SOLO.   Go on!
CHORUS.   Play as ye are wont there in the shades.
SOLO.   Ay!
CHORUS.   A bird of plumage gay is watching you.
SOLO.   A game of ball-throwing with Karaia'!
CHORUS.   A game of ball-throwing with Kumu-tonga'!
And her sister Karaia-i-te-ata.
The quick movements of the fingers are invisible.

Of the sky-fairies, 'Ina and Matonga were the most expert at this game, but both were vanquished by Ngaru.   'Ina is beaten in the first and third stanzas, Matonga in the second and fourth.   At the conclusio he is trying his skill against the Peerless Ones of the netherworld with equal success.

In the dance the performers imitated the movements of

the ball-throwers, but without the balls. The contemptuous language of the fourth stanza is in direct contradiction to the orthodox belief in their peerless beauty. It is a sly hit at certain women in the dance personifying the two sets of fairy women. Proud of their assumed name, Tapairu, they are really the butt of the whole assembly.

Death Ceremonies in Mangaia

Upon the death of an individual on Mangaia a messenger, called " bird " from the swiftness of his going, was sent round the island. At the boundary line of each district he paused to give the war-shout, adding, " So and so is dead." Near relatives would start at once for the house of the deceased, each carrying a present of cloth. Most of the young men of the island united on the following day in a series of mimic battles, called *te i a mauri*, or slaying the ghosts.

The district where the corpse lay represented the *mauri* (ghosts). Early in the morning the young men belonging to it arrayed themselves as if for battle, and, well armed, started off for the adjoining district, where the young men were drawn up in battle-array under the name of *aka-oa*, or friends. The war-dance performed, the two parties rushed together, clashing their spears and wooden swords, as though in real earnest. The sufferers in this bloodless conflict were supposed to be malignant spirits, who would thus be deterred from doing further mischief to mortals.

The combatants joined forces, and were collectively called *mauri*, and passed on to the third district. (Throughout the day their leader carried the sacred *iku kikau* (coconut-leaf) at the pit of his stomach, like the dead.) Arrived at this village, they would find the young men ready for the friendly conflict. The battle of the ghosts was fought again, and, the forces once more joining, they passed to the fourth, fifth, and sixth districts. In every case it was supposed that the ghosts were well beaten. Returning in an imposing body to the place where the corpse was laid out in state, the brave ghost-killers were given a feast, and all except near relatives returned to their homes ere nightfall.

333

So similar was it to actual warfare that it was appropriately named " a younger brother of war."

The ghost-fighting took place immediately after the death, and was common to all; the dirge was sung months afterward, and was reserved for persons of distinction. Sometimes the friends of the distinguished dead preferred a grand tribal gathering for the purpose of reciting songs in their honour. This was called a death-talk, or talk about the devouring, for when a person died it was customary to say he was eaten up by the gods, and this may have originated the belief in the common mind, which is apt to be extremely literal, that the souls of the dead were devoured by Miru.

A death-talk, like the festive *kapa*, or dance, took place at night; but while the *kapa* was performed under long booths, the death-talk took place in large houses, built for the purpose, well lighted with torches.

As many as thirty songs, called *tangi* as in the Maori and generally, with the usual letter-modifications, throughout Polynesia, were often prepared for a death-talk. These were the ' weeping songs,' and each one was supplemented with another song, called a *tiau*—a word meaning a light shower, and hence, metaphorically, a ' partial weeping.' The songs varied greatly in merit; each adult male relative must recite a song composed by himself, or, if unable to compose it, must pay some one to furnish an appropriate song.

A near relative started the first *tangi*, the chorus taking up the words at the proper pauses and carrying on the song. In the *tangi* the weeping was reserved for the close, when the whole of those assembled abandoned themselves to passionate cries and weeping. A song of this kind always began, " Sing we . . ."

The appropriate *tiau*, or *pe'e*, followed. The songs relating to Vera were *tiau*, or ' showery ' songs. In these the chief mourner took the solo; and whenever, as indicated, the whole assembly took up the strain the solo wept loudly until it was his duty again to take up his part in a soft, plaintive voice.

The accompaniments of this performance were the great wooden drum called *kaara* (the awakener) and the har-

334

(1) DRESS WORN BY CHIEF MOURNER AT TAHITIAN BURIAL RITES
(2) CLUB WITH SHARKS' TEETH CARRIED BY THE MOURNER

British Museum

(See page 334)

monicon, the *pau* being sometimes added. The musical instruments were called into use between every two songs; and in the 'showery' songs the great drum accompanied the grand chorus. The true accompaniment of the *tangi* was the passionate weeping of all present.

The most touching songs were the most admired and the longest remembered. Several months were required for the preparations for a death-talk; for not only had the songs, and dresses, and complexions to be thought of, but a liberal provision of food for the guests had to be made.

If a person of consequence in the same tribe died within a year or two the old performance might be repeated, with the addition of a few new songs. It was then termed *e veru*, or 'second-hand.' Some of the best modern songs belong to the " death-talk of Aro-kapiti," says Gill, who made a most excellent collection of these songs; and he adds naïvely that the eldest son of Aro-kapiti " was the first to embrace Christianity, which necessarily put an end to this high effort of heathen poetry."

Some months after the death of a person of note funeral games, called *eva*, were performed in his honour. These took place during the day. There were four varieties of the dirge proper :

(1) The *eva tapara*, or dirge with blackened faces, streaming blood, shaved heads, and malodorous garments; this Gill designates as a " most repulsive exhibition," which " well expressed the hopelessness of heathen sorrow"; its refinement, among civilized people, is the sable hearse, the funereal plumes, the " customary suits of solemn black."

(2) The *eva puruki*, or war-dirge, for which long spears were made of a brittle wood, and the inhabitants, armed with these, divided into two companies facing each other at a distance of about eighty yards. The performance began by an animated conversation between the leaders of the two parties of supposed enemies as to the grounds for war, to excite a lively interest in what was to follow. When this was concluded the person most nearly related to the deceased began the history of the heroic deeds of the tribe by slowly

chanting the introductory words. At the appointed pause both companies took up the strain and vigorously carried it forward. The mighty chorus was accompanied by a clashing of spears and all the evolutions of war. At the close of each short story a momentary pause took place, then a new story was taken up by the soft musical voice of the chief mourner, caught up and recited in full chorus by both companies as before.

(3) The *eva toki*, or axe-dirge. In this iron-wood axes were used, for cleaving the cruel earth which had swallowed up the dead. In cleaving the earth the wish was expressed that an opening might be made through which the spirit of the departed might return. This dirge was appro-priate only for artisans, who enjoyed great privi-lege, seeing that their knowledge was the special gift of the gods.

(4) The *eva ta*, or crashing-dirge, in which each person of the two parties was furnished with a flat spear or a wooden sword a fathom long. It differed from the war-dirge in the style of the com-position and the weapons used.

Songs and Music

These dirges proper, dancing-festals, reed-matches, and death-talks were all comprehended under the general name of *eva*, called by Captain Cook *heava*. He also gives some account of their songs, more of their dances, some of the descrip-tions in his *Voyages* being especially detailed and fine.

MAORI
PUTORINO
(Bugle-flute)

He speaks of the accompanying instruments, the drum formed of a hollow block of wood, cylindrical in form, and covered at the open end with shark's skin, beaten with the fingers, not with sticks. He said that every two verses, or couplet, of a song were called *pehay*, which is probably the same word as *pe'e* above. He said that the songs were often, though not always, in rime, and when pronounced by the natives they appeared to be in metre. The rime was

336

probably more apparent than real. The opening of the
dirge for Vera is given here to show how the closing vowel-
sounds of the lines will suggest rime:

SOLO.   Turokia i Vai-rorongo;
Noo mai koe i te aiai
Ka aere au, e Manga e,
CHORUS. I te ara taurere ki Iva ē!
SOLO.   Pare mai Vera i te kau ara,
Ariua te mata i Mangaia.
Te karo nei i o metua,
Te roe nei i te ao ē!
CHORUS. E niaki i te tere i Anakura e aere ei.
SOLO.   Turokia ē
CHORUS.   i tona are ē!
I tona are, e manga kai nā Vera.
Tu a rau kura Tueva akatapu.
SOLO.   Tu a rau kura Tueva akatapu.
Kua tangi te ike a Mueu
Kua taroe ua miringa, e Vera ē!
Ka aere au, e Manga ē!
CHORUS. I te ara taurere ki Iva ē!

In this, as in Polynesian generally, the predominance of
vowels allows the soft gliding of the voice from syllable to
syllable, allows the sustaining of sound to which the Polynesians are so addicted, the ē, so often occurring, being the
equivalent, if it has any foreign equivalent, of " Ay me ! "
Preceding a proper name it is a vocative ; and its depth of
pathos is revealed in the last two line-ends of the solo :

Weeping we follow thee, O Vera, ay me !
I go far away, O Manga, ay me !
By the perilous path to Iva, ay me !

Here the solo, the voice that represents Vera, and the
chorus end their lines with the melancholy sustained ē! or
" Ay me ! " and at the second singing of the solo three lines
end in the a sound.

As regards their being in metre, they may be partially so.
The music is no doubt of the same character as Maori music,
or at any rate of a similar character. There is melody in
Maori music, but usually not of a kind to appeal to the

337

average civilized ear.   The music of songs heard by tourists and casual visitors, and usually called Maori music, is not Maori, but largely an adaptation of European tunes, often hymn tunes : the same is true as regards much that passes for Hawaiian music.   An early writer, Davies, states that Maori melody is based on the scale of the Greek modes ; but it is not based on that or any scale.

They had a few musical instruments—instruments that

WOODEN
KOAUAU

WOODEN KOAUAU, WITH
TOGGLE FOR SUSPENDING

produced real music—the flute of three holes being one. The present writer concluded that if the Maori recognized a scale at all that scale might be ascertained from their flutes.   The first thing was to hear the flute played, but after repeated visits to various parts, and seeing thousands of Maori, it was found that the flute is no longer played, and that the only old Maori flutes now known are in museums.

Experiment revealed a method of blowing, and comparison revealed the fact that in no two flutes do the intervals agree; this is probably because all tried were from different

338

localities ; but it should not have mattered had the scale been the same.

The Maori had no melody without words ; that is, melody, as melody only, was unrecognized by him ; it was the words he appreciated, the speech-melody, each singer singing on his best note, and rising or falling a little above or below as the nature of the words demanded. Few melodies include more than four tones ; most are comprised within three, some are confined to one ; yet within one tone, so minutely will the Maori subdivide it, may be had the effect of several tones. A half-caste was singing a Maori song for a musician who wished to note it down. " Do you know, you are singing within the range of a tone? " said the musician to the singer, who was himself a musician. " No ; surely not." " Sing it again." He did so. " Yes, it is within the range of a tone." " Do you know," said the other, " to me it seems that I am ranging over the octave? " So conscious were the Maori, and are still, of minute subdivisions of a tone.

Among the flutes I found some that had one or more holes plugged and new holes bored. I judged here that the maker was seeking certain definite intervals, and thought they were intervals of a scale. They were not.

Each flute was made to play a certain air, and it could play no other that did not contain the same intervals ; and the explanation was suggested by another Maori friend. " I expect he was sick of that song and wanted another." And in one flute where one hole had been bored twice and another three times the melody had been changed more than once.

Yet while the words were the important part of a song, and the melody secondary only, some tunes became very popular, and, as in our own old ballads, other sets of words would be written to them. The writer has heard a melody composed on the east coast of the North Island of New Zealand sung to different words by a distant tribe, almost the only alteration in the melody being in the embellishments. In embellishing some of the tribes are as expert as the Highland piper, and some of the melodies thus become bafflingly intricate. Some of their songs do fall on the notes of our scale; but a great many use intervals that do not conform, and are quarter-tones or less. Yet the Maori ear is keen to detect and appreciate these fine tones, while at the same time the singers are able to sing perfectly and thoroughly appreciate European songs also.

The songs into which melody enters are their laments (*tangi*), their love-songs (*waiata-aroha*), and in a less degree their watch-songs (*whakaaraara*), and in these there is no metre. When they sing with action, however, as in the song when swinging *poi*-balls (*waiata-poi*), or in their *haka* of various kinds, metre enters in, and in the *haka* melody disappears. Some of the *poi*-songs of modern times have modern tunes, when they are a blending of the old and new, but usually the songs with action are in monotone, and with perfect metre. Here, too, enter in all manner of rhythms, some of them very complicated; and the Maori can be taught nothing in the way of syncopation—he had it long ago. There is an intermediate class of songs, sung on a level monotone without action, which tends to be in metre; in this class are comprised their incantations and invocations of various kinds (*karakia*) and their lullabies (*oriori*). These lullabies seem extraordinary compositions; they consist largely of a recital of family and tribal history, so that the child in arms becomes familiar with his ancestors and their doings at the very dawn of understanding. The Maori knew the attentive and retentive nature of the young mind. These *karakia* and *oriori* have a decided rhythm, the syllables being uttered as if to quavers, occasional syllables, sometimes two or more in succession, being lengthened to the value of two quavers; and the lengthening occurs at such regular intervals that the whole chant is broken into portions like bars of music. There is no pause in the delivery, however; no stoppage; and the writer has sat listening to one of these strange chants, which may take a quarter of an hour or more in delivery (though that delivery

THE SPIRIT WORLDS

is very rapid), and after a minute or two a most strange
feeling has been induced; a feeling of subjection to the
chanter, till the very heart seemed to beat according to the
rhythm of his chant, the will to subdue itself to his. The
Maori songs, too, are apt to end their lines with an *ē* or an *ī*,
or with both, *ēī*, long drawn out; the *e* with the vowel-sound
in ' net,' prolonged, the *i* with the sound of *ee* in ' sweet.'
The style of the *karakia* is also adopted when a body of
people sings a song of welcome in unison. The people
stand and utter it in a rapid monotone, the great object
being to complete the whole as it were in a breath; that
is, there is never any pause in the sound; one man takes
a breath while the others are still chanting, then he picks
it up again. Moreover, as is natural with a people who
had no written language, they had no perception of words
as separate and distinct entities; a sentence was to them
a word; it expressed an idea. ' Man ' might be a word,
but ' abigman ' was likewise a word, and ' youhavecometo-
usfromafar ' was equally a word—that is, it expressed one
idea. When a breath was to be taken, therefore, it might
be taken in the middle of a word as naturally as anywhere,
and after a pause the song might be taken up again in the
middle of a word; no incongruity was felt. So, too, when
dictating the words of a song, the dictator will break anywhere. For instance, if he said " In the hurricane he caught
us," and he were asked to repeat it a little at a time, he would
see nothing amiss in " In the hurri " and then " cane he
caught us." This was possibly how Captain Cook and
others came to record many words incorrectly; when asked
the word for their fortified village, for instance, they would
naturally say *he pa*—a fortified place—and as naturally
hippah was written as the word. These remarks do not, of
course, refer to the modern educated Maori, who with his
perfect English can put many of us to shame.

To the Maori, as to the Polynesian, song was as natural
as speech. A party visiting a neighbouring village was
received with speech and song, and replied with speech and
song, the exchange of courtesies often lasting several hours.

Whoso feels inclined may, in order of precedence, make a speech; and it is rarely that a speech is finished without the introduction of one or more appropriate songs. On the song starting, too, all join in. The number of songs in their *répertoire* is amazing, each, too, having its particular tune.

Native Ideas regarding the Spirit World

It is a matter of difficulty to know what is the exact idea of the Polynesian regarding the spirit world. He is supposed to have recognized upperworlds, perhaps incorrectly rendered as heavens, and also netherworlds, most certainly incorrectly rendered as hells. He knew of no place of torment other than that described by Milton:

> The mind is its own place, and in itself
> Can make a Heaven of Hell, a Hell of Heaven.

For any offences against the gods he made recompense while still on earth—the rigorous law of *tapu* saw to that; but the wrath of his gods did not pursue him beyond the grave. He feared their power, but he did not endow them with vindictiveness. The spirit world held few terrors for him, and his worst fate was gradual extinction. He had apparently not yet, however, arrived at any definite idea as to his ultimate end: it was enough to know that a spirit world awaited him, not very different from the one upon earth, a world where he would rejoin his friends, his relatives. As regards his enemies, some of the stories of gods and demigods seem to indicate that there were wars there too; but, as by the Norsemen of old, fighting was numbered among the pleasures of life. In Valhalla the Einheriar went out each day to fight, but all were whole again in the evening; and so in the Polynesian spirit world the death by slaying was but a temporary affair. In the myth of Rata the dead warriors were restored to life by means of a powerful *karakia*, showing that death never had the meaning of finality; it was a shadow that fell and was lifted again, even as the sun set and rose again.

342

ENTERING TE REINGA, THE WORLD OF SPIRITS
(See page 342)

NORTH CAPE, NEAR THE SPIRITS' LEAPING-OFF PLACE FOR TE REINGA

N.Z. Government Publicity Photo

(See page 344)

The entrance to the upperworlds and to the netherworlds might be by the same gateway—at the place where the skies hang down to the earth; and in many of the islands the spirit took the shimmering pathway across the sea, entering the netherworlds together with the setting sun.

The name Te Reinga has been applied to the Maori netherworld, the name Rerenga-wairua to the entrance. Both words Reinga and Rerenga are, however, from the same root, *rere*, one meaning of which is ' a leap,' the *nga* making the verb a noun, ' the place of leaping.' *Wairua* is ' a spirit,' so that Rerenga-wairua means Leaping-place of the Spirit. In New Zealand this place is at the north-west extremity of the North Island; and, arriving there, the spirits tarried awhile, looking back for the last time on the islands of delight with a last affectionate greeting. They then proceeded to the extremity of the cape, where a *pohutu-kawa*-tree stood, a long root reaching down the cliff. Down this root the spirits descended to the base of the cliff, where they stood upon a rock, watching until the swirl of the water parted the rising kelp and disclosed the chasm which was the entrance to the netherworld. Into this they plunged, and found themselves in the world of spirits.

Accounts differ as to what was found, and how the spirit proceeded, but at length it reached a land where the sun shone, trees waved, and people were engaged much as in the upperworld, and before long friends and long-lost relatives thronged around the spirit with greeting. Food was offered, and most of the accounts agree in saying that if the spirit partook of that food, then all power to return to the earth, except as a spirit, was lost.

Often the descent to the spirit world seems synonymous with the return to Hawaiki, the old homeland—in the words of one farewell, " My father, farewell. Go to the spirit world, to the spirit world, to the spirit world. Go to Hawaiki, to your ancestors, to your elders. Farewell the breast-work of the people, the shelterer from piercing winds, the shade-giving *rata*-tree! Farewell to Tawhiti-pamamao. My protector, farewell! . . ."

343

The account of the passing by way of the road of the setting sun is more detailed. The destination is the distant land of Irihia, and the house is Hawaiki-nui. Four paths lead to the house, one from the north, one from the south, one from the east, one from the west, and along these the four winds enter the house. Every spirit faring to this place fares on the wind that blows from his earthly abode. While four paths lead to the house Hawaiki-nui, only two paths leave it, one leading up, one down. When it enters the house some purifying rites are performed over the spirit, which then is given a choice as to which of the two paths it wishes to take; those who wish to remain with the old earth-mother pass down Tahekeroa to the netherworlds, those who prefer the celestial spirit world pass along Aratiatia to the upperworlds. After residing for a time in the upperworlds all memory of the former life passes away; the spirit has returned to the realm of Io the parent, from whom all things originated. It is hardly to be expected that any coherent account of what is supposed to take place after death could be given by such a folk as the Polynesians; how many among ourselves could give an account of our own after-existence? No doubt the highest of the priests could have done so, but it is hardly likely that the early, unlearned voyagers could have understood the account even had the priests divulged it, and these certainly would not have divulged it to those later comers many of whom were at pains in the first place to assure the "savages" that all their beliefs were wickedness and error. There are a few exceptions, such, perhaps, as R. Taylor among the Maori, but it is only in later days, when men with wider tolerance and wider sympathies have lived long among them, that a little of what philosophy has survived the wreck of belief has been gleaned.

Maori School of Learning

As regards such knowledge as he had, the Polynesian did not disseminate or transmit this in any haphazard fashion. There was a regular school of learning, whose object was the preservation and accurate teaching of all desirable knowledge. A great deal of valuable information regarding the Maori school of learning, the *whare-wananga*, has been put on record by Percy Smith and Elsdon Best; only the briefest reference to it can be made here. A study of this school shows the Maori to have been highly appreciative of learning in the best sense, an appreciation that is markedly apparent in his descendants of the present day. As all knowledge was from the gods, everything connected with the school was *tapu* in the strictest sense. Most of us hold our Bible and Church in some veneration, so we are better able to understand the extreme veneration of the Maori for the learning of his teachers and the school where it was taught.

The most intensely *tapu* matter was that relating to the Supreme Being, the origin of man, the higher versions of their myths or beliefs; and we can in a measure realize the feelings of the earnest Maori, and Polynesian in general, when strangers came and assured him that all his belief was error, and worse than error. When in the year 1819 the Rev. Samuel Marsden visited New Zealand for the second time he recorded in his journal discussions with various Maori regarding their beliefs, and the astuteness and penetration of the " savage " often baffled the missionary. Marsden had been telling them of the Creation as recorded in Genesis, when a Maori assured him that he was in error. Marsden disputed the point, saying that the facts in the Bible had been recorded by the holy men of old. The Maori conceded that that may have been the way of creation in that part of the world; but it was different in New Zealand. And, indeed, the Maori had as much ground for his faith, for he too held it by tradition. If it be said that the Maori was an uneducated savage, the missionary a cultured, civilized man, it may be pointed out that for many years most of the civilized men who came in contact with the Polynesians were as savage as the savages; and if among the nations from whom these lawless adventurers had come there were men of high character and noble nature, so among the Polynesians there were men high and noble; and the extent

345

of a people's development is judged by the highest point reached—it is unjust to hold in contrast the high of the one, the low of the other.

The Maori had all his knowledge orally, as did we ourselves until within the last few hundred years, and it was this fact that made the *whare-wananga* such an important institution; it was his university. The original school was known as Rangiatea, and it was situated in the uppermost of the twelve upperworlds. It was sacred to Io, the Supreme Being, and it was guarded by his attendants. After it was named the island of the same name in the Pacific, one of the Society group, now known as Ra'iatea, and on it was situated one of the most *tapu* of all places in Polynesia.

Noted houses of learning were scattered throughout Polynesia, the names of many of them having been preserved through the centuries. They were open during the winter months only, and at different times according to which class of learning was being taught. The highest class, including the higher forms of religious teaching, ceremonial connected with the enlightenment of man, and with the preservation of his physical, mental, and spiritual welfare, was taught from sunrise until midday; nothing of this was taught after midday, as the declining sun was connected with decay and death. The second class related to tribal history of all kinds, and this was taught from midday until sunset. The third class included all kinds of black magic, and it began at sunset. This syllabus may have been the ideal, but it was not strictly adhered to. In some districts, apparently, all teaching was at night.

The many details regarding the building of these houses, and their appointments, may be gathered from works entering more into particulars than the present one, as, for instance, those of Percy Smith, Best, and Fornander. There, too, may be learned the ceremonies through which novitiates must pass before being admitted, and while receiving instruction. Before being allowed to enter their powers of memory were tested, and only those with retentive memories were selected. The great aim of the institute was to transmit the ancient lore unchanged, the penalty exacted by the gods from a *tohunga* for making a mistake or omitting a word in a *karakia* being death. The gods were always jealous in this respect; and we read in Landor's *Pentameron*, " On the first Sunday of August a thunderbolt fell into the belfry of the Duomo, by the negligence of Canonico Malatesta, who . . . omitted a word in the Mass." Even were the fact controvertible, the belief in its possibility cannot be denied.

On entering the house the scholars left all their ordinary clothing outside, putting on other used only within the building. Each one had chosen from the three *kete o te wananga*, the receptacles of knowledge, the knowledge he desired to acquire; the *kete aronui*, the *kete tuauri*, or the *kete tuatea* representing the three classes above specified. The scholars being assembled, on the appearance of the first rays of the rising sun the principal officiating *tohunga*, or priest, uttered an invocation to Io, the Supreme Being, praying that the scholars might be enabled to acquire and retain the sacred teachings. The language of this and other invocations used is extremely archaic, containing many obsolete expressions. The concluding portion of the fine opening invocation is as follows :

> Enter deeply, enter to the very foundations,
> Into the very origins of all knowledge,
> O Io of the Hidden Face!
> Let penetrate to the very roots of the understanding
>   of thy neophytes,
> Thy sons, the desired knowledge.
> Let fall on them thy knowledge, thy thoughts,
> To the very foundations of the mind,
> O Io the Wise! O Io of all Holy Knowledge!
> O Io the Parentless!

This invocation made the building and all within it exceedingly *tapu*, as if the gods themselves were present, and themselves imparted the instruction.

As the teaching progressed, the students were constantly examined, so that any fault might be corrected at once, a final searching examination taking place at the end of the course for the season. Certain invocations were intoned over the scholars before dismissal, and these must be delivered without a pause or break in the continuity of the recital. The invocation was begun by the chief officiating *tohunga*, who continued as long as his breath held out, his assistant taking up the recital on the very instant of his stopping, so that there was a continuous flow of sound.

Part of the third receptacle of knowledge, the *kete tuatea*, was the power of *makutu* (witchcraft); and the price the scholar sometimes had to pay for the acquisition of this knowledge was heart-searching. He might be told to cause the death of a flying bird; to wither a living tree; to reduce to powder a pebble held in his hand; or he might be told to cause the death of a person, sometimes a slave, sometimes a relative, sometimes the very teacher who had taught him; and had he assimilated the lore with which he had been endowed these acts could be performed by him, and tradition says that they were performed. Nor, if we admit the possibility of the occurrences we call miracles, are we able to deny that the Polynesian may have possessed such power. It is an admitted fact that one *tohunga* turned a withered *ti*-palm blade green in the sight of a missionary; and to most the fire-walking ceremony of Fiji and other islands is a miracle and a mystery.

CHAPTER XI: IO, TANGAROA, AND CREATION

MOST of the information regarding the belief in Io, the Supreme Being, has been derived from Maori sources. It may be that the Maori formed the more virile division of the Polynesian stock, or it may be that his superior virility is the result of his leaving the semi-tropical regions and settling in the temperate islands of New Zealand. Be the reason what it may, the Maori is usually regarded as the best developed, mentally, of the Polynesian race.

It is difficult for us, in whose hearts religion sits more or less lightly, to realize the intense veneration of the Maori, and the Polynesian in general, for things *tapu*, or sacred. So *tapu* was the thought of Io that even the name was used only on rare occasions among the initiated, and only in invocations used in a few of the highest ceremonies. The people as a whole knew nothing at all of the cult of Io ; it is doubtful if they even knew the name. So, too, of the higher beliefs or myths ; one version was known to the people generally, one to only the inner circle of those trained as repositories of the lore of the race. Of most of the myths there is the esoteric version and the common or fireside version ; it is the latter with which most Europeans have come in contact, but it is acquaintance with the former that induces a high respect for the Polynesian as a mystic and a philosopher.

There is no fireside version regarding Io. As the name of the Supreme Being, the word occurs in Tahiti in the forms Iho-iho and Io-i-te-vahi-naro. In Hawaiian *io* means 'truth,' *iu* 'to dwell in some sacred place,' and Iao is the name of Jupiter the planet as the morning star. In Mangaia *io* is the name commonly used for a god, Motoro being called Te Io ora (the Living God), because he would not permit his worshippers to be offered in sacrifice. The other gods were called *io mate* (gods of death), as their worshippers might be offered on the altars of Rongo of the shades. " Most appropriately and beautifully," wrote Gill, " do the natives transfer the name Io ora, or *The-living-god*, to Jehovah."

349

As in one of the Maori legends Tawhaki is permitted to ascend to the upperworlds on a spider's delicate thread of web, so on the name Io the searcher is taken as on a beam of light away into the dim past of time.

Through the inscription on an old Phœnician coin, a quarter-shekel of 350 B.C., it is known that the name Iao is the triliteral form of the name Jehovah. The coin represents Jehovah under the guise of Zeus. In a Theban papyrus is an incantation which begins:

> Come, foremost angel of great Zeus, Iáo,
> And thou too, Michael, who holdest heaven,
> And, Gabriel, thou archangel, from Olympos.

Even in that dim past the name was venerated as it was among the Polynesian Maori; and in Roman times the oracle of Apollon Klarios near Colophon in Asia Minor was once questioned as to the nature of the dread, mysterious Iao, giving as an answer, according to Macrobius:

> "They that know mysteries should conceal the same.
> But, if thy sense be small and weak thy wit,
> Mark as the greatest of all gods Iao—
> In winter Hades, Zeus when spring begins,
> Helios of the summer, autumn's soft Iao."

The precept of the first line was well observed by the learned among the Maori.

Zeus is regarded as a solar deity. Homer mentions Iao as one of the horses of the sun-god. Further, Io was a priestess of Hera, a moon-deity, of whom Isis, the Egyptia cow-goddess, was by the Greeks considered the counterpart. In Alexandrine times Io was commonly identified with Isis, so that Io also becomes a moon-goddess. At Gaza, in South Palestine, where the quarter-shekel mentioned above is considered to have been struck, there was an image of Io the moon-goddess with a cow beside her; and Iao, the supposed sun-god, was early represented by a golden calf. The Cretans had deified the sun and the moon as a bull and a cow respectively, and here is some clue to the story of Zeus and his love for Io, whose wanderings, on her being transformed

350

to a cow, are the wanderings of the moon ; and it may be that Argus the hundred-eyed, who was by Juno set as a guard to watch her, represents the starry heavens.

In Babylonia the moon-god was Sin ; is it possible that this name links up with Sina of Samoa, the Hina of the Maori and other Polynesians?

The sun- and moon-deities are sometimes male and female respectively, sometimes female and male. In Polynesia the moon, as 'Ina, Hina, or Sina, is usually female ; when regarded as male the name is one of the many forms of Rongo ; and it has been noted that in Hawaii, while Hina was a female deity upon earth, on her deserting the earth for the moon she became Lono-moku, a male. So in Ovid the sex of Iphis was changed, and Iphis as a male offered to the gods the presents which he had vowed as a female. It was to Isis, too, that the presents were vowed, Isis who effected the metamorphosis. In one Maori myth the moon was a male, who took up the maiden Rona and her *ngaio*-tree.

Iao is, as noted, the name given by the Hawaiians to the same planet that Europeans named Jupiter ; and if the name was independently given it is one of those strange coincidences that cause the searcher to pause and wonder ; for Jupiter is the Latin form of the name Zeus, who was Iao, both Latin and Greek names being derived from the Hindu Dyaus-pitar, as Max Müller showed. The three letters also appear in Tariao, a name in Maori of the planet Jupiter.

Can there be any doubt that the Maori deity Io is the same as the circum-Levantine Iao? If the two are identical, another clue is furnished for the threading of the labyrinth built by the Polynesians in their wanderings. Have the names, on the other hand, come into existence independently?

It has been supposed, too, that the Polynesians had been in contact with Egyptians, because of the one name Ra, the sun-god ; but Amen-Ra of Egypt and Tama-nui-te-ra of Polynesia have nothing in common but one syllable of their names. It is known that names are persistently tenacious of life, and certainly the name Io takes us back to a past that we possibly shall never see more clearly than we do now.

351

In one account the names of Io are given as the twelve following : (1) Io-nui (Io the Great), (2) Io-roa, (3) Io-take-take (Io the Eternal, the Unchanging), (4) Io-te-wananga (Io the Source of all Knowledge), (5) Io-matua (Io the Parent), (6) Io-matua-te-kore (Io the Parentless), (7) Io-mata-ngaro (Io of the Hidden Face), (8) Io-mataaho (Io the Invisible), (9) Io-te-waiora (Io the Source of Life), (10) Io-tikitiki-o-rangi (Io the Supreme), (11) Io-mata-kana (Io the Vigilant), (12) Io-te-kore-te-whiwhia (Io the Withholder).

The eighth name signifies that he cannot be looked upon directly, but only as the beams of light are seen ; practically he is the sun. The seventh name has a similar meaning ; he cannot be looked in the face—a familiar concept of the brightness of the divine. Other names besides these twelve are, however, current in various *karakia*.

There were likewise twelve heavens or upperworlds, Io dwelling in the uppermost. Their names were (1) Te Toi-o-nga-rangi, (2) Tiritiri-o-matangi (Tiritiri-ki-matangi was the name of the fishing-line of Maui'), (3) Rangi-naonao-ariki, (4) Rangi-te-wawana, (5) Rangi-nui-ka-tika, (6) Rangi-mataura, (7) Rangi-tauru-nui, (8) Rangi-matawai, (9) Rangi-maire-kura, (10) Rangi-parauri, (11) Rangi-tamaku, (12) Rangi-nui-a-tamaku. The lowest is the sky above us, wherein move the heavenly bodies. The Whatu-kura and Mareikura are two companies of supernatural beings, male and female, who dwell in the highest upper-world, and act as the attendants of Io. They act as couriers and guardians, and are able to visit the other upperworlds and all other realms, reporting to Io on the condition of things. The other upperworlds have similar companies, every company numbering twelve beings ; but those of the inferior upperworlds cannot enter the highest.

There were apparently no teachings as to the origin of Io ; he was the Parentless, the Eternal, and he caused the existence of all realms, of all beings. He was of an entirely beneficent nature, and while he had no connexion with evil, and could be invoked only with regard to the welfare of the

IO, TANGAROA, AND CREATION

people, yet as all things flowed from him, and evil came into
existence, it too must have flowed from that highest upperworld, Te Toi-o-nga-rangi.   Nor is this any more inconsis-
tent than in the Christian religion as we know it.   Through
him Rangi' and Papa' had their origin, and through them
he created the gods and mankind.

There is a fine fragment remaining of an ancient Maori
chant of creation, translated by Hare Hongi:

> Io dwelt within breathing-space of immensity.
> The universe was in darkness, with water everywhere.
> There was no glimmer of dawn, no clearness, no light.
> And he began by saying these words,
> That he might cease remaining inactive,[1]
> " Darkness, become a light-possessing darkness."
> And at once light appeared.
> He then repeated those self-same words in this manner,
> That he might cease remaining inactive,[1]
> " Light, become a darkness-possessing light."
> And again intense darkness supervened.
> Then a third time he spake, saying,
> " Let there be a darkness above,
> Let there be a darkness below.
> Let there be a darkness unto Tupua,
> Let there be a darkness unto Tawhito;
> It is a darkness overcome and dispelled.
> Let there be one light above,
> Let there be one light below.
> Let there be a light unto Tupua,
> Let there be a light unto Tawhito.
> A dominion of light,
> A bright light."
> And now a great light prevailed.
> Io then looked to the waters which compassed him
>   about, and spake a fourth time, saying,
> " Ye waters of Tai-kama, be ye separate.
> Heaven, be formed."
> Then the sky became suspended.
> " Bring forth thou Tupu-koro-nuku."
> And at once the moving earth lay stretched abroad.

[1] My friend Hare Hongi has thus translated the words *Kia noho kore noho ia*
(literally, " That he might abide without an abiding-place "). All these genuinely
ancient *karakia* are very difficult to translate ; dictionary meanings cannot be
taken, but the meanings sometimes emerge in comparative work.

353

'Tis Io,
The A-io-nuku of Motion,
The A-io-rangi of Space,
The A-io-papa of Earth,
The A-io-matua the Parent,
The Primeval Darkness,
The Continuous Darkness,
The Groping Darkness,
Sleep-impelling Hine',
The Great Firmament,
The Night,
The Day,
Rangi' and Papa', Space and Matter,
    Sky-father and Earth-mother,
Who begat
Tama-rangi-tauke,
Aitua,
Rongo-ma-Tane,
Tane-mahuta,
Tawhiri-matea,
Rua-ai-moko,
Ngana,
Haumia-tiketike,
Tu-matauenga,
Tangaroa.

From Ngana sprang the sun, moon, and stars. When the sky became suspended it was evidently but a little way above the earth. On Rangi' being thrust upward by Tane', the props or poles (*toko*) used by him were the long and powerful sunbeams.

A most interesting genealogical origin of the primal parents was collected from a Waikato chief:

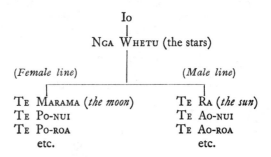

Io
|
Nga Whetu (the stars)

(*Female line*)   (*Male line*)

Te Marama (*the moon*)   Te Ra (*the sun*)
Te Po-nui   Te Ao-nui
Te Po-roa   Te Ao-roa
etc.   etc.

IO, TANGAROA, AND CREATION

Here the Supreme Being first brought the stars into existence, and from them sprang the moon and the sun, the moon heading the female line of descent, the sun the male line. The female line signifies darkness and death, the male line light and life. The twentieth name from Te Marama is Papa-tu-a-nuku, the twentieth from Te Ra is Rangi-nui-e-tu-nei, or Papa' and Rangi', the earth and the sky.

There are many other cosmogonic versions of the origin of the primal parents, and while they are perhaps of the nature of secondary or inferior versions, they reveal the poetical nature of the Polynesian, and the lofty heights to which his imagination had soared. In one version the following ages or existences evolved: (1) Te Kore (the Void), (2) Te Kore-tuatahi (the First Void), (3) Te Kore-tuarua (the Second Void), (4) Te Kore-nui (the Vast Void), (5) Te Kore-roa (the Far-extending Void), (6) Te Kore-para (the Sere Void), (7) Te Kore-whiwhia (the Unpossessing Void), (8) Te Kore-rawea (? the Delightful Void), (9) Te Kore-te-tamaua (the Void Fast-bound), (10) Te Po (the Night), (11) Te Po-teki (the Hanging Night), (12) Te Po-terea (the Drifting Night), (13) Te Po-whawha (? the Moaning Night), (14) Hine-ruaki-moe (the Daughter of Troubled Sleep), (15) Te Po (the Night), (16) Te Ata (the Morn), (17) Te Ao-tu-roa (the Abiding Day), (18) Whaitua (Space). The meanings are at times doubtful. Every one of these ages lasted two, three, ten, a hundred, a thousand, and unlimited years; every one was an eternity. In Whaitua floated two existences, without definite shape: Maku (Moisture), a male, and Mahora-nui-a-rangi (Great Expanse of Heaven), a female. From these sprang Toko-mua, Toko-roto, and Toko-pa, parents of winds, clouds, and mists, and finally Rangi', the heavens, and Papa', the earth, male and female. It is no mean concept, Void through Void giving birth to Night, Night acquiring movement and giving birth to that final Night whose flowering is Morn, broadening through Day to the bright illimitableness of Space. Then the Greek idea enters, of brightness or warmth and moisture producing the gods or parents of man.

Some versions give the number of the upperworlds as ten, and the netherworlds as ten ; and here again is revealed that curious swaying of the human mind between the numbers ten and twelve. Originally the Polynesian year was divided into ten months ; latterly into twelve ; and if ten was derived from the number of the fingers, whence was the twelve? Nor has the swaying yet ceased ; for among civilized people to-day there is a hesitation between the two—between a decimal system of measures and a duo-decimal. Archdeacon H. W. Williams hazards that the ten-heaven cult was that permitted to the common people, the twelve-heaven version being reserved for the cult of Io.

In New Zealand Awatea or Atea takes the place of Whaitua as the eighteenth age. While here it is apparently regarded as an age or existence only, in other parts of the Pacific it is given personality. In Mangaia there are two traditions of Avatea or Vatea, one the fireside version, the other with more of the higher characteristics. The latter is much the more ancient, and is allied to the Hawaiian tradition of Wakea—the same name, with the usual letter-changes. The name has the same meaning as the Maori Atea, Watea, or Awatea—the broad, open space of noonday. The older version has not escaped personification, for Vatea is spoken of as a man possessed of two resplendent eyes. These eyes are not often visible at the same time ; for while the one, called the sun by mortals, is visible in this world, the other, the moon, shines in Avaiki.

Here, again, the Polynesian and Greek mythologies mingle, or mirror like concepts. More than once in papyrus documents and in the recorded sayings of oracles is the sun called the eye of Zeus—and Zeus was originally the bright sky. In an Orphic hymn, too, in which Zeus is identified with various parts of the cosmos, it is said:

> As eyes he has the sun and the shining moon.

Creation (Mangaia)

The Mangaian fireside version of creation may be given, to show the place assigned to Vatea, father of gods and men.

IO, TANGAROA, AND CREATION

The universe is thought of as the hollow of a huge coconut-shell, whose interior is called Avaiki, and contains the underworlds. At the top is an aperture communicating with the world where mortals dwell, and at various depths within are different floors, as it were, or lands communicating with each other. At the bottom of the shell, where the husk would taper in to the stem, is a thick root gradually tapering to a point, representing the very beginning of all. This point is a spirit, without human form, and is named Te Aka-ia-Roe (Rohe)—the Root of All Existence.

Above the extreme point, still in the tapering root, is Te Tangaengae, or Te Vaerua—that is, Breathing, or Life. The thickest part of the root, that at the bottom of the shell, is Te Manava-roa (the Long-lived). These three constitute the foundation of the universe; they are sentient spirits, ever stationary, and ensure the permanence and well-being of the rest of the universe.

In the lowest depth of Avaiki, the interior of the shell, lives a woman or demon, of flesh and blood, named Vari-ma-te-takere (the Very Beginning). So narrow is her territory in the tapered shell that she can sit in only one position, knees and chin touching. She was most anxious for progeny, so one day plucked off a portion of her right side, and it became a human being—the first man, Avatea, or Vatea. This being was half-man, half-fish; on his left side he had a half-human head, with human eye, arm, leg, and foot; on his right side he had a half-fish head, a fish eye, a fin, and a half-fish tail—a gruesome variant of our Northern merman.

The home of Vari-ma-te-takere was called Te Enua-teki (the Silent Land). In Maori *teki* means ' to drift with the anchor down, but not touching the bottom,' *whaka-teki* ' to suspend so as not to touch the ground.' *Enua* is the Maori *whenua* (the earth), and the Suspended World seems a good descriptive name of this home of the Mother of All.

The land assigned to Vatea by Vari' was called Te Papa-rairai (the Thin Land), and it was the division within the shell immediately below the surface, the first of the six divisions into which the interior was divided. Another name of his land was Te Enua-marama-o-Vatea (the Bright Land of Vatea), implying the contrast between the brightness of *avatea*, or noonday, and the gloom of *po*, or night, the equivalent of Avaiki.

On another occasion Vari' plucked off a second portion from her right side, and it became Tini-rau, who, like his brother, had a second and fishlike form. The fish which composed his half-fish body was of the sprat kind; that of Vatea was of the whale or porpoise kind. This dual form of Vatea and Tini-rau probably means that, Proteus-like, they could assume either the human form or the fish form at will. To Tini-rau Vari' gave the land of Motu-tapu, the next division below Te Papa-rairai.

Again, Vari' took a portion from her left side, and it became Tango, whose land was Enua-kura (the Land of Red Parrot Feathers), the third division from above, immediately below Motu-tapu.

A fourth child was produced, from her left side, Tumu-teanaoa, or Echo, whose land was Te Parai-tea (the Hollow Grey Rocks), the fourth division from above.

A fifth child was produced, from the left side, Raka, who presided over the winds, and whose home was Moana-irakau (Deep Ocean). Raka received from Vari' a basket (or receptacle) in which the winds were confined; also the knowledge of many useful inventions. The children of Raka are the many winds and storms which distress mankind. To each child is allotted a hole at the edge of the horizon, through which he blows at pleasure. The various holes from which the winds blow were as well known to the Polynesians as are the points of the compass to the mariner; and the number of holes is the same as the number of named points—thirty-two. The 'head' of the winds is in the east; veering with the wind, the 'tail' is reached at S.W. by W., dying away until, in the S.S.W., it is merely an *uru*, or like the touch of a feather. Cyclones begin in the N.E., and go on increasing in violence until, on reaching Iku, S.W. by W., they moderate; and passing on to Uru there is perfect calm. The east is Marangai; and shifting a point to the north, E. by N., it becomes Marangai-anau. *Anau* signifies ' giving birth '; the east gives birth to the new wind, E. by N. This, shifting to E.N.E., becomes Marangai-akavaine (the East as Gentle as a Woman). N.E. by E. is Marangai-maoake (East becoming North-east). N.E. is Maoake; N.E. by N. is Maoake-anau (Maoake giving Birth). N.N.E. is Maoake-ta (the Terrible Maoake), so called on account of the extreme violence of this wind when a cyclone blows. N. by E. is Maoake-ma-akarua—that is, north-east (Maoake) and north (Akarua). For purposes of priestly exorcism " that inverted bowl the sky " was represented by a calabash in which a series of small holes was made to correspond to the various wind-holes at the edge of the horizon. The holes were all stopped with cloth; and should the wind be unfavourable for an expedition, the chief priest began his incantation by removing the plug from the aperture through which the unfavourable wind was blowing. Rebuking this wind, he stopped up the hole, and advanced by all the intermediate holes, removing plug after plug, until he reached the one desired. This was left open, as an indication to the children of Raka that a steady wind was desired from that quarter. As he would have a good knowledge of the ordinary course of the winds, and the various indications of change, the invocation usually resulted in the coming of the wind desired. There was an unfailing natural indication of the approach of a cyclone expressed in the saying, " *Kua taviriviri te kao o te maika* "—" Twisted is the core of the banana." This twisting takes place some weeks before the coming of a hurricane, and at the same time there is an unusually luxuriant growth of food.

Finding that her left side had suffered more than her right, Vari-ma-te-takere took a third piece from her right side, and named the sixth being Tu-metua (Remain by the Parent). This favourite child lived, as the name implies, with her mother in Te Enua-teki, where the only language known is that of signs—nods, elevated eyebrows, grimaces, and smiles. Tu-metua is Tu-papa in Ra'iatea, and became the wife of the sun-god Ra. Her name was usually shortened to Tu', and as Tu' she was tutelary goddess of Moorea.

In his dreams Vatea several times saw a beautiful woman; but, waking from sleep, he could discover no trace of her. At length it occurred to him that her home might be in some land other than his own, and that she visited him by way of one or other of the dark chasms communicating between his and the lower land. He scraped a quantity of coconuts, and scattered handfuls down all the chasms in his country, and some time afterward found that from the bottom of one, named Taevarangi (the Celestial Aperture), the white food had disappeared. He scattered a fresh lot of the dainty food, hiding behind a crag and cautiously peering down. It was not long before a slender hand was extended toward the coveted morsels, and Vatea concluded that this must be the hand of the woman whom he had seen in his dreams. With a favouring current of wind he descended, and caught her. She confessed that she had again and again ascended to his home, wishing to win him as her husband, guessing that once having seen her he would never rest until he found her. Her name was Papa, the daughter of Timate-kore and his wife Tamaiti-ngavaringavari. Vatea thus went to a far country and found a wife, and by another eddy of wind both ascended through the chasm to Te Enua-marama-o-Vatea.

The following song of creation was composed for the festal of Potiki, about the year 1790:

> *Call for the dance to begin with music.* The home of Vari' is the
> narrowest of all,
>> Knees and chin ever meeting—
>> It was reserved for Rongo to ascend.
> SOLO.   Go on!
> CHORUS. 'Twas in the shades Vatea first saw his wife
>> And fondly pressed her to his bosom.
> SOLO.   Ay!
> CHORUS. When asked who was her father,
>> Papa said, " Timate-kore."

SOLO.   Truly, Timate-kore.
          But we no father knew whatever:
          Vari' alone made us.
          That home of Vari' is
          The very narrowest of all!

CHORUS. The home of Vari' is the narrowest of spaces;
          A goddess on raw *taro* feeding
          At periods of appointed worship!
          Thy mother, Vatea, self-existent is.

SOLO.   Vatea sprang into existence.
          Bright as the morn is Papa.
          Vari-ma-te-takere
          To Papa gave safe shelter.

FINALE

Call to begin.   Let the storm be restrained
          In favour of Vatea, O thou god of Winds!

SOLO.   Go on!

CHORUS. Awake the gentle breeze of 'Ina
          That bore her to her lover.

SOLO.   Oh for as soft a wind to bear me, Vatea,
          Prosperously on my way
          Below there!
          Be lulled, ye winds.

CHORUS. The winds are lulled; no storm
          Now sweeps the treacherous sea.

SOLO.   Ye winds inconstant of the netherland,
          To her abode the gloomy bear me down.

The expressed idea by means of which Vari' produced new beings—that is, by plucking off portions of her body— seems on first thought extremely crude; but the same idea is expressed when it is said that Brahma, himself an emanation from the Supreme Being, caused other beings to issue, one from his mouth, one from his right arm, one from his left, one from his right thigh, one from his left, and two from his feet. Coming nearer home, is not the same idea expressed in the creation of Eve?

Wakea of Hawaii

In Hawaiian legend there is a Wakea who with his wife Papa has been identified with the Vatea and Papa of Mangaia. The Papa of this legend conceived and bore a calabash, including bowl and cover. Wakea threw the cover upward, and it became the heaven. From the inside and seeds of the calabash he made the sun, moon, stars, and sky, and from the bowl he made the land and sea. This is supposed to be a corrupted fragment, a fireside version, of a legend now lost. The fragment states that an immense bird laid an egg on the water, which burst and produced the land of Hawaii. Shortly afterward a man, a woman, a hog, a dog, and a pair of fowls came in a canoe from the Society Islands, landed on the eastern shore, and were the progenitors of the present inhabitants.

Later there lived another Wakea and his wife Papa ; and these are historical, not mythological personages. Wakea, known also as Makea or Akea, is said to have ruled in Hihiku, his wife being a chiefess from O-lolo-i-mehani, an island supposed to be one of the Moluccas, called by the Spanish, Dutch, and English navigators Gi-lolo, Ji-lolo, Dji-lolo, and I-lolo. He was one of the earliest ancestors of the Hawaiians to enter into the Pacific, at about A.D. 190. His was evidently a time of great unrest and disturbance. He warred with his brother Li-haula ; he was conquered by Kaneia-Kumuhonua, and was by him driven to seek a new home away in the Pacific. He changed the religious and social institutions of his people, not, apparently, because he was a reformer, but because they interfered with a love he had conceived for his own daughter. In order to conceal this from Papa he introduced, with the aid of a priest, the laws of *tapu* ; certain nights were made *tapu* to him, certain nights to Papa, so that they could conveniently be separated. Temples for the gods were built, for Ku, for Lono, for Kane, for Kanaloa, and to them the firstfruits were devoted. Then certain days were made *tapu* or consecrated to the gods. Wakea accomplished his purpose, but his transgression was detected by Papa, and quarrels and strife arose. Wakea in wrath imposed certain restrictions upon Papa, prohibiting her from eating pork, and bananas, and coconuts, and certain kinds of fish. He also decreed that a man and a woman should not eat together in the same house, but each in a

362

separate place for the purpose. He then spat in her face, the recognized indication of divorce in Hawaii, and left her. The origin of the *tapu*, and of the restrictions as regards the food of which women may partake, may be in accordance with this legend, or it may not; certainly both existed, and among other peoples in the Pacific besides the Hawaiians.

In another legend Wakea is said to have had illicit intercourse with a woman Hina, and she gave birth to the island which Wakea named Molokai. In return for this unfaithfulness Papa cohabited with a man Lua, and gave birth to the island Oahu; and in commemoration of this these two islands of the Hawaiian group were known as Molokai-Hina and Oahu-a-Lua. In this myth is thought to lie embedded the reference to the Gi-lolo chief Wakea and the neighbouring island Morotai, after which the Hawaiian Molokai was doubtless named.

Wakea, expelled from his Moluccan home, went south and settled in Fiji, where his people remained for about thirteen generations; and when expulsion from those islands took place in due course, several streams of migration issued simultaneously, or nearly so, to the Samoan, Tongan, Tahitian, and other eastward and northward groups.

When these wandering migrants eventually reached Hawaii, from the south, they found the group already occupied by Polynesians of their own race—a people who had probably reached it directly from the west some hundreds of years earlier, and who had lived there quite isolated from the rest of the world. The lack of any history regarding them seems to indicate that they had lived in peace, and during their time of isolation they had undertaken works of considerable magnitude, the relics of which long survived. Among them were the temples (*heiau*) of truncated pyramidal form found in various parts of the group, and the fishponds (*loko-ia*) of cyclopean structure along the coasts of Molokai and other places, of which tradition says no more than that they were the work of the Menehune people.

363

MYTHS OF THE POLYNESIANS

The names of Wakea and Papa occur in more than one genealogy of recognized authenticity, and many names precede them; in one genealogy they are the thirty-seventh generation, which seems to leave no doubt as to their historical, not mythological, character.

The Awakening of Philosophic Thought

Many of the more serious minds among the olden Polynesians must have regarded the springing of god from god, of power from power, of existence from existence, as more than mere material begetting. Hints and more than hints of this are caught from old laments and *karakia*, handed down from generation to generation. In one of these laments, collected in New Zealand, occurs the following:

> From germ of life sprang thought,
> And God's own medium came:
> Then bud and bloom; and life in space
> Produced the worlds of night—
> The worlds where bowing knee
> And form in abject crouching lost
> Are lost—for ever lost.
> And never now return ye
> From those worlds of gloom.
>   'Twas Nothing that begat
> The Nothing unpossessed,
> And Nothing without charm.
> Let priests attention give
> And all I state dispute.
> I may be wrong; I but rehearse
> What was in Whare-kura taught.
>   'Twas Rangi who, with Atutahi,
> Brought forth the moon:
> And Rangi Werowero took,
> And, yet unseen, the sun produced.
> He, silent, skimmed the space above,
> And then burst forth the glowing eye of heaven
> To give thee light, O man!
> To wage thy war on fellow-man.
>   Turn and look this way;
> On Tararua, distant peak,
> Now shines the light of coming day.

IO, TANGAROA, AND CREATION

There is much in these semi-philosophical chants to indicate that a divine light was already shining in these untutored minds; fitfully, it may be, but doubtful dawn is ever the precursor of day. Thoughts such as these, while numerous, are all too fragmentary; nor perhaps could more be expected; a reasoned philosophical discussion in so early an age would be a *lusus naturæ*. Gleams of inspiration are not lacking, but gleams can reveal only portions of truth. Nevertheless, the thoughts sprung from these gleams show how much attracted was primitive man by the truths he was not yet able to comprehend, and so could utter only brokenly.

Inquirers, too, must be careful not to attribute more comprehension to these Stone Age thinkers than they possessed. Like children, they uttered fragments of truths, apprehending, but not comprehending their nature—hence they remained fragments; not knowing the key, they could not piece them together. We must not conclude that the key was in their possession and that great portions of a philosophical system have been lost to us, the later comers. It may equally well be—more probably is—that the system never was complete, that the key never was in their possession, any more than it is in our own. Indeed, I have heard well-informed Maori folk speaking on this very head. Of certain writers they have said, "They put more thought into our minds than we ever had; the old fellows had never evolved all that philosophy; but never mind—it won't hurt to make us out better than we are." The Maori was right; it will not hurt; quite the contrary. There is no doubt at all that the birth of philosophy and true religion had taken place; the unfolding must slowly follow in the ordinary course of nature.

The wonderful thing to the writer is the contemplation of this young thought; watching it soar, watching it plunge, watching it take all media as its element; it does not know, though it feels, when its inspiration is lofty, when it is lowly; it does not know when it is virile, when it is puerile; its chief concern is the exercise of its wings, the exploration of regions to which it can find no limits.

365

Again, it is well known that the poet does no more than give utterance to apprehensions that are in the hearts of thousands; apprehensions that in some clarify so that they are able to take on the power of thought. By the poet the thought is crystallized in words, and the thousands now comprehend; the poet has given sight to the almost blind, speech to the almost dumb; he is understood at once, or, if not in his generation, in the generations following. More than once or twice two poets, or more, have simultaneously given utterance to the same message; a comprehension, the lightning of apprehension, has discharged at more points than one. Cannot we imagine the same regarding a myth —the poetical expression of an observed phenomenon? The mind-stuff is the same throughout, its environments differ; according as the environment is more or less the same, so the shaping myth may be more or less the same. The very first articulate sounds of the speech-organs are automatic, mechanical, and some of these persist among our best-known words; cannot we imagine the very first essays of thought to be likewise automatic, with results whose parallelism at first astonishes us? We seek contact and intercommunication to explain them; the explanation may be much simpler.

It was deemed advisable to make a few observations before speaking of some of the Polynesian fireside versions of creation; if they appear puerile, it must be remembered that they are the utterances of the child-mind of the Stone Age. We do not ridicule the imaginings, the fantastic stories, of the child; rather we augur an active and a fertile intellect; we may refrain from ridicule here if we remember that the Polynesian intellect is like the childhood of our own. Moreover, we do not know how much of these fireside versions was deliberately permitted; the *tohunga* were well aware of them, but took no trouble to contradict them or replace them with the higher teaching. Nor is this without parallel in modern religion; the higher truths would, to many, be only bewilderment.

IO, TANGAROA, AND CREATION

The Separation of Rangi' and Papa' (New Zealand)

Probably the best known of the fireside stories of creation is the Maori version as related by Grey. Rangi' and Papa', the heaven and the earth, were regarded as the source from which all things, gods, and men originated. There was darkness, for these two still clung together, not yet having been rent apart; and the children begotten by them were ever thinking what the difference between darkness and light might be. They knew that beings had multiplied and increased, and yet light had never broken upon them, but ever darkness continued. Hence these sayings were found in old *karakia* : " There was darkness from the first division of time, to the tenth, to the hundredth, to the thousandth "—that is, for a vast space of time ; and each of these divisions of time was considered as a being, and each was termed Po, and it was because of them that there was yet no bright world of light, but darkness only for the beings which then existed.

At last, worn out with the oppression of darkness, the beings begotten by Rangi' and Papa' consulted among themselves, saying, " Let us now determine what we shall do with Rangi' and Papa' ; whether it would be better to slay them, or to rend them apart." Then spoke Tu-matauenga, the fiercest of the sons of Rangi' and Papa', " It is well ; let us slay them."

Then spoke Tane-mahuta, the father of forests and all things inhabiting the forests, or that are constructed of trees, " Nay, not so. It is better to rend them apart, and to let Rangi' stand far above us, and Papa' lie beneath our feet. Let Rangi' become as a stranger to us, but the earth remain close to us as a nursing mother."

To this proposal the brothers consented, with the exception of Tawhiri-matea, the father of winds and storms ; and he, fearing that his kingdom was about to be overthrown, grieved at the thought of their parents being torn apart. Five of the brothers readily consented to the separation ; but one of them would not consent.

Hence, also, these sayings of old are found in the *karakia* :
" The Po, the Po, the Light, the Light, the seeking, the
searching, in Chaos, in Chaos," these signifying the way in
which the offspring of Rangi' and Papa' sought for some
mode of dealing with their parents, so that human beings
might increase and live. So also the saying, " The multitude, the length," signifying the multitude of their thoughts
and the length of time they considered whether they should
slay their parents so that human beings might be called into
existence; for it was in this manner they talked and consulted among themselves. Their plans having been agreed
to, Rongo-ma-Tane, the god and father of cultivated food,
arose, that he might rend apart Rangi' and Papa'; he
struggled, but he did not rend them apart. Next Tangaroa,
the god and father of fish and reptiles, arose, that he might
rend apart Rangi' and Papa'; he also struggled, but he did
not rend them apart. Next Haumia-tikitiki, the god and
father of food that springs without cultivation, arose and
struggled, but quite ineffectually. Then Tu-matauenga,
the god and father of fierce human beings, arose and
struggled, but he too struggled ineffectually. Then at last
Tane-mahuta, the god and father of forests, of birds, and of
insects, arose and struggled with his parents; in vain with
hands and arms he strove to rend them apart. He paused;
firmly he planted his head on his mother Papa', the earth,
and his feet he raised up against his father Rangi', the sky;
he strained his back and his limbs in mighty effort. Now
were rent apart Rangi' and Papa', and with reproaches and
groans of woe they cried aloud, " Wherefore do you thus
slay your parents? Why commit so dark a crime as to slay
us, to rend us, your parents, apart?" But Tane-mahuta
paused not; he regarded not their cries and their groans;
far, far beneath him he pressed down Papa' the earth; far,
far above him he thrust up Rangi' the sky. Hence the
saying of old time, " It was the fierce thrusting of Tane'
which tore the heaven from the earth, so that they were rent
apart, and darkness was made manifest, and light made
manifest also."

IO, TANGAROA, AND CREATION

No sooner were Rangi' and Papa' rent apart than was discovered the multitude of human beings they had begotten, who had hitherto lain concealed between the bodies of the two. Then, also, there arose in the breast of Tawhiri-matea, the god and father of winds and storms, a fierce desire to wage war with his brothers, because they had rent apart their common parents. He from the first had refused to consent to their mother being torn from her husband and their children ; it was his brothers only who had wished for this separation, and desired that Papa-tu-a-nuku alone should be left as a parent to them.

The god of hurricanes and storms also feared that the world would become too beautiful ; so he arose, followed his father to the realms above, and hurriedly sought the sheltered hollows in the boundless skies ; there he clung and hid, and nestling in this place of rest he consulted long with his parent ; and as great Rangi' listened to the suggestions of Tawhiri-matea thoughts and plans were formed in his breast, and Tawhiri-matea also understood the things he should do. Then by himself and by Rangi' were begotten a numerous brood, and they rapidly increased and grew. Tawhiri' dispatched one of them to the west, one to the south, one to the east, and one to the north ; and he gave corresponding names to himself and to his progeny, the mighty winds.

He next sent forth of his children Apu-hau, and Apu-matangi, and Ao-nui, and Ao-roa, and Ao-pouri, and Ao-potango, and Ao-whetuma, and Ao-whekere, and Ao-kahiwahiwa, and Ao-kanapanapa, and Ao-pakakina, and Ao-pakarea, and Ao-takawe—that is, Fierce Squalls, Whirlwinds, Dense Clouds, Massy Clouds, Dark Clouds, Gloomy Thick Clouds, Fiery Clouds, Clouds which precede Hurricanes, Clouds of Fiery Black, Clouds reflecting Glowing Red Light, Clouds wildly drifting from all Quarters and wildly bursting, Clouds of Thunderstorms, and Clouds hurriedly flying ; and in the midst of these Tawhiri-matea himself swept wildly on.

Behold! behold! then raged the fierce hurricane ; and while unconscious of evil Tane-mahuta and his mighty

369

forests still stand, the blast of the breath of Tawhiri-matea smites them; the great trees are snapped across the bole; behold! behold! they are rent and riven, dashed to the earth with branches splintered and shattered; and, lying on the earth, trees and branches alike are left for the insect, the grub, and loathsome rottenness.

From the forests and their inhabitants Tawhiri-matea next swept down upon the seas, and in his wrath lashed the ocean. Behold! behold! waves sheer as cliffs arose, whose summits were so lofty that to gaze from them would make the beholder giddy; these toppled and eddied in whirlpools, and Tangaroa, the god of the ocean, fled through his seas affrighted; but before he fled his children consulted together how they might secure their safety, for Tangaroa had begotten Punga, and he in his turn had begotten Ika-tere, father of fish, and Tu-te-wehiwehi, or Tu-te-wanawana, father of reptiles.

When Tangaroa fled for safety to the ocean, then Ika-tere and Tu-te-wehiwehi and their children disputed as to what they should do to escape from the storms; and Tu-te-wehiwehi and his party cried aloud, "Let us fly inland"; but Ika-tere and his party cried aloud, "Let us fly to the sea." Some would not obey one order, some would not obey the other, and so they escaped in two parties; the party of Tu-te-wehiwehi, or the reptiles, hid themselves ashore, the party of Punga and Ika-tere rushed to the sea. This is what is called the separation of Tawhiri-matea. Hence these traditions have been handed down: Ika-tere, the father of things inhabiting the waters, cried aloud to Tu-te-wehiwehi, "Let us escape to the sea"; but Tu-te-wehiwehi shouted in answer, "Lo! let us rather fly inland." Then Ika-tere warned him, saying, "Fly inland, then; and the fate of you and your race will be that when they catch you, before you are cooked, they will singe off your scales over a lighted wisp of dry fern"; but Tu-te-wehiwehi answered him, saying, "Seek safety, then, in the sea; and the future fate of your race will be that when they serve out little baskets of cooked vegetable food to each person you will be laid on the top of the food to give it a relish." Then the two separated without delay; the fish fled to the sea, the reptiles sought safety in the scrub and in the forest.

Tangaroa, enraged at some of his children thus deserting him and finding shelter in the forests on dry land, has ever since waged war with his brother Tane', who in turn has waged war against him. Hence Tane' supplies the offspring of his brother Tu-matauenga with canoes, with spears, and fish-hooks made from his trees, and with nets woven from his fibrous plants, that they may destroy the offspring of Tangaroa; while Tangaroa, in return, swallows up the offspring of Tane', overwhelming canoes with the surges of his seas, swallowing up the lands, the trees, the houses that are swept off by floods, and ever wastes away, with the lapping and sapping of his waves, the shores that confine him, so that the giants of the forests may be washed down and swept out into his boundless ocean, and so that he may swallow up the insects, the birds, and the creatures that inhabit the trees, the numerous progeny of his brother Tane'.

Tawhiri-matea next rushed on to attack his brothers Rongo-ma-Tane and Haumia-tikitiki, the gods and progenitors of cultivated and uncultivated food; but Papa', to save these for her other children, caught them up and hid them in a place of safety; and so well were these children of hers concealed that Tawhiri-matea sought for them in vain.

Having thus vanquished all his other brothers, Tawhiri-matea next rushed against Tu-matauenga, to try his strength against his; he exerted all his force against him, but he could neither shake him nor prevail against him. What did Tu-matauenga care for his brother's wrath? He was the only one of all the brothers who had planned the destruction of their parents; he had shown himself fierce and brave in war, when his brothers had yielded at once before the tremendous assaults of Tawhiri-matea and his progeny. Tane-mahuta and his offspring had been broken and shattered; Tangaroa and his children had fled to the depths of the ocean or the recesses of the shore; Rongo-ma-Tane and Haumia-tikitiki had been hidden from him in the earth ; but Tu-matauenga, or man, still stood erect and unshaken upon the breast of his mother Papa'. And now at length the hearts of Rangi' and Tawhiri' became tranquil, and their passions were assuaged.

Tu-matauenga, or fierce man, having thus successfully resisted his brother, the god of hurricanes and storms, next took thought how he could turn upon his brothers and slay them, because they had not assisted him or fought bravely when Tawhiri-matea had attacked them to avenge the separation of their parents. As yet death had no power over man. It was not until the birth of the children of Taranga and Makea-tutara that death had power over men. If that goddess had not been deceived by Maui-tikitiki-a-Taranga men would not have died, but would have lived for ever.

This statement reveals one of the many inconsistencies in Maori mythology, though such inconsistencies occur in all mythologies. It will be remembered that it was because man must suffer the indignity of death that Maui' determined to attempt the overcoming of Hine-nui-te-po, so that man might not die, but live for ever.

Tu-matauenga continued to brood upon the cowardly manner in which his brothers had acted in leaving him to show his courage alone ; and he first sought some means of injuring Tane-mahuta. Not only had Tane' failed to aid him in his combat with Tawhiri', but he had had a numerous progeny that might at last prove hostile to Tu', and cause him injury. He therefore collected fibrous blades of the *whanake*, one of the trees of Tane', and these he split and twisted into nooses, with which he made snares. He set them in the forests—aha ! the children of Tane' fell before him ; no longer could any of them move or fly in safety.

Next he determined to be revenged on his brother Tangaroa, who also had deserted him in the combat. He sought for his offspring, and found them leaping or swimming in the water. He cut many blades of flax, split them in strips, and knotted nets, and, dragging these through the water, he hauled the children of Tangaroa ashore.

372

After that he determined to be revenged on his brothers Rongo-ma-Tane and Haumia-tikitiki. He soon found them by their peculiar leaves ; he shaped digging implements, he plaited baskets, he dug in the earth and pulled up all kinds of plants with edible roots ; the roots he kept, and the plants withered in the sun.

Thus Tu-matauenga consumed his brothers, in revenge for their having deserted him and left him to fight alone against Rangi' and Tawhiri-matea. He then assumed the several names Tu-ka-riri, Tu-ka-nguha, Tu-kai-taua, Tu-whakaheke-tangata, Tu-mata-whaiti, Tu-matauenga, one name for each of his attributes displayed in the victories over his brothers. Four of his brothers were entirely deposed by him and became his food ; but one of them, Tawhiri-matea, he could not vanquish, nor make him common and degrade him by using him as food ; he, therefore, the last-born child of Rangi' and Papa', was left as an enemy for man; and still, with a rage equal to that of man, he ever attacks him in storms and hurricanes, endeavouring to destroy him alike by sea and land.

Now the meanings of these names of the children of Rangi' and Papa' are as follows : Tangaroa signifies fish of every kind ; Rongo-ma-Tane signifies the *kumara* and all vegetables cultivated as food ; Haumia-tikitiki signifies fern-root, and all kinds of food which grow wild ; Tane-mahuta signifies forests, the birds and insects which inhabit them, and all things fashioned from wood ; Tawhiri-matea signifies winds and storms ; and Tu-matauenga signifies man. For each of his vanquished brothers Tu-matauenga assigned *karakia* to make them common and serve for his food. There were also *karakia* for Tawhiri-matea to cause favourable winds, and to Rangi' for fair weather, and to Papa' for the plentiful production of all things.

The bursting forth of the wrathful fury of Tawhiri-matea against his brothers was the cause of the disappearance of a great part of the dry land ; during that contest a great part of Papa' was submerged. The names of the beings who then caused that submergence were Ua-nui and

Ua-roa, Ua-whatu and Ua-nganga; that is to say, Great
Rain, Long-continued Rain, Rain turning to Hailstorm,
Furiously Raging Rain; and their progeny were Hau-
maringi, Hau-marotoroto, and Tomai-rangi—that is to say,
Mist, Heavy Dew, and Light Dew. These together submerged the greater part of Papa', the earth, so that only a
small portion of the land projected above the sea.

From that time clear light increased upon the earth, and
all the beings hidden between Rangi' and Papa' before they
were separated now multiplied upon the earth. The first
beings begotten by Rangi' and Papa' were not like human
beings; but Tu-matauenga bore the likeness of a man, as
did all his brothers, as also did a Po, and an Ao, and a Kimihanga, and Runuku, and so it has continued to this day.

The children of Tu-matauenga increased, and continued
to multiply, until at last was reached the generation of
Maui-taha, and of his brothers Maui-roto, Maui-waho,
Maui-pae, and Maui-tikitiki-a-Taranga.

Rangi' has ever remained separated from Papa'. Yet
their mutual love still continues—the soft, warm sighs of
her loving bosom ever rise up to him, ascending from the
wooded mountains and valleys, and men call these mists;
and Rangi', as he mourns through the long nights his
separation from his beloved one, lets fall frequent tears upon
her bosom; and men, seeing these, call them dewdrops.

The Wives of Rangi'

This version is shorn of all complications. It mentions
the multitude of beings who had come into existence, and
who were prisoned in the darkness between Rangi' and
Papa', but it names none of them, nor does it touch on their
genealogy—and wisely; for it is confusion worse con-
founded. Papa' was not the only wife of Rangi'; and it
would even appear that she should not have been his wife
at all, as she was already the wife of Tangaroa, given as a
son in the above version.

His first wife was Pokoharua-te-po, a younger sister of
Tangaroa. Their progeny consisted of winds and storms.

374

The first-born was Hanui-o-rangi, father of winds, whose son was Tawhiri-matea, the strong north-west wind, whose son Tiu also ruled the north-west wind, and these two were chief of all the winds. From Tiu sprang Hine-i-tapapauta, mother of Hine-tu-whenua, both gentle western winds that calm the seas and lull the rougher winds. From Hine-tu-whenua sprang Hakona-tipu, and he begat Pua-i-taha. These were blustering south and south-west gales. Later born was Awhiowhio, god of whirlwinds. The second family by this wife were " the multitude of Tahu "—rites and *karakia*—connected with whom were " the multitude of Space," including Anu-matao, and Anu-whakarere, and Anu-whakatoro, and Anu-mate—that is to say, Cold Space, Space of Extreme Cold, Cold Space creeping on, and Space of Cold Death ; also many of the deformed generation, who, disobedient to Rangi', were swept by him to the darkness of Te Po, and by whom mankind is drawn into the glooms of the netherworlds.

His second wife was Hekeheke-i-papa. Among their progeny were lords great in the upperworlds and on the earth. Their first-born was Tama-i-waho; later came Tama-nui-a-rangi, from whom sprang Haumia-tikitiki, god of fern-root.

His third wife was Hotu-papa, and from them sprang Tu', the god of war, Rongo-ma-Tane, the god of the *kumara*, and many of lesser note.

From his fourth and fifth wives, Ma-ukuuku and Tu-hara-kiokio, came no influential offspring.

His sixth wife was Papa-tu-a-nuku. Their first-born was Rehua, whose coming was as the flashing of light; then came Hakina, his sister, and Tane', the great artificer. Ru', god of earthquakes, was never born, but still lives within Papa', ever and anon struggling for light and air. From Rangi' and Papa' sprang also Rauru, god of the head, Rongo-mai, god of the whale, and Paikea, god of sea-monsters.

From these wives sprang innumerable other lesser-known deities, but there is great confusion, not only in the order of their origin, but also in the order of the wives, and in their number. Tangaroa held a less important place with the Maori than with other branches of Polynesians in the Pacific. One legend states that he was a son of Rangi' by a second wife, Papa-tu-a-nuku, and committed adultery with a third wife of Rangi', also named Papa'; but in more legends it is said that Papa-tu-a-nuku was the wife of Tangaroa, that Rangi' took her to wife during the absence of Tangaroa, begetting Rehua, Tane', and others, and that on the return of Tangaroa he and Rangi' engaged in a duel with spears in the windy fields of space, when Rangi' was wounded in the thighs and long lay enfeebled in the blueness of Watea. When so lying he begat the Whanau-tuoi, a family of offspring inferior and deformed.

In another legend the first wife of Rangi' was Hine-ahupapa, whose offspring were sky-powers, the fourth being Haronga. Haronga took Tongotongo to wife, and from them sprang a son 'Ra, the sun, and a daughter, Marama, the moon. In one genealogy this first wife was Atutahi, which is the name of the star Canopus, and she was the mother of Marama, the moon, Whetu, stars, Atarapa, daydawn, and Ata-hiku-rangi, full day; the second wife was Werowero, with whom Haronga begot 'Ra, the sun.

The more detailed these genealogies are, the more confused they become; and the mythology of many a race that seems simple may be so because only one version has been collected or has survived.

Tangaroa and Rongo in Mangaia

In Mangaia Tangaroa and Rongo were twin children of Vatea and Papa; and, as in Maori, these beings, offspring of the primal pair, were the first to have human form. Tangaroa should have been born first, but gave precedence to his brother Rongo. A few days after the birth of Rongo his mother suffered from a large boil on her arm. On being pressed, the core flew out—it was Tangaroa. Another account stated that Tangaroa came up through the head of Papa. The point of issue is indicated by the ' crown ' with which all their descendants have since been born. This is reminiscent of the birth of Minerva, who sprang full-armed from the head of Jove.

The third son was Tongaiti, whose visible form was the white and black spotted lizard. Under the name of Matarau he was a deity in the Hervey group. The fourth son was Tangi'ia, the fifth and last Tane-papa-kai ('Tane' the Piler-up of Food).

The home of Rongo was Auau (Ahuahu)—afterward named Mangaia—in Avaiki. As an individual consists of two parts, a body and a spirit, so this island had an essence, or spirit, the secret name of which was Aka-tautika, used only by priests and highest chiefs of ancient days. When in aftertimes the earthly form, or body of Auau, was dragged up to light there remained behind in the dimness of the netherworld the ethereal form or spirit, Aka-tautika. This duality of names may be the cause of some confusion in traditions. The two names, for the material and ethereal forms, may be taken as the names of two different islands instead of the alternative names of one. Thus in the Hervey group the spirit name of Rarotonga is Tumu-te-varovaro; of Auau Aka-tautika; of Aitutaki Araura; of Atiu Enua-manu; of Mauki Aka-toka; of Mitiaro Nuku-roa; of Manuae Enua-kura; and it was said that the spirit name of Tahiti was simply Iti.

Tangaroa was altogether the cleverer son of Vatea; he instructed Rongo in the art of agriculture, and their father wished to make him lord of all they possessed; but the mother objected, because as parents they dared not taste the food or touch the property of Tangaroa, the elder by right, and the mother had her way. When the body of a man was offered as a sacrifice to Rongo the decayed body was cast to her, dwelling with Rongo in the shades. Government, the arrangement of feasts, the drum of peace—all the sources of honour and power were secured to Rongo through the partiality of Papa.

Most kinds of food, too, fell to the share of the younger brother. The division was made in this manner: every-

377

thing red on earth or in the ocean was dedicated to Tangaroa; the rest, which meant the great bulk, was dedicated to Rongo. Thus of the various kinds of *taro* only one was sacred to Tangaroa; the rest were sacred to Rongo. Among the very many varieties of banana and plantain only the plantain belonged to Tangaroa on account of its redness and the uprightness of its fruit. Bananas of all kinds belonged to Rongo. The very name of the plantain, *uatu*, the upright fruit, testified to the dignity of the eldest of the gods. The plantain, being the *kokira*, or head of the great *meika* family, including the banana and plantain, does not bend its head, just as Tangaroa is the *kokira* or first in the family of the gods.

Of three kinds of chestnuts only one, the red-leafed, was sacred to Tangaroa; of the two kinds of yam his was the red; of the double variety of coconut one was his; all bread-fruit was sacred to Rongo. In regard to the wealth of the ocean, too, Rongo was the gainer; only four kinds of fish, all scarlet, besides lobsters, fell to Tangaroa. The silvery, the striped, the spotted, the black all fell to Rongo.

Thus Rongo became very rich; Tangaroa was comparatively poor. The twin gods made a grand feast, each collecting only his own food, to which Vatea and Papa were invited. Tangaroa made one great pile of red *taro*, yams, chestnuts, coconuts, the top garnished with red land-crabs, and all the red fish he could find in the sea. The pile of Rongo was immensely greater; all the treasures of the earth and ocean were there. The parents declared that Tangaroa excelled in beauty, Rongo in abundance.

In after ages all fair-haired children were considered to belong to Tangaroa, the god himself having sandy hair; while the dark-haired, who formed the majority, belonged to Rongo, who was black-haired. Very few Mangaians had fair hair—a colour they disliked for themselves, but thought suitable for foreigners; and a golden-haired child would, in playful allusion to this myth, be addressed as " the fair-haired progeny of Tangaroa." Hence when Cook discovered Mangaia the islanders were surprised at the fair

378

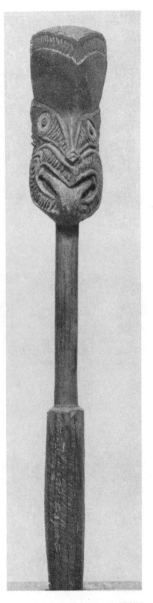

(1) FIGURE OF TANGAROA UPAO VAHU, SUPREME GOD OF POLYNESIA
(2) WOODEN IMAGE, PROBABLY REPRESENTING MARU, GOD OF WAR

British Museum
(See page 378)

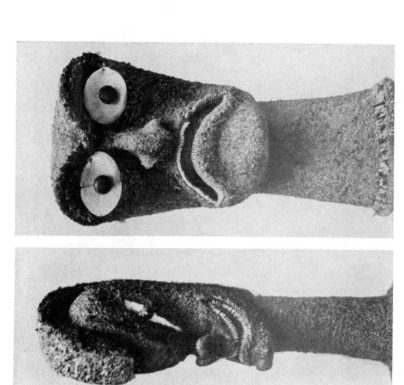

HAWAIIAN EFFIGIES OF THE WAR-GOD KUKAILIMOKU

Of wicker covered with feather-work, with dogs' teeth and composite eyes of shell and wood.

British Museum

hair and skin of the visitors, and concluded that they were some of the long-lost fair children of Tangaroa.

Tangaroa became displeased at the preference always shown for Rongo. He therefore collected a supply of red food of all kinds, and set out on a voyage to some other land where he could reign alone. He made a long journey, touching at many islands, and scattering everywhere the blessings of food, piled up for the purpose in his canoe. Finally he settled on Rarotonga and Aitutaki, leaving Auau, or Mangaia, as it was afterward called, in the quiet possession of Rongo.

In winter tree-fruits disappear, whereas *taro*, bananas, and the like are in season all the year round. The reason for this is that the former belong to Tangaroa, who permits his gifts to be seen and tasted in the land of Rongo while they are on their way, in winter, to the lands where he reigns undisturbed. On this account these fruits were not regarded as private property, but as belonging to all the inhabitants of the district in which they grew.

The home of Rongo was in the netherworld, and there his wife Taka bore him a daughter, Tavake, who when she grew up gave birth to Rangi, to Mokoiro, and to Aka-tauira. Rongo wished his three grandsons, who were likewise his sons, to live with him in Auau. But Rangi was resolved to pull up this land from Avaiki. This was an arduous task, but with the aid of his brothers he succeeded in dragging the island to the light of day, when it was known as Mangaia. The three brothers took up their abode on the island in this upper world, and they were thus the first inhabitants of Mangaia, giving rise to the original tribes that peopled the island.

Rongo continued to live in Avaiki, on the invisible or nether Auau, of which the island of Mangaia was the material expression. He directed Rangi to offer sacrifices in his courtyard in the upper world, throwing the decayed corpses aside for Papa.

Mangaia thus became the centre of the universe, its central hill being accordingly called Rangi-motia (the Centre of the Heavens). Vatea, or Avatea, was in this way the father of gods and men, the three original tribes being regarded as the direct offspring of Rongo; all subsequent settlers and visitors were regarded as interlopers, to be, if possible, slain and offered in sacrifice.

Creation in the Marquesas

The Marquesans have a legend called *Te Vanana na Tanaoa—The Prophecy* or *Record of Tanaoa* ('Tana'oa = Tangaroa)—which relates that in the beginning there was no life, or light, or sound; that a boundless night (Po) enveloped all space, over which Tanaoa (Darkness) and Mutu-hei (Silence) ruled supreme. In course of time the god Atea (Light) evolved himself, sprang from or separated himself from Tanaoa, made war on him, drove him away, and confined him within limits. After Atea had thus evolved from Tanaoa, the god Ono (Rongo) evolved from Atea, and he destroyed or broke up Mutu-hei. From this struggle, of Atea with Tanaoa, and Ono with Mutu-hei, arose Atanua, or the dawn. Atea took Atanua to wife, and from them sprang Tu-mea.

This fine conception of creation is embodied in a very ancient chant :

> In the beginning, space and companions.
> Space was the high heaven.
> Tanaoa filled and dwelt in the whole heavens,
> And Mutu-hei was entwined above.
> There was no voice, there was no sound;
> No living things were moving.
> There was no day, there was no light.
> A dark, black night.
> O Tanaoa he ruled the night.
> O Mutu-hei was a spirit pervading and vast.
> From within Tanaoa came forth Atea.
> Life vigorous, power great.
> O Atea he ruled the day,
> And drove away Tanaoa.
> Between day and night, Atea and Tanaoa,
> Sprang up wars fierce and long.
> Atea and Tanaoa, great wrath and contention.

IO, TANGAROA, AND CREATION

Tanaoa confined, Atea soared onward,
Tanaoa dark as ever.
Atea very good and very active.
From within Atea came forth Ono.
O Ono ruled the sound
And broke up Mutu-hei.
Here was made a great division
In the company of Atanua.
Atanua was beautiful and good,
Adorned with riches very great.
Atanua was fair, very rich and soft.
Atea and Atanua embraced each other.
Atanua produces abundantly of living things.
Atea took Atanua for wife.
Atea and Ono pass onward, pass upward.
Atea the body, Ono the spirit.
Atea with Ono in one place.
Atea the substance, Ono the [? soul].
Atea produces the intense fire.
Ono is powerful and great,
Atea is adorned with riches changeable and dazzling,
Ono is adorned with princely wealth and power.
The two the same glory.
Atea the body, Ono the spirit.
Atea the substance, Ono the [? soul].
And dwelt as kings in the most beautiful places,
Supported on thrones, large, many-coloured, wondrous.
They dwelt above, they dwelt beyond.
They ruled the space of heaven,
And the amplitude of sky,
And all the skyey powers,
The first lords dwelling on high.
O wondrous thrones, good and bright!
O wondrous thrones, whereon to seat the great lord
    Atea!
O thrones placed in the midst of the upper heavens!
O thrones whereon to seat the lord of love!
The great lord Atea in love established,
To love the fair Atanua.
Atanua shades the neck of Atea,
A woman of great wealth is Atanua,
Which she brought from out of night,
Gathered for Atea.
Nothing was given again to night,
Atea gave nothing again to Tanaoa,
Who thus was driven to distant regions,

Where the light of day was unknown;
No wealth; no warmth;
Confined, lying beneath the feet of Atanua,
Very cold, dark, dreary, without companions;
Nothing of all his wealth remained.
Cold, shivering, engulfed; behold, indeed!
O dark Tanaoa, engulfed in the long nights,
Secure sits Atea on his wondrous throne,
And dwells as chief in his domains.
Born is his first son, his princely son.
O the great prince, O the sacred superior!
O the princely son, first-born of divine power!
O the lord of all, here, there, and always!
O the lord of heavens and amplitude of sky!
O the princely son, first born of the exalted power!
O the son, equal with the father and with Ono!
Dwelling in the same place.
Joined are they three in the same power.
The father, Ono, and the son.
From those three was one tree formed.
The tree producing in the heavens.
All the good and wondrous families in love.
The tree of life, firm rooted in the heavens.
The tree in all the heavens producing
The bright and sprightly sons.
From Atea as his sons were they born.
O Atea, the exalted lord of all!
O Atea, their life, their body, their spirit!

In spirit the opening of this lofty hymn of creation is like a similar opening in the Elder Edda:

It was Time's dawn,
There nothing was,
Nor sand, nor sea,
Nor cooling billows.
There was no earth,
No arching heaven;
Life there was none,
Only a vast profound.

In another Marquesan legend the progenitors of the Marquesans were Atea and his wife Owa.

Tangaroa seems to have been one of the oldest of the gods. Even in Maori mythology he is spoken of sometimes as a son of Rangi', sometimes as a coeval deity, dwelling elsewhere in the immensity of space where Rangi' lay.

Among the Marquesans, as Tanaoa, he was the origin of all things; among the Society Islanders, as Ta'aroa, he fished up the earth from the ocean, and was father of gods and men. Among the Samoans, as Tagaloa, he was also the origin of all, using as helpers in creation Gai-tosi (Gai the Marker), Gai-va'a-va'ai (Gai the Seer, or Beholder), also called Tagaloa-va'a-va'ai, as though these names represented himself in varied manifestations. Many of the Polynesian deities have these alternate or group-names; indeed, there is a like Trinity in the Christian religion itself, the mystery being explained in the Nicene Creed.

Creation in Samoa

The son of Tagaloa was Tuli, and he in the shape of a bird went down from the heavens to the surface of the ocean, but finding no place to rest he returned and complained to his father, who thereon threw down a stone, which became land, or, according to another account, fished up the stone from the bottom of the sea with a fish-hook. The son took possession of this his dwelling-place, but found that it was partly overflowed by the swell of the ocean, so that he had to move from place to place to avoid becoming wet. This annoying him, he returned to the skies and again complained, when Tagaloa by means of his fish-hook raised the rock higher. The name of it was Papa-taoto (the Reclining Rock); it was succeeded by Papa-sosolo (the Spreading Rock), and Papa-tu (the Upright Rock). The rock was covered with earth, or mould, which was then overspread with grass. After this a *fue* (convolvulus) grew and overcame the grass. Having obtained his land, Tuli returned to Tagaloa, as there was no man to reside on it. His father said to him, " You have got your land; what grows on it? " Tuli answered, " The *fue*." His father bade him go and pull it up, which he did; and on its rotting it produced two grubs, which moved a little as Tuli watched them, when again he returned to the heavens and told Tagaloa what had taken place. Upon this he was told to return, taking with him Tagaloa-tosi (or Gai-tosi) and Tagaloa-va'a-va'ai (or Gai-va'a-va'ai), who were set to work on the two grubs. They shaped them into the forms of men, beginning at the head, and naming each part as finished. Both were males. One day, while net-fishing, one of them was injured by a small fish called the *lo*, which caused his death.

Again Tuli returned to the heavens, and complained that one of his inhabitants was lost to him. Gai-tosi was told to return to earth and reanimate the dead body, first changing the sex from male to female. The two beings formed from the grubs then became man and wife, and from them sprang the human race.

Following the example set by Tuli, the descendants from these two made occasional visits to Tagaloa, returning to earth with some benefaction. Losi in this way is said to have brought the *taro* to man.

Tuli is also known as Kuri, when he is called a daughter of Tagaloa, and as a bird flew down to look for dry land. She found a spot, visiting it frequently as it extended, and at one time brought down the earth and the creeping plant to grow in it.

Quite a different impression is produced by the version following, translated direct from the Samoan in the *Journal of the Polynesian Society*. It should be said that in the alphabet fixed for Samoan the letter *g* has the sound of *ng*; there is no *g* sound, so that symbol was adopted for *ng*, which has the same sound as the *ng* used in Maori. Tagaloa is the Maori Tangaroa, in pronunciation as well as in fact.

" The god Tagaloa dwelt in the Expanse; he made all things; he alone was; not any sky, not any country; he only went to and fro in the Expanse; there was also no sea, and no earth; but at the place where he stood there grew up a Rock. Tagaloa-fa'atutupu-nu'u was his name. [In Maori *whakatupu* (*fa'atupuputu*) is 'to cause to grow'; *nuku* (*nu'u*) is 'space,' or 'the earth.'] All things were about to be made, by him, for all things were not yet made;

384

the Sky was not made, nor anything else; but there grew up a Rock, on which he stood.

"Then Tagaloa said to the Rock, 'Be thou split up.' Then was brought forth Papa-taoto; after that Papa-sosolo; then Papa-lau-a'au; then Papa-'ano-'ano; then Papa-'ele; then Papa-tu; then Papa-'amu-'amu and his children.

"But Tagaloa stood facing the west, and spoke to the Rock. Then Tagaloa struck the rock with his right hand, and it split open toward the right side. Then the Earth was brought forth (that is the parent of all the people in the world), and the Sea was brought forth. Then the Sea covered Papa-sosolo; and Papa-nofo said to Papa-sosolo, 'Blessed are you in your sea!' Then said Papa-sosolo, 'Do not bless me; the Sea will soon reach you too.' All the rocks in like manner called him blessed.

"Then Tagaloa turned to the right side, and the Fresh Water sprang up. Then Tagaloa spoke again to the Rock, and the Sky was produced. He spoke again to the Rock, and Tui-te'e-lagi was brought forth; then came forth Ilu [Immensity], and Mamao [Space] came (that was a woman); then came Niuao.

"Tagaloa spoke again to the Rock; then Lua'o, a boy, came forth. Tagaloa spoke again to the Rock, and Lua-vai, a girl, came forth. Tagaloa appointed these two to the Sa-tualagi.

"Then Tagaloa spoke again, and Ava-lala, a boy, was born, and Gao-gao-le-tai, a girl; then came Man; then came the Spirit; then the Heart; then the Will; then Thought.

"That is the end of the creations of Tagaloa which were produced from the Rock; they were only floating about on the Sea; there was no fixedness there.

"Then Tagaloa made an ordinance to the Rock, and said, 'Let the Spirit and the Heart and Will and Thought go on and join together inside the Man'; and they joined together there, and Man became intelligent. And this was joined to the Earth [*eleele*], and it was called

385

Fatua-ma-le-'Ele'ele as a couple: Fatu the Man, and 'Ele'ele the Woman.

" Then he said to Immensity and Space, ' Come now; you two be united up above in the Sky with your boy Niuao.' Then they went up; but there was only a void, nothing for the eye to rest upon.

" Then he said to Lua'o and Lua-vai, ' Come now, you two, that the region of Fresh Water may be peopled.'

" But he ordains Ava-lala and Gao-gao-le-tai to the Sea, that those two may people the Sea.

" And he ordains Le Fatu and Le 'Ele'ele that they people this side; he points them to the left-hand side, opposite to Tualagi.

" Then Tagaloa said to Tui-te'e-lagi, ' Come here now, that you may prop up the sky.' Then it was propped up; it reached up on high. But it fell down because he was not able for it. Then Tui-te'e-lagi went to Masoa and Teve; he brought them and used them as props; then he was able. (The *masoa* and the *teve* were the first plants that grew, and other plants came afterward.) Then the Sky remained up above, but there was nothing for the sight to rest upon. There was only the far-receding Sky, reaching to Immensity and Space.

" Then Immensity and Space brought forth offspring; they brought forth Po and Ao [Night and Day], and this couple was ordained by Tagaloa to produce the Eye of the Sky [the Sun]. Again, Immensity and Space brought forth Le Lagi [Rangi']—that is, the Second Heavens; for Tui-te'e-lagi went forth to prop it up, and the Sky became double; and Immensity and Space remained there, and they peopled the Sky. Then again Lagi brought forth, and Tui-te'e-lagi went forth and propped it up; that was the Third Heavens; that was peopled by Immensity and Space. Then Lagi bore again; that was the Fourth Heavens. Tui-te'e-lagi went forth to prop it up; that heaven was also peopled by Ilu and Mamao. Then Lagi bore again; that was the Fifth Heavens. Then went forth Tui-te'e-lagi to prop it up; that heaven also was peopled by

386

Ilu and Mamao. Lagi brought forth again; that was the Sixth Heavens. And Tui-te'e-lagi went and propped it up; that heaven was peopled by Ilu and Mamao. Then Lagi bore again; that was the Seventh Heavens. And Tui-te'e-lagi went forth and propped it up; that heaven was peopled by Ilu and Mamao. Then Lagi again brought forth; that was called the Eighth Heavens. Tui-te'e-lagi went to prop up that heaven; and that heaven was peopled by Ilu and Mamao. Then again Lagi brought forth; that was the Ninth Heavens; and it was propped up by Tui-te'e-lagi; and that heaven was peopled by Ilu and Mamao. Then ended the productiveness of Ilu and Mamao; it reached to the Ninth Heavens.

" Then Tagaloa sat; he is well known as Tagaloa-fa'a-tutupu-nu'u; then he created Tagaloa-le-fuli, and Tagaloa-asiasi-nu'u, and Tagaloa-tolo-nu'u, and Tagaloa-savali, and Tuli also, and Logonoa.

" Then said Tagaloa, the creator, to Tagaloa-le-fuli [the Immovable], ' Come here; be thou chief in the heavens.' Then Tagaloa-le-fuli was chief in the heavens.

" Then Tagaloa, the creator, said to Tagaloa-savali [the Messenger], ' Come here; be thou ambassador in all the heavens, beginning from the Eighth Heavens down to the First Heavens, to tell them all to gather together in the Ninth Heavens, where Tagaloa-le-fuli is chief.' Then proclamation was made that they should go up to the Ninth Heavens, and then visit below the children of Night and Day in the First Heavens.

" Then Tagaloa-savali went down to Night and Day in the First Heavens, and asked them thus : ' Have you two any children appointed to you?' And they answered, ' Come here, these two are our children, appointed to us, Lagi-'uli and Lagi-ma.' [In Maori Rangi-uri, the Dark Heaven, and Rangi-ma, the Bright Heaven.]

" All the stars also were their offspring, but we have not the names of all the stars (the stars had each its own name), for they are forgotten now, because they dropped out of use. And surely the last injunction of Tagaloa, the creator,

to Night and Day was that they should produce the Eye of
the Sky. That was the reason Tagaloa-savali went down
to ask Night and Day in the First Heavens [if they had any
children].

"Then answered Night and Day, 'Come now; there
remain four boys that are not yet appointed—Manu'a,
Samoa, La ['Ra, the Sun], and Masina [Mahina, the Moon].'

"These are the boys that originated the names of Samoa
and Manu'a ; these two were the children of Night and Day.
The name of the one is Satia-i-le-moa [Obstructed by the
Chest], the meaning of which is this : the boy seemed as
if he would not be born, because he was caught by the
chest; therefore it was that he was called Satia-i-le-moa
—that is, Samoa. The other was born with one side
abraded [*manu'a*]; then said Day to Night, 'Why is this
child so greatly wounded?' Therefore the child was
called Manu'a-tele.

"Then said Tagaloa-savali, 'It is good; come now; go up
into the Ninth Heavens, you four ; all are about to gather
together there to form a Council ; go up you two also.'
Then they all gathered together in the Ninth Heavens, the
place where dwelt Tagaloa-fa'a-tutupu-nu'u and Tagaloa-le-
fuli ; the Council was held in the Ninth Heavens ; the
ground where they held the Council was Malae-a-Toto'a
[the Council-ground of Tranquillity].

"Then various decrees were made in the Ninth
Heavens ; the children of Ilu and Mamao were appointed
all of them to be builders ; and to come down from the
Eighth Heavens to this earth below ; perhaps they were
ten thousand in all that were appointed to be builders ;
they had one name, all were Tagaloa. Then they built
houses for the Tagaloa, but the builders did not reach to the
Ninth Heavens—the home of Tagaloa-le-fuli—which was
called Fale-'ula [the Bright House].

"Then said Tagaloa, the creator, to Night and Day,
'Let those two boys go down below to be chiefs over the
offspring of Fatu and 'Ele-'ele.' But to the end of the
names of the two boys was attached the name of Tagaloa-le-
388

fuli, who is *tupu* [king] of the Ninth Heavens; hence the *tupu* [kings] of Samoa were named ' Tui o Manu'a tele ma Samoa atoa.'

" Then Tagaloa, the creator, said to Night and Day, ' Let those two boys La [the Sun] and Masina [the Moon] go and follow you two; when Day comes, let La follow; also, when Night comes, Masina also comes on.'

" These two are the shades of Tagaloa; they are well known in all the world; Masina is the shade of Tagaloa; but thus runs the decree of Tagaloa, the creator, ' Let there be one portion of the heavens in which they pass along; in like manner also shall the Stars pass along.'

" Then Tagaloa-savali, the Messenger, went to and fro to visit the land; his visit began in the place where are [now] the Eastern groups; these groups were made to spring up; then he went off to cause the group of Fiti [Fiji] to grow up; but the space between seemed so far off that he could not walk it; then he stood there and turned his face to the sky, to Tagaloa, the creator, and Tagaloa-le-fuli; Tagaloa looked down to Tagaloa-savali; and he made the Toga [Tongan] group spring up; then that land sprang up.

" Then he turns his face to this Manu'a; and looks up to the heavens, for he is unable to move about; then Tagaloa-fa'a-tutupu-nu'u and Tagaloa-le-fuli looked down, and caused Savai'i to spring up; then that land grew up.

" Then Tagaloa-savali went back to the Heavens, and said, ' We have now got countries, the Eastern group and Fiti and Toga and Savai'i.' Then, as all these lands were grown up, Tagaloa, the creator, went down in a black cloud to look at the countries, and he delighted in them; and he said, ' It is good '; then he stood on the top of the mountains to tread them down, that the land might be prepared for people to dwell in. Then he returned. And Tagaloa, the creator, said, ' Come now; go back by the road you came; take people to possess the Eastern groups; take Atu and Sasa'e '—that is, a pair; they were called conjointly Atu-Sasa'e; these two people came from the heavens from among the children of Tagaloa.

"Then Tagaloa-savali went again to Fiti; he also again took two persons, a pair—their names were Atu and Fiti—from among all the children of Tagaloa; so that group of islands was called Atu-Fiti.

"Then he turned his face toward Toga; he took a couple; their names were Atu and Toga; these two peopled that group of islands; their names were the Atu-Toga; these two were the people of Tagaloa.

"Then Tagaloa-savali came back to this Manu'a, to Le Fatu and Le 'Ele-'ele and their children, because of the command of Tagaloa, the creator, from the Heavens, that Le Fatu and Le 'Ele-'ele should go there to people this side of the world. Then went out Valu'a and Ti'apa to people Savai'i; these two are the children of Le Fatu and Le 'Ele-'ele; these two people are from this Manu'a; Savai'i and this Manu'a are one; these two were the parents of I'i and Sava; I'i was the girl, and Sava was the boy; that island was peopled by them, and was named Savai'i.

"And Tagaloa-savali went again to this Manu'a; then he stood and faced the Sky, as if he were making a prayer; Tagaloa, the creator, looked down, and the land of Upolu sprang up. Then Tagaloa-savali stood again and faced the Heavens toward Tagaloa-fa'a-tutupu-nu'u; and Tagaloa, the creator, looked down from the Heavens and the land of Tutuila sprang up.

"Then Tagaloa-savali turned to the Heavens, and said, 'Two lands are now gotten for me to rest in.' And Tagaloa, the creator, said, 'Come now, go you with Fue-tagata [the Man-begetting Vine]; take it and place it outside in the sun; leave it there to bring forth; when you see it has brought forth, tell me.' Then he took it and placed it in Salea-au-mua, a council-ground, which is now called Malae-la [Marae-ra—Council-ground of the Sun]. Then Tagaloa-savali was walking to and fro; and he visited the place where the *fue* was; he went there, and it had brought forth. Then he went back again to tell Tagaloa, the creator, that the *fue* had brought forth. Then Tagaloa, the creator, first went down; he went to it; he

390

looked, and it had brought forth something like worms; wonderful was the multitude of worms; then Tagaloa-fa'a-tutupu-nu'u shred them into strips and fashioned them into members, so that the head, and the face, and the hands, and the legs were distinguishable; the body was now complete, like a man's body; he gave them heart and spirit; four persons grew up; so this land was peopled; there grew up Tele and Upolu, which are the children of the *fue*; four persons, Tele and Upolu, Tutu and Ila. Tele and Upolu were placed to people the land of Upolu-tele; but Tutu and Ila, these two were to people the land now called Tutuila.

" Fue, the son of Tagaloa, that came down from Heaven, had two names, Fue-tagata and Fue-sa; he peopled the two flat lands.

" Then Tagaloa gave his parting command thus; ' Always show respect to Manu'a; if anyone does not, he will be overtaken by calamity; but let each one do as he likes with his own lands.' "

The story of the creation of Samoa ends with this parting command, which was given at Malae-la.

How much of the collector's own personality has entered into this it is difficult to say; it always is difficult to say this as regards myths and traditions collected from uncivilized peoples, and it is therefore always preferable to preserve the tradition in the literal original, as has been done in this instance. It is certain, too, that the finer receptacle will receive the finer wine of thought, preserving the mellowness imparted to it by age.

Hawaiian Mythology

Dibble has much to say on the subject of Hawaiian mythology, but he seems to have been prejudiced by asceticism, and his accounts are unreliable. He mentions Kanaloa as one of the four Hawaiian gods, or one of the four hundred thousand; other writers with less unchristian charity, but yet with some Christian bias, reduce these gods to three, wishing to show that the Hawaiian mythology was in reality Christian in origin, and that the ancient Hawaiians at one time believed in and worshipped one god, comprising three beings, Kane, Ku, and Lono, equal in nature, but distinct in attributes. Of these one was considered superior to the other two, and they formed a triad, commonly referred to as Ku-kau-akahi (Ku stands alone, or Ku established). Another ancient name was Oi-e, or Kane-oi-e. These existed before chaos, from eternity, by an act of will breaking or dissipating the all-pervading night or chaos, Po, and causing light to enter the darkness. They then created the heavens, three in number, as their dwelling, " and the earth to be their footstool," also creating the sun, moon, and stars, and a host of spiritual ministrants. Last of all they created man in the likeness of Kane. The body of the first man was made of red earth and spittle, his head of whitish clay, brought from the four ends of the earth by Lono. When the earth-image was ready the three breathed into its nose and called upon it to rise, and it became a living being. Afterward the first woman was created from one of the ribs, taken from the man as he slept. Even the Garden of Paradise and the Deluge are found in these old Hawaiian legends, but apparently only by those anxious to find traces of the Hebrew mythology in the Hawaiian. Two chants, said to be ancient, are quoted by Fornander:

> O Kane, O Ku-ka-pao [an epithet of Ku as constructor],
> And the great Lono dwelling on the water,
> Brought forth are Heaven and Earth,
> Quickening, increasing, moving,
> Raising up into Continents.
>> The great Ocean of Kane,
>> The Ocean with dotted seas,
>> The Ocean with the great fishes,
>> And the small fishes,
>> Sharks and *niuhi* [large sharks],
>> Whales,
>> And the large *hihimanu* of Kane.
> The rows of stars of Kane,
> The stars in the firmament,
> The stars that have been fastened up,
> Fast, fast, on the surface of the heaven of Kane,

And the wandering stars,
The tabued stars of Kane,
The moving stars of Kane;
Innumerable are the stars;
The great stars,
The small stars,
The red stars of Kane.   O infinite Space!
   The great Moon of Kane,
   The great Sun of Kane,
   Moving, floating,
   Set moving about in the great space of Kane.
The great Earth of Kane,
The Earth gathered together by Kane,
The Earth that Kane set in motion,
Moving are the stars, moving is the moon,
Moving is the great Earth of Kane.

The second chant reads:

Kane of the great Night,
Ku and Lono of the great Night,
Hika-po-loa, the king,
   Who tabued Night that is set apart,
   The poisonous Night,
   The barren, desolate Night,
   The continual darkness of Midnight,
   The Night, the reviler.
O Kane, O Ku-ka-pao,
And great Lono dwelling on the water,
Brought forth are Heaven and Earth,
Quickened, increased, moving,
Raised up into Continents.
   Kane, lord of night, lord the father,
   Ku-ka-pao, in the hot heavens,
   Great Lono with the flashing eyes,
   Lightning-like lights has the lord
   Established in truth, O Kane, master-worker;
The lord-creator of mankind:
Start, work, bring forth the chief Ku-honua [a
    name of the first man],
And Ola-ku-honua the woman;
Dwelling together are they two,
Dwelling in marriage with the husband, the brother.

There is no mention of animals in the chants, but from
the prose tradition the world when produced was evidently

393

stocked with animal and vegetable life. The animals specially mentioned are hogs, dogs, and lizards, or reptiles (*mo'o*, or *moko*). As in New Zealand, in Hawaii there are legends of reptiles of a far greater size than any now found in the islands, as though they were a memory of creatures encountered in a traditional past—unless, indeed, they, together with the monsters of the old metrical romances, are merely poetic imaginings, or such playful exaggerations as are common in the childhood of thought awakening to a perception of its own magical powers.

When the Garden of Paradise, or Pali-uli, is described, and is said to have contained a tabued breadfruit-tree, and a sacred apple-tree, and a lying serpent, then the doubt of the antiquity and genuineness of these traditions becomes strengthened. They appear to be grafts on an old stock, as much of the tradition of the group, the Hawaiian, is a graft due to the Tahitian migration.

The three gods Kane, Ku, and Lono are sometimes regarded as the personifications of light, stability, and sound respectively; again, they are regarded as the originator, the architect and builder, and the executor and director of the elements, and as a trinity were known as Hika-po-loa, named in the second chant above. Kanaloa was altogether deposed, being transformed to a Lucifer, leading other evil spirits to rebellion, and being thrust by Kane into uttermost darkness, where he ruled with the evil Miru. When Kane made the first man, Kanaloa made a similar figure, but was unable to endow it with life, for which reason he said, " I will take your man, and he shall die."

In New Zealand Tangaroa, the Maori form of the name Kanaloa, was regarded as a god of the sea and tutelary deity of fishes; he was father of the famous Tini-rau. He shared with Rona, the moon-god, in the control of the tides, being then known as Tangaroa-whakamau-tai, Rona being known as Rona-whakamau-tai. He was very little known in the South Island of New Zealand, where he was said to be seen occasionally in the spray of the sea when the sun shone.

This exalting of a god at one time, debasing him at

another, is a universal occurrence; even the God of the Old Testament has given way to the God of the New. " The god of whom I speak is dead," said a witness in a native land-court in New Zealand. " Gods do not die," said the court. " You are mistaken," said the witness; " gods do die unless there are *tohunga* to keep them alive." The remark embodies a whole philosophy, and explains the wax and wane of the deities here as elsewhere. As a sea-deity Tangaroa had an altar at the stern of sea-going canoes, a custom observed since the coming from Hawaiki. And since the puncturing instrument used for tattooing was made of whalebone, the person being tattooed would not eat fish or shellfish without first holding it before his face so that Tangaroa might see the tattoo, or the pattern might be warped out of proportion.

Cosmogony of Society Islands and Tuamotu

The French voyager Moerenhout, dealing particularly with the Society Islands and the Tuamotu archipelago lying to the east of them, writes with great *empressement* of the loftiness of the cosmogonic conceptions of the people of these regions. The savage, lost in the regenerating influence of meditation, conceives the deity in the act of creating the universe, hears the word that causes all things to be: " You —pivots, and rocks, and sands ! We are. . . . Come, you who are about to form this earth."

He urges them, he urges them again, but they have no wish to unite. Then with his right hand he sets the seven heavens to form the first foundation. Light is created, darkness is no more. All is revealed; the universe shines in sphering light. God rested, rapt in ecstasy on beholding immensity. The task of the harbingers is fulfilled; the mission of the speaker is accomplished; the pivots are fixed; the rocks are in place; the sands are settled. The heavens revolve, the skies are lifted up, the sea fills the depths, the universe is created.

Moerenhout thinks that these are not the ideas of a mere savage dancing on the shore in a defiant brandishing of arms against an as savage enemy. They are the ideas of a Zoroaster, a Pythagoras, who, having long meditated on the marvels of nature, sees in them the work of some divine creator ; they are the ideas of a theist who, recognizing God in His works, is exalted in a religious fervour to the apprehension and adoration of an omnipotent being.

The other fragments of creation myths call for a similar interpretation. Moerenhout thinks them perhaps an indication of some higher state of civilization, of which the scattered Polynesian peoples were but the broken wreckage. So man was considered a fallen angel, bearing within him attributes of the divine and memories of his divinity. These divine attributes may, however, be the flowering birth of a creature mounting from a lowlier state to a higher ; the exalted ideas not a recollection, but a fore-vision of divinity to come and glory to be enjoyed. The religious fervours are the ever-strengthening wings bearing the aspiring soul higher and higher ; there may be resting-places, there may be occasional drooping and despondency ; but the course, the desire, are ever upward.

Moerenhout found that the people had a considerable knowledge of astronomy, of the motion of the heavenly bodies, and that they believed the moon to be a globe similar to the earth, inhabited like the earth, and producing an abundance of similar growth and life. He quotes a song-fragment on the birth of the stars, which, while couched in enigmatic language, reveals an exalted imagination, an aptitude for scientific speculation :

> Roua—
> Great is his origin—
> Slept with his wife
> The gloomy earth:
> To her *arii*, the sun,
> She gave birth;
> Then was born the day;
> Then shadows,
> Obscure and dark;
> Then Roua
> Put from him
> This woman.

IO, TANGAROA, AND CREATION

Roua-touboua—
Great is his origin—
Slept with the woman
Named Taonoui [Great Reunion].
Then were born *arii*,
The stars appeared,
The moon,
The star Faiti.

The king,
The golden heavens,
Slept with his wife
Fanoui;
Of her was born
The *arii* Faouroua,
Faouroua,
Star of the morning,
To the night lawgiver,
And to the day,
To the sun, and to the moon,
And guide to seafarers.

To the left he soars,
To the north, and there,
With his wife sleeping,
The guide to seafarers,
Is born the red star,
The red star of evening,
Two-visaged,
The red star, the god
Who seeks the west,
Preparing his pirogue [1]
The great day,
Which sails toward heaven,
Spreading his sail
At sunrise.

Rahoua
Into space advances,
Into limitless horizons,
Sleeps with his wife
Oura-taneipa.
Then are born
The Twins,
Over against
The Pleiades [Matariki].

[1] As it were, the chariot of Apollo.

MYTHS OF THE POLYNESIANS

In this song the deity Roua is once translated Roua-
touboua, and the word *touboua* follows his name wherever
occurring in the original text. This is equivalent to the
Maori Rua-tupua. The name does not connect this with
other creation myths, though Rua-tipua (or Rua-tupua)
was the name of one of the " props " used in the separation
of Rangi' and Papa' ; but a note by Moerenhout does
connect it, for he says that this god is often confused with
Ta'aroa (Tangaroa), and that some say that it was he who
created the earth, the sky, the stars. He believed that
Faiti was intended as the evening star, Faouroua as the
morning star. Of the names occurring in the original text
he says that Houi-tarara, or the Twins, were the same as
Castor and Pollux of the constellation Gemini ; Atouahi
was the evening star, and Naunou-oura, shining with two
faces, was Sagittarius. Rahoua also was a star, the year
commencing when it appeared in the evening—that is,
toward October. Some of these names occur elsewhere.
Atutahi, or Autahi, was Canopus in New Zealand, and was
regarded as a very *tapu* star. It is said to have been one of
the most useful guides to voyagers from other parts of
Polynesia to New Zealand, and its varying appearance gave
weather-indications. To it offerings of food were made,
and songs sung. Fanoui is the Maori Whanui, the star
Vega. While the other names are not among those collected from the Maori, *hui*, or *huihui*, is a cluster of stars,
and the first part of the name Houi-tarara is the same as the
Maori *hui*. Then in the song quoted by Moerenhout the
word *arii* (*ariki*) constantly occurs in connexion with one
or other of the heavenly bodies. In Maori the term
whanau ariki is applied to the heavenly bodies as a whole,
to denote their superior status. In the last stanza quoted
the name Roua is spelt Rahoua, which brings it very near
Rehua, a well-known star-name in New Zealand. The
French represented the Polynesian *u* sound by their *ou* ; it
is the same as our *oo*.

Of the twins, Houi-tarara, it is said that they were originally mortal children of Borabora. Hearing their parents

398

speaking of separating them, they left their home and fled together, first to Ra'iatea, then to Ouhaine, then to Eimeo, and then to O-taiti (Tahiti). Their mother followed after in search of them, but always arrived at the different islands just too late. However, on Tahiti she heard that they were still there, hiding in the mountains; she followed and discovered them, but they fled to the summit of a lofty mountain; and when she, following them, believed that she at last had caught them they flew upward toward the skies, where they have since remained among the constellations.

There is a similar story in the Hervey Islands, where the two twin children were a girl, Piri-ere-ua (Inseparable), and her younger brother. Their mother Tara-korekore was a scold, and she gave them no peace. After fishing on the reef till midnight she returned home with her basket of fish, woke her husband, and they cooked and ate a meal. She would not agree to the husband's suggestion that they should wake the children to share the savoury meal, but put away their portions in their baskets.

Now the children were awake, waiting for their mother to bring them their share of the good things, and hearing that they were to get none until the morning they wept in silence. When the parents were asleep the girl proposed that they should leave them for ever; and while at first the boy hesitated, at last he agreed to his sister's proposal. Cautiously they started off, and upon reaching an elevated point of rock again they sat down and wept, each filling a little hollow in the rocks with parting tears, but without in the least swerving from their purpose. At last they leaped into the sky, Piri-ere-ua keeping tight hold of the end of her brother's girdle.

As soon as the morning star appeared the mother went to rouse the children, so that they might eat their fish and *taro*; but they were gone. Their little bed of fragrant dry grass was cold, and moist with tears. Hastily calling her husband, with him she went out in search of the children, tracing the path they had taken by their tears. The little sparkling hollows revealed where they had last rested on

399

earth, no further trace being discoverable. In utter perplexity the now sorrowful parents looked up into the sky, where the sun had not yet risen, when to their surprise there they saw the two children, shining brightly. Vainly they called on them to return ; but as the children gave no heed to their calls they leapt up in pursuit of the twins. But the children had the start of their parents, and made their way across the shining skies, where the parents still vainly pursue them. All four shine brightly ; but the parents Potiki and Tara-korekore, being bigger, exceed the children in brilliancy. These stars are not in the constellation Gemini, but in Scorpio, the parents being the two bright stars forming the sting of the tail, the children the double star close to the claw that lies on the same side as the tail.

The Story of Pipiri ma in Tahiti

The same story is known in Tahiti, but the details differ. There the father's name is Taua-tiaroroa, the mother's Rehua. The children are Pipiri, the boy, and his sister Rehua, the same name as the mother's. They are not said to be twins, and the sister is the feebler of the two. In the story they are referred to as Pipiri ma, the word *ma* being simply a sign of the plural ; in Maori it signifies plurality— three or more.

One beautiful clear night the parents went fishing by torchlight, and on their return the husband prepared fire for cooking some of the fish for supper. The appetizing smell of the cooking fish, and other delicacies being prepared by the mother, whetted the appetites of the two children, who lay awake listening to what was going on. The mother suggested that the children should be awakened to share the delicious meal ; the father hesitated, but decided that it would be a pity to waken them, and the disappointed children wept quietly. They determined to leave their parents, crept from their bed, and noiselessly slipped away.

Their meal finished, the parents retired. The mother, whose thoughts had been with her children, felt for them and perceived that they were no longer there ; their bed was deserted. Searching about, the parents found the aperture by which they had escaped; they hastened outside, and in the half-light of early dawn they saw the children fleeing in the distance, the less active sister helped by the brother, who held her hand. " O Pipiri ma ! " they cried; " Pipiri ma ! " " Return to our parents," said the sister to her brother ; " return." The brother, who had conceived the escapade, wept, but made no response.

The parents came nearer and nearer ; seeing which, Pipiri ma climbed on to a stag-beetle happening to pass at the moment, and on its back they were carried up into the skies.

The parents saw them rapidly receding, and cried, " O Pipiri ma ! Pipiri ma ! return, return to us."

" No," answered the children ; " unpalatable is the fish caught by torchlight ; not even one fish for the children." And an evil spirit, meeting them by the way, encouraged them in their flight.

Again the parents called as before ; and, as before, the children answered them. Then said Taua-tiaroroa, " It is no use following them ; let us return."

But Rehua did not hear her husband, repeating, full of sorrow, " O Pipiri ma ! return, return to us ! " But from afar came faintly the cruel words :

" No ; unpalatable is the fish caught by torchlight ; not even one fish for the children."

Since that time, when the glorious constellations of the South appear in the sparkling sky the gentle-hearted Tahitians say, pointing to the shining sweep of the Scorpion :

" There they move, Pipiri ma, changed to stars. One night they were borne aloft by the stag-beetle, who also was changed to a star, the redly glowing torch yonder."

Their spirit saddened for a moment by the legend, they pause as they gaze above, then resume their steps as they murmur on their breath the plaintive words : " O Pipiri ma ! "

The very children of Tahiti may be heard singing the little song :

" O Pipiri ma,
Return to us."
" No, never will we return:
Unpalatable is the fish caught by torchlight;
Not even one fish for the children."
They have departed; twin clusters of rosy flowers
    in the sky.

The brother and sister are seen in the last two stars of the tail of the Scorpion, Pipiri preceding the tinier sister Rehua; the redly glowing torch is the bright Antares, the heart of the Scorpion.

CHAPTER XII: TANE' AND RONGO

Stars spread on Rangi'

THERE are more varied embodiments of Tane' in natural objects than of any other god. In New Zealand particularly he was the personification of light and fertility; he it was who caused the light to dawn when he separated Rangi' from Papa'. One version says that it was because of his being wounded by Tangaroa that Rangi' lay close to Papa'; he was unable to stand. When they were parted Tane' looked upward, and saw that Rangi' lay naked. He took red colouring, and with it covered the body of his parent, but, dissatisfied with the result, swept it away. There were certain cloaks of darkness that had stars for fastenings, and these twinkling fastenings he thought would look well if disposed over the body of Rangi'. Some say these fastenings were beings; that they were the shining offspring of Kohu, which is mist, and Ika-roa, the Milky Way.

Some, again, say that when he went a-star-gathering Tane' heaped the shining ones in a receptacle, and that that receptacle was the Milky Way. One was left hanging outside; that was Atutahi, which is Canopus. The receptacle was placed in the *waka* Uruao, generally known as Te Waka-o-Tama-rereti, which is the tail of the Scorpion.

There are other wonder-tales concerning these heavenly lights. It is said that while Tane', having searched for and found the stars, lay and slept a younger brother named Wehi-nui-a-mamao caught them and fixed them as ornaments to his houses Hira-uta and Hira-tai, Pari-nuku and Pari-rangi, where Tane' on awakening beheld them shining. His younger brother agreed that they should be placed on the body of their father Rangi', for its adornment, and there accordingly they were placed, their coming and going ordered, and the coming and going of the sun and moon.

Trees set on Papa'

Rangi' had been now made beautiful; and so that the body of their mother Papa' might not be bare Tane' went

403

and sought trees that he might cover her with the whispering shadow and the shimmering coolness of the forests. At first the trees stood as men, with feet firmly set on earth; but their appearance did not please Tane'; he thought how he himself had lain with legs upthrust when he had separated his parents, and he set the trees with their heads in the earth, their limbs pointing upward. Roots sprang from the hair, branches and leaves from the body and limbs, and what once seemed men seemed men no more.

Has this act of Tane' an appearance of strangeness? It should have none to us, for six hundred years ago, in about 1340, Richard Rolle of Hampole, in *The Pricke of Conscience*, wrote:

> As says the great clerk Innocent.
> In shape, what is man but a tree
> Turned upside down as men may see?
> Of which the roots that from it spring
> Are hairs that from the head down-hing;
> The stock that next to the root grows
> It is the head, whose neck follows;
> Thereby the body of the tree
> Are breast and belly as men see;
> The boughs the arms are and the hands,
> The legs, the feet, whereon man stands;
> The branches men may rightly call
> The toes and the fingers all.

The Greeks were perfectly familiar with the transformation of men and women into trees—the laurel still breathes her story to the winds, the poplars whisper theirs, and the shivering reeds—but these were not inverted when they struck root, as is proved in the old cuts illustrating the *Metamorphoses*. It is a whimsical fancy, yet does it not seem evident that it has come independently to two widely separated races? And if this, why not others? The diffusion of thought, of culture, is not overlooked, nor is its importance underestimated; but unless a predisposition were there even diffusion would be difficult, if not impossible. It must be remembered that the mind of man, the spirit of man, is as a great sea, ever flowing, ever circulating,

BUSH OF NORTH ISLAND, NEW ZEALAND
Showing the big trees that made such a difference to the Polynesian Maori.
N.Z. Government Publicity Photo
(See page 404)

TANE' BREATHING LIFE INTO HINE-AHU-ONE
(See page 407)

sometimes hidden in darkness, sometimes flashing in light; here and there poets and philosophers give expression to the great sea of thought and emotion, and are comprehended by all. Is it strange if at times they give independent utterance to the same thoughts, the same emotions, and in the same way?

It will have been remarked that most of the important Polynesian deities were males; the female element was considered inferior; indeed, while the male element was regarded as the source of life, the female element was regarded as the source of death. It was also known as *te whare moenga*—the house of rest, the passive element.

Tane' obtains Sacred Knowledge from Io

Tane', in order that Rangi' might be further beautified, had called on the god of winds, Tawhiri-matea, to marshal his clouds and spread them here and there above, like the unrolled *tapa* of Hina'. There had evidently been some kind of reconciliation between Tane' and Tawhiri', for when Tane' was selected as the one to take down to earth the occult knowledge and the lore of Io Tawhiri' assisted him in his ascent by way of Ara-tiatia, which is the whirlwind. Or it may be that the conflict as described between the two belonged only or principally to the fireside version of the story. Another great protagonist in the shadowy scene, however, a veritable adversary of Tane', was Whiro, said also to have sprung from Rangi' and Papa'. He did not wish the parents to be parted, but wished darkness to remain. As noted, Whiro is the personification of darkness, evil, and death. These two, Tane' and Whiro, are as Ormuzd and Ahriman of the Zoroastrians.

When messengers were sent from Io to seek out one to whom the occult knowledge should be imparted, Whiro desired that he might be chosen, and was angered when the choice fell on Tane'. Before ascending Tane' prepared a suitable place for the preservation of the *wananga* (lore), and went to the second of the twelve upperworlds, to Rangi-tamaku, in order to see the pattern on which the house should be built. So was erected the first *whare-wananga* in this world; its name was Whare-kura.

Meanwhile, Whiro had begun the ascent by scaling the side of the heavens; but when he reached Rangi-tamaku he learned that Tane' had already reached the third upperworld, and sent his hordes to attack him and beat him back; but the wind deities came to the assistance of Tane' and beat back the hordes of Whiro.

Tane' went on to the tenth upperworld, where all his companions but two returned to the earth. In this region he was purified before ascending to the highest of the upperworlds, and at Pu-motomoto, the entrance to the twelfth upperworld, he was met by Rehua and other attendants of Io, his two companions retiring to the eleventh upperworld.

He was conducted to Io, and after further purification he was given the three receptacles of knowledge. He was escorted to the eleventh upperworld, where his companions rejoined him. On reaching the ninth upperworld he was again assailed by the hordes of Whiro; but these were once more dispersed, some of them being taken prisoner and brought to the earth. Hence the mosquito, sandfly, bat, owl, and other creatures still torment mankind.

Eventually Whiro was overcome by Tane', and was compelled to descend to the netherworld, where he still dwells; it is he who instils thoughts of evil into human minds. He also it is who controls the deities of sickness and disease, sending them covertly up from their dark lairs to assail mankind. The representative of Whiro upon earth is the lizard, which signifies death.

Tane' begets Trees

The acts of beautifying by Tane' seemed but the precursors of a desire to beget; his creations had so far been no more than the work of his hands. He asked of the earth-mother, of Papa', where a mate for him might be found. She bade him seek Mumu-hango; he did so, but the child that sprang from her was the *totara*, a forest tree.

He sought Pu-whakahara, but she produced the *ake-rau-tangi*, also a tree. So Ata-tangirea produced a *maire*; Kuraki a *kahikatea* (white pine); Otunairanga a *nikau*; Ngaore the *toetoe*; Pakoti the *harakeke* (New Zealand flax); Kui-uku the *matai*; Tuwaerore the *rimu* and the *tanekaha*; Maiteata the *manuka*. Rangahore produced mountain stones; Hine-tu-a-maunga the rusty pools of water in the hills; Haere-awaawa the bird called *weka*; Uru-tahi the *tui*; Papa the *kiwi*.

In the superior version of the myth the gods sought through the heavens for the female element from which mortal man might be produced. The female deities could produce only deities, and that was not what was desired. They sought everywhere, and in vain. Then it was that Tane' mated with the various goddesses enumerated, and with others, but mortal man was not produced.

Tane' creates a Female Being

Tane' created, but his creations did not give him the satisfaction he desired. Hitherto he had produced trees, shrubs, birds, and objects unresponsive; he desired progeny in his own form, but mortal. Then certain of the gods called to Tane', bidding him seek the beach Kura-waka, where rose the *mons* of the earth-mother, of Papa'. There he was to gather sand and shape a body similar to his own. He did so. He completed the figure, extended himself upon it, breathed life into it, and a living being quivered to warmth and motion, and he named her Hine-ahu-one. In the degraded version the name appears as Hine-haone and Hine-hau-one.

Here the same problem confronted the Maori mind that confronted the Greek mind, as it no doubt has confronted every mind awaking from the slumber of unself-consciousness; in the Greek it found expression in the pastoral idyll *Daphnis and Chloe*, in the Maori it produced the less-known chant of Tane'. First his mate produced an egg, from which sprang birds, and Tane' feared a repetition of the old unsatisfying begettings; but the second child was a maid,

407

who was first named Tiki-kapakapa, and afterward Hine-a-tauira, the Pattern Maid.

As she grew in beauty the heart of Tane' was gladdened, since he had thus obtained as companion a living, moving being, fashioned like himself. As she matured Tane' loved her; and as his love for her increased so his love for Hine-ahu-one diminished, and she sank back to earth, leaving Tane' the father and lover with his Pattern Maid. In the same way Rongo of the Mangaian legend took his daughter Tavake to wife, one of their children being Aka-tauira, a name reminiscent of Hine-a-tauira. Such consanguineous unions were not always regarded with reproach; in Hawaii, on the contrary, they were rather regarded with favour, a chief wedding with his sister, or his niece, or his daughter, often thereby exalting the royalty of his line, and adding honour to his house; apparently no deterioration resulted from such unions.

The Maori, however, did not favour consanguineous marriages; he held that at any rate three generations from a common ancestor should separate any couple desiring to mate.

The Daughter of Tane' becomes the Mother of Death

While Tane' was living happily with his daughter he paid a visit to his elder brother Rehua in the upperworld. They wept over each other in greeting, and Rehua ordered that food be prepared. Calabashes were brought, and Rehua then loosened his long locks, shook them, and out flew flocks of *tui*, which were caught and prepared for food. But Tane' would not eat of this food, since the birds had fed on the sacred head of his elder brother. He took some of the living birds, however, and placed them in his forests. This incident is sometimes related in connexion with the search of Rupe for his sister, and it is an instance of the sometimes inextricably tangled nature of these myths. It is an ultra-fireside version of some finer myth, glimpses of which may be caught when it is remembered that Rupe is a personification of the pigeon and that Tane' is lord of the forests. As for Rehua, the word in Maori is used only for the beneficent deity, or for a star or planet, probably Jupiter. In Hawaii, however, the word *lehua* is the name of a tree, and at one time meant forest; so that the shaking of the locks of Rehua is the shaking of the forest branches. Moreover, another version tells how the birds liberated by Tane' were fed on the *kutu* (parasites) of younger deities than Rehua, of Maire and Miro, and Kahika, and others, all names of trees, where the parasites clearly mean the fruits.

During the absence of Tane' Hine-a-tauira, led by natural curiosity, inquired of the people regarding her parentage. She knew Tane' as her husband, and when she learned that he was also her father she fled in shame to the netherworlds, so that on his return he found her gone. In troubled sorrow he followed. She had arrived at the place of Hine-a-te-ao in the netherworld, who had said, " Return; I am Hine-a-te-ao, the daughter of light, and this is the division between night and day." Hine-a-tauira took no heed, but persisted in her desire and passed on. Then Tane' arrived, and Hine-a-te-ao asked of him, " Where are you going?" " I seek my wife," said he. " She will not be overtaken by you," said the *tipua*; " she has rushed on recklessly; she will not be overtaken by you." " Nevertheless, let me pass," said Tane'. " Come, then," said Hine-a-te-ao. " Follow after your wife."

On Tane' went until he came to the darkness, the Po, of Hine-a-te-po. " Where are you going?" said she. " I seek my wife," said Tane'. Said this *tipua*, " I have spoken thus to her, ' Return from this place, as I, Hine-a-te-po, am here. I am the barrier between night and day '; but she would not hearken to me." " Let me pass on," said Tane'; and the *tipua* allowed him to pass.

When Tane' arrived at the darkness of Hine-ruaki-moe his wife had for some time been in the house of Tu-kai-nanapia. He came to the house, but he could not enter; he tried to pass, but in vain.

" O mother," he cried, " come; let us two return to our place above." She replied, " Do you return to the world of day, there to nourish some of our children; and leave me here in the world of night, so that I may drag some of them here to me." She would not listen to his entreaties. "You go to the world of light," said she; "I will for ever dwell in the house of Tu-kai-nanapia, in Poutere-rangi."

Tane' grieved for his wife, and sang this song of love to her:

> "Art thou a child
> To put away the fondling of years?
> Am I a parent
> That we are severed by Rohi-te-kura?
> Throbbing is my solitary heart,
> Being by you forsaken.
> In Te Rangi-pohutukawa
> Will I enter and mourn;
> I will pass from sight through the doorway
> Of the house called Poutere-rangi.
> Ay me!"

And Hine', whose love was less only than shame, sang her love in reply to Tane':

> "Art thou Tane',
> And art thou my father,
> The food-provider at Hawaiki?
> The *tohunga* of sacred rites
> Of the *kumara* harvest
> Left by me in Rangi-pohutukawa?
> I will depart and weep
> At the door of the house Poutere-rangi.
> Ay me, *ai*!"

Tane' returned to the darkness of Hine-a-te-ao, where he slept, and in one legend it states that it was now that, on waking, he saw some of the beautiful offspring of Ira, the trembling stars. Joyfully he admired their beauty, and said to the *tipua*, to Hine-a-te-ao, "Those are beautiful things standing yonder." "What would you do with them?" asked Hine-a-te-ao. "Clothe and beautify my father," answered Tane'. "Have you a desire to go where they are?" "Yes." The *tipua* said, "O young man, there is no road thither; but go by the way that you made when you went to close up the rents in Rangi'—that is, the road to Te Pae-tai-o-te-rangi. But, O Tane', you may catch all the stars, but one you will not catch, as it rests on the very lip of the cave." "The reason I wish to go where those things are," said Tane', "is because they appear so good." She said, "Go; but I do not know if they are kept in houses or not." Tane asked, "What are the names of the houses?" "Koro-riwha-te-po is one," said she, "Koro-riwha-te-ao the other; and the mountain on which the stars rest and display their light is called Mahiku-rangi." Again she said to Tane', "O young man, go! and if you catch the stars, keep fast hold of two of them to be a sign for winter." Tane' came back to his home called Te Rangi-pohutukawa; and having slept two nights there he left and went out to see the offspring of Te Pae-tai-o-te-rangi, and of Ira, and of Tonga-meha; but on his arrival his younger brother Wehi-nui-a-mamao had already caught the stars, as has been told. The stars he set to rule the winter were Wero-i-takokoto and Wero-i-te-ninihi; Wero-i-te-ao-marie was set to rule the summer, and Puanga (Rigel) and Taku-rua (Sirius) to rule the season of planting and harvest. Matariki (the Pleiades), the chief group of the spring or planting season, was known throughout the Pacific.

In the netherworld Hine-a-tauira changed her name to Hine-nui-te-po—the Great Woman of Night, the Mother of Death; and there she gave birth to Po-uriuri, to Po-tangotango, and to Pare-kori-tawa. The first two seem to be personifications of dark night and gloomy night. Po-tangotango, or Tangotango, was the goddess who visited Tawhaki as a lover, though this is in some legends said of Pare-kori-tawa. When she and Tawhaki ascended to the upperworlds they are said to have left a black moth behind them, as token of the relinquished mortal body. Here again the thoughts of Maori and Greek meet in imaginative conception. When toward the spring the sky is covered with small clouds it is said, "Pare-kori-tawa is tilling her garden"—a sign that the time for planting the *kumara* has

411

arrived. In one legend this goddess is mother of Uenuku (the rainbow) and Whati-tiri (the thunder).

Creation of Man (Maori)

Tane' now contemplated the creation of man; and as before he had formed the shape of a woman from earth, so now he formed the shape of a man. There are many variants of this myth. In one it is said that the aquatic plant *makaka*, or *paretao*, growing in swamps, was the male element that engendered the red clay seen in landslips, and that from this red clay Tane' formed the man into whom he breathed the breath of life and whom he named Tiki. The creation of man is also ascribed to Tu-matauenga, who from earth fashioned a form like his own, endowing it with life by means of certain rites, naming him Tiki. Again, Tiki himself is said to have been a deity and to have made the first man; but when the legend says that he also lifted and propped up heaven from the earth it is evident that Tiki and Tane' are being confused.

There are traces of phallic worship in various parts of Polynesia; it apparently preceded the worship of the gods Tane', Rongo, Tu', and Tangaroa, or it may have been coeval, dying out while the worship of the gods persisted, leaving survivals here and there. Many of the myths bear traces of it. In a variant of the Maui'-Raukura-Tuna-roa legend Tiki, the first man, takes the place of Maui'. Tiki, being alone, sought a being as companion, but could find none like himself. Sitting one day beside a clear pool of water, and seeing his own reflection therein, he concluded with delight that he had discovered another person of the same form as himself. He plunged into the pool to secure this companion, but the shadow and his hopes were shattered together. Some time afterward he awoke from sleep, and again saw the image in a little pool of water in the ground near him. He covered it with earth so that it might not escape, and there as from a chrysalis the image developed, and issued as a living companion for him. They lived together for some time without knowledge of the meaning of sex, until

412

one day the woman entered the stream to bathe. An eel came to her, and she became aware of desire. She in turn excited Tiki, and so came about what has in modern times been called the fall of man. The man was incensed against the subtlety of the eel; he sought it, slew it, and cut it into six pieces, from whence sprang the six kinds of eels. This, too, explains why woman is the source of misfortune and death, and why Maui', in attempting to overcome death, made the offending member the point of attack.

Polynesian Phallic Worship

Tiki, again, was a personification of the phallus, the source of fertility; and the charm worn by women round the neck to ensure fertility was named *tiki* after him. In shape it is like a human fœtus, and was also regarded as a charm against the spirits of unborn children; for these, never having known human love, were more than usually malevolent. The pendant has survived the cult in which it originated. From the shape, too, of the *palaoa*, a carved charm worn round the neck by the Hawaiians, it would almost seem as if this had a similar origin.

On Cape Kumukahi, in Puna, Hawaii, there are two pillars of stone, the Pohaku-a-Kane, which, from their shape, and from the ceremonies known to have been observed in connexion with them, are believed to have been phallic stones, dating back to the earlier occupation of the islands. One bore the name of the cape, Kumukahi, the other was called Makanoni.

Similar stones were found in Fiji, near Vuna, Naloa, and other places. Williams, who records the fact, calls them consecrated stones, where offerings of food were sometimes made, but it cannot be gathered that he realized their significance. Their true nature is revealed by the illustration he gives, especially by the one named Lovekaveka, situated near Thokova, Na Viti Levu. He describes it as like a round black milestone, slightly inclined, with a *liku* tied round the middle. The *liku* is a band with a close-set fringe as shown in his illustration, and its presence accentuates

MYTHS OF THE POLYNESIANS

the phallic character of the stone. Such stones might be from six to eight feet high.

Tane' himself has six, sometimes twelve, names which indicate that in the confusion of tongues he was sometimes regarded as the personification of the phallus. The names were given because of the six forms he assumed in his desire for creation of one like himself; they were as follows: Tane-tuturi (Tane the Recumbent), Tane-pepeke (Tane the Bowing), Tane-uetika (Tane Straight as a Tree), Tane-ueka (Tane Strong as a Tree), Tane-te-wai-ora (Tane of the Living Water), and Tane-nui-a-rangi (Great Tane' of Heaven).

In the Rua-tahuna district of the North Island of New Zealand was a phallic tree, known as Te Iho-o-Kataka, whose magical properties had been known for twenty generations. Childless women resorted to this tree, a *hinau*, in order to become fruitful. A woman would be taken to the tree by her husband and a *tohunga*, who would recite the necessary charm while she clasped the tree in her arms. The east side of the tree was the male side, the west the female side, and the woman would make her choice of east or west according as she desired a boy or girl. There seemed to be no doubt as to the efficacy of the ceremony; a belief could scarcely endure for twenty generations without justification to keep it alive.

To the west, at Kawhia, was a boulder called Uenuku-tuwhatu, endowed with similar powers; it too was resorted to by childless women.

At one time flutes were played to women in cases of difficult parturition, and there are old flutes existing which are shaped like a double phallus, apparently a survival of the ancient cult (see p. 338).

Creation of Man, Hawaiian and Other

The Hawaiian account of the creation of man is similar to the Maori account, but more Biblical parallels are introduced. It is almost certain that these details were not in the earlier traditions; and it is usually recognized that there

414

has been much borrowing on the part of the Hawaiians, not only in their traditions, but in their genealogies. For some reason the old lore failed to be transmitted from generation to generation with the scrupulousness usually observed, and the borrowings were from the Hebrew as well as from the Polynesian.

In Vaitupu (Tracey Island, of the Ellice group, north of Fiji), whose inhabitants trace their origin to Samoa, they say that the heavens and the coral rocks of the earth were at one time united, and that vapour from the rocks caused the heavens to ascend. From the same vapour a man was formed, and from the sweat of the man came a woman. The giant brood of the frozen North arose in a similar manner. Between Niflheim, the world of mist and cold, and Muspelheim, the world of fire, lay Ginnunga-gap, where eleven streams, having their source in Niflheim, united and met a poison-stream, congealing to ice. A great thaw hung in Ginnunga-gap between these two worlds, and from the thaw fell drops that took form and received life—a giant human form, named Ymer. As he slept, he fell into a sweat; and from under his left arm issued a man and a woman, while one foot begot with the other a son. From these sprang the Hrimthussar, the frost-giants.

Creation of Woman (Maori)

The Maori myth of the creation of woman is as imaginative, but more beautiful. A wife of 'Ra, the sun, was Arohi-rohi—that is, mirage, or quivering heat. From the warmth of the sun and Paoro (Echo) she formed a woman, Ma-rikoriko; but as the woman was not formed by a god she was not considered of divine origin. To Tiki Ma-rikoriko was given as wife, and to them was born Hine-kau-ataata. Clouds then began to skim over the sky; the clouds stood, they flew. They were dark clouds—black clouds—very black clouds. Water began to flow, and the banks of rivers were seen, and dry land was preserved from floods. Then was the earth seen in the dawn of day. There was lightning, rivulets were, and streams flowed on to the rivers of water.

415

Then came the full light of day, and Tane' propped up the heavens; great Rangi' was seen above; then light and day were complete.

Tane' and the Dawn-maid

After having separated Rangi' and Papa' and made them beautiful with stars and trees, after having introduced love, with the glory of its joy and its pain, and after having created man, Tane' withdrew to the upperworlds. There seems hardly a doubt that Tane' was a personification of light, and as the light of day he separated his parents, propping up the sky, as may be seen morning and evening, with his long beams. His daughter is the dawn, and she ever flees from him, after the brief hesitancy of earliest morning, seeking refuge in the darkness of the west, the netherworld, whither Tane' follows, reappearing to continue the pursuit that never ends while full day follows dawn. In this aspect, too, the Dawn-maid as Hine-nui-te-po acquires another character; Tane' nourishes their offspring on earth, and when in the natural course they seek her land of shadows the Dawn-maid will nourish and care for them there.

In one version of the legend, when the Dawn-maid, fleeing to the underworld, turns and sees Tane' following in sorrow, she says, as she looks on him for the last time, " Return, O Tane', to our offspring. I have abandoned the upperworld as a realm for you; my realm shall be the night beneath us. Turn back, that you may bring up our children to the light of day and that I may guard their spiritual welfare in the spirit world." Who then, losing life, shall fear death? It is a sleep, but not altogether a forgetting, that birth to the spirit world.

The Living Waters of Tane'

Throughout the Polynesian world there is, too, an attribute of Tane' that seems never to suffer degradation. Somewhere, in some serene region, lies Te Wai-ora-a-Tane', usually spoken of as the Living Waters of Tane'. Bathed in these waters, the weary find renewal of strength, the sick

416

are healed, the dead find life. In Maori myth these living waters lay in Hauora, the fourth upperworld, being also known as the Lake Aewa. Here Marama, the moon, when wasted in waning, bathed and gained new strength, coming as Hina-uri (Dark Hina) and emerging as Hina-keha (Pale Hina). Here came the fairy mothers whom Tura found in O-tea, dead from their birth-giving, finding healing and life in the sacred waters. From here the souls of new-born mortals descended to their earthly home.

In Hawaiian myth the region where the lake lay was known by many names, the oldest of which is said to be Kalana-i-Hauola (Kalana with the Living Dew). Hauola is the same as the Maori Hauora. It was also known as Aina-i-ka-kaupo-o-Kane (the Land of the Heart of Kane (= Tane)) and as Aina-wai-akua-a-Kane (the Land of the Divine Water of Kane). It had other names, among which is the beautiful one Pali-uli (the Blue Mountain), but the foregoing clearly connect it with the Maori. In the legends it is often called Aina-waiola-a-Kane, which is still nearer the Maori name. The waters came from a clear overflowing spring, broadening into a pool, as it were a pool of Bethesda. It had three outlets, one each for Kane, Ku, and Lono. The waters had the virtue of healing the sick and restoring the dead to life. It is said that in this region the first man and woman were created.

Among the songs of the Hawaiian *hula* dances there is one of particular beauty. It is called *The Water of Kane*. As the medieval religious feeling flowered in the legend of the Holy Grail, so in most of the Polynesian islands the fervour of the finer religious imagination has risen superior to environment in the legends of the mystical Water of Tane', as if the old and the new were destined to unite—the Sacramental Water to be held in the Grail of Christ. It will be remembered that the best of the myths often appear in two forms, the popular and the esoteric; this Hawaiian song, this *mele*, is on the border-line, but with more than gleams of exaltation :

417

MYTHS OF THE POLYNESIANS

A query, a question,
I put to you:
Where is the Water of Kane?
At the Eastern Gate,
Where the Sun comes in at Haehae;
There is the Water of Kane.

A question I ask of you:
Where is the Water of Kane?
Out there with the floating Sun,
Where cloud-forms rest on Ocean's breast,
Uplifting their forms at Nihoa,
This side the base of Lehua;
There is the Water of Kane.

One question I put to you:
Where is the Water of Kane?
Yonder on mountain peak,
On the ridges steep,
In the valleys deep,
Where the rivers sweep;
There is the Water of Kane.

This question I ask of you :
Where, pray, is the Water of Kane?
Yonder, at sea, on the ocean,
In the driving rain,
In the heavenly bow,
In the piled-up mist-wreath,
In the blood-red rainfall,
In the ghost-pale cloud-form,
There is the Water of Kane.

One question I put to you :
Where is the Water of Kane?
Up on high is the Water of Kane,
In the heavenly blue,
In the black piled cloud,
In the black, black cloud,
In the black-dappled sacred cloud of the gods ;
There is the Water of Kane.

One question I ask of you :
Where flows the Water of Kane?
Deep in the ground, in the gushing spring,
In the ducts of Kane and 'Loa,

TANE' AND RONGO

A well-spring of water to quaff,
A water of magic power—
The water of life!
Life! Oh, give us this life!

Haehae was the name of the Eastern Gate, the portal in the solid vault of blue through which the sun entered at morning. At sunset the sun, seeming to float on the water, was given the name Kaulana-ka-la (the Floating of the Sun). 'Loa is an abbreviation for the Kanaloa of the original *mele*. Kane and Kanaloa were once journeying together, and when Kanaloa complained of thirst Kane thrust his staff into the cliff near at hand, and out gushed a stream of pure water that has continued to the present day. The place is at Keanae, on Maui.

In this interpretation the coloured clouds, the rains, the continually flowing brooks in the valleys, the limpid lakes, the fresh abounding waters—these are the Waters of Tane'. Other students, however, being asked the same question that elicits the *mele*, would say that, as Tane' is light and life, his living waters are the floods of sunshine that brighten the skies and drench the earth-mother with vigour and fill her with the life of tree, and flower, and moving, joyful creature; and it is this sunshine, too, that gives life to Marama herself, the waning and waxing moon.

The Polynesian Paradise

These waters are also connected with the abodes of bliss. In Futuna (Horne Island) the abode of the gods was known as Pulotu, in the midst of which grew an immense tree, the *puka-tala*, the leaves of which supplied all wants, for on being cooked they changed into all kinds of delicious foods. In this region was the Lake Vai-ola, and if the happy denizens of Pulotu felt themselves growing old they had but to bathe in the waters of Vai-ola and they emerged full of life and beauty.

Pulotu was also the name of the netherworld on Savai'i, the largest of the Samoan Islands. Luao, or Luaoo (the Hollow Pit), was the name of the place down which the

419

spirit went on the death of the body. At the bottom of this Hollow Land there was a running stream, which floated the spirits away to Pulotu, the dominions of Saveasiuleo (Savea of the Echo). All floated away together, well- and ill-favoured, young and old, sound and sick, chiefs and commoners; they must look neither to right nor left, nor attempt to reach either side, nor must they look back. Little more than half alive, they floated on until they reached Pulotu, where they bathed in the waters of Vai-ola, when all became lively, bright, and vigorous, every infirmity vanishing, and even the aged becoming young again. Everything went on in Pulotu much as in the world of life, except that here their bodies were singularly volatile, so that they were able to ascend at night, becoming luminous sparks, or vapours, revisiting their former homes, but retiring again in early dawn to the bush or to Pulotu.

The lake lay at the foot of a tree, the *puka-tala*; and, as in Futuna, the leaves furnished a food, exquisite and varied as fancy might desire. In Maori the lake was known as Waiora, or Te Waiora-a-Tane; in that tongue *purotu* means 'pure,' 'clear,' 'transparent' as water; it also means (as it does, too, in other parts of Polynesia) a handsome or beautiful person; for instance, Tawhaki was said to be a *purotu*.

These beautiful myths cannot but call to mind the descriptions of heaven in the Younger Edda, where it is said that the great ash-tree, Ygdrasil, has three roots stretching far out, one to the abode of the gods, one to the land of the giants, one to the world of mists. At each of the three roots is a lake or spring. At the third root, in the world of mists, is the spring Hvergelmer, where the serpent Nidhug gnaws at the root; at the second, in the land of the giants, is Mimer's spring, wherein are concealed wisdom and understanding. It was here that Odin gave an eye to the guardian Mimer for a draught of the waters:

I know all, Odin!
Where now your eye is;
'Tis in the limpid
Fountain of Mimer.

At the first root, in the abode of the gods, is Urd's spring. Here dwelt the Norns, or Destinies, Urd (the Past), Verdande (the Present), and Skuld (the Future). Every day the Norns sprinkle the tree with the waters of the spring, keeping it perpetually green and vigorous, and the dew that falls from the tree, Honey-rain, is the food of the bees. Everything bathed in the spring, too, becomes clear and pure, so wholesome are the waters. The gods did not, however, depend only upon Urd's spring for the perpetual renewal of youth ; they had also the apples of Idun, gathered by her from the tree itself.

In the Tongan belief concerning Bulotu (Pulotu) there is yet another parallel with the Eddic Valhalla. The plants of this region were always perfect in growth, always bearing the richest fruit and the most beautiful and fragrant flowers, others taking their place immediately on any being plucked. It was well stocked with birds and hogs, and these were so far immortal that immediately one was killed for food another took its place. So in Valhalla the hog Saehrimner, though cut up for food one day, was whole again the next. Were Bulotu by chance visited by mortal men, they were unable to pluck the fruit any more than if they were shadows, and they walked through trees and houses, feeling no resistance, as if they were shadows too. Those who dwelt in Bulotu had no need of canoes or other means of conveyance ; they had but to wish to be in a place, and they were there. In Fiji the region was called Mbulotu.

There is an all-pervading beneficence and kindliness, too, in the myths of Tane', his elder brother Rehua, and the supreme Io that make manifest the innate nobleness and elevation of ideal of these Polynesian myth-makers. Their netherworlds, in Te Reinga, have been miscalled hells, places of unhappiness ; of worse—of torment. The Maori knew no such places ; his departing to Te Reinga was mournful only because it was a parting with friends, and all partings are melancholy, however temporary ; but his anticipations found joy in the thought of meeting with friends and relatives who had preceded him, and who would welcome him.

421

MYTHS OF THE POLYNESIANS

The Polynesian did not fear death; for him it held no terrors. It is true there were debasements, permitting of Miru and her witchcraft; but the fiery realm of Pele, the fierce goddess of volcanoes, which might indeed have been a hell, was the reverse; for there the spirits enjoyed themselves, bathing and surf-boarding on the billowy flames like mortals on the billowy seas.

It must be repeated, however, that the beliefs regarding the future had no definiteness of outline; they could have no definiteness any more than can our own; but the faith was as firm as ours, the conceptions were as lofty. The light had of course its contrasting shadow; that too is only natural; and the brighter the light, the darker the contrast.

Whiro and Tu', the Source of Evil

Whiro, the personification of darkness, was in perpetual strife with Tane'. Tu-matauenga, the god of war, also constantly stirred discord, and conspired with other spirits of darkness to overwhelm the upperworlds and the deities of light dwelling therein. He and Whiro play similar parts; and from Tu' and the hosts of Anu came the discord that sets at enmity man, and fish, and bird, so that evil fills the world. Tu' took counsel with Rongo-maraeroa, seeking how they could best overthrow the gods. Like most of the gods, Rongo' had many names according to his various attributes. In Rongo-ma-Tane he is apparently connected with Tane' as god of the *kumara* and cultivated food, Tane' being god of fertility in general. Rongo-maraeroa was the mystical name of the *kumara*. Tu' had degraded his brothers by using their offspring as food, and now one of the degraded ones, the personification Rongo-maraeroa, assisted him in his ambitious projects against his brothers in the upperworlds. Now, assisted by the abjects, the hosts of Anu, who had been thrust into darkness from the upperworlds, Tu' swept upwards, unresisted, the first stubborn resistance being encountered at the battle Puke-nui-o-hotu. Another hill lay above, and it too the hordes of Tu' surmounted, winning a second victory at Puke-nui-papa.

422

The natures of the two deities appeared in this; as they ascended Rongo' continually counselled Tu' to slay as he went, not merely defeat; but the aim of Tu' was apparently conquest only, not destruction. Upperworld after upperworld was won, but there is little coherence in the story, as there could be but little coherence in the thought of it. The battle Taku-tai-o-te-raki was won, the seventh upperworld was attained, but on the eighth being entered the first defeat was suffered at the battle Awa-rua, and Tu' fell, reproached by his ally Rongo-maraeroa for not having followed his advice to destroy as they ascended; for defeat was partly due to the conquered gods following them on recovery and overwhelming them with numbers in the final battle Te Uru-rangi.

Tu' fell to Kai-hewa, and from that abode in the darkness of the underworlds he ceaselessly incites mankind to evil and rebellion. Tu' is widely known, yet there is not so much known of him or told of him as of the other primary gods, even in Hawaii, where the three gods Kane, Ku, and Lono (Tane', Tu', and Rongo') were sometimes spoken of as one, Ku-kau-akahi (Ku stands alone). In Maori myth he was the one who stood alone in that he made war on all his brothers, but through that enmity he seemed to win no more than ignominy. It seems strange, too, that so warlike a branch of the race as the Maori should not have held the war-god in greater esteem; in the South Island of New Zealand, indeed, his place is largely taken by Maru; but the fact that he holds, on the whole, an inferior position would seem to indicate that the Polynesian race was not primarily a warlike race, though certainly capable of warlike genius when occasion arose. War was, as with the Scandinavians, a pleasure, a pastime, not a main object in life. Proverbs are the concentrated wisdom of a people, and there are many Maori proverbs against entering on war, many in praise of peace.

Rongo' as God of Agriculture

Of much greater importance than Tu' was Rongo', whose name appears in the various parts of the Pacific as Ro, Ro'o,

Rono, Lono, Longo, Oro, Orongo. The name Oro is
doubtful; when it appears as O Ro or O Ro'o, then it clearly
is the equivalent of Rongo; but as Oro it is supposed rather
to be the equivalent of Koro ('Oro).

In New Zealand he was god of cultivated food, especially
of the *kumara*, as whose deity he was called Rongo-ma-Tane.
There appears to be great confusion in his names. He is
god of agriculture, and as Rongo-maraeroa he was also
closely connected with the *kumara*; yet *maraeroa* (the extended *marae*, or common) was a name of the sea, so that
the name seems to apply to his other character as male
personification of the moon. Rongo of the Wide Sea, too,
seems a fine title for the moon, and one natural to be conceived by a people familiar with wide ocean spaces. One
genealogy makes Rongo' and Rongo-maraeroa brothers,
sons of Rangi-potiki (another form of Rangi') and Papa-tu-
a-nuku. Many of the names which are compounded of
Rongo and a qualifying suffix are not names of the deity,
and attributes have been given to mortal heroes that properly belonged to the deity, and *vice versa*, so that stories of
deity and mortal have become almost inextricably mingled.

The story has been told of how the first *kumara* were
brought to New Zealand; but that was only one of many
variants of the story; another follows wherein Rongo'
appears.

The *kumara* brought to New Zealand

When Kahu-kura landed in New Zealand he found Toi'
and his people living there. The people cooked food for
Kahu-kura and his friend, the food consisting of root of the
ti-tree, *ponga* (tree-fern), and *roi* (fern-root). Of this they
partook, and in return the people of Kahu-kura cooked
food which they had brought from Hawaiki. The friend
of Kahu-kura, who was called Rongo-i-amo, loosened his
belt, and out of it poured *kao* (dried *kumara*) into seventy
calabashes. This was mixed with water and squeezed into
a pulp with the fingers. Toi' and his people smelt the aroma
of the *kao* as they partook of it, and asked, " What is the

424

name of this food?" Kahu-kura answered, "It is *kumara*."
"Perhaps it can be brought to this land?" said Toi'.
Kahu-kura said, "It can be brought here." Pointing to
a shed, he asked, "What is that over which a shelter is
built to protect it from the sun and rain?" "It is a canoe,"
said Toi'. "By that the *kumara* can be brought here," said
Kahu-kura.

It was at once determined that the canoe, whose name was
Horouta, should go to Hawaiki for *kumara*. That night the
people met; ceremonies were performed and incantations
chanted so that the gods might close up the holes out of
which the wind blew, and calm the waves of the sea, and
attend and guard and uphold the canoe on the voyage, that
she might skim swiftly to Hawaiki.

Horouta was put to sea, with a crew of twice seventy
paddlers, Kahu-kura accompanying them. It was midnight when they landed in Hawaiki, and the *kumara* crop
had been taken up and stored. Therefore Kahu-kura dug
on the cliffs of the coast to obtain *kumara*, and caused them
to fall into the canoe. He remained in Hawaiki, and the
canoe returned, the priest commanding the crew to carry
no other food than *kumara*, as it was sacred to the gods of
peace. She landed at Ahuahu, and when she left that
island one of the crew obtained a bundle of *aruhe* (fern-root)
and took it on board. When the canoe arrived at Whakatane the gods who had charge of her were angry because of
the *aruhe* (which food was used by war-parties), and caused
a great wind to arise. To appease the gods the crew threw
a woman overboard, but she rose to the surface and caught
hold of the bows of the canoe. The crew called on her to
let go or the canoe would capsize; but she would not, and
the canoe turned over. It was damaged, and the piece
spliced on to make it longer, the *haumi*, was broken off, and
drifted ashore. The people wept because of the injury to
their canoe, and they determined to procure another *haumi*.
The people were divided into parties; some to guard the
canoe, some to secure the timber required, some to spear
birds and provide food. The names of the leaders of these

various parties are given in the legend, and many other doings of the people, but these are of no particular interest here.

The legend goes on to explain why *kumara* is not stored with fern-root, or used with it. The *kumara* is called Rongo-maraeroa, and fern-root is called Ariki-noanoa, and both were children of Rangi' and Papa'. Rongo-maraeroa was ordained to be the god of Tu-matauenga, and Ariki-noanoa to be food for man in time of war. When an enemy is on the way to attack a *pa* the inhabitants of the *pa* take some *kumara* and place them on the road over which the enemy will come. If the war-party come near these *kumara* the warriors will be taken with panic, and flee back to their home. The *kumara* is also chanted over by the experts (*tohunga*) previous to the crop being planted, and then taken to a stream, placed in it, and offered to Kahu-kura, as he is the supreme god of crops. When a few of the *kumara* which are to be planted have had the ceremonies and incantations performed and chanted over them, and have been set, the experts go and perform ceremonies at the sacred place (*tuahu*, sometimes *raua*, especially in the South Island). If the god Kahu-kura, represented by a small wooden image, is seen to tremble and shake the experts know by this that he ensures that the crop will not be destroyed by floods, or an enemy, or the gods. The whole crop is then planted.

In another version it was Rongo-i-tua, whose appearance was like that of the rainbow, who came from Hawaiki. On the return voyage some act similar to the one related in the foregoing version displeased the gods, for it was found that after a day's paddling the canoe was still in the same place, and so for days the canoe remained in the one spot. " Let some of you strike me," said Rongo-i-tua, " that this evil may not continue, and that some of you may get back to your home." They struck him and performed the sacred ceremonies over him. He stood up and clung to the clouds, and from thence he swung himself back to his home in Hawaiki. When he got to the clouds his name was changed, and he was called Rongo-tiki.

In this version Rongo-i-tua remained in Hawaiki, but

426

MAORI GREENSTONE AXES
Photo Dominion Museum, Wellington, N.Z.

MAORI WEAPONS ON FLAX CLOAK WITH TANIKO BORDER

Bone-handled tomahawk ; long wooden-handled tomahawk ; *tewha tewha* ; two *taiaha*, with ornament of *kaka* feathers and *mani* dog's hair, diagonally across the cloak ; mere (greenstone or stone) suspended at crossing of the *taiaha*.

Photo Dominion Museum, Wellington, N.Z.

(See page 426)

one day the Kahui-tipua, the then inhabitants of New Zealand, saw a rainbow, which suddenly assumed the form of a man, and Rongo-i-tua stood among them; hence he was ever after known as Rongo-tikei (Rongo the Strider).

Quarrel between Rongo' and Tu'

One legend relates that Rongo-maraeroa quarrelled with his younger brother Tu-matauenga on account of a *kumara* plantation called Pohutu-kawa. Tu' went to Ruru-tangi-akau to procure weapons, and Ruru' gave his own child Te Ake-rau-tangi as a weapon. This child had two mouths, four eyes, and four ears, and four nostrils to his two noses. Then the battle between Rongo' and Tu' began in earnest, and Rongo' and his people were killed. Tu' baked his elder brother in an oven and ate him. Now the interpretation of these names in common words is that Rongo-maraeroa is the *kumara*, and Tu-matauenga is man.

The legend explains thus much, but does not explain the other names. Te Ake-rau-tangi is a tree, *ake-rau-tangi* (*Dodonea viscosa*), commonly called *ake* or *akeake*. From the tough wood of this tree were made *ko*, the digging implement of the Maori—a long, pointed implement, with a step lashed on the side for forcing it into the ground. At the top was carved a double head, a face turned both ways, signifying that the workman must watch both before and behind to guard against surprise. The *ko* was made so that it might be used as either an implement of peace or a weapon of war. *Taiaha*, the characteristic two-edged weapon and emblem of rank among the Maori, were also made from this timber, and one end of this weapon is in the form of two conventionalized faces with four *paua*-shell eyes and long, carved protruding tongue—a deadly striking and jabbing weapon.

While this makes the fable clear, however, it does not resolve the mystery of Rongo-maraeroa.

Rongo-mai a Different Deity

Rongo-mai appears to be a different deity altogether, a son of Tangaroa and father of Kahu-kura; though here

427

again, since Kahu-kura is the rainbow, he is in some way connected with Rongo'.   Rongo-mai was god of the whale, and sometimes took on the form of a whale, as Maru the war-god discovered.   Rongo-mai himself was known as a war-god in the Lake Taupo districts of New Zealand.   His appearance was sometimes in the guise of a comet or meteor.

Again, Rongo-mai was a demigod ancestor of some Maori tribes, and it is told how he with Ihenga and other friends paid a visit to Miru in the lowest netherworld, where they learned magical charms, witchcraft, religious songs, dances, games, including *whai*, or cat's-cradle, from the deities of those regions.   They also learned the charm *kaiwhatu*, whose use is to avert witchcraft.   Ihenga was so unfortunate as to be captured by Miru and retained by her as a sacrifice in *utu* (payment) ; the others got safely back to earth.   This is reminiscent of the Mangaian Miru, whose daughters were so expert in dancing and ball-juggling, besides being of peerless beauty.

Rongo' in Mangaia and Tahiti

The Rongo of Mangaia has already been spoken of.   In that island, too, he was a god of agriculture, having been instructed in that art by Tangaroa.   His *marae* (courtyard, or village common) in Mangaia was called O-Rongo.   It was first set up on the east side of the island, but was afterward moved to the west, where it was at the time of the visit of Captain Cook.   The ' O ' before the name, used so often by Cook, was, as Forster discovered, not part of the name, but a prefix meaning ' the place of,' as in Maori, sometimes being a prefix that has no European grammatical equivalent. Thus the name Rongo appears as O-Rongo, O-Ro, where the long *o* represents two letters with a slight catch between them (Ro'o = Ro(ng)o), the extreme and doubtful form appearing as Oro.

Rongo was also an important deity at Tahiti and the Leeward Islands, and through the Tuamotu group ; indeed, he appears to have been the principal god over a great part of the Polynesian Pacific, his brother Tangaroa supplanting

428

him in Samoa, his brother Tane' in New Zealand. There are certain indications, however, that Tangaroa was the chief god of the earliest migrants into the Pacific, the others coming into prominence as the later migrants appeared, all the gods retaining positions more or less prominent according to the manner in which their worshippers, if they can be called so, were scattered. In Tahiti, too, there was a Romatane, a name that seems the same as Rongo-ma-Tane, as it should properly be Ro'omatane; but both gods, Oro and Romatane, or perhaps the same god in two aspects, were invoked on the death of an Areoi, as will be seen in the chapter following.

Apart from his interest as a mythological figure, Rongo', or Lono, is of especial interest because of the connexion between him and Captain Cook. There was some kind of prophecy that Lono was one day to appear to them, and the Hawaiians apparently thought he had come in the person of the great navigator. The revulsion of feeling experienced by them, partly brought about by the sickness and death of one of the marines, resulted in the catastrophe of the death of Cook.

So far as Europeans are concerned, the two greatest and longest-remembered fatalities that have occurred during the exploration of the Pacific are the death of Captain Cook in 1779 and the loss of La Pérouse in 1788. The latter, because of the uncertainty that enmists the event, is rather haloed with romance; the former, because of the certainty of the details, is shadowed in tragedy.

Lawlessness of Adventurers in the Pacific

To the island natives of the Pacific the incursions of the Old World explorers and traders had from the beginning the shadowy menace of tragedy. Well has it been said of the adventurers that on entering the Pacific they hung their consciences upon Cape Horn; many of them, lawless and turbulent in their own country, rejoiced to come to a part of the world where laws might be utterly disregarded; and those who refused to respect laws that their white fellows

429

could enforce certainly would not respect laws of so-called savages, who were quite unable to enforce them, and suffered fearful retaliation if they attempted to do so. Many instances of this are known; how many are not known? It is idle to say that the white men were welcomed because of the benefits derived from them, the chief of which was iron. The more savage-natured among the islanders—and there were such, as there were equally savage-natured men among the whites—welcomed them because of the firearms they could obtain; and many of the early whalers and traders were nothing nobler than abettors of bloodshed and murder. Even Captain Cook, the mildest commander among them all, writes that the natives always seemed anxious for them to go away. He could see that they were always more or less apprehensive; the white men with their firearms had the power at any moment to pour death among the natives, to whom it seemed no more than caprice that stayed their hands.

The death of the first circumnavigator of the globe, Magellan, was due to a conflict brought about by his attempting to punish the natives for refusing to acknowledge the sovereignty of the King of Spain, many deaths following a futile attempt to wrest a barren glory from ignorant children of nature. One incident may be briefly told to show the barbarity of which the traders were capable.

Captain Metcalf at Hawaii

In 1790 a snow, commanded by Captain Metcalf, anchored off the island of Maui, in the Hawaiian group, and trading was commenced. Native accounts state that he was an irritable and harsh man, liberal in his use of the rope's-end on trifling provocation; yet trade was continued and his ill-usage submitted to for the gain the people thought they obtained in the barter.

Kalola, widow of Kalaniopuu, with her new husband Kaopuiki, was among those who brought hogs and other produce for trade. It is not known that these received ill-usage from Captain Metcalf, but others did; and noticing

430

that the ship's boat was left towing astern during the night, Kaopuiki resolved to possess himself of the boat. This was effected on the following night; the boat was cut adrift, the watchman, who had fallen asleep in her, was killed, and the boat towed ashore and broken up for the sake of the iron fastenings.

When the loss of the boat and the death of the seaman were discovered in the morning Captain Metcalf fired on the people on shore, and took two prisoners, from one of whom it is thought that he received information as to who had stolen the boat. In a day or two the vessel went to another anchorage, but no canoe came to her for three days, owing to a *tapu* that had been put on the place by Kalola. On the *tapu* being lifted, however, canoes crowded to the vessel for the purpose of trade, supposing that recompense for the loss of the boat had been taken in the attack on the inhabitants at the anchorage lately left.

As the canoes collected around the ship the Captain ordered the guns and small arms to be loaded. The unsuspecting natives were ordered to keep their canoes off the waist of the ship, and when any strayed either to the bows or the stern they were driven off until they rejoined the fleet lying off either broadside of the ship waiting for trade to commence. When all was ready Captain Metcalf mounted on the rail and gave orders to open the ports of the ship. The guns, loaded with small shot, were fired into the crowd of canoes lying within easy range on both sides. Over a hundred were killed outright, and several hundred more or less seriously wounded. Captain Metcalf then lifted anchor and sailed for Hawaii.

CHAPTER XIII : THE AREOI SOCIETY AND THE HULA DANCE

CONNECTED with the deity Rongo' was that curious institution the Areoi Society, known only in the Tahitian group and the adjacent islands. It was semi-religious, and was said to be of divine origin. Through Hina' Ta'aroa created and produced Oro-tetefa and Uru-tetefa. They were called the brothers of Oro (? O Ro'o = Rongo), the son of Ta'aroa, and were considered to rank as divinities.

Oro desired a wife from among the daughters of Ta'ata (Tangata), the first man created. He sent his brothers Tufara-pai-nu'u and Tufara-pai-rai to seek a suitable companion for him. They searched through the islands, but not until they came to Borabora did they find a woman fit to become the wife of Oro. Here, near the foot of Moua-tahuhu'ura (the Red-ridged Mountain), they saw Vai-raumati. "This is an excellent woman for our brother," the one said to the other.

Returning to the skies, they hastened to Oro, and told him of their success; they described the place where she lived, and represented her as a woman possessed of every charm. Oro fixed the rainbow in the heavens, one end of it in the skies, the other resting in the valley at the foot of the Red-ridged Mountain, and this formed his pathway to the earth.

When he emerged from the cloud-like vapour which encircled the rainbow he discovered the dwelling of Vai-raumati, and she became his wife. She bore him a son, named Hoa-tabu-i-te-ra'i (Hoa-tapu-i-te-rangi—Sacred Friend in the Heavens). This son became a powerful ruler among men.

The absence of Oro during his visits to Vai-raumati in the valley of Borabora induced his two younger brothers Oro-tetefa and Uru-tetefa to leave their abode in the skies and commence a search for him. Descending by means of the rainbow fixed by Oro for his own passage, they alighted

432

on earth near the base of the Red-ridged Mountain, and soon perceived him and his mortal wife in their terrestrial habitation. Ashamed to offer him their salutations without a present, one of them was transformed into a pig and a bunch of red feathers. These acceptable presents the other brother offered to the inmates of the dwelling, as a gift of congratulation. Oro and his wife expressed their satisfaction ; the pig and the feathers remained, but the brother of the god assumed his original form.

Oro, in his turn, to mark his appreciation, made his brothers gods, and constituted them as Areoi by saying " *Ei Areoi orua i te ao nei, ia noaa ta orua tuha'a* "—" Be you two Areoi in this world, that you may have your portion [in the Government, etc.]." In commemoration of this the Areoi in all public festivals carried a young pig to the temple of the gods, strangled it, bound it in the *ahu haio* (a loose, open kind of cloth), and placed it on the altar. They also offered the red feathers, which they called the *uru maru no te Areoi* (the shadowy feathers of the Areoi).

The brothers thus constituted as Areoi lived in celibacy, and had no descendants ; and on this account, while they did not enjoin celibacy upon their devotees, they prohibited their having any offspring, the result being the practice of infanticide. By the direction of Oro, the first company of Areoi was nominated by Oro-tetefa and Uru-tetefa, and comprised the following individuals : Huatua, of Tahiti ; Taura-atua, of Moorea, or Eimeo ; Temaiatea, of Sir Charles Saunders Island ; Tetoa and Atae, of Huahine ; Taramanini and Aripa, of Ra'iatea ; Mu-taha'a, of Taha'a ; Bunaru'u, of Borabora ; and Marore, of Maurua. These were always the names of the principal Areoi from each of these islands, and to them the brother-gods delegated their authority, they being empowered to admit to their society such as were desirous of joining them, provided they complied with all necessary observances.

Forster, who was with Cook, records that the Areoi were recruited from the highest ranks, that the men were in general stout and well made, and were all professed warriors.

He gathered that, while the institution originally required their living in perpetual celibacy, this law, being no doubt repugnant to the impulses of nature, which must, in the climate of the islands, be exceptionally strong, was soon transgressed ; but the object of the law was observed in the destruction of any offspring that might ensue. One probable reason for the existence of the society, according to Forster, was the maintaining of a body of able warriors ; another was the prevention of a too rapid propagation of the chiefs. While at first the existence of the society seemed to the visitor injurious to the rest of the people, he supposed that, among a people so far removed from barbarism as the Tahitians, it could not have existed unless its advantages were more considerable than its disadvantages. While they appeared to live in continual sensuality their indulgence did not go so far as to reduce their vigour ; their wrestling, dancing, and the requirements from them as warriors ensured the maintaining of a high standard of physical fitness.

Moerenhout suggested that the origin of the society might be in sun-worship, interpreting Rongo', the Oro of Tahiti, who originated the society, as a sun-god. He stated that from April or May until the vernal equinox, in September, the Areoi in the Marquesas suspended their performances, mourning the absence of their god, whom they called Mahoui—that is, Maui'. He considered Rongo' and Maui' alternate names of the same god.

In Maori mythology Rongo' is the god of agriculture and fruitfulness ; he is also the male as Hina' is the female personification of the moon. Maui' is without doubt a personification of the sun, though some of the fireside stories concerning him, such as that of his snaring of the sun, may seem to contradict this.

Again, as the names of Rongo' and Tane' are combined in Rongo-ma-Tane, the god of cultivated food, so the names of Rongo' and Maui' appear to be combined in Rongo-maui, the names in both instances combining the two luminaries, the moon and the sun. Rongo-maui was said to be the younger brother of Whanui, the star Vega, which star was connected with agriculture. Rongo-maui obtained *kumara* from Whanui, but was not able to produce it himself. He took to wife Pani, or Pani-tinaku, called the mother of the *kumara*, Rongo-maui being the father. There is much doubt as to the position of Pani in the Maori pantheon, and some confusion. It is not made clearer when it is known that she is spoken of in myth as the aunt and foster-mother of the Maui' brothers. She gave birth to the *kumara* in water, and this appears to be quite anomalous, as the *kumara* has a repugnance to water, growing best in dry, stony soil. It may be that she was at one time connected with the rice-crops, and she seems to be in some way analogous to Ceres.

The names Oro and Mahoui may therefore be seen in Rongo-maui—especially when it is observed that the French represented the *u* sound with *ou*—and they may well have been regarded as gods of the sun and fertility. One of the objects of the Areoi Society seems to have been the representation of the fertility of nature, to which representation was due the indulgence in excesses; though here again it must be remembered that what to European onlookers appeared excesses did not appear so to them, their outlook being entirely different. They took a joy, and an unconcealed joy, in what is one of the miracles of human existence; and if they denied themselves the fruits of that miracle, so far as the Areoi themselves were concerned, there was no doubt some potent reason—as there may be in the present-day denials in civilized society.

The Eleusinian mysteries seem in a similar way to have had their origin in festivals celebrating the return of spring, or fertility, and there seems always to have been a danger of such festivities degenerating into unrestrained excesses.

The kindred society in the Marquesas was called Hoki, or Kaioa. It was composed of a wandering body of poets, musicians, and dancers, and there were regular *tahua* (stone-laid platforms), where they performed, as did the Areoi, before the people. Around the *tahua* were tiers of low,

435

raised terraces serving as seats for the spectators. The *tahua* was, in fact, a kind of open-air colosseum or amphitheatre; and one of them, a particularly large one, is said to have been capable of accommodating ten thousand spectators. It might also be compared with the open-air theatre of the Greeks.

There was this difference between the Areoi and the Kaioa—the members of the former were respected and esteemed; those of the latter were rather despised because of their effeminacy. This difference of attitude, if it really did exist, may be due to the differences in the two peoples, the Marquesans being much more energetic, more well-developed physically, than the Tahitians. The dances of the Kaioa were accompanied by the beating of drums and the singing of a chorus numbering as many as a hundred and fifty. While the entertainers were not so highly esteemed, the entertainments were; and the longest journeys would be taken from all parts of the islands in order to be present. While the entertainment was in progress a general compulsory truce was observed; so that men fresh from engagement with one another in warfare might be spectators together, observing mutual peace, but ready to resume the warfare on the entertainment being ended.

There is no record of exactly similar societies in other parts of the Pacific, unless the Uritoy of the Caroline Islands be considered akin.

In Maori the word *karioi* occurs, and means ' to loiter,' ' to be idle '; in Mangarevan it also occurs, and has been translated ' lewdness '; also in Tuamotuan, where it has been translated ' immodest ' or ' indecent.' It must be remembered, however, that these are European meanings; there were no words with such meanings as our ' lewd ' and ' indecent ' among the Polynesians, for there was no thought or feeling among them requiring such words.

On this question Cook remarks, " Privacy, indeed, is little wanted among people who have not even the idea of indecency. . . . Those who have no idea of indecency with respect to actions, can have none with respect to words;

it is, therefore, scarcely necessary to observe that in the conversation of these people, that which is the principal source of their pleasure is always the principal topic; and that everything is mentioned without any restraint or emotion, and in the most direct terms, by both sexes."

It was some time before the islanders discovered that their white visitors regarded certain things in a different light from themselves; nor is this to be wondered at, remembering one of the chief reasons for the visits of the early adventurers. These things, too, are largely a matter of climate; in a region where the temperature necessitates the covering of the body the covering comes to be regarded as the natural thing; but it is at the dictation of necessity, not modesty. So, too, in the more torrid regions it is at the dictation of necessity, not immodesty.

In a manner the Areoi Society combined the characteristics of the medieval minstrels, and in modified form of the actors in the mystery and morality plays. Their recitals were sometimes in recitative, sometimes in cadence, generally accompanied by the drum and the music of flutes. They sang of the creation of the universe, of the wonders of nature, of the great achievements and exploits of the demigods and heroes, of the voyages of their people, of their battles, their victories, adding expressive gestures to eloquent words; they performed pantomimes, and danced, and their coming was eagerly anticipated, and intensely enjoyed.

In May 1774 Cook saw sixty canoes and upward leaving Huahine at daylight for Ulietea, the occupants being a company of Areoi visiting the neighbouring islands. Forster says there were seventy canoes, and that there were more than seven hundred Areoi on board.

Great preparation was necessary before they set out. Pigs were killed and presented to Oro, and large quantities of plantains, and bananas, and other fruits were offered upon his altars. The preliminary ceremonies occupied several weeks. The concluding part of the preparations was the erection, on board the canoes, of two temporary temples or altars for the worship of Oro-tetefa and Uru-tetefa, the symbols of the gods being perhaps no more than a stone and a few red feathers.

On landing at the place of destination they proceeded to the residence of the principal chief, and presented their offering (*marotai*); a similar offering was also sent to the temple, as an acknowledgment to the gods of the preservation they had experienced at sea. If they remained in the neighbourhood preparations were made for their dances and other performances.

On public occasions they sometimes wore a girdle of yellow *ti* leaves, or a vest of ripe yellow plantain leaves, their heads being adorned with the bright yellow and scarlet leaves of the *hutu* (*Barringtonia*); or their only adornment might be the black and scarlet stain with which they painted their bodies and faces, their faces especially being stained with the *mati*, a scarlet dye.

In reciting a legend or song in honour of the gods or some distinguished Areoi they sometimes sat in a circle on the ground, the leader standing in the centre, introducing the recitation with a kind of prologue, when those that sat around began their song in a low and measured tone, which increased in volume and speed as they proceeded, till it became vociferous and unintelligibly rapid. It was accompanied by movements of the arms and hands, in exact keeping with the tones of the voice, until they reached the highest pitch of excitement.

Their public entertainments frequently consisted in delivering speeches, accompanied by every variety of gesture and action; and their representations on such occasions assumed something of a histrionic character. The priests, and others, were fearlessly ridiculed in these performances, in which ludicrous allusion was made to public events. In a performance, somewhat of this kind, that was witnessed by Cook the story was enacted of a girl who had accompanied the ship with Cook to visit other of the islands; and whatever the nature of the story so enacted was, it brought the girl to tears, and it was with difficulty that she could be persuaded to stay to its conclusion.

Sometimes the Areoi gave exhibitions of wrestling, but never of boxing—a favourite exercise with others, both men and women. Dancing was one of the most popular performances. In this they were led by the chief Areoi, their bodies being stained with charcoal, their faces with scarlet, and the dances often continued through the greater part of the night. Their movements were accompanied by their voices and the music of the flute and hand-drum. The performances might last for several days and nights at the one place, when they moved on to the abode of the next chief, where the performances were repeated.

Substantial, spacious, and sometimes highly ornamented houses were erected in several districts throughout most of the islands, principally for their accommodation and the exhibition of their performances. These might be regarded as theatres. Sometimes they performed on their canoes as they approached the shore, and this was quite possible, as in the fleet were many double canoes with their connecting platform. This they did especially if they had on board the king of the island or any principal chief. When one of these companies thus approached the land, with streamers floating on the wind, bright with red and yellow colours, flutes and drums sounding, the Areoi, attended by their chief, who acted as their prompter, appeared on a stage erected for the purpose, and sang their songs, accompanied with gesture and posture and the sounds of music. The whole, with the deeper accompaniment of the dashing sea, and the rolling and breaking of the surf on the adjacent reef, must have presented an imposing spectacle. Ellis, from whom many of these details are derived, viewed these things with different eyes, as in Stuart times the Puritans viewed the playhouses and singing; and he says it " must have presented a ludicrous, imposing spectacle "; but there are many ceremonies that are imposing to some, ludicrous to others; there are almost as many measures of conduct as there are minds of men.

In such exhibitions the Areoi passed their lives, going from the habitation of one chief to another, and from island to island, welcomed and held in high estimation by the chiefs, but not, according to Ellis, by the cultivators, who must supply the food for their entertainment. But it is probable that even the cultivators derived pleasure from the visits, as in civilized countries the populace derived pleasure from royal progresses, when entertainments were held such as are described in *Kenilworth*. Indeed, Forster, who was an eye-witness long before Ellis was in the islands, says that " their presence seemed to enliven the whole country, and to inspire all the people with extraordinary cheerfulness." Of the Areoi he says, " They frequently shifted their garments, made of their best kinds of cloth ; they passed their time in luxurious idleness, perfuming their hair with fragrant oils, singing and playing on the flute, and passing from one entertainment to another ; in short, they enjoyed the blessings of their island to the utmost extent ; and so much resembled the happy indolent people whom Ulysses found in Phæacia, that they could apply the poet's lines to themselves with peculiar propriety " ; and he quotes from Pope's *Homer* :

> " To dress, to dance, to sing, our sole delight,
> To feast or bath by day, and love by night."

The Areoi fraternity was divided into distinct classes, each of which was distinguished by the kind or situation of the marking on their bodies. The first or highest class, called *Avae parai* (painted leg), had the leg blackened from the foot to the knee ; the second class, *Otiore*, had both arms marked, from the fingers to the shoulders ; the third class *Harotea*, had both sides of the body, from the armpits down, marked with stain ; the fourth class, *Hua*, had only two or three small figures on each shoulder ; the fifth class, *Atoro*, one small stripe on the left side ; the sixth class, *Ohemara*, a small circle round each ankle ; the seventh class, *Poo*, which included all novitiates, was usually called the *Poo fa'arearea* (pleasure-making class), as by them the most laborious part of the pantomimes was performed.

In addition to the seven classes, there were others who

APPROACH OF THE AREOI
(See page 440)

attached themselves to the fraternity, preparing their food and dress, travelling with them, and performing various menial services. They were called *Fanaunau*, because they did not destroy their offspring as was required of the regular members.

Every Areoi had his own wife, who was also a member of the society, and while his own conduct was unrestrained, any improper conduct by others toward his wife was punished, sometimes with death. The members were recruited from any rank or grade of the community ; but, while thus accessible to all, admission as a member was attended with a variety of ceremonies ; a protracted novitiate followed, advancement to the superior classes being possible only by progressive steps.

It was supposed that those who became Areoi were generally prompted or inspired to do so by the gods. When any individual wished to be admitted to the society he presented himself at some public exhibition in a state of apparent *nenewa*, or derangement. He generally wore a girdle of yellow plantain or *ti* leaves, his face was stained with the scarlet dye, his brow decorated with a curiously plaited shade of yellow coconut leaves, his hair perfumed with strongly scented oil, and ornamented with fragrant flowers. He rushed through the crowd assembled round the house in which the actors were performing, and leaping into the circle joined with seeming frantic wildness in the dance or pantomime, continuing with the performers until the close. This was considered an indication of his desire to join the company ; and if approved he was appointed as a servant to wait on the principal Areoi. After a considerable trial of his natural disposition, docility, and devotedness in this occupation, if he persevered in his desire to join he was admitted with all the attendant rites and observances.

This admission took place at some great meeting of the society, when the chief Areoi presented him to the assembled members, arrayed in the *ahu haio*, a curiously stained native cloth, the badge of their order. Every Areoi had his distinctive name, and at his introduction the new candidate

441

received from the chief Areoi the name by which he was in future to be known among them. He was now in the first place directed to destroy any offspring he might have. He then bent his left arm, struck his right hand upon the bend of the left elbow, which at the same time he struck against his side, while he repeated the invocation for the occasion. He was then commanded to seize the cloth worn by the chief woman present, and by this act he completed his initiation, and became a member of the seventh class. There are all kinds of initiations and ordinations, and every one is a solemn ceremony to its own members, while it may be a meaningless display to all others.

The advancement of an Areoi to a higher class also took place at some public festival, when all members were present. The gods were called on to sanction the advancement, and the members were taken to the temple and solemnly anointed in the presence of the gods, the forehead of each being sprinkled with fragrant oil. The sacrificial pig, wrapped in the *haio*, or cloth of the order, was next put in his hands, and offered to the gods. Each individual was then declared by the person officiating on the occasion to be an Areoi of the class to which he was raised. If the pig was killed, as was sometimes done, it was buried in the temple; but if left alive its ears were ornamented with the *orooro*, or sacred braid, of coconut fibre. It was then liberated; and, being regarded as sacred to the god to whom it had been offered, it was allowed to range the district uncontrolled till it died.

The artist was now employed to imprint the distinctive badges of the rank or class to which the individuals had been raised. As this operation was attended with considerable suffering, it was usually deferred till the termination of the festival which followed the ceremony. The marks were indelibly tattooed; which means that the members of the various classes must bear the marks, not only of their class, but of all below them in addition. The festival was one of extravagant profusion; and bales of native cloth were also provided as presents to the Areoi, among whom they were divided. The greatest peculiarity connected

442

with the entertainment was that the restrictions of the *tapu* which prohibited females, on pain of death, from eating the flesh of animals offered in sacrifice to the gods were removed, and they partook with the men of the pigs, and other kinds of food considered sacred, which had been provided for the occasion. Women here, as in other parts of the Pacific, were prohibited from eating bananas, coconuts, the sea-turtle, and certain fishes; if they infringed this *tapu* they were liable to suffer death. Music, dancing, and pantomime exhibitions followed.

On the death of an Areoi the general lamentation (*otohaa*) continued for two or three days, during which time the body remained at the place of death, surrounded by relatives and friends of the deceased. It was then taken by the Areoi to the temple where the bones of kings were deposited. Soon after the body had been brought into the sacred place the priest of Oro came and, standing over the corpse, repeated a long prayer to his god. This prayer and the accompanying ceremonies divested the body of all the sacred and mysterious influence received from the god at the time of the sprinkling of the fragrant oil when the Areoi was raised to the order of the class in which he was when he died. The influence thus returned to Oro, from whom it came, and the body was afterward buried as that of a common man, but within the precincts of the temple in which the bodies of chiefs were interred.

The continuance of the ceremonies was now taken over by the priest of Romatane. He stood by the dead body, and offered his petitions to Urutaetae, the god who conducted the spirits of Areoi and others to the spirit world of happiness, Rohutu-noanoa (Rohutu the Fragrant). This region was supposed to be near a lofty mountain in Ra'iatea and to be called Te Mehani-unauna (Te Mehani the Splendid). It was invisible to mortal eyes, being in the *reva*, or aerial regions. The country was described as most lovely and enchanting in appearance, beautiful with flowers, and fragrant with odours. The air was pure and sweet, and free from noxious vapours. Every enjoyment to which the Areoi had been accustomed on earth was experienced here by him and other favoured classes, with food and fruit in abundance.

Had their objects, their actions, been different, how like the Areoi Society was to societies of the civilized world! And the objects and actions were different through circumstances of environment only. Ritual, ceremony, vestments —throughout the study of mythology it may be seen how the human mind evolves and creates or is apprehensive of like beings, like actions, like legends.

There is another aspect of the Areoi fraternity, however, that must not be ignored. They have been traduced as inhuman and unnatural because of their enforcing infanticide on their members. It is not only the savages of the Pacific that have practised this custom; and if it has been stamped out among the kindly and more amenable Polynesians it has hardly been affected in civilized lands.

In Vaitupu (Tracey Island) infanticide was ordered by law; only two children were allowed to a family; the people were afraid of a scarcity of food. In Nuku-fetau (De Peyster Island) it was also the law, only one child being allowed in a family. It is clear that necessity was the reason for it, not inhumanity. It is well known that the Polynesians were and are fond of children, and as kind to them as any human beings could be. If the extent of the islands be considered, and the number of the population at the time of Cook's visit, it is evident that if the islands did not then support all the population possible they were very near the limit. Infanticide was one means of reducing the numbers; war was another. When Cook visited Tongatabu (Amsterdam) he was struck with the neatness of the plantations and enclosures, the orderliness of everything, plots fenced and pathways fenced off, houses with their grass plots; everything ordered so that, fertile as the island was, its fertility was fully conserved. The whole of the island Middelburg was cultivated, and there is little doubt that the Areoi Society was partly for the inculcation of the need for controlling the number of the population. There was no such

444

society and no trace of its teaching in New Zealand, for instance, where there was ample area for the spreading of the people.   Infanticide was practised more or less through the Pacific—but hardly more than in other parts of the world ; not that this is said in palliation, but to suggest that the universality of the practice argues a necessity rather than a depravity.

The Hula Dance

In Hawaii the place of Areoi as entertainers in great part was taken by the *hula* dancers.   The *hula* was also semi-religious in its nature, and appealed very widely and power-fully to the Hawaiian emotions and imagination.   It was combined song or recitative and dance, the songs and recitations relating to mythology, with which was naturally interwoven the history of the people and their everyday life, as naturally as gods and goddesses mingled with mortals.

The *halau* was the special hall for the performance of the *hula*, a large building, containing a *kuahu* (shrine) for the deity whose presence was invoked at the performances. The goddess-mistress of the *hula* was Laka :

> In the forests, on the ridges
> Of the mountains, stands Laka;
> Dwelling in the source of the mists.
> Laka, mistress of the *hula*,
> Has climbed the wooded haunts of the gods,
> Altars hallowed by the sacrificial swine,
> The head of the boar, the black boar of Kane.
> A partner he with Laka;
> Woman, she by strife gained rank in heaven,
> That the root may grow from the stem,
> That the young shoot may put forth and leaf,
> Pushing up the fresh enfolded bud,
> The scion-thrust bud and fruit toward the East,
> Like the tree that bewitches the winter fish,
> *Maka-lei,* tree famed from the age of night.
> Truth is the counsel of night—
> May it fruit and ripen above.
> A messenger I bring you, O Laka,
> To the girding of the *pau.*

445

An opening festa this for thee and me;
To show the might of the god,
The power of the goddess,
Of Laka, the sister,
To Lono a wife in the heavenly courts.
O Lono, join heaven and earth!
Thine alone are the pillars of Kahiki.
Warm greeting, beloved one,
We hail thee!

The altar was decorated with leaves and flowers, the ones most in favour being the bines of the wreathing and fragrant *maile*, the fronds and the ruddy drupe of the *ieie* (*kiekie*) and *hala-pepe*, the scarlet pompoms of the *lehua* and *ohia*, ferns in many varieties, the lemon-coloured hibiscus, royal yellow *ilima*, and others. While twining these about the shrine a song-prayer would be sung to the goddess:

Here am I, O Laka from the mountains,
O Laka from the shore;
Protect us
Against the dog that barks; [1]
Reside in the wild-twining *maile*
And the goddess-enwreathing *ti*.
Ah, the joyful pulses
Of the woman Ha'i-ka-manawa!
Thou art Laka,
The god of this altar;
Return, return, abide in thy shrine.

There were many of these prayers, so that if one were finished before the decoration of the altar was completed another was begun.

Emerson has written on the many forms of the *hula*, of the songs and ceremonies connected with it, of the gods and goddesses: of what nature were the gods of the old times, says he, and how did the ancient Hawaiians conceive of them? As of things having the form, the powers, and the passions of humanity, yet standing above and somewhat apart from man. One sees, as through a mist, a figure standing, moving; in shape a plant, a tree, or vine-clad stump, a bird, a monster, a rock carved by Pele the fire-

[1] An evil omen.

queen, a human form, a puff of vapour—and now there is nothing. It was a goddess, perhaps the goddess of the *hula*. In the solitude of the wilds one meets a youthful being of pleasing address, godlike wit, of elusive beauty; her gestures commands, the charm of her countenance unspoken authority. She seems one with nature, yet commanding it. Food placed before her remains untasted; the oven in which the fascinated host has heaped his abundance, preparing a feast, when opened is found empty; the guest of an hour has disappeared. Again it was a goddess; perhaps the goddess of the *hula*. Or a traveller meets a creature of divine beauty, all smiles and loveliness. Smitten with infatuation, the mortal offers blandishments; he finds himself by the road-side embracing a rock. It was a goddess; perhaps the goddess of the *hula*. It was her of the prayer:

> O goddess Laka!
> O wildwood bouquet, O Laka!
> O Laka, queen of the voice!
> O Laka, giver of gifts!
> O Laka, giver of bounty!
> O Laka, giver of all things!

A long course of training and study was needed to qualify an aspirant as a dancer; songs must be learnt, prayers, an infinity of gesture and posture, for every song had its appropriate movements; the younger and more active dancers were called for the vigorous movements, the more mature for the less energetic, kneeling or sitting with flute and drum.

The principal article of dress of the *hula* dancer, man or woman, was the short *hula*-skirt (*pau*), this being worn in addition to that of daily wear. In its simplest form it might be only a close-set fringe of ribbons stripped from the bark of the hibiscus, or blade of the *ti*, or a fine rush, strung upon a thong to encircle the waist. In the more elaborate and formal style it consisted of a strip of fine *tapa* several yards long, and of a width to reach almost to the knees, often delicately tinted or printed on the outer parts with stamped figures.

447

MYTHS OF THE POLYNESIANS

The woman who set the fashion for the many-folded *pau* was Lu'ukia; her *pau* was of five thicknesses; and she is referred to in a prayer offered by a visitor at the shrine in the *halau*, this prayer being one of many used on occasion:

> Thy blessing, O Laka, on me the stranger, and on the residents, teacher and pupils. O Laka, give grace to the feet of Pohaku; and to her bracelets and anklets; comeliness to the figure and *pau* of Lu'ukia. To each one give gesture and voice. O Laka, make beautiful the *lei*; inspire the dancers when they stand before the assembly.

The Lu'ukia referred to is the Rukutia of the Maori; she too was a noted dancer, as has been told in the story of her and Tu-te-Koropanga.

For the lower limbs there were the anklets (*ku-pe'e*), of whales' teeth, bone, shells, plaited fibre, or other material; for the neck the long necklet of feathers (*lei*); and garlands of flowers for the head, the long, glossy hair flowing free. As one writer has expressed it, the natural garb of these children of the sun is flowers and sea-foam; they were as unself-conscious, as innocent, as Adam and Eve before the Fall—the serpent that ruined their Paradise was the early white adventurer.

The *halau* itself was the dressing-room, and those waiting to see the dancing might know by the songs being sung behind temporary screens the state of the preparation, for each act in dressing had its appropriate song. Some of the songs were in partial rime; such was the following, sung while all stooped in unison to tie on the anklets:

> Fragrant the grasses of high Kane-hoa.
> Bind on the anklets, bind!
> Bind with finger deft as the wind
> That cools the air of this bower.
> *Lehua* bloom pales at my flower,
> O sweetheart of mine,
> Bud that I'd pluck and wear in my wreath,
> If thou wert but a flower!

The fixing of the *pau* was a more intricate business, the ends being brought together after the folding round the waist so as to hang in an artistic way. The leader and others

448

THE AREOI SOCIETY AND THE HULA DANCE

sang the accompanying song, which was partly descriptive of the *hula* itself, partly descriptive of the *pau* and its donning. The following is part of such a song:

> Gird on the *pau*, garment tucked in one side,
> Skirt lacelike and beauteous in staining,
> That is wrapped and made fast about the oven.
> Bubbly as foam of falling water it stands,
> Quintuple skirt, sheer as the cliff Kupe-hau.
> One journeyed to work on it at Honokane.
>
>   •   •   •   •   •
>
> Wondrous the care and toil to make the *pau*!
> What haste to finish, when put a-soak
> In the side-glancing stream of Apua!
> Caught by the rain-scud that searches the glen,
> The tinted gown illumines the *pali*—
>
> The sheeny steep shot with buds of *lama*—
> Outshining the comely *malua-ula*,
> Which one may seize and gird with a strong hand.
> Leaf of the *ti* for his *malo*, Umi stood covered.
>
> Look at the *olona* fibres inwrought,
> Like the trickling brooklets of Wai-hilau.
> The *olona* fibres knit with strength
> This dainty immaculate web, the *pau*,
> And the filmy weft of the *kilo-hana*.
> With the small bamboo the *tapa* is finished.
>
> A fire seems to bud on the *pali*,
> When the *tapa* is spread out to dry,
> Pressed down with the stones of Wai-manu—
> Stones that are shifted about and about,
> Stones that are tossed here and there,
> Like the work of the hail-thrower Kane.

The song is full of allusions, well known to the hearers. The word 'oven' is used figuratively for the parts covered by the *pau*. The *pau* is likened to a cliff (*pali*) with poetical effect. *Malua-ula* was a coarser *tapa* than that from which the *pau* was made. *Malo* is the belt, and the reference to Umi and the belt of *ti*-blades relates to an amour of Liloa; he left his *malo* as pledge with the woman, who became the mother of Umi. The *olona* was a vegetable fibre sometimes added to the *tapa* to give it strength. The *kilo-hana* was

449

the outside, ornamented part of the *pau*; part of the ornamentation was printed on with a bamboo rod cut in a
pattern.

After the ceremony of the *pau* came that of the *lei* for
the neck and shoulders and the wreath for the head. There
was no over-adornment; the outlines of the figure must
not be hidden; and as the adornments were put on
the wearers sang:

> " Kaula wreathes her brow with the ocean;
> Niihau shines forth in the calm.
> After the calm blows the wind Inu-wai,
> The palms of Naue then drink in the salt.
> From Naue the palm, from Puna the woman—
> Ay, from the pit Kilauea."

This song was first heard when Hiiaka', sister of Pele, the
goddess of volcanoes, went to bring Lohiau to his divine
lover the goddess. Hiiaka' and her friend Omeo (or Wahine-
oma'o), standing on the heights overlooking the beach at
Kahakuloa, Maui, saw the figure of a woman, maimed in
hands and feet, dancing in fantastic glee on a flat rock by
the ocean. She sang as she danced, pouring out her soul
in an ecstasy unaccountable in one in her pitiable condition;
and as she danced her shadow-dance—for she was but a
ghost, poor soul!—these were the words she repeated:

> " Alas, alas, maimed are my hands!
> Alas, alas, maimed are my hands!"

Omeo, lacking spiritual sight, saw none of this; but
Hiiaka', in pure pity and goodness of heart, impulsively
plucked a *hala* fruit from the string about her neck and threw
it so that it fell before the poor creature, who eagerly seized
it with the stumps of her hands and held it up to enjoy its
odour. At the sight of the woman's pleasure Hiiaka' sang
a short song, in answer to which the desolate creature,
grateful for the recognition and kind attention of Hiiaka',
sang the above *mele*, beginning

> Kaula wreathes her brow with the ocean;

and this was adopted by the *hula* folk as a wreath-song.
450

THE AREOI SOCIETY AND THE HULA DANCE

The girls, having finished their preparations, sang a spirited song as with lively action they came out to bloom in their natural charms and adornments before the waiting assembly:

> The rainbow stands red o'er the ocean;
> Mist steals from the sea and covers the land;
> Far as Kahiki flashes the lightning;
> A reverberant roar,
> A shout of applause
> From the four hundred.
> I appeal to thee, Laka!

It is not impossible to imagine the effect of a body of young men and women in the flush of youth coming thus adorned and singing, ranging themselves before the expectant spectators, the youngest and most active and pliant slightly in advance, the musicians half kneeling, half sitting.

They await the signal to begin, the left hand resting on the hip, the right extended, the *pau* hanging in swelling folds, the *lei* glowing on breast and neck, the flowers gleaming in the hair—and, more vital than these, the eyes glancing and flashing from the smiling flower-faces.

The leader, who sits with the musicians, calls the *mele*—that is, begins the recitation of the song. The joining in of the dance-leader standing with the dancers is the signal for all to begin, and the *hula* is set free with its entrancing murmur, and movement, and colour, and fragrance, all thrilling both dancers and beholders to exaltation.

There was great variety in the various *hula*, from grave and stately to gay and vivacious. All manner of subjects were introduced—love, war, history, mythology, descriptions of nature. A favourite topic was the love of Pele for Lohiau, and the adventures of this honoured but unfortunate mortal and the loving, kindly natured Hiiaka', the youngest sister of the fiery Pele; but every song contained references that were as windows to the soul and wings to the imagination.

CHAPTER XIV : RELIGIOUS OBSERVANCES

IN the ancient, beautiful *hula* dances of Hawaii, in the highly poetical and emotional death-dirges of Mangaia, in the histrionic recitals and dances of Tahiti and the Marquesas, may be seen the luxuriant flowering of nature-worship, from which flowering in due course fall the germs of the older dramatic and religious fervours.

In both these later efflorescences—drama and religion—dance and song and music, man's expression of the nature-worship welling up within him, were found in close union. Even in the *hula*, the death-dirge, and the Areoi entertainment development had proceeded so far that the mass of the people had resigned their active part in the ceremonies (they were ceremonies as much as exhibitions). The various songs, dances, and actions had become so definite that trained bodies of performers were necessary for their production. The acting, however, was still mass-acting, the dance mass-dancing, the song mass-singing. There are indications, as in the occasional recitative or sung directions of the leaders, of solo and chorus; as in the Greek drama, of priest and congregation.

Drama and religion are twin seeds from one flower, and this flower was fragrant in the Pacific when it was roughly shaken by the more advanced, more sophisticated European. The Areoi carried with them on their canoes an altar to the god Rono; the *hula* dancers erected a shrine to Laka, daily renewing it with flowers during the time of their performances. Dancing, music, song, and flowers still play an important part in our drama, and in our religion too.

The direct worship of the gods had not fully developed, but the evolution was in progress. The fact, however, that in most parts of the Pacific a brotherhood of three or four principal gods had come to be recognized, while the innumerable minor deities of the Polynesian pantheon still existed, shows that the thoughts of these Stone Age poets and philosophers were turning toward monotheism; while the cult of Io, seen clearly in the Maori philosophy, and more dimly here and there elsewhere in the wide Pacific, shows that the idea, the ideal, of monotheism had already taken root.   The Polynesian was on the path that was trodden by the man of the Bronze and Iron Ages, who had outstripped him in the Old World.   Given the advantages of metals and a temperate climate, the Samoan and the Maori especially have shown that the Polynesian can in a generation step from the Stone Age to the Iron Age and hold his own, in energy and in intellect.

The principal gods and demigods are those whose names are known more or less throughout Polynesia, and the greatest interest attaches to the stories and legends current concerning them ; the lesser gods possess less interest, as in many instances they are no more than names.

There were deities of various fish, shellfish, birds, reptiles, dogs, besides deities of peace, war, revenge, music, unintelligible noises, trees, winds, rain, clouds, darkness, light, deities invoked when fishing, journeying, deities haunting deserted houses, the sick, the demented—their number was legion ; and it was these more numerous and more mundane *atua* or spirits that were invoked or placated, but not worshipped, with *karakia* and exorcism in everyday life.   They may almost be paralleled with the saints, images of whom King Louis XI of France wore in his hat, as related in *Quentin Durward*, adjuring first one, then another, as whim or circumstance dictated, rewarding them or reviling them as they granted or denied the boon prayed.   There seemed to be an unbroken series, from the spirits of ancestors to the primal gods—ancestors became heroes, heroes demigods, and the lines of demarcation grow fainter and fainter with the lapse of time.

The deities known most widely are no doubt the deities that all knew before the dispersal through the Pacific ; the inferior deities, or tribal gods, are the ones who have sprung into being during the time of isolation or semi-isolation. Remembering the remark of the Maori who said that gods died if there were no *tohunga* to keep them alive, it is evident that as the gods created man, so man reciprocally creates gods. The process is even to-day in progress in the canonization of saints.

In many instances mortals who have become heroes or demigods have become confused with gods of the same or a similar name. This has possibly taken place, for instance, in the case of Rongo' and Maui'. There is an actual instance from Mangaia, where Tane-papa-kai is a god, and Tane-ngakiau (Tane striving for Power) was a warrior deified on his death. Were the fact of this deification lost, no doubt in time Tane-ngakiau would be regarded as one of the many names of the god Tane'.

In the different groups of the Pacific religion was developing along somewhat different paths ; or it may be that it was the inherent differences in their modes of thought that caused the different groups to hive off, each developing its own thought and religious emotion in its own way. These differences may be seen in considering the evidences of the trend of their evolution that were noted down especially at the time of their first contact with Europeans.

The evidence of greatest value is that of the more intelligent of the navigators and explorers who placed on record what they actually saw and actually heard ; their speculative interpretations as often conceal clues as yield them. Cook, one of the ablest observers among them, confesses that owing to his ignorance of the language and the customs of the people he can say very little of their religion. Had he been perfectly acquainted with both the language and the customs he would still probably have found a difficulty in giving a coherent account of an emotion and its formal expressions that varied, not only in the different groups of islands, but in the individual islands of the different groups. We have only to consider what kind of account of our own religion would be given by an intruding foreigner who might visit us, overcoming our unwillingness only by a continual show, and occasional exercise, of superior force, who disregarded our customs, though it might be only in ignorance, who was unceasingly urgent for provisions, and whose followers were continually seeking the favours of our women.

Even such benefits as he might bring would hardly abate our desire for him to be gone—and in his accounts Cook confesses to feelings of this kind.

Many of the accounts of the Polynesian religion upon which we must rely in default of others were written by missionaries, unsympathetic, if not openly and bitterly contemptuous. One of the kindest-hearted writers is Gill, and Ellis is often sympathetic in spite of himself, when the man speaks and not the missionary; from these two we gather much, more especially from Ellis, who covers a far wider field. Men expressing themselves in so unchristian a way as Dibble does of the Hawaiians could expect little return of sympathy from those he paints in such diabolic and untrue colours.

If, as Spencer said, temples are derived from tombs and gods from dead men, the religious structures and observances of the Polynesians, so far as we are able to interpret the one and understand the other, show the actual transition in progress. Most of these structures were found in the southern groups of islands—the Society Islands, the Marquesas, and the Friendly Islands. Their general name was *marae*, often misspelt *morai* in early authors, and they usually consisted of two parts, an open, oblong area, enclosed at the narrow ends with stone walls, a low fence running along the longer front, the area being paved with flat stones, and a pyramidal structure erected at one of the narrow ends. This was a solid, stepped structure, one seen by Cook on Tahiti measuring 267 feet by 87, rising in a series of eleven steps or terraces, each 4 feet in height. The steps on the long sides were broader than those at the ends, so that the oblong narrowed as it rose. The edges of the steps were formed of solid blocks of coral, neatly squared and joined, without cement of any kind, the interior being filled with rounded pebbles. Some of the blocks were $3\frac{1}{2}$ feet long and $2\frac{1}{2}$ feet wide. The steps along the long sides were not perfectly straight, but dipped in the middle, so that the edge formed a slight curve, like the ridge of some Chinese temples. This pyramid formed part of one side of

455

an enclosed area 360 feet by 354. The area and pyramid were open to the sky, and in the former, though paved, trees were growing, some of great size and considerable age.

These *marae* differed very much in size and in detail. One at Opoa, on Ra'iatea, about 138 feet by 26, was enclosed to a height of 6 feet 7 inches by a wall of gigantic coral blocks standing side by side. These were hewn from the inner reef, the outer surface being smoothed, the inner left rough. One block stood over 11 feet high, besides what was buried in the soil, and was 12 feet wide, and 2½ feet thick. If the island itself did not furnish the stone, it would be brought from other islands in great double canoes. On Borabora alone, a small island only ten miles in circumference, in the Society group, there were two hundred and twenty of these *marae*. The missionaries, regarding them as reminders of heathendom, caused the destruction of a great many. In some earth took the place of rounded pebbles for filling; in some the uppermost terrace was filled with only the finest white sand.

In front of the pyramids were fixed altars, though some pyramids were without them, and there the images, when present, were kept. These images were of wood or stone, some rudely carved, some nothing more than logs of wood, ornamented, perhaps, with red feathers. They were, however, regarded simply as emblems, and were no more worshipped than are the emblematic images, carved or coloured, plain or adorned, in our own sacred edifices. The altars were wooden stages, some quite low, some up to 10 feet in height, and at these were made offerings of all kinds—prayers, food, and occasionally human sacrifices.

In parts of Polynesia, as at Hawaii, these sacred enclosures were regarded as houses of refuge; once within their walls fugitives were safe from their enemies, so long as they remained within. Even inveterate enemies must there meet as friends, for the place was *tapu*, and bloodshed was a violation of the *tapu*, its violation meaning death. In other parts, as at Tahiti, trespassers were put to death.

In the Society Islands (Tahitian) the pyramids were with-

MARAE TOOARAI, MAHAIATEA, TAHITI

From *A Missionary Voyage in the Ship "Duff," 1796–98*, by courtesy of Mrs Scoresby Routledge and the Royal Anthropological Institute.

(See page 456)

WOODEN FIGURE OF A HAWAIIAN GOD
From a sacred enclosure.
British Museum
(See page 458)

out buildings of any kind ; in the Friendly Islands (Tongan) one or more houses often occupied the top terrace. Moreover, the pyramid might take the form of a gently sloping green, which Cook thought must be much used as the grass was always short, as if much sat or trodden upon. At the top of the slope stood the house, oblong in form, built like a dwelling-house. Sometimes this was no more than a roof raised on posts ; sometimes it was quite enclosed with woven walls, there being no opening of any kind. One house visited by Cook was on a green eminence about 16 feet high. The house measured about 20 feet by 14, and was surrounded by a fine gravel walk, the floor of the house too being laid in fine gravel, except in the middle, where there was an oblong of blue pebbles, raised about 6 inches higher than the floor. The eminence, enclosed with a low stone wall 3 feet in height, stood in a grove, open only on the side fronting the roadway.

There were apparently two kinds of these houses, one kind consecrated to the gods, and one kind being the tomb of a dead chief, these being regarded as both tomb and temple. They were called *faitoka* (often misspelt *fiatooka*) as well as *marae*, *faitoka* signifying a burial-place : they were called *marae* only in the Society Islands. The *faitoka* were of two kinds ; the one above described was the burial-place of an inferior chief. For the chiefs of divine descent much more elaborate structures were built—structures more nearly resembling the Society Island *marae*. The house on the top of the pyramid covered, not a simple grave, but a stone vault, wherein the chief's body was laid, the mouth of the vault being covered by a huge slab of coral rock, measuring sometimes 8 feet long, 4 broad, and 1 thick.

These imposing tombs were, like the Great Pyramid of Cheops, prepared by the chiefs during their lifetime. It took from a hundred and fifty to two hundred men, pulling on ropes, to raise the stone lid when the vault was to be opened for the burying of the body. While the forest was cleared for the building of the monuments, once they were occupied the vegetation was allowed to grow again, and for

457

this reason most of these great structures are now almost hidden in a luxuriance of forest growth.

In the Marquesas stone platforms seemed to take the place of the pyramids, and here the body might be deposited in a vault or simply in a hollowed log coffin resting on the floor under the shelter of the roof. These were called *marae*, and while the pyramids themselves were not used for burial in the Society Islands, chiefs and noted warriors were buried in the open paved area, so that apparently the *marae* throughout was tomb and temple in one. Although no remains of pyramids have been seen in the Marquesas, Melville has described stepped platforms built against a hillside, the ruins, like those in the Friendly Islands, being buried in tangled forests. In New Zealand the name *marae* was applied to the open space or common in the village, with no idea of temple or tomb.

The ruinous state of these memorials of the past, and the magnitude of the ruins, has led some to suppose them the work of a race more numerous than the Polynesians, more advanced in civilization, and hence more capable of undertaking their construction. But the natives had traditions regarding the building of at least some of them.

Among the largest of them in Tongatabu is one known as Telea, which is said to contain no body. The sacred chief Telea, who had it built as his tomb, was dissatisfied with it when completed, and had another built next to it, also of great size; and here he is said to lie buried. There is a tradition that Takalaua, one of the chiefs of the island, was assassinated about A.D. 1535 because he was a tyrant who compelled the people to drag great stones from Liku at the back of the island to the burial-place Mooa (the Maori *mua*), a distance of about a mile and a half. At times the chiefs would make voyages of hundreds of miles in order to obtain slabs of stone suitable for these great structures. The largest measured had a base of 156 feet by 140, and had four steps to the top, the lowest step 4 feet in height, the other three 3 feet 9 inches, each step 5 feet 6 inches wide. One stone composed the height of each step, part

458

being sunk in the ground. The corners were at times composed of huge rectangular stones ; one of these was measured and found to be 24 feet by 12 by 2 feet thick. These were said to have been brought in double canoes from Lifuka, an island in the northern part of the group, a distance of about 120 miles. The later Tongans had given up building these huge structures, as they had given up their former long sea-voyages.

There were some paved enclosures in the Hawaiian Islands, but no *marae* such as those found in the southern groups. The temples, equivalents of the *marae*, were here called *heiau*, and consisted of walled enclosures, of from 1 to 5 acres, generally irregular in form. The walls were sometimes 10 feet thick and 20 feet high, the material being unhewn stone, without mortar or cement. They narrowed slightly from the base upward, and were sometimes capped with hewn slabs of coral.

Within this enclosure was an inner stone or wooden temple of small dimensions, and before it stood the altar, a raised stone platform. Sometimes the altar was on an elevated platform of large dimensions. One such was seen by Captain King. It was a solid platform of stone, about 40 yards long and 20 broad, and 14 feet high, the top flat and neatly paved, and surrounded with a wooden rail. At one end was a scaffold supported on poles more than 20 feet high, at the foot of which were twelve images ranged in a semicircle, with a sacrificial table or altar in front of them. It was on this scaffold that Captain Cook stood, swathed in a red cloth, when he received the adoration of the Hawaiians.

In some of the enclosures, near the altar, Cook and his people also saw obelisks, 4 feet square at the base and about 20 feet high, made of poles and wicker-work covered with grey *tapa*, or bark-cloth, and open from top to bottom. It is supposed that the priests stood within these when deliver· ing oracles from the gods.

The Samoan temples were houses like ordinary dwellings, but always set on stone platforms. They were called *fale- aitu*, and were not used for burial. There were no stone houses in Samoa at the time of the discovery of the islands, but there are the ruins of a stone house said to have been built by Fe'e (the war-god) on his arrival from Fiji. The ruins are about ten miles inland from Apia, in Upolu, and the central posts, side-posts, and rafters all appear to have been of stone. The house or temple was shaped like the ordinary Samoan house, the ellipse measuring 50 feet by 40. The two central pillars are each a single block of worked stone about 13 feet high, 12 inches wide, and 9 thick. The rafters were in lengths of 12 feet and 6 feet, and 4 inches square. The side-pillars, of which eighteen were standing when the building was described, were 3 feet high, 9 inches wide, and 6 inches thick. All were quarried from an adjoining bluff. The ruins are called Fale-o-le-Fe'e—that is, House of the Fe'e. Watson, writing of these ' ruins ' in 1918, says that none of the stones shows signs of having been worked, and not one is too big or too heavy for a man to lift. They are simply columns that have fallen from a basaltic cliff, about thirty feet high, in the near vicinity! The stones are very roughly put in place.

In the mountainous interior of the same island, hidden in dense forest-growth, is another ruinous stone structure, roughly circular in shape, but apparently built in tiers like the Tongan tombs, and with chambers or vaults as if for a like purpose. Of these ruins little is known but their existence.

In Tongatabu, besides the many great pyramidal stone erections, there is another megalithic erection that has given rise to much speculation. This is a trilithon—two upright blocks of stone, with a third resting horizontally across their tops. All three are coral rock, and for size they are compared with similar trilithons at Stonehenge, but the space between the uprights is wider, and the horizontal block is more deeply mortised into the tops of the uprights. These are 10 to 12 feet apart, from 14 to 16 feet in height, 8 to 10 feet wide from front to back, and 4 feet thick. They taper upward, and the cross-block is about 24 feet long, by 4 or 5 feet wide, and 2 feet thick. The purpose of this trilithon cannot even be conjectured, and the explanation given by native tradition is as likely as any other. The Tongan tradition says it was erected by the chief Tui-ta-tui. His time was a time of assassination, people rebelling against the slavery imposed on them in the erection of the many *marae* required by successive chiefs. He caused this trilithon to be erected as his seat, to be occupied by him during the ceremonious *kava*-drinking, so that he might be out of reach of any hand that might desire to take him off as others had been taken off. The *kava*-drinking apparently gave the assassins their opportunity, and it is said to be because of them that the custom originated of the chief sitting at the narrow end of the oval, with every person present in sight before him. There is, too, a depression about the size of a *kava* bowl in the centre of the horizontal block; but this, while it may give probability to the legend, may as well be the cause of its origin.

There may, indeed, be no need for any elaborate theory regarding its origin or the origin of like structures. It is one of the simplest of architectural forms; the pyramid is another; their inevitableness may be seen even in the play of a child with blocks or dominoes.

There were extensive stone structures of another kind—artificial fish-ponds (*loko-ia*, Maori *roto-ika*), built in the water of the sea itself, as along the coasts of Molokai in the Hawaiian Islands. The story of Tini-rau and his pet fish no doubt had its origin in the keeping of fish in such ponds by some great chief of long ago. One of the Hawaiian kings, Kamehameha, built a series of these ponds, which were overwhelmed in a lava-flow in the year 1801.

Structures that appear to be of another kind are found in the Caroline Islands, a group of islands now no longer purely Polynesian, though at one time in small part occupied by Polynesians. These look like quays, or the walls of great houses that were actually built in the water, as were the fish-ponds, or were built on a shore that has since sunk. Buried in the forests on these islands, too, stone buildings are found comparable with the *marae* of the Society and Friendly Islands.

461

At the extreme east of the Polynesian area, too, on the solitary Easter Island, occur ruins of great stone structures. The island is triangular in shape, each angle occupied by a dead volcanic peak, the highest, in the south, a little over 1700 feet in height. It is thirteen miles long, its greatest width is seven miles, and its circumference thirty-four miles. Being altogether volcanic, its soil consists principally of decomposing lava. It lies 2000 miles west of Chili, and over 1000 miles east of the Tuamotu group, the nearest inhabited archipelago. It has none of the luxuriance of vegetation possessed by other parts of Polynesia; it has no trees and few bushes, the greater part of its surface being clothed only with grass. Its population now numbers about 250; it was 700 or more on Cook's visit in 1774; a great many were taken away by slave-raiders from Peru in 1862. The only permanent water is in the various crater-lakes. Though the rainfall is good, there are no streams, the water sinking underground and issuing in the sea below tide-level.

It is more remarkable that an island now so barren should be so rich in mystery. Judging from the number of *ahu* (burial platforms), the island would seem at one time to have been as thickly populated as the Tahitian or Tongan Islands. On most parts of the coast, except the great eastern and western headlands, these *ahu* are found, to the number of two hundred and sixty. They are mostly situated at the edge of the shore, on the low-lying parts, or at the edge of the cliffs in those parts where the sea has eaten in; about thirty are situated well inland.

The platforms may be 300 feet in length or more. The construction is quite different from that of the *marae* of the southern groups or the *heiau* of Hawaii. The proportions of one, 300 feet long, at the sea-edge are as follows: the outer wall is 14 feet high, the central part projecting for 100 feet of its length 10 feet beyond the two wings, each 100 feet in length. The level surface of this central 10-foot width is for the reception of the statues, numbering as many as fifteen. From the inner side of this 10-foot pro-

462

POLYNESIAN WOOD-CARVING

(1) Head of a national idol of Raratonga ; (2), (3), and (4) wooden ceremonial weapons and staff from the Hervey Islands.

British Museum

(See page 460)

STONE STATUES ON EASTER ISLAND
From *The Mystery of Easter Island*, by Mrs Scoresby Routledge.
(See page 462)

jection, which is in line with the two wings, there is a steep slope of 20 feet, to a wall 3 feet in height. From half the height of this wall a paved area slopes very gently landward, tapering to a wedge-edge where it meets the slope of the land. This edge is about 250 feet from the sea-edge of the seaward wall, and in this paved area, contained between its surface and the underlying sheet of lava, mortuary vaults are built. Beyond the edge of the area the ground has been levelled for 50 or 60 yards; it is traversed by a pathway about 12 feet wide from the edge of the paved area. The lower stones of the sea-wall are huge blocks as much as 9 feet high, irregular in shape, the interstices filled with smaller stones, and the top levelled off with layers of slabs of lava or cubes of basalt. The images are, with few exceptions, hewn from compressed volcanic ash mined from the interior of a crater. Within the crater Rano-raraku, 540 feet in height, in the eastern angle of the island, is the crater-lake, and the slopes above this lake formed a well-used quarry from which many statues were obtained; and here about a hundred and fifty still lie, in all manner of positions, and in all stages of completion or incompletion. They are mostly about 30 feet in height, and up to 36 feet; a few are only 6 feet or less. One, unfinished, is very much more; it is 66 feet in length—a solitary colossus among giants.

They were shaped at the same time that they were quarried, and the manner of the quarrying can be seen. A trench was cut round each figure being worked, niches showing where each man stood while working, so that it can be seen how many men were engaged on the figure. When the front and the sides were finished, the back was undercut until the figure was supported on a thin strip of rock like a keel along the spine. Calculations made from the number of men at work and the amount they could probably do in a day show that a statue could be roughed out in about fifteen days. Even the tools with which the work was done have been found; the common and less valuable tools in great numbers, the well-wrought, more valuable stone axes or great chisels in much smaller numbers. Statues lie in all

463

sorts of positions in the crater, outside the crater, and on the slopes to the sea. Some appear to have been set up, partly sunk, on the hillside, as if there were intended to be image-lined roadways, like colonnades of sphinxes or man-headed winged bulls.

Very different conclusions are arrived at concerning these remains; some think they must have taken thousands of workmen many years; but while there are about two hundred and sixty of the *ahu* on this island, on Borabora, only ten miles in circumference, there were two hundred and twenty *marae*. No doubt these were smaller, but a comparison may be made, and a similar origin may be conjectured. It is believed, too, that the *ahu* were used for religious ceremonies when the island was discovered by Roggewein in 1722. Many of the statues were then standing, but most have since been thrown down, some through weathering, some through vandalism.

When placed in position many of the statues were crowned with a huge head-piece like a hat, from 3 feet 10 inches to 6 feet high, and 5 feet 6 inches to 8 feet across, topped with a knob from 6 inches to 2 feet high. It was only the statues on the *ahu* that were found with crowns. Their stability on the platforms, where they apparently stood facing inland, was so insecure—as is shown by the ease with which they have been overturned—that it has been conjectured that they were intended to be fixed elsewhere —slightly sunk in the shore, facing the sea, with their backs to the outer wall. Then, however, another mystery is added—why were some set in place upon the platforms?

It cannot be conjectured how the statues, which weigh from 30 to 40 tons, were transported from the crater to the shore, or how they were erected on the platforms once they were transported, and the crowns placed on their heads. La Pérouse thought that a hundred people would be able to set a statue in place, and no doubt there was as great difficulty in the transport and placing of the great blocks and slabs of the Tongan and Tahitian *marae*. If timber were used, it must have been transported, unless it originally grew on the island under different conditions from those now prevailing; but if so no signs of it remain.

While the Easter Islanders were the only ones of the Polynesians who made great images of stone, great images in wood were made by the Maori, and the Easter Islanders probably chose stone only because no wood was available; and, as has been seen, the stone chosen was soft. The type of features may signify nothing, but be arbitrary, as the type chosen by the Maori was arbitrary. There was evidently a bias in the Polynesians toward the creation of huge structures, different branches of the race showing their differences in the result—the *ahu*, the *marae*, the *heiau*. Lesser images, up to 9 feet in height, were hewn from a red stone in other parts, such as the Austral Islands.

In yet another respect, however, do the Easter Islanders differ from Polynesians in other parts of the Pacific; they had, some suppose, evolved a form of script. In other parts of the Pacific there are at any rate traces of a form of communication by knotted cords, and this appeared to have been in general, if not common, use by the Polynesians; but only in Easter Island has a script been found—curious characters inscribed on wooden tablets, that have so far defied interpretation. It would seem as if the script were a local development, and not brought from the original home, as presumably the knotted cord was. So different, however, is the script from anything found elsewhere in Polynesia that it is perhaps doubtful if it was ever used by the Easter Islanders themselves. It is possible that the tablets were a legacy from earlier occupants, dispossessed by the Polynesians; and it is not impossible that these earlier occupants, the so called 'long-eared' race, came from South America, bringing the script with them.

While poor in its people, Easter Island is rich in its relics; as has been said, its present is its past, and the great statues guard that past with a greater imperturbability than even that of the Sphinx of the Egyptian desert.

In New Zealand the art of working in stone has been lost or neglected altogether. This may be because there was no stone suitable such as was obtained from the coral reefs in other parts of Polynesia; it may be that the Maori had no inclination toward the mason art, especially in the presence of unlimited timber, while the former inhabitants of Easter Island developed an inclination for the carving of huge stone figures possibly because of the absence or dearth of timber. That the Maori was quite able to work in stone is shown by his manufacture of *tiki* and beautifully shaped *mere* from greenstone, one of the hardest of stones. He manufactured stone clubs also, and fern-root pounders; but the only stone figures carved were the small representations of Rongo', twelve to eighteen inches in height or a little more, sacred emblems used on the *kumara* plantations at the time of setting the seed.

There were great differences in the rank of the priesthood in the various groups. In Samoa, where the gods were many minor local deities rather than a few primal, universal gods, every householder was a priest, and superintended the family worship, if the formal intercession or propitiation observed can be called worship. There were priests for a few of the gods more widely recognized, such as the war-gods, but the priestly class was not the powerful body it was in other groups.

In New Zealand the priesthood was a powerful class, but there were no temples, and there was no worship, all ceremonies being performed in the open, a small space being set aside for the performance of general ceremonies, which else were performed wherever circumstances demanded.

In the Friendly Islands the priests belonged to the lower order of chiefs, the office being usually hereditary. They were paid no special deference, however, except during such time as they were possessed by the god when being used as the mouthpiece of that god.

In the Society Islands, and in the Hawaiian Islands, the priests and great chiefs were closely allied, so that religion and government went together. The divine right of kings was here believed in as firmly as ever in Stuart times in England, and the chiefs were inclined to be despotic in consequence. In both groups the religion was more formal than elsewhere; in both human sacrifices were often made. Ellis remarked on the deep religious feeling of the Society Islanders, though he called the feeling superstition, saying that they offered a prayer before food—was not this grace before meat?—when the first fruits were offered—was not this a harvest thanksgiving?—when they built their houses —why should not a dwelling be consecrated as well as a church?—when they launched their canoes, or began a journey—was not this a kind of Litany?

Nowhere, however, was such ceremony observed as in Hawaii; and indeed it would appear as if the rulers themselves found this religion oppressive; for in the October of the year 1819, six months before the first Christian missionaries arrived in the islands, an extraordinary occurrence took place which can only be likened to the Reformation of the Old World. The great king Kamehameha died, and his successor, Liholiho, under the inspiration of Kaahumanu, one of the widows of his father, in the presence of the people broke the *tapu* by partaking of food from vessels from which women were feasting, and the same day decreed the destruction of every temple and idol in the kingdom. He was abetted by the high priest Hewahewa, and in a few weeks temples, altars, images, and a priesthood which had held rulers and people in awe for centuries were swept away.

It has been noted how susceptible the Polynesians are to new ideas, to new customs. It was enough for the people if their ruler led the way; they would follow; and so it was in Hawaii, though the old religion did not fall without champions. Kekuaokalani, a cousin, or half-brother, of Liholiho, called together those who would join him in defence of the gods; but he was defeated, and the old religion passed away. How different Ellis found it in Tahiti, where Pomare, the ruler, granted him permission to teach, but would not himself be converted, and whose people adhered loyally to him. Ellis confessed that Pomare, the more he learned of his objects, the less he liked them.

467

MYTHS OF THE POLYNESIANS

The missionaries who came to Hawaii in March of 1820 found a people ready for a new teaching; but they presented Christianity as a severe, harsh religion; not one of dignity, beauty, and tenderness; a religion rather of the Old Testament than of the New; and they introduced a *tapu* system more stringent and more intolerable than the one they abolished. It is through their discouraging the preservation of the old myths that the accounts of the Hawaiian legends are so meagre and distorted.

There seems now, alas! little more original matter to be gathered, though, as regards New Zealand, Elsdon Best's recent volumes, *The Maori*, show what may still be gleaned by a sympathetic harvester. The writer has accompanied Mr Best in some of his later quests, and particularly remembers the significant remark of an old blind Maori who found great joy in speaking of the old days with this Maori-learned *pakeha*. Best rendered in Maori is Peehi; and one evening, sitting smoking and chatting by the fire, after a pause such as falls when the reminiscent thoughts are busy, the old man said—in Maori, of course—" *E!* Peehi, you are making me remember things that your fellows have been forty years trying to make me forget!" There is, too, another significant remark by a humorous old-time Maori who has adapted himself to the present time. " While our eyes have been fixed on heavenly things, our earthly things have slipped from under our feet." They have their humour, these old Polynesians; they have their memories; and they are not irresponsive to the invading *pakeha* whose breast carries the loadstone of sympathy. I greet them; there are more to-morrows, here and in Te Reinga.

AUTHORITIES

BEST, ELSDON: *The Maori* (2 vols., Wellington, 1924).
—— *Maori Religion and Mythology*, Part I (Dominion Museum Bulletin No. 10, Wellington, 1924).
CHURCHILL, W.: *The Polynesian Wanderings* (Washington, 1911).
—— *Sissano : Movements of Migration within and through Melanesia* (Washington, 1916).
COOK, A. B.: *Zeus : a Study in Ancient Religion* (Cambridge, 1914; vols. i and ii only issued).
COOK, CAPTAIN JAMES: *A Voyage to the Pacific Ocean* (London, 1784).
ELLIS, WILLIAM: *Polynesian Researches* (2 vols., London, 1829; 4 vols., 1831).
EMERSON, N. B. : *Unwritten Literature of Hawaii* (Smithsonian Institution, Bureau of American Ethnology Bulletin No. 38, Washington, 1909).
FENTON, F. D.: *Suggestions for a History of the Maori People* (Auckland, 1885).
FORNANDER, A.: *An Account of the Polynesian Race* (3 vols., London, 1880).
—— *Fornander Collection of Hawaiian Antiquities* (Honolulu, 1916–17).
FRAZER, SIR JAMES G.: *The Belief in Immortality and the Worship of the Dead* (vol. ii, *The Belief among the Polynesians*; London, 1922).
GILL, WILLIAM W.: *Myths and Songs from the South Pacific* (London, 1876).
GREY, SIR GEORGE: *Polynesian Mythology* (London, 1855; 2nd edition, with Maori originals, Auckland, 1885).
HANDY, E. S. CRAIGHILL : *Polynesian Religion* (Bernice P. Bishop Museum Bulletin No. 34, Honolulu, 1927). (*Note.* This book is an excellent *résumé* of the subject.)
KALAKAUA I, King of the Hawaiian Islands: *The Legends and Myths of Hawaii* (New York, 1888).
KER, A.: *Papuan Fairy Tales* (London, 1910).
KRAEMER, A.: *Die Samoa-Inseln* (2 vols., Stuttgart, 1920).
MOERENHOUT, J. A.: *Voyages aux îles du grand océan*, (2 vols., Paris, 1837).
RIVERS, W. H. R.: *The History of Melanesian Society* (2 vols., Cambridge, 1914).
SMITH, S. PERCY: *Hawaiki : the Original Home of the Maori* (4th edition, Wellington, 1921). (Smith's *Lore of the Whare-wananga* appeared first in the *Journal of the Polynesian Society*, and was issued by the Society as *Memoirs* 3 and 4 in 1913 and 1915.)
STAIR, J. B.: *Old Samoa* (London, 1897).
STUEBEL, O.: *Samoaische Texte* (Berlin, 1896).
THRUM, THOMAS G.: *Hawaiian Folk-tales* (Chicago, 1907).
TREGEAR, EDWARD: *The Comparative Maori Dictionary* (Wellington, 1891).

MYTHS OF THE POLYNESIANS

Turner, George: *Nineteen Years in Polynesia* (London, 1861).

—— *Samoa* (London, 1884).

Watson, R. M.: *History of Samoa* (Wellington, 1918).

Westervelt, W. D.: *Legends of Ma-ui, a Demigod of Polynesia, and of his Mother Hina* (Melbourne, 1913).

White, John: *The Ancient History of the Maori* (6 vols., Wellington, 1887).

Williams, T.: *Fiji and the Fijians* (2 vols., London, 1858).

Williamson, R. W.: *The Social and Political Systems of Central Polynesia* (3 vols., Cambridge, 1924).

Bulletin de la société des études océaniennes (Papeete, 1917–23).

Journal of the Polynesian Society (Wellington and New Plymouth, 1892, and yearly).

Transactions of the New Zealand Institute (Wellington, 1869, and yearly).

Note. This is not intended as a bibliography, and many good books have not been included in the list as, while they may have been read, no facts have been drawn directly from them; many of them are nevertheless better books than some of those included.

GLOSSARY AND INDEX

GLOSSARY AND INDEX

473

GLOSSARY AND INDEX

GLOSSARY AND INDEX

HAWAIKI-NUI. House in Spirit Land, 344

HAWK. Brown feathers of, caused by fire, 206

HEAD. Custom of preserving, 110

HEAVA. Cook's descriptions of, 336

HEIAU. Of Hawaii, 363; description of, 459

HEKEHEKE-I-PAPA. A wife of Rangi', 375

HEL. Norse goddess; Miru the Pacific equivalent of, 122

HELIOS. A name of Iao, 350

HELL. Maori knew no such place or idea, 421

HEMA. Son of Tawhaki, 158–159; in several Polynesian genealogies, 190; child of Ai-kanaka and Hina', 263

HERMES. His mischief like that of Maui', 232

HERON. Combat of, and snake, 184

HERVEY ISLANDS. *See* COOK ISLANDS

HEWAHEWA. In religious revolution in Hawaii, 467

HIHI. A New Zealand bird, the stitch-bird (*Pogonornis cincta*); origin of colours of, 200–201

HIHIMANU. A Hawaiian fish, the spotted sting-ray (*Mobula japonica*); in chant, 392

HIIAKA-I-KA-PALI-O-PELE (HIIAKA'). Sister of Pele, 268 *et seq.*; in song of Pele, 285; in song of the Water of Kane, 286; song heard by her at Kahakuloa, 450; story of, a favourite subject in the *hula*, 451

HIKA. Term for generation, 218

HIKA-PO-LOA. Name in chant, 393

HIKITA. Name invoked in *karakia* of Paikea, 107

HIKITAIOREA. Name invoked in *karakia* of Paikea, 107

HIKU. A man who brought back Kawelu from the netherworld, 302

HIKU-RANGI. Mountain on which canoe of Maui' grounded, 203

HIKU-TOIA. A netherworld, 207

HILO. Place where Hiiaka' met a demon, 272

HINA'. *See* HINA-URI

HINA. Mother of island Molokai, 363

HINA. Wife of Ai-kanaka; went to the moon, 263

HINA. Mortal mother of Hiku, 302

HINA-HELE. Wife of Ku-ula, 263; known as La-ea and Hina-ulu-ohia, 264

HINA-I-KA-MALAMA. A name in the chant of Kualii, 265

HINA-KEHA. Personification of the moon in its bright phases, 234

HINAKI. Maori eel-trap, 208

HINA-TE-IWAIWA. *See* HINE-TE-IWAIWA

HINA-TU-MOANA. Sailed into the moon, 261–262

HINAU. A Maori tree (*Elæocarpus dentatus*); berry of, used as food, 30; a phallic, 414

HINA-ULU-OHIA. A name of Hina-hele, 264

HINA-URI (HINA'). Sister of Maui' and wife of Ira-waru, 209; goddess of the moon, 212; personification of the moon in its dark phases, 234; story of her love for Tini-rau, 236–238; and origin of Areoi Society, 432

HINE-AHU-ONE. The first woman created by Tane', 407

HINE-AHU-PAPA. A wife of Rangi', 376

HINE-A-TAUIRA. Name of daughter of Tane', 408; changed name to Hine-nui-te-po, 411

HINE-A-TE-AO. A goddess guardian of the netherworld, 409

HINE-A-TE-PO. A goddess guardian of the netherworld, 409

HINE-A-TE-REPO. A wife of Maui', 208

HINE-HAONE. A form of the name Hine-ahu-one; the first woman, 407

HINE-HAU-ONE. A form of the name Hine-ahu-one; the first woman, 407

HINE-HEHE-I-RANGI. Name in chant, 93

HINE-I-KUKU-TE-RANGI. Name in chant, 93

HINE-I-TAPAPAUTA. A wind-goddess, 375

HINE-I-TAPEKA. Personification of subterranean fire, 218

HINE-I-TE-IWAIWA. Story of her visit to Tini-rau, 236–238

HINE-KAIKOMAKO. The Fire-maid, 218

479

GLOSSARY AND INDEX

GLOSSARY AND INDEX

KAI-HEWA. The place to which Tu' fell defeated, 423

KAIKOMAKO. A Maori tree, the Maori-fire (*Pennantia corymbosa*); used for fire-making by friction, 206, 207

KAILUA. A locality in Hawaii, 303

KAINGA. A dwelling-place, or village, 168, 198

KAINGA-ROA. Plains in the North Island, New Zealand, 140

KAIOA. The name of Areoi Society in Marquesas, 435–436

KAITAKA. An ornamental cloak, 298

KAI-TANGATA. Ancestor of Tawhaki, 157

KAI-WHAIA. Abode of Matuku, 177

KAI-WHAKARUAKI. A *taniwha* of New Zealand and Society Islands, 145

KAIWHATU. A charm to avert witch-craft, 428

KAKA. A Maori bird, the brown parrot (*Nestor meridionalis*), 143; red feathers of underwing of, used for cloaks, 153, 297

KAKAALANEO. Chief of Maui; wore first feather cloak, 293

KAKAHO-ROA. The old name of Wha-katane, New Zealand, 91

KAKARIKI. A Maori bird, the green parakeet (*Cyanorhamphus novæ-zea-landiæ*); cause of red feathers of, 208

KALAMAINU. A lizard-woman, 273

KALAMAKUA. Lover of Kelea; story of, 72 *et seq.*

KALANA-I-HAUOLA. Region where lay the Living Waters of Tane', 417

KALANIOPUU. Husband of Kalola, 430

KALAU-PAPA. Landing-place on Molo-kai, Hawaii, 73

KALOLA. And traders in Hawaiian group, 430

KALONA-IKI. Father of Lo-Lale, 84

KAMA-HUA-LELE. Astronomer and poet, 48, 56

KAMA-PUAA. Lover of daughters of the god of the mirage, 286

KAMEHAMEHA. Seen in procession of spirits, 305; built fish-ponds, 461; revolution in religion at death of, 467

KA-MOHO-ALII. Name in song of Pele, 285

KANAE. One of the Ponaturi, 164

KANAKA. Word meaning ' a man,' the Hawaiian form of the Maori *tangata*; in chant, 69

KANALOA (Maori Tangaroa). One of the chief gods, 362; in chant, 265; abbreviated to 'Loa in *hula* song, 418

KANAPU. Ancestor of Tawhaki; ancestor of Tuna', 168

KANAWA. An *atua* in story of Uenuku, 100

KANAWA. A man who saw the forest elves, 133–135

KANE. The Hawaiian deity (the Maori Tane'), 362, 392; in chant, 284, 285, 392; song in *hula*, *The Waters of Kane*, 417; region of the Waters of, 417; caused waters to come from cliff, 419

KANE-HOA. Locality on Oahu; in chant, 84; in *hula* song, 448

KANE-HOALANI. Father of Pele, 283

KANE-HUNA-MOKU. In journeying of Pele, 283

KANEIA - KUMUHONUA. Conquered Wakea, 362

KANE-MILOHAI. A relative of the vol-cano-deities, 278

KANE-OHE. A locality on Oahu, 57

KANE-OI-E. The Hawaiian deity triad, 392

KANIKANI-AULA. A girl restored to life, 296

KANI-O-WAI. A wife of Rata, 100 *n.*, 180

KAO. The star Antares; in navigation, 78

KAO. Dried *kumara*; as food, 90, 424

KAOAHI. A woman mentioned by Pele, 283

KAOIO POINT. On western side of Oahu, Hawaii, 79

KAOPUIKI. Husband of Kalola, 430

KAPA. A dance performed in long booths, 334

KAPA. *Tapa* elsewhere; Hawaiian bark-cloth, 51, 293

KAPAA. Locality on Kauai, 49

KAPENGA. The dwelling-place of a *taniwha*, 140

KAPUKAULUA. A cave occupied by Koona, 264

483

GLOSSARY AND INDEX

KI. *See* TI

KIEKIE. A Maori epiphyte (*Freycinetia banksii*) among whose leaves lived the fairies, 116, 127; leaves of, used for garments, 63

KIHEI. A mantle, 50

'KIJIKIJI. *See* Maui-kijikiji

KIKI-AOLA. Place where Pi built dam, 137

KILA. Sailed from Hawaii to Tahiti, 55

KILAUEA. Volcano of Hawaii; home of Pele, 267; called the navel of the earth, 278; in *hula* song, 450

KILIOA. A lizard-woman, 273

KILO-HANA. Outer ornamental part of *pau*, 449

KILU. A Hawaiian game, 282

KIMIHANGA. A primal existence, 374

KING, CAPTAIN. Paved enclosures and altars of Hawaii seen by, 459

KIORE. Maori rat; introduced to New Zealand, 29

KIORE-TA. An attendant of Ngararahuarau, 148

KIORE-TI. An attendant of Ngararahuarau, 148

KITE. Tawhaki mounted to upperworld by means of, 170; flown from under the water, 180

KITE-ORA. Wife of Rua-tapu, 109

KIWA. Father of shellfish, 285

KIWI. A flightless Maori bird (*Apteryx*), 133; feathers of, used for cloaks, 297; begotten by Tane', 407

KNOTTED CORDS. Used for communication, 465

KO. Maori digging implement, 198; made from *akeake*, 427

KOA. A Hawaiian tree (*Acacia koa*), 302; used for canoe-building, 75

KOAUAU. The Maori flute, 240, 338

KOHARA. Ancestor of Tuna', 168

KOHI-WAI. Relative of Tama-nui', 60

KOHU. Mist personified; parent of stars, 403

KOITI. One of the fire-children, 217

KOKAKO. A Maori bird, the crow (*Glaucopis*); reason for long legs of, 201; seen by Kupe, 37

KOKII KURA. A poison, 321

KOKIRA. A term applied to the plantain, 378

KOKO. The *tui* when fat, 174

KOKOMUKA-HAU-NEI. Man who saw fairies, 126

KONA-HUA-NUI. Mountains on Oahu, 278

KONO. Little platters for food plaited from green flax, used for only the one meal, 96

KONUI. One of the fire-children, 217

KOONA. An eel of Hawaii, equivalent of Tuna, 264

KOPU. Venus as the morning star, 148

KOPURU. A fragrant New Zealand moss, 298

KORARI. Flowers of the Maori flax (*Phormium tenax*); their nectar sipped, 307

KORE. The first primal void, 355

KORE-NUI. The fourth primal void, 355

KORE-PARA. The sixth primal void, 355

KORE-RAWEA. The eighth primal void, 355

KORE-ROA. The fifth primal void, 355

KORERO-TARA. Wife of Tangaroa, 168

KORERO-URE. Wife of Tangaroa, 168

KORE-TE-TAMAUA. The ninth primal void, 355

KORE-TUARUA. The third primal void, 355

KORE-TUATAHI. The second primal void, 355

KORE-WHIWHIA. The seventh primal void, 355

KORIPI. Knife edged with sharks' teeth, 158

KORIRO. A fish led by 'Ina, 225

KOROA. One of the fire-children, 217

KORO-MAU-ARIKI (KORO'). Son of Tini-rau and 'Ina, 247; the dancing of, by moonlight, 247–249

KOROMIKO. A greatly diversified Maori shrub (*Veronica* or *Hebe*); used for roasting Tutu-nui, 239

'KOROPANGA (TU-TE-KOROPANGA). A Maori character; his story, 58 *et seq.*; the Hawaiian Olopana, 68

KORO-RIWHA-TE-AO. A house of the stars, 411

GLOSSARY AND INDEX

GLOSSARY AND INDEX

GLOSSARY AND INDEX

GLOSSARY AND INDEX

493

GLOSSARY AND INDEX

song of creation, 354; in separation of
Rangi' and Papa', 368; son of Rangi',
375; connexion of, with Tu', 422;
as god of agriculture, 423; various
forms of the name, 423–424; Romatane a Tahitian form of the name, 429;
connected with Maui', 434; representations of, in stone, 466

RONGO-MAUI. A combining of Rongo'
and Maui', 434; younger brother of
Whanui, 434–435; in production of
kumara, 435

RONGO-MUA. A skid used in the slaying of Tuna', 208

RONGORONGO. Upper jaw of the fish of
Maui', 203

RONGO-ROTO. A skid used in the slaying of Tuna', 208

RONGO-TIKI. Later name of Rongo-
i-tua, 426

RONGO-UA-ROA. Son of Uenuku, 94

RONO (RONGO). Probably a form of
Rongo-ma-Tane, 424; an altar to, on
the Areoi canoes, 452

RO'O (RONGO). Probably a form of
Rongo-ma-Tane, 423

ROPA-NUI. Son of Uenuku, 94

ROPES. First plaiting of, 200

ROTO-MAHANA. A lake in the North
Island, New Zealand, 140

ROTORUA. Slaying of *taniwha* near, 140

ROTU. A flower (unidentified) of Te
Reinga, 63; evidently fragrant, 65

ROTU. A charm to soothe wind, 91;
a spell inducing sleep, 240

ROTUMA, 13

ROUA (RUA). In chant of creation, 396;
spelt Rahoua, 397; full name Roua-
touboua usually given in chant, 398;
a name given to Tangaroa, 398

ROUA-TOUBOUA (RUA-TUPUA). In
chant of creation, 397

RU. Father of Maui' (Mangaia), 214;
propped up the sky, 222; pumice the
bones of, 223, 234; brother of Hina-
tu-moana, 262

RU'. God of earthquakes. *See* RUAU-
MOKO

RUA-AI-MOKO. God of earthquakes; in
song of creation, 354

RUA-HIKIHIKI. Son of Manawa, 111

RUAHINE-MATA-MORARI. Guardian of
fairies, 116

RUA-MANO. Helped Paikea in his
swim, 108

RUAMANO. Wife of Malu, 189

RUA-NUKU. The deity; known in
Atia, 35

RUA-O-MIRU. Entrance to netherworld, 305

RUA-O-TE-RA. The cave of the sun, 199

RUA-PUPUKE. A man whose son was
carried off by sea-fairies, 138

RUA-RANGI. A man whose wife was
carried off by fairies, 135–136

RUA-TAHUNA DISTRICT. Phallic tree
in, 414

RUA-TAPU. Son of Uenuku, 103 *et seq.*

RUA-TE-ATONGA. A great chief of old,
35

RUA-TIPUA. A "prop" used in separation of Rangi' and Papa', 398

RUAU-MOKO (RU'). God of earthquakes; an unborn god, 234; son of
Rangi' and Papa', 375

RUKUTIA. Wife of Tama-nui'; her
story, 58 *et seq.*; the Hawaiian
Lu'ukia, 68, 448

RUNUKU. A primal existence, 374

RUPE. Brother of Hine-i-te-iwaiwa,
237; brother of 'Ina (Mangaia), 243

RUPE (LUPE, LUBE). Word for pigeon
in Pacific, 237

RURU. An owl, the Maori morepork
(*Ninox novæ-zealandiæ*), 154

RURU-ATAMAI. Bird guardian of the
pools of Tini-rau, 237

RURUKU. A charm to make vessel
seaworthy, 91

RURU-TANGI-AKAU. Gave Tu' weapons
to war with Rongo', 427

RURU-TEINA. The winner of Roanga-
rahia, 146 *et seq.*

SACRIFICE. Of first man killed in war,
101

SAEHRIMNER. The inexhaustible hog,
421

SAGITTARIUS. In creation chant, 398

SAILS. Of Polynesian canoes, 31

SAINTS. *Atua* almost parallels of, 453;
canonization of, 453–454

SALEA-AU-MUA. A council-ground (Samoa), 390

SA-LE-FE'E. Home of Mafui'e, 216; home of Fe'e, 284

SAMOA, 13, 24; early visits to, 26; Maui' and Mahuika in, 216–218; Maui' and winds in, 218–219; origin of coconut in, 250–253; the name Manono in Mangaian drama, 330; origin of name of, 388; temples of, 459–460

SAMOANS. Characteristics of, 15; Samoan migration, 33, 36

SANDFLY. Origin of, 406

SASA'E. A person used in the creation of islands, 389

SATIA-I-LE-MOA. A name of Samoa, 388

SA-TUALAGI. A name in Samoan creation, 385

SAVA. A boy who with the girl I'i peopled Savai'i, 390

SAVAI'I. Canoe built at, 186; 'Ina and the eel in, 251; Mangaian drama brought from, 330; peopled by Sava and I'i, 390

SAVAIKI (or SAVAI'I). A variant of Hawaiki, 35

SAVEASIULEO. In the Samoan spirit world, 420

SAWAI-LAU. Home of the bird Ngani-vatu, 131

SCENT. See MOKIMOKI, PERFUMES, ROTU

SCORPION. The constellation; is the fish-hook of Maui', 216; tail-stars of, were two children, 400; tail of, was Te Waka-o-Tama-rereti, 403

SCRIPT. Of Easter Island, 465

SEASONS. Stars ruling, 411

SEA-TEMPERATURE, 16

SEX. Eel taught knowledge of, 412–413

SEXTANT. Polynesian, 42

SHADOWS. Of jewels taken by forest elves, 135

SHARK. Carried 'Ina toward Motu-tapu, 246; reason for protuberance on forehead of, 246

SHELLFISH. Offspring of Kiwa, 285

SHONGI. A form of Hongi, 262

SHOURAKI. A form of Hauraki, 262

SINA ('INA). Story of, and the eel (Samoa), 250–253; and the moon, 262

SIR CHARLES SAUNDERS ISLAND. Areoi of, 433

"SKIDBLADNER." The ship of Frey, 225

SKIRNER. His wooing of Gerda, 225

SKULD. One of the Norns, 421

SKY. Raised by Maui', 222–223

SMITH, S. PERCY. On origin of Polynesians, 21; on Polynesian migrations, 32–33; on the name Atia-te-varinganui, 35; on Tangaroa, father of Maui', 227

SNAKE. Combat of heron with, 184; and owl, 187; eel takes place of, in Polynesia, 250 et seq.

SOCIETY ISLANDS, 13, 24; early visits to, 26; first missionaries in, 26; in Polynesian migrations, 33; cosmogony of, 395 et seq; religious feeling of, 467

SOLOMON ISLANDS. In Polynesian migrations, 33

SONGS AND MUSIC, 336 et seq.

SPANIARDS. In Pacific, 25–26

SPENCER, H. On temples being derived from tombs, 455

SPIDER'S WEB. Ascent of Tawhaki to upperworld by, 181

SPIRIT WORLDS, THE, 288 et seq., 343–344

SPORTS AND GAMES. Originated in Atia', 35

STARS. Knowledge of, 36, 86, 396; used in navigation, 41–43, 77–78; Pleiades used in navigation, 77; the planets known, 78; Canopus a guide in navigation, 398; names of, 398, 403; gathered by Tane', 403, 410; the offspring of Ira, 410, 411; the offspring of the seasons, 411

STONE. Various marae of, 455 et seq.; tools of, quickly discarded, 27

STRING-FIGURES. Of Maori, 92

SUBSIDENCES. In Pacific, 24, 48

SUMMER. Stars ruling, 411

SUN. Snared by Maui', 199–200; rays of, the ropes of Maui', 215; and moon brother and sister, 234; delayed by Tangaroa, 310; setting, and road to Spirit Land, 344; and moon as bull and cow, 350–351; varying sex of,

GLOSSARY AND INDEX

505

MYTHS OF THE POLYNESIANS

TEIIRI. A god who taught ball-throwing, in drama, 330

TEKOTEKO. Carved figure at gable of house, 138, 149, 165

TELE. A child of the *fue*, 391

TELEA. Stone platform in Tongatabu, 458

TEMAIATEA. One of the first Areoi, 433

TEMPERATURE. Of sea, 16

TEMPLES. Derived from tombs, 455

TERARANGA. A god who taught ball-throwing, in drama, 330

TETOA. One of the first Areoi, 433

TEVE. A prop of heaven (Samoa), 386

TEVE. A Mangaian tree on which the sky rested, 222

THEATRE. Of the Areoi, 439; of the *hula*, 445

THOKOVA. Phallic stone at, 413

THOR. The fishing of, 231–232

THUNDER. Whai-tiri personification of, 157; caused by 'Ina throwing aside her *tapa*-stones, 261

TI (or KI, or I). A Hawaiian tree (*Dracæna* sp.); blades of, used for *malo* (girdle), 447; in *hula*, 449

TI. A Maori tree, the palm-lily or cabbage-tree (*Cordyline* sp.); used as food by the Maori, 30, 89, 307, 424

TIARE. A scented flower (Pukapuka), 256

TIAU. A mourning song, 334

TIEKE. A Maori bird, the saddleback (*Creadion carunculatus*); origin of saddle on, 200

TIGI. Parent of Tigilau, 242

TIGILAU. A boy in a variant of the Tini-rau story, 242

TIGILAU-MA'OLO. Full name of Tini-rau, 242

TI'ITI'I-A-TALAGA. Name of Maui' in Samoa, 216

TIKI. First man, or creator of first man, 412; created woman, 412; personification of phallus, 413; the *tiki* named after him, 413; wife of, was Marikoriko, 415

TIKI. Sister of Veetini, 308, 311

TIKI. Greenstone neck ornament and charm, 134, 466; object of, to ensure fertility, 413

TIKI-KAPAKAPA. Name of daughter of Tane', 408

TIKI-TAPU. A district in the North Island, New Zealand, 144

TIKO-KURA. A monster attacked by Ngaru, 318

TIMATE-KORE. Father of Papa, 360

TINILAU. See TINI-RAU

TINI-RAU. A fish-deity; sought by Hina', 236 *et seq.*; Tinilau in the Samoan story, 241–242; full name of, 242; son of Vari', 358; and fish-ponds of Hawaii, 461

TIOBA. A New Guinea tree, the corkwood, 254

TIPORO. A fruit used in juggling, 225

TIPUA. A goblin or demon, 139, 150, 409

TIRANGI. A mountain; in song of forest elves, 134

TIRI-KAWA. A mountain; in story of Uenuku, 101

TIRITIRI-KI-MATANGI. The fishing-line of Maui', 202

TIRITIRI-O-MATANGI. One of the heavens, 352

TIU. A wind-god, 375

TI-WAI-WAKA. A being in the spirit world, 289

TIWAIWAKA. A Maori bird, the black fantail; variant of the name *tiwakawaka*, which see

TIWAKAWAKA. A Maori bird, the black fantail (*Rhipidura fuliginosa*); seen by Kupe, 37; spelt *tiwaiwaka* in *karakia* on death of Maui', 214

TOA. A Samoan tree, 217, 256

TOATOA. A tall Maori tree, the celery-topped pine (*Phyllocladus trichomanoides*); reason for red sap of, 208

TOBOGGAN. Used for sport in Hawaii, 267

TO'ELAU. The trade-winds, 218

TOETOE. A drooping Maori plume-grass (*Arundo conspicua*), 96; reason for drooping of, 175; begotten by Tane', 407

TOFOA. A well in Tonga, 222

TOGA (TONGA). In Samoan creation, 389; the name of a turtle, 242

MYTHS OF THE POLYNESIANS

Tu-MANAWARU. Killed by Te Rangi-whakaputa in satisfaction for a wrong, 110

TUMATAKURU. A stiff, thorny Maori shrub, the 'wild Irishman' (*Discaria toumatou*), 59

Tu-MATAUENGA (Tu'). God of war; ancestor of Uenuku, 93, 101; in song of creation, 354; at separation of Rangi' and Papa', 367; various names assumed by, 373; son of Rangi', 375; created man, 412; the source of evil, 422; quarrel of, with Rongo-maraeroa, 427

Tu-MATA-WHAITI. A name assumed by Tu', 373

Tu-MAUNGA. Ancestors of Tama-nui', 60

Tu-METUA. Child of Vari', 359

TUMU-I-TE-ARE-TOKA. A monster attacked by Ngaru, 318

TUMU-TEANAOA. Child of Vari', 358

TUMU-TE-VAROVARO. Spirit name of Rarotonga, 377

TUNA. The eel personage, probably the equivalent of the Maori Tuna-roa; in Tuamotu, 256–258; in Mangaia, 258–260

"TUNA-MOE-VAI." Name of a canoe, 189

TUNA-ROA (TUNA'). A water-monster, half man half eel; face of, on the coconut, 29; met by Tawhaki, 168; killed by Maui', 208–209; a parallel of Python, 234; Tuna in Tuamotu, 257–258; Tuna in Mangaia, 258–260

TUONE. A Maori dance, 288

Tu-PAPA (Tu'). Child of Vari' and wife of 'Ra, 359–360; tutelary goddess of Moorea, 360

Tu-PARARA. Name invoked in *karakia* of Paikea, 107

TUPARI-MAUNGA. Mother of Para-whenua-mea, 286

TUPEKE-TA. Man speared by Whaitiri, 158

TUPEKE-TI. Man speared by Whaitiri, 158

TUPUA. Name in song of creation, 353

TUPU-KORO-NUKU. Name in song of creation, 353

TURA. His life with the fairies, 115 *et seq.*

TURAKI-HAU. Fairy wife of Tura, 116 *et seq.*

TURAKI-RAE. The head of the fish of Maui', 203

TUREHU. A race of Maori fairies, 126, 288

TURI-WHAIA. Ancestor of Tawhaki, 157

TUTAE-PUTAPUTA. A locality in Canterbury, New Zealand, 110

TUTAMAOTAMEA. A name of Rata, 187

TUTAPU. Son-in-law of Malu, 189

Tu-TATA-HAU. A supernatural being met by Tura, 116

Tu-TE-HEMAHEMA. Son of Tama-nui', 59

Tu-TE-KOROPANGA ('KOROPANGA). A Maori character; story of, 58 *et seq.*

Tu-TE-NGANA-HAU. A deity who called to Tawhaki in the upperworlds, 169

Tu-TE-RANGIATEA. A great voyager, 36

Tu-TE-RANGI-MARAMA. A great chief of old, 35

Tu-TE-WEHIWEHI (or Tu-TE-WANA-WANA). God of reptiles; sprung from Tangaroa, 370

TUTU. A child of the *fue*, 391

TUTU. A Maori shrub (*Coriaria* sp.) with poisonous properties, 68

TUTUILA. Name in dirge, 317; origin of the island, 390; peopling of the island, 391

TUTU-NUI. Pet whale of Tini-rau, 236; death of, 239

TUTU-WATHIWATHI. Sister of Rokoua, 130

TUWAERORE. Mother of the *rimu* and *tanekaha*, 407

Tu-WHAKAHEKE-TANGATA. A name assumed by Tu', 373

Tu-WHAKAPAU. Father of Ahua-rangi, 111

Tu-WHAKARARO (TUWHAKA'). Son of Rata, 180; son of Tu-huruhuru, 241

Tu-WHENUA. Ancestress of Tama-nui', 60

GLOSSARY AND INDEX

509

VARI. An old name for rice, 30, 227

VARI-MA-TE-TAKERE (VARI'). A primal being, 357; in drama as Vari-Origin-of-all, 327

VASCO DA GAMA. In East Indies, 19

VATEA. Father of gods and men, 356, 357; in festal song, 124; in ballthrowers' song, 332; discovers Papa, daughter of Timate-kore, 360

VAVAI. A scented flower (Pukapuka), 256

VAVAU. The spirit land, in dirge, 316

VEETINI. Ceremonies at the death of, 308–311

VEGA. The star Whenui, 398

VENGEANCE. Held in high estimation, 108, 109; a curious form of, 111; taken by traders on natives, 430–431

VERA. Son of Ngara; dirge for, 312–314

VERDANDE. One of the Norns, 421

VITI LEVU. In Polynesian migrations, 33; a name of the Polynesian homeland, 35

VOYAGES IN PACIFIC. In open boats, 28; routes of, 32; beginning of Polynesian, 36; provisioning for, 55–56; long, abandoned, 89; from New Zealand to Hawaiki, 89; from Samoa, 188–189. See also NAVIGATION

VUNA. Phallic stone at, 413

WAHIE-LOA. Hawaiian form of Wahieroa, 190; husband of Pele, 283

WAHIE-ROA. Son of Tawhaki, 161, 174, 185; in several Polynesian genealogies, 190; a comet, 191

WAI-A-HIKU. A water-hole on Hawaii, 303

WAI-A-LUA. Locality on Oahu, 56, 72

WAIANAE MOUNTAINS. On Oahu, 83

WAIATA-AROHA. A love-song, 340

WAIATA-POI. A song sung while swinging poi-balls, 340

WAI-HEMO. Ancestor of Tawhaki, 157

WAI-KALAI. A water-hole on Hawaii, 303

WAIKATO. A river in the North Island, New Zealand, 133, 140, 143

WAI-KOLOA. Locality on Oahu; in chant, 84

WAI-LAU. Home of Koona, 264

WAILUA. A name in song of Pele, 286

WAI-MANU. A valley mentioned in hula song, 449

WAIMEA. Home of Pi, 137

WAI-O-PUA. Locality on Oahu; in chant, 84

WAI-ORA-A-TANE'. The Living Waters of Tane', 416; renewed the moon, 212, 417; known also as Aewa, 417

WAIPAPA. Locality in Canterbury, New Zealand, 110, 113

WAIPIO. A valley of Hawaii, 46, 305

WAIRANGI. A name of Tura, 117

WAI-RARAPA. A lake near Wellington, New Zealand; an eye of the fish of Maui', 203

WAI-RARAWA. Home of Hina-uri; mentioned in her tangi, 211; place where she drifted ashore, 236

WAITAHA. An extinct tribe of New Zealand, 129

WAI-TOREMI. Name of a haka, 240

WAKA. Means receptacle as well as canoe, 219, 403

WAKA-O-TAMA-RERETI. The tail of the Scorpion, 403; also known as Uruao, 403

WAKEA. In genealogy of Moikeha, 52; in song of Pele's coming to Hawaii, 279; in story of creation, 361–363

WALLIS, S. In Pacific, 26

WAOLENA. A wife of Laa, 57

WAR. Polynesians not primarily fond of war, 423; gods of—see MARU, TU-MATAUENGA

WARO-URI. A water-hole, home of a taniwha, 143

WARS. Of dispersal in Atia', 35

WATERS OF LIFE. Te Wai-ora-a-Tane', 417

WATSON, R. M. Described ruins of Fale-o-le-Fe'e, 460

WAWAU. An early home of the Polynesians, 115

WEATHER-LORE. Of Polynesians, 86, 359

WEEDS OF TURA. Grey hair, 118

WEHE-LANI. In genealogy of Moikeha, 52

GLOSSARY AND INDEX

511

MYTHS OF THE POLYNESIANS

WITCHCRAFT. Taught in school of learning, 348; practised by Miru, 422; learned from Miru by Rongo-mai, 428; averted by charm *kaiwhatu*, 428

WOMAN. Created by Tane', 407–408; sprang from warmth of the sun and echo, 415

WOOD ELVES. Built canoe for Rata, 174–176

WOOD-PIGEON. *See* KERERU

WORD-SENSE. Primitive, 341

WORSHIP. Direct, in course of development, 452

WRITING. Unknown to Polynesians, 465

YAM. Carried to New Zealand, 29; regional limit of, 30

YASAWAS. A region on Fiji, 131

YGDRASIL. The ash-tree of Norse mythology, 420

YMER. Creation of, 415

ZEUS. And the name Iao, 350